Perspectives on Coping and Resilience

Perspectives on Coping and Resilience

Editors
Venkat Pulla, Andrew Shatté & Shane Warren

AUTHORSPRESS

₹ 1200

Worldwide Circulation through Authorspress Global Network
First Published 2013
by
Authorspress

Editorial
Q-2A Hauz Khas Enclave
New Delhi-110 016

Marketing
E-35/103, Jawahar Park
Laxmi Nagar, Delhi-110 092

e-mails: authorspress@rediffmail.com; authorspress@hotmail.com
Website: www.authorspressbooks.com

Copyright © 2013 Editors

Perspectives on Coping and Resilience
ISBN 978-81-7273-715-3

Printed in India at Tarun Offset, Delhi.

Dedications

To the authors of individual chapters for their trust in us
—*Venkat Pulla, Andrew Shatte, Shane Warren*

To Srinivas Arka, my spiritual mentor, and to my wife Nisha Rao for her three decades of coping and understanding
—*Venkat Pulla*

To Veronica, Vivien & Julian—my perpetual source of resilience.
And to my editorial colleagues, Venkat & Shane, for their vision, hope, faith and trust
—*Andrew Shatte*

To my partner and children—Lewis, Jonathan, James and Jacob. Thank you for teaching me the art of resilience daily
—*Shane Warren*

Introduction

Humanity's need for resilience has rarely been greater. We live in a troubled world, in troubled times. As we write, there are 35 major military conflicts and wars raging on this planet. Thirteen per cent of the world's population is unable to find enough food. And global warming is threatening our very survival as a species.

The global recession has tested our mettle—tested our resilience—for the last five years. In the United States, each and every day since 2008, 8,000 people lost their jobs and 2,500 families lost their homes. This is not a uniquely American phenomenon. The economic contagion has spread throughout much of the globe. In the Eurozone, unemployment now stands at a record high of 11.1 per cent. In the first year of the recession alone, China saw 670,000 of its businesses close their doors.

But as tough as these times are, and as immediate as our need for resilience is, the reality is that resilience is an evergreen ability, ever in demand, almost as much a basic human need as air to breathe and water to drink.

Consider the fishermen in India's Bay of Bengal. Every year, year after year, the monsoons batter and swamp their meager boats. But day after day, holding tightly to their dinghies, they return to the sea, fighting the wet and the tides, forever hopeful for that big catch. Consider the people of the Oddar Meanchey province on the Cambodian-Thai border, who live their entire lives tending their disputed lands, under a pall of conflict and uncertainty—and who manage, through their resilience, to settle into some kind of normalcy. Drive through some of these dusty villages where farmers continue to cultivate their fields amidst chaos, and one is struck by the improbable serenity. Or, if you will indulge us, consider the lives of the average citizen of our industrialized nations. They have food and, by and large, they have peace. What they lack is peace of mind. Day in and day out they are told to do more with less at work, face impossible deadlines, are torn between work and home, watch their retirement plans go up in smoke in the great recession, juggle kids and deal with aging parents—all under the threat of downsizing.

And so we see that the need for resilience is a basic human need. And as a truly global phenomenon, it demands a global voice. And that is why we have gathered together a cadre of people from around the world to share with us, and with you the reader, their important work on resilience. *Perspectives on Coping and Resilience* examines the interplay of individual, family, community and social factors, and deepens our understanding of the human ability to 'bounce back'—a vital competency for success. This unique collection of trans-disciplinary writings on human coping and resilience is the collaboration of distinguished practitioners and academics in the diverse fields of psychology, management science, art, social work and spirituality.

Coping and Resilience have become core issues in a multiplicity of social science disciplines, as they have in our societies today. Taking a social work perspective the very first chapter on contours of coping and resilience by Venkat Pulla explains the core elements in coping and resilience, and suggests a strengths approach, promoting resilience from the remedial to the empowering. The intention of this chapter, and this book, is to facilitate change by examining what has worked, what has not worked and what might work in boosting resilience in our clients.

If we are going to take a deeper dive into resilience, we must first examine what the concept of resilience is. Thomas Dukes, the Director of School Counselling at Rhode Island University in the United States takes us on a philosophical examination of resilience and its meaning.

We learn that Emotion Regulation—the ability to control negative feelings in the wake of an adversity—is a critical component of Resilience. Shane Warren, a Director of the International Resilience Institute of Sydney, opens us up to what emotion regulation is. Jennifer Hudson and Venkat Pulla, from Social Work at Charles Sturt University in Australia, expand on the topic and show us how emotion regulation develops from birth through the first six years of life, pointing to possible prescriptions for our children along the way.

We learn of the importance of Self-efficacy in Resilience—the belief that one has control or even mastery in one's world. Anndrea Wheatley shares with us her important work in the schools of Sydney, Australia, as she co-opts the old narrative of 'the little engine who could' to assess the current state of self-efficacy in the students she serves and to help them boost their sense of mastery and control for greater resilience.

Several of our marvelous contributors demonstrate the power of resilience in the lives of individuals and the importance of personal resilience to better deal with adversity. Sharalyn Drayton, in her Sydney practice, writes of the use of resilience to change self-defeating behaviors in the cycle of addiction and co-dependence. In a truly multinational collaboration (Canada-Australia-New Zealand-Malaysia), Nur Aishah Hanun, Lynne Briggs and Wayne Hammond present case studies illustrating exactly how and when to deploy a resilience intervention with youth with disabilities. Anne Riggs, a practitioner in Victoria, Australia, relates her creative use of art therapy to help the female victims of childhood sexual abuse move from victimhood to recovery. Linda Douglas of the New Hampshire Coalition Against Domestic Violence offers riveting anecdotes that demonstrate the key role of resilience in predicting who recovers from domestic violence and how this knowledge should guide the services we provide to victims of abuse and Sindisio Zhou and Nhlanhla Landa proffer a moving chapter on how the 18 per cent of Zimbabwean women afflicted with HIV-AIDS are able to cope.

Some of our authors reflect the advances made by the positive psychology movement in their work. In their powerful and important work, practitioners Pamela Trotman and Leisha Townson from the Northern Territory, Australia, introduce us to the concept of the *Survivor Self.* They outline how we in the healing professions have come to medicalize and clinicalize the normal, human response to trauma with our very language. Instead of remediating victims, they help their clients—like the woman who was held hostage and threatened for hours with death by machete—identify the very moment in time when they became a survivor rather than a victim, and use that kernel to help resilience bloom and flourish. Richard Hill posits that humans may experience as much growth as trauma after a traumatic experience. Jeanne Broderick challenges us to tap into our emotional guidance systems for the positive as much as we do the negative. And Jo Kelly writes of how we can inject resilience into the normal, positive, social and emotional development of our adolescent children.

Of course, individuals are part of wider networks—work organizations, communities, societies, and nations—and several of our contributors have shared their work on resilience at this broader level. Robin Hills and Doug Haynes of the United Kingdom have developed an innovative method of opening up conversations with employees about their attitude to organizational change and adversity. Using 16 cards depicting adversity and resilience scenarios, they explore the resilience metaphors we bring to the table and begin to build stronger individuals in more resilient organizations as a result. Similarly, Linda Hoopes, a corporate consultant from the United States, explores how to create individual resilience in an organizational setting. Alyce White and Venkat Pulla encourage us to consider resilience as more than just a list of personal strengths. They outline a theory of how family, school, community, and even national and cultural mores shape the resilience of the person—reminding us of the old African proverb that it takes a village to raise a child. Linda Hoopes and her colleague, Lynne Varagona have developed a system to provide a snapshot into the resilience of a community and Lynne Varagona details her remarkable discovery that, in the developing nations, the resilience of the country's leaders, people, and social context are able to predict changes in GDP above and beyond the metrics of the World Bank.

In our final chapter, Andrew Shatté of the College of Medicine at The University of Arizona in the United States and a Fellow with the Brookings Institution outlines the 20-year history of his and his colleagues pursuit of the concept of resilience and how to boost it in children, adolescents and adults. Consider this chapter, and this book, as a celebration of all of our contributors and countless others around the world who have dedicated their careers to understanding people, their adversities big and small, the human capacity for resilience, and how we can help people heal, survive, and thrive.

This book is dedicated to them all.

Venkat Pulla, Andrew Shatté, Shane Warren
23 November, 2012

Our Contributors

Alyce White, completed her Bachelor of Social Work (Honours) this year. Alyce has experience working in family support and now works with Barnardos Australia in the Intensive Family Support Program. Alyce has studied the concept of resilience and has a passion for strengthening children and creating a safe and supportive environment for them to grow and develop., Email: alycewhite@hotmail.com

Andrew Shatté is the President of Phoenix Life Academy—a company that trains and coaches Resilience. He is a research professor in the College of Medicine at The University of Arizona, a highly-decorated teacher from the University of Pennsylvania, and a Fellow with the Brookings Institution. He co-authored "The Resilience Factor"

Anndrea Wheatley B.Arts Psychology, Postgrad Dip. Psych., M.A.C.A., is director, Resilience Training Programmes. 475 Great Western Highway, Faulconbridge, NSW 2776, Australia. Email: anndrea_oasis@yahoo.co.nz

Anne Riggs is an exhibiting visual artist, community artist and educator with PhD in art and wellbeing with victims of sexual abuse. She is a co-founder of Artists in Community International, providing arts, creative education, and professional development training. She lectures in BA Community Mental Health, Drug, Alcohol and Other Addictions course. ariggs@alphalink.com.au; www.anneriggs.com

Doug Haynes, has a BSc in Statistics, MA in Operational Research, PGCert in Business & Executive coaching. In the last 20 years, he has held several senior roles at Liverpool Business School (Liverpool John Moores University), including Director of the School of Business Information and Chair of Quality for the Faculty of Business & Law. dough@ei4change.org.uk

Jeanine Broderick, founder, Happiness 1st Institute, where knowledge and skills necessary to become adept at utilizing one's emotional guidance system are easily learned. Ms. Broderick has conducted more than five years of self-directed study on human thriving across many scientific disciplines including advanced research in philosophy, positive psychology, sociology, quantum physics, and other sciences as they relate to what cultivates human thriving. JeanineBroderick@Happiness1st.com

Jennifer Hudson currently works in a rural location with a Child & Adolescent Mental Health Service, and is passionate about working systemically with children and families. She is a Social Work graduate from Charles Sturt University, and is due to complete a Masters in Social Work (Advanced Practice) in 2012. She grew up in Papua New Guinea, has lived and worked in London as well as in both city and rural locations in Australia. She has worked in the areas of domestic violence, community development, substance use, mental health, policy, media and youth work. Email: jennicol1@bigpond.com.au

Jo Kelly, MMH (Art Therapy) AThR, Diploma in Counselling, MAIPC, QMACA, Bachelor of Education (Hons), Postgraduate Certificate in Health Promotion, is a doctoral student at the School of Education, Southern Cross University, Lismore, NSW, Australia. Jo is a mother, artist, art therapist, counsellor and educator. She has lived and worked mainly in developing countries, including India, Bangladesh and Papua New Guinea. She is also a supervisor for students on the Masters of Mental Health (Art Therapy) program at University of Queensland, as well as a lecturer in the Diploma of Transpersonal Art Therapy in Brisbane, through Ikon Institute. Email: jokelly@iinet.net.au

Leisha Townson and **Pamela Trotman** (social workers) have worked extensively with people who have experienced trauma (adult and child sexual assault, family and political violence, natural disasters and accidents). In recent years they have developed the concept of the Survivor Self™ and its role in promoting post-trauma recovery and growth. They have presented at national (Australian) and International conferences and have developed a training package: Recognising, Nurturing and Strengthening the Survivor Self™

Linda A. Douglas M.Ed., MLADC, is the Trauma Specialist for the New Hampshire Coalition Against Domestic and Sexual Vio-lence working to enhance the capacity of domestic violence programs, and local communities, to address the affects of trauma and the complex needs of victims with mental health and substance abuse problems. Ms. Douglas is a master licensed alcohol and drug counselor in the State of New Hampshire. She can be reached at: ladoug@msn.com; linda@nhcadsv.org

Linda Hoopes is the founder and president of Resilience Alliance, a training and consulting firm that provides tools and materials to help individuals, teams, and organizations thrive in turbulence, and the author of Managing Change with Personal Resilience. She holds a PhD in industrial/organizational psychology from the University of Tennessee, has served on the faculties of Rutgers

University, Georgia Tech, and Colby College, and has extensive experience in organizational change consulting. She is a licensed psychologist, and is currently an adjunct faculty member in Philadelphia College of Osteopathic Medicine's Organizational Development and Leadership program. She is currently working on her second book. Email: linda@resiliencealliance.com

Lynn Varagona, MBA, Ph.D. is a licensed psychologist and founder of Trust Capital Institute, a principle-based consultancy that helps leaders build the trust behind top performance. A thought leader in the field of organizational and leadership development with over 20 years' experience, Lynn is adept at developing methodologies to create top-performing organizations, leaders, and teams. She created the Trust Infusion™ methodology based on timeless truths backed by research and experience, to help leaders build a foundation for lasting success. lynn.varagona@lvglobal.com

Lynne Briggs: Associate Professor at Griffith University, Australia and adjunct status with University of Otago, New Zealand. Email: l.briggs@griffith.edu.au

Nhlanhla Landa is a freelance writer, editor and communications consultant in Zimbabwe. He is interested in gender and language issues and reports on gender, children, development and climate change. He is a holder of a BA Hons. in English and Communication Degree and an MA in Applied Linguistics from Midlands State University, also in Zimbabwe. He is currently studying towards a PhD in Linguistics. Email. landamasuku@gmail.com

Nur Aishah Hanun Manager of Taska Permata UPSI, National Child Development Research Centre (NCDRC), Sultan Idris Education University, Malaysia. She is currently undertaking her doctoral work at the School of Human Services and Social Work, Griffith University, Australia. Email: nuraishahhanun.azizi @griffithuni.edu.au

Richard Hill, M.A., M.Ed., Dip. Prof. Couns Richard Hill MA, MEd, MACA practices psychotherapist in Sydney, specialising in neuroscience. He lectures internationally and has authored books, papers and articles that are published worldwide. Richard is a board member of the Global Association for Interpersonal Neurobiology Studies; a select member of the International Psychosocial Genomics Research Team and director of the Mindscience Institute. Email: richhill@iinet.net.au

Robin Hills, is a science graduate from Durham University with the Chartered Institute of Marketing diploma and holds the British Psychological Society Certificate of Competence in Occupational Testing—Ability and Personality (trait, type and behaviour). For the last 6 years he has been running his own business specialising in Emotional Intelligence, recognised in 2012 by the Association of Business Psychologists. robin@ei4change.org.uk

Shane Warren is a psychotherapist in private practice in Sydney, Singapore and Hong Kong. He is a Director of the International Resilience Institute Sydney and facilitates of leadership development programs within a resilience framework for multinational corporations, not-for-profit groups and small businesses throughout the Asia Pacific Region. Email:shane@irisconsulting.com.au

Sharalyn Drayton is Director and Senior Therapist of ARISE Counselling Solutions Sharalyn has been working in this field for the past 14 years. Trained in Clinical Pastoral Counselling and Drug and Alcohol work, Sharalyn holds a Masters Degree in Theology specialising in Addiction and Spirituality. She has also trained in a number of leading Sydney hospitals and has worked with clients covering a large range of issues from addiction to trauma and abuse. www.arisecounsellingsolutions.com.au

Sindiso Zhou is a Lecturer in the Humanities and Social Sciences Faculty at Africa University in Zimbabwe. She is also a PhD student at the University of Fort Hare in South Africa and a holder of a BA Hons. in English and Communication Degree and an MA in Applied Linguistics from Midlands State University, in Zimbabwe. Sindiso is also a practicing journalist with a keen interest on women, children and vulnerable groups. Email: sindisolorraine@gmail.com

Thomas W. Dukes, MSW, EdD is Assistant Professor of Counseling at Rhode Island College and Director of the School Counseling Graduate Program in the Department of Counseling, Educational Leadership, and School Psychology. After more than a dec-ade of practice as a child, adolescent, and family therapist, Dr. Dukes returned to graduate school at Boston University's School of Education to complete a doctorate in Human Development and Education. His doctoral research examined the promotion of resilience among adolescents through increasing self-understanding in a small group intervention. Email: tdukes@ric.edu

Venkat Pulla is a Tata Dorabji Merit Scholar from the Tata Institute of Social Sciences India. Currently he teaches social work at Charles Sturt University, Australia. His research interests are in human coping and resilience, spirituality and social work, and green social work. He is the founder of the Brisbane Institute of Strengths Based Practice (www.strengthsbasedpractice.com.au)

Wayne Hammond is President of Resiliency Initiatives and holds an adjunct status with the School of Medicine at the University of Calgary, Alberta Canada. Email: wh@resil.ca

Contents

Introduction ... vii

Our Contributors ... xiii

1. Contours of Coping and Resilience: The Front Story ... 1
   Venkat Pulla
2. Toward a Philosophy of Resilience ... 25
   Thomas W. Dukes
3. Using Metaphors to Develop Resilience ... 46
   Robin Hills and *Doug Haynes*
4. Developing Personal Resilience in Organizational Settings ... 79
   Linda L. Hoopes
5. Emotion Regulation in Children: Towards a Resilience Framework ... 100
   Jennifer Hudson and *Venkat Pulla*
6. Strengthening the Capacity for Resilience in Children ... 122
   Alyce White and *Venkat Pulla*
7. Resilience Building Using Art Therapy with Adolescents in Australia ... 152
   Jo Kelly
8. Out of the Shadows: Into the Light: Resilience and Coping Skills through Arts Practice ... 176
   Anne Riggs
9. Resiliency and Recovery from Intimate Partner Violence ... 202
   Linda A. Douglas

10. Resistance to Resilience: Addiction, Co-dependency
   and Doing Life Differently 217
   Sharalyn Drayton

11. Trauma–Creating Beneficial Change 235
    Richard Hill

12. Trusting One's Emotional Guidance Builds Resilience 254
    Jeanine Broderick

13. The Role of Language in Promoting
    Trauma Recovery and Resilience 280
    Pamela Trotman and *Leisha Townson*

14. The Community Resilience Profile: A Framework
    for Assessing Community Development Efforts 307
    Lynn Varagona and *Linda Hoopes*

15. What World Bank Metrics Don't Tell Us About
    Per Capita GDP: How a Nation's Resilience Affects
    Its Prosperity 333
    Lynn Varagona

16. Building Resilience in the Next
    Generation and the Power of Higher Self-efficacy 362
    Anndrea Wheatley

17. Revisiting Emotional Regulation:
    Evidence from Practice 388
    Shane Warren

18. Life Narratives Mirroring the Feminization of
    HIV and AIDS Trauma: Zimbabwean Perspectives
    of Coping and Resilience 399
    Sindiso Zhou and *Nhlanhla Landa*

19. Resilient Reintegration during Adversities:
    Case of Young People with Disabilities 419
    Nur Aishah Hanun, Lynne Briggs and *Wayne Hammond*

20. "Resilience at Work and in Life" 444
    Andrew Shatté

Index **480**

CHAPTER 1

Contours of Coping and Resilience: The Front Story

Venkat Pulla

Abstract

This chapter presents an introduction to the two concepts of *coping and resilience,* with their varied dimensions, in order to unravel the concepts. The chapter begins with brief stories that show how individuals, groups, communities and nations display both coping and resilience every day. The analysis, after shifts to the meaning of every day stress and adversity that have become inevitable parts of our daily *jigsaw puzzle of life*; defines the contexts of coping and resilience, and brings in strengths perspective into resiliency and finally signals the efficacy of an inner strengths approach.

Key Words

Coping, resilience, stress management, strengths approach, social work

The Collective Stories

Bwera, a Ugandan city on the banks of the Rubirihiya River, separates the Democratic Republic of Congo (DRC) and Uganda, east of the Beni region. Ugandans and Congolese sell from the same stalls. They all discuss products and prices in "Kinande," their shared mother tongue but carry transactions in shillings on the Ugandan side, and in francs on the Congolese one. The same merchants do their market rounds on both sides of the border. Truck drivers with bananas and palm oil from the Congo cross the border and unload their merchandise in Uganda, but on the other side of the border, they show Ugandan ID papers. The same goes for the Ugandan drivers who enter the Congo through Kasindi. When they go through customs loaded with beer, bags of grey cement, corn starch and other products, they pull out Congolese ID, which exempt them from certain taxes ((Kokonyange & Syfia International 2012). This is a fundamental example of coping and resilience.

Amidst cross border tensions, fears of militancy, constant destabilisation people continue to live in the strife-torn border districts of Jammu in India. At sunrise they move to their fields and till their farms and return to their homes as the sun sets. These people remain cautiously apprehensive about an unpredictable future and the mood of most people living in these towns and villages is summarised as: how far can one run from one's own land? Again, this is coping and resilience.

While recession continues to hurt business around the globe, many industries in India have come out unscathed. Among BRIC countries (Brazil, Russia, India and China), China and India never went into recession. Brazil briefly did, but its recovery seems pretty strong. India defied the global recession by posting a very healthy GDP growth rate of 7 per cent. The fact that the Indian industry, so far, has remained insulated from the global recession can be attributed to its value systems, entrepreneurship and its spiritual traditions and coping and resilient entrepreneurship (Panchanatham 2011). Panchanatham acclaims these above characteristics to spell the competitive edge for India. These qualities might also be described as 'ingredients' of coping and resilience

The Individual Stories

Over the years I heard these two terms, coping and resilience, resonate quite clearly through various conversations and brave stories that many people told me. There was something heroic about some of them, but with some others it was plain and simple.

Their strategies for plain survival recognise an essential will to thrive and some others recognised a will to flourish and move ahead. Tewodros Fekadu, a friend of mine, an artist, community worker and a writer now lives on the Gold Coast in Australia. Teddy, as he is fondly called, recounted the challenges and triumphs of surviving a poverty-stricken childhood in the streets of Ethiopia. With the backdrop of the civil war he spent years as an orphan, struggled with his loneliness—his only companion—and the need for love. His life brought him as a refugee to Japan for another ten years until he moved as a more permanent refugee to Australia. His journey spanned five countries and three continents, with sometimes meaningless and sometimes meaningful contact with the Catholic Church, the police, the law and life in Japanese detention centres. His story is a story of family love—unacknowledged by his wealthy father—and his pride and being abandoned by his desperate, poor mother, but is also a story of one man's defiance and triumph, that is beautifully presented in a book called, *No One's Son* (Fekadu 2012).

John Dommett told me his story of how epilepsy and a misdiagnosis of intellectual disability in his case upshot very quickly into a loss of his social roles and his dreams and brought the end results of assumption of incompetence, rapid devalued status and an income of 20 dollars a fortnight from a sheltered workshop and how many years it took him to reclaim his life (Dommett 2010)

Pamela Trotman and Leisha Townson, social workers, featured in this book had conversations with me around tapping the inner resource or their inherent inner energy that they described as 'survivor self' that continues to exist before, during and after a traumatic event (Trotman & Townson 2012).

Group Stories

Braj Bhushan, talked to me about how elderly men and women handle anxiety, depression, somatisation and cognitive competence rather proactively in India, while Coralie Graham, in her conversations at a conference talked about the adaptability, positive outlook that predicted better mental health of the elderly men and women in Australia (Bhushan 2010; Graham 2010). Anne Riggs, an art therapist talked about people living on the brink of suicide and how she observed her subjects delve into what hurts, disturbs and stultifies in order to offer something back that reveals, transforms and restores (Riggs 2010) In all the above narratives resilience as it emerges is best understood as a process and also as an idea more typically referred to as "resiliency". (Leadbeater et al. 2005)

The central message from the above stories is that recovery from any calamity does not involve restoration of the status quo but instead requires development of pathways leading forward to possible and preferred futures. In response to both man made and natural disasters, individuals and collectives face the challenge of 'What now? What next?' amidst the damage, loss or irrevocable changes. We are witness to profound and unanticipated disruptions of all sorts playing out again and again around the globe. Compelling questions and concerns arising from this stream of natural and man made disasters and these questions are: What helps people cope with disaster? What aids in their recovery? What factors support capacity for individuals and communities to build positive futures 'out of the ashes'?

Stress and Coping

The two central themes common to all of the above living stories are coping and resilience. The purpose of this chapter is to tease these two concepts with their varied dimensions and unravel the ingredients that come within their conceptualisations. A place to start this discussion is with the stresses and strains that we have all experienced. Life is not often like still waters. I have always thought there are ripples whose sound and gaze we miss under the still waters. In most simple terms, stress is a load, a burden that one can carry without a disruption, but it can tear a muscle or stretch our emotional abilities as we struggle to withstand its weight. Thus there are sudden, acute stresses that we can see or describe and there are others that we might not feel in the beginning, but whose symptoms slowly appear. Stress, adversity and challenge have become inevitable parts of our daily *jigsaw puzzle of life*—and sometimes out of control. However the way we think about stress appears to me as being very much in our control and this could make a big difference in how we can handle ourselves when we find ourselves at the cross roads of unseen stresses. Some people feel helpless in the face of stress and adversity and easily give up attempts to change or improve their conditions while others manage and move on. Research is suggesting that an option exists. People can learn to cope and resiliency can be acquired (Masten & Coatsworth 1998; Revich & Shatté 2002; Schneider 2001; Abramson, Seligman & Teasdale 1978; Siegel 1999). The types of stress reactions that are noticed across various stages of life appear to be physiological, emotional, cognitive and behavioural and starting with childhood these reactions vary by age, maturity and exposure.

According to Folkman & Lazarus (1984), managing stress includes accepting, tolerating, avoiding or minimising the stressor as well as gaining mastery over the environment seem to be the central processes in the management of stress. Anything that we do to adjust to the challenges and demands of stress, by way of adjustments made to reduce the impacts of stress, could be defined as coping. Thus coping can be viewed as constant changes in our cognitions and the use of behavioural effort to mitigate both external internal demands that are appraised as 'taxing' (Cummings 1991) or 'exceeding the resources of the person' (Folkman & Lazarus 1984). Do early life stressful events produce a better rate of resilience in later life? DuMont, Widom and Czaja (2007) reported from their study of a large sample size (n=676) that resilience that was evident throughout adolescents and early adult life was associated with a low rate of stressful life events.

They also reported paradoxically, that those who became resilient only after adolescence had experienced more negative life events, so therefore it may not be conclusively said that stressful events provide life experience with positive steeling effects or negative effects that evade psychological resources (DuMont et al. 2007)

Coping is also explained as conscious effort to solve personal and interpersonal problems, and seeking to master, minimize or tolerate stress or conflict (Snyder 1999; Weiten, & Lloyd; 2008 Zeidner, & Endler 1996). In literature on coping there are a number of adaptive or constructive coping strategies, i.e., those strategies that appear to be reactive to stress and that reduce stress levels. This contrasts with proactive coping, in which a coping response aims to head off a future stressor.

Coping strategies

Coping responses are partly controlled by personality (habitual traits), but also partly by the social context, particularly the nature of the stressful environment (Carver & Connor-Smith 2010). While there are a number of ways by which people cope, most of these mechanisms can be classified as:

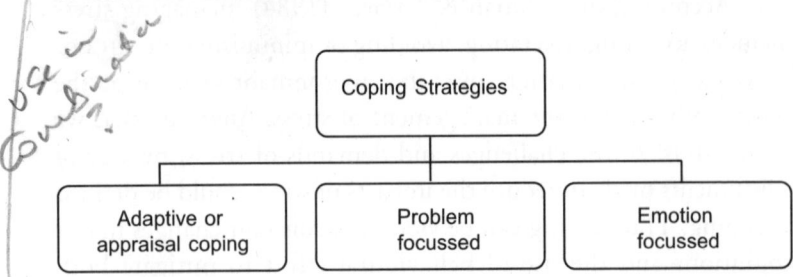

The basic distinctions are often made between various contrasting strategies, for example: problem-focused versus emotion-focused; engagement versus disengagement; cognitive versus behavioural. Weiten (2008) has provided a useful summary of three broad types of coping strategies:

- appraisal-focused (adaptive cognitive),
- problem-focused: Any coping behaviour that is directed at reducing or eliminating a stressor, adaptive behavioural
- emotion-focused: Directed towards changing one's own emotional reaction to stressor

Appraisal-focused strategies assist with personal modifications of the way we think occur when the person modifies the way they think, for example: employing denial, or distancing oneself from the problem. People may alter the way they think about a problem by altering their goals and values, such as by seeing the humour in a situation. Laughter Yoga is being taught around the world today as a simple and profound. An exercise routine, it is sweeping the world and is a complete wellbeing workout. The brainchild of Dr. Madan Kataria an Indian Physician has forwarded laughter as the best medicine and clinical research on Laughter Yoga methods, conducted at the University of Graz in Austria; Bangalore, India; and in the United States has proved that Laughter lowers the level of stress hormones (epinephrine, cortisol, etc.) in the blood. It fosters a positive and hopeful attitude. It is less likely for a person to succumb to stress and feelings of depression and helplessness, if one is able to laugh away the troubles (Kataria, M. Laughter, Yoga International 2012).

Meditation for instance and practice of mindfulness is being seen not only a technique to calms one's emotions, but can bring humanity to come and feel more 'together' as it tends to a assist acquiring inner quietness and peace and bring some sense of balance in oneself.

Depending upon individual perceptions and the nature of stress, people combine the above coping strategies. While both seem to have their own advantages, counsellors and social workers tend to work with and encourage problem-focused coping mechanisms as it allows for a greater perception of individual control over one's own problem, while emotion-focused coping may lead to a reduction in perceived control.

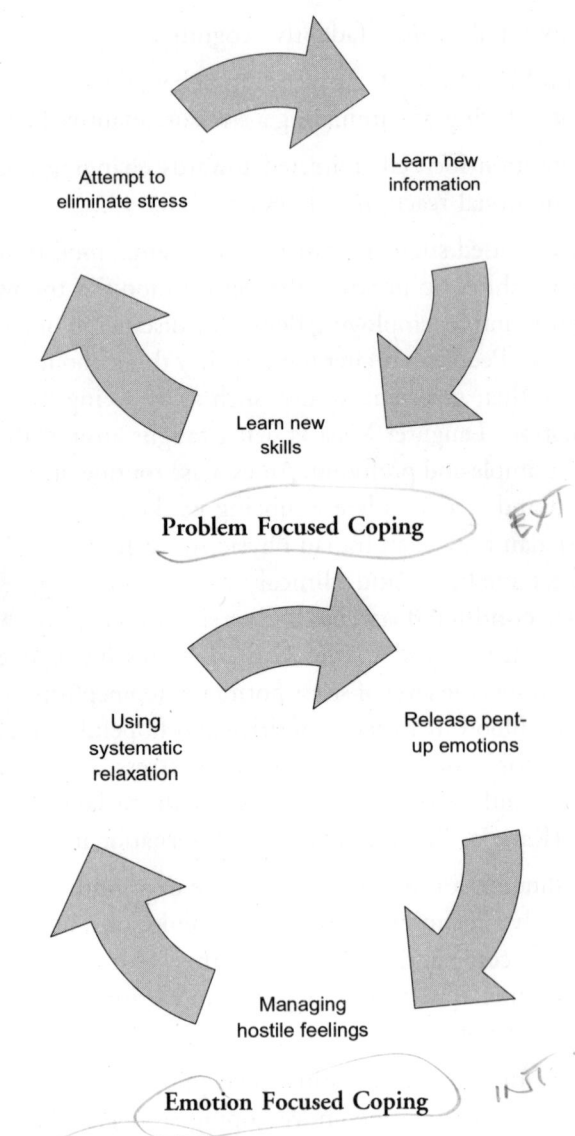

Folkman and Lazarus (1984) identified five emotion-focused coping strategies:

- Disclaiming
- Escape-avoidance

- Accepting responsibility or blame
- Exercising self-control
- Positive reappraisal

They also highlight problem-focused coping strategies. Seeking social support attends to the problem. "...taking action to try to get rid of the problem is a problem-focused strategy, but so is making a list of the steps to take". Lazarus notes, "... the connection between his idea of 'defensive reappraisals' or cognitive coping and Freud's concept of 'ego-defenses' coping strategies thus overlapping with a person's defense mechanisms." Anticipatory Coping is also known as proactive coping. Society makes great efforts in this direction. City councils remind us to prepare for summers as well as monsoons, but there is a limited amount that individuals can do to reduce the stress of some difficult challenge just by anticipation.

Stoeber & Janssen (2011) examine the benefits of positive reframing as an adaptive strategy. Their research focussed on the issue of perfectionism and the benefits of cognitively reframing negative attitudes by questioning the perfectionist expectation and criticism. This is another pathway into opening up new ways of thinking that solve problems by erasing the thoughts that are creating the problem. Religious coping has been found to be the most common coping response, with one study reporting that 17 per cent use religion as a coping response. Women mentioned religious coping more frequently than did men

Maladaptive Coping

Due to work and life stresses people also tend to adopt negative or maladaptive coping. While adaptive coping methods improve functioning, a maladaptive coping mechanism may assist in immediate symptomatic reduction, but maintains and even contributes to the growth of the disorder. Maladaptive techniques can seem to be effective in the short-term, which can give the false impression of being a successful technique, but maladaptive processes will fail as a long-term coping process.

Examples of maladaptive behaviour strategies include dissociation, desensitization, reckless behaviours; anxious avoidance and escape behaviours including as over consumption of alcohol as well as self-medication and doping. Unfortunately such maladaptive coping mechanism interferes with the person's ability to unlearn, or break away the existing relationship between the presenting problem and the associated symptoms. They only exacerbate to serve and to maintain the disorder. Dissociation is the ability of the mind to separate and compartmentalize thoughts, memories, and emotions. This is often associated with post-traumatic stress. Further examples of maladaptive coping strategies include: self-distraction, denial, substance use and self-blame.

Do Women Cope Better?

Gender differences in coping strategies are the ways in which men and women differ in managing psychological stress. There is evidence that males often develop stress due to their careers, whereas females often encounter stress due to issues in interpersonal relationships (Wang et al. 2007). In general, such differences as exist indicate that women tend to employ emotion-focused coping and the response to stress, whereas men appear to be utilising more of problem-focused coping and the response, perhaps because societal standards encourage men to be more individualistic, while women are often expected to be interpersonal. Whether or not this has anything to do with the genetic composition of is still debated, thus preferences in coping strategies are seen as a result of social conditioning and child-rearing: for instance, as boys as they grow up are encouraged to be independent, while girls are expected to comply, which may influence each gender's choice of coping mechanism.

Hormones also play a part in stress management. *Cortisol*, a stress hormone, was found to be elevated in males during stressful situations. In females, however, the same hormone levels were decreased in stressful situations, and instead, an increase in limbic activity was discovered. Many researchers believe that these results underlie the reasons why men administer a fight-or-flight reaction to stress; whereas, females have a tend-and-befriend reaction. The "fight-or-flight" response activates the sympathetic nervous system in the form of increased focus levels, adrenaline, and epinephrine (Wang et al. 2007). However, the "tend-and-befriend" reaction refers to the tendency of women to protect their offspring and relatives. These qualities can well be discussed as coping mechanisms, but it is important not to forget the quality of resilience and how this in intertwined in the processes of management of stress, adversity management.

Resilience—Bits

In most simple terms "resilience" refers to the notion of an individual's predisposition to cope with stress and adversity. This coping may result in the individual "bouncing back" to a previous state of normal functioning, or simply not showing negative effects (Masten 2009). Resilience crops up in situations of adversity and risk and negative life circumstances that are known to lead to poor outcomes (Luthar & Cicchetti 2000). There are several theories and approaches that seek to address and promote resilience. Current research suggests that interventions need to address both individual and environmental factors. Such an approach allows for a holistic multi-systemic approach supports all ages and all situations (Luthar & Zelazo 2003; Ungar 2011; Walsh 2006).

While individualised interventions seek to strengthen a person in resisting and persisting through adversity sometimes individual may also require suitability of behavioural changes in combination with interventions to affect the immediate social environment of the person (Jaffee et al. 2007). A similar view is expressed by Walsh (2006) who supports multisystemic, strengths-based understanding of family resilience and interventions, that reign in the frontier of social and social cultural ecology. Most writings in resilience refer to the result of individuals being able to interact with their environments and the processes that either promote well-being or protect them against the overwhelming influence of risk factors (Zautra et al. 2010).

Another form of resilience, referred to as posttraumatic growth, is discussed by Richard Hill (2012) in this book. Traumatic affects that impact the foundation of safety and security of an individual leaving the sufferer floundering in an unfamiliar and unsafe psychosocial environment (Calhoun and Tedeschi 2006; Hill 2012). Adversity, dealt with in this positive, strength-based way can lead to better functioning, making it possible for us to relate to resilience as more of a process exhibited by an individual in *reaction* to a situation rather than just an *innate trait* of an individual (Rutter 2008). Recently there has also been interesting evidence that resilience can indicate a capacity to resist a sharp decline in functioning even though a person temporarily appears to get worse (Boyden & Mann 2005; Castro & Murray 2010). Sometimes, what we see in surface behaviour may not be a true reflection of the inner workings of resilience.

Commonly used explanations about resilience are hardiness, resourcefulness, and mental toughness, but it may be that a wiser way of looking at resilience is to see it as a dynamic process whereby individuals exhibit positive behavioural alternation when one encounters major adversity, trauma, tragedy, threats, or even considerable sources of stress. It is different from innate strengths that individuals, groups and communities or entire populations possess regardless of the level of adversity they face. Under adversity, assets function differently (e.g. a good school, or parental monitoring) and can have a great deal more influence in the life of a child from a poorly resourced background than one from a wealthy home with other options for support, recreation, and self-esteem (Masten & Obradovic 2006). Thus "resilience" is defined here as the ability to produce an individual biological, psychological and social resistance through adaptation that produces the strengths within to fight the adversity to withstand a crisis. Thus, in medium term it should produce the ability to fight back.

Constructing Resilience

For the purposes of this chapter we will view resilience as a two-dimensional construct that concerns itself with exposure to adversity and resultant positive adjustment (Ungar 2004). This two-dimensional construct implies two judgments: one about a "positive adaptation" and the other about the significance of risk (or adversity). One point of view about adversity could define it as any risks associated with negative life conditions that are statistically related to adjustment difficulties, such as poverty, children of mothers with conditions of mental illness or families and communities that have experienced disasters. Positive adaptation, on the other hand, must demonstrate behaviours that suggest social competency after witnessing distressing events. Once again such competencies differ from society to socially and suggest vast differences across cultures as well. In a previous study Pulla and Bharadwaj looked at the 'love thy neighbour' community resiliency demonstrated by Mumbai residents in India on three occasions in the city: the dreadful bomb explosions in Mumbai suburban trains in 2006 that claimed 188 lives; the devastating floods of 2007 when the city was halted for six days; and the and 26/11 terror attacks of 2008 that shook global humanity. These events raised three questions: *Is resilience* an expression of mutual generosity; is it remarkable heroisms in the face of adversity and crisis; and finally, *is resilience* historically a public resource for solace? (Pulla & Bharadwaj 2010).

Ungar and his colleagues at the Resilience Research Centre (2008, 2012) argue that this standard definition of resilience could be problematic because it does not adequately account for cultural and contextual differences in how people in other systems express resilience. They have shown that cultural and contextual factors exert a great deal of influence on the factors that affect resilience amongst population. Resilience has been shown to be more than just the capacity of individuals to cope well under adversity often localised to those societies where adversity occurred. Resilience, as 'public resource of solace', does not appear to be an indefinitely renewable when crisis hits the world today and links Mumbai, Kashmir, Madrid, London, Karachi, Wall Street and Washington, together (Pulla & Bharadjwaj 2010). Thus resilience is better understood as the opportunity and capacity of individuals to navigate their way to psychological, social, cultural, and physical resources that may pull together during crisis and provide them an opportunity and capacity individually and collectively to negotiate for life following adversity in appropriate and culturally meaningful ways.

Most recent researchers on resilience have devoted to discovering the protective factors that explain people's adaptation to adverse conditions, in various situations. For example a sample of areas in which research has been carried on in recent years includes homelessness and health in a nationwide Australian study (Nirui 2010); refugees resettlement in third countries, (Murray 2010); natural disasters, (Hargreaves 2010); natural calamities such as drought on vulnerable populations with disabilities, (Crichton & Chenoweth 2010) and man made disasters such as 26/11 in Mumbai, (Pulla & Bharadwaj 2010). The focus of empirical work then has been shifted to understand the underlying protective processes.

Andrew Zolli and Ann Marie Healy in their latest book, *Resilience: Why things bounce back* (2012), bring in a radically new definition of resilience in rather simple words: "if we can not control the volatile tides of change, we can learn to build better boats. We can design- and redesign- organisations, institutions and systems to better absorb disruption, operate under a wider variety of conditions, and shift more fluidly from one circumstance to the next".

The following illustration summarises to me that resilience expectations in all human endeavours have considerably changed and there is not a reservoir of resilience from which we can draw upon in all adversities.

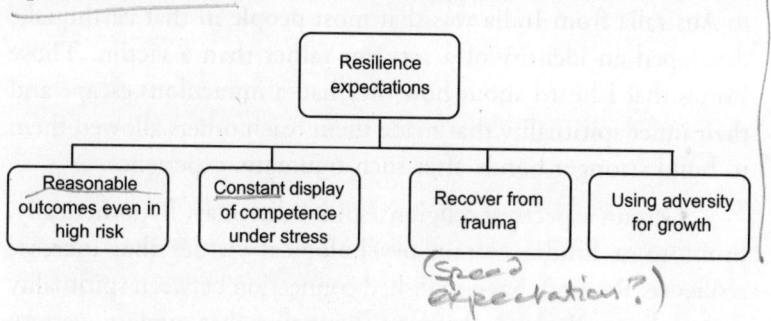

```
                    Resilience
                    expectations
    ┌──────────────┬─────────────┬────────────┬──────────────┐
 Reasonable     Constant display   Recover from   Using adversity
 outcomes even in  of competence    trauma         for growth
 high risk       under stress
```

(Speed expectation?)

Thus, in these days of turbulence, the ability of people, communities and the systems to maintain their 'core purpose integrity' (Zolli, & Healy 2012) amid unforseen shocks and surprises expects of us to adapt successfully in spite of experiencing risk factors. There are always challenges in this fragile world of ours, we have persistent poverty, increased susceptibilities to human disease and pestilence, climate changes and growing lack of paid employment that could possibly prevent poverty. While in the west equality, solidarity and social justice, true cornerstones of post-war welfare states are being replaced by inequality, exposing differences between 'us' and 'them', between natives and foreigners, rich and poor, those on top and those at the bottom (Leskošek 2005: 247), these differences are likely to grow further asking for more creative ways of ensuring a purpose life and a life.

In my experience as a social worker in floods and community recovery in Queensland, Australia, I often found it was useful to work and facilitate competency development to cope with stress effectively and in a healthy manner. Locating the strengths in clients that we work with such as their problem-solving skills, their ability to seek help in addition to their capacity to offer help to others were very important. Reflecting back on earth quake in Latur, Maharashtra, in India, a country where there are no social security measures for people except some immediate relief measures, it was amazing to see how people bounce back to some form of normal routine. One of the lessons that I brought back to Australia from India was that most people in that earthquake developed an identity of a survivor rather than a victim. Those stories that I heard about how they had a miraculous escape and their inner spirituality that made them reach others allowed them to build stronger bonds after such traumatic experience.

Certain aspects of religions/spirituality may, hypothetically, promote or hinder certain psychological virtues that increase resilience. Research has established connection between spirituality and resilience. Indeed, there is a suggestion that modern western cultures have become neglectful of family and thereby reduce opportunities for children to acquire spirituality and resilience. Further, Benson & Thistlethwaite (2008), argue that Western culture and thus its communities have become focused on perfection and fail to view "pain, suffering, mistakes and failure" as normal components of life. Financial and personal successes are now valued and failure is not viewed as a learning experience that improves problem solving skills.

'This has led to increased feelings of guilt and shame for many Westerners who are unable to acknowledge mistakes and mend relationships. This in turn has led to reduced community and empathy for others and increased feelings of hopelessness and reduced connections to others.' (Benson & Thistlethwaite 2008, p.94)

The suggestion that people are now learning skills of resilience (problem-solving, self-belief, realistic expectations, confronting mistakes and relationship skills) from psychotherapists, social workers rather than family, society and culture as these traditional supports are becoming less effective or are no longer available is certainly not questionable.

The Strengths Perspective and Resiliency

"The strengths perspective does not require one to discount the grip and thrall of addictions or the humiliating, frightening anguish of child abuse, or the unbidden disorganization and confusion of psychosis. But from the vantage point of a strengths perspective, *it is as wrong to deny the possible just as it is to deny the problem.* And the strengths perspective does decry the intemperate reign of psychopathology and illness as the central civic, moral, and medical categorical imperative. Adherents of the strengths perspective *do not* believe, with good reason, that most people who are the victims of abuse or their own rampant appetites, or that all people who have been traumatized inevitably become damaged goods"(Saleebey 2000).

That the world has adversity and it produces challenges which are associated with diverse negative consequences is accepted. Nevertheless, despite negative outcomes predicted and making our lives functional ensuring that there is a purpose, sense of well being and meaning in life, communities and organisations is the whole purpose of utilising the strengths approach to resiliency development in people. It starts with the primordial recognition that everybody has the capacity for resiliency and that every body can bounce back.

Masten (2001) affirms, "[w]hat began as a quest to understand the extraordinary has revealed the power of the ordinary. Resiliency does not come from rare and special qualities, but from the everyday magic of ordinary, normative human resources in the minds, brains, and bodies of children, in their families and relationships, and in their communities" (p. 235).

This view point represents the shift from a pathological preoccupation with risk. Most of us manage to have positive lives and develop successfully; including the most challenged ones from troubled families and disadvantaged communities. Even if we were to see this only in the context of children most research shows that an average of 70 per cent to 75 per cent of children who seemed at a greater risk for later problems to make it and make it well (Benard 2004). As strengths practitioner I believe that all human processes have the intrinsic capacity to direct people toward a healthy development and to bring their full potential. By utilising a strengths perspective that allows them to assess attainable goals, mobilizes resources to promote change and self-esteem, and finally become resilient. Common to resiliency theory and the Strengths Perspective is the faith in human beings capacity to cope and design his or her future. Social workers and counsellors who are interested in this perspective, and committed to the core values of their profession challenge to explore their attitudes, beliefs, biases, and their own selves in order to generate a shift in the way they perceive themselves, their clients, and their relationship with them.

Approaching Inner Strengths

Be it coping or resiliency development, the core business in our societies today, we seek empowering alternatives to traditional methods. Our attention is to facilitate change by helping to look at what has worked, what does not work and what might work presently. It is important for those who facilitate and those desiring change to be integral to this process of change. As helping professionals we pride ourselves with the skill set to deal with our existence and manifestations of the state of un-satisfactoriness; suffering; stress; anxieties and tensions (Pulla 2010).

I am aware that the Buddhist perspective presents a couple of themes that appear to me as being useful in influencing human behaviour. They are internalised verbalisations and visualisations. Internal verbalisations are the talk and chatter that constantly invade the human consciousness while internal visualisations are mental pictures that are produced in the human mind. Therapists believe both need taming. One method of taming internal verbalisations is to overwhelm them and replace them with diversions including mindfulness, meditative practices, engaging in good companionships and suitable conversations (Pulla 2010). The taming of internal visualisations is to constantly hold in one's *spiritual purpose for life?*

mind a higher image of him or herself, even an imaginary higher image for the moment that one is comfortable with. With the taming of the 'swinging monkey' there is a possibility to draw into the present instead of living in the past. We do need a paradigm shift: seeking solutions from inside to seeking solutions from outside. Would the seeking solutions from within be at the level of the individual, group or collective or society is a matter of detail. But inward looking demands a rigorous approach altogether.

My recent visits and conversations in Tuzla and Sarajevo in Bosnia and Herzegovina with mental health professionals confirm that a great number of people are withdrawing into the past, but I also saw a growing number of people attempting to reduce their stresses and anxieties through acceptance of events as they are rather than as what they would like them to be. It appears to me that we need to work on our capabilities as helping professionals to engage in conversations that allow us to go into the cause that leads us to the rot that is currently manifested in the world. Perhaps we need to ask this question in a different way: Are we actually perpetuating and indulging in coping and resilience skills to deal with effects and neglecting a discourse on returning to the causes of the effects in the first place? For the last five years I have been working on these themes and pondering over the roots of our business in human services and I started feeling that we are loosing the plot. Problems appear to be more fundamental: *The gradual erosion of human values, few people's greed over many people's need, anomie and the growth of human alienation in our civil societies are some of the main issues that we are* not *dealing with.*

These are problems we need to confront. How do people live with economic and social inequality? The short answer is that they don't, not if they can help it. They walk miles, dragging their bodies and meagre possessions including children in the hope of finding food, water and safety. They have done that for many years in many parts of Africa. Or brave the seas in dinghies to afar shores, miles away from their countries of birth. While being compassionate may be virtuous, practice of obligatory compassion in the face of illegitimate suffering, appears to me as a cop out that converts societal guilt into a false responsibility.

As helping professionals with an obligatory humanitarian and social justice response to human suffering, we also need to wake up to our professional responsibilities to see the truth, i.e. *the ultimate cause of suffering in the world today*. The task is in front of us and I am sure we are capable of moving centre stage not only to show how people organise themselves in the face of suffering and global inequality today but how this might be made more just. This involves a fundamental critique of current practices and use of the opportunity to ponder over the roots of our crisis and make decisions about 'where to from here'.

Works Cited

Abramson, L.Y., Seligman, M.E.P., & Teasdale, J.D. (1978). Learned Helplessness in humans: A critique and reformulation. *Journal of Abnormal Psychology, 97* (1).49-74.

Benard, B. (2004). *Resiliency. What we have learned.* San Francisco: WestEd.

Benson, J. & Thistlewaite, J. (2008). *Mental health across cultures: A practical guide for primary care.* Sydney: Radcliffe Publishing.

Boyden, J. & Mann, G. (2005). Children's risk, resilience, and coping in extreme situations. In M. Ungar (Ed.), *Handbook for Working with Children and Youth: Pathways to Resilience Across Cultures and Contexts* (pp. 3-26). Thousand Oaks, CA: Sage.

Bhushan, B. (2010) Psychiatric profiling of the Indian geriatric population: Implications for possible interventions, (p. 8) Coping Resilience and Hope Building, Asia Pacific Regional Conference, 9-11 July 2010 Abstracts.

Castro, F.G. & Murray, K.E. (2010). Cultural adaptation and resilience: Controversies, issues, and emerging models. In J.W. Reich, A.J. Zautra & J.S. Hall (Eds.), *Handbook of Adult Resilience* (pp. 375-403). New York: Guilford Press.

Calhoun, L. G. & Tedeschi, R.G. (2006). *Handbook of Posttraumatic Growth: Research and Practice.* New York: Erlbaum.

Carver, C. S.; Connor-Smith, J. (2010). "Personality and coping". *Annual Review of Psychology*, 61, 679-704.

Crichton, M and Chenoweth, L. (2010). *Drought- Intellectual disability and resilience in rural Australia* (p.14) Coping Resilience and Hope Building, Asia Pacific Regional Conference, 9-11 July 2010 Abstracts.

Cummings, E.M., Greene, A.L. & Karraker, A.H. (1991). *Life-span Developmental Psychology: Perspectives of stress and coping.* Hillsdale, NJ: Erlbaum.

Dommett, J. (2010). From being devalued and powerless to coping and resilience: a personal story of recovery (p.37) Coping Resilience and Hope Building, Asia Pacific Regional Conference, 9-11 July 2010 Abstracts.

Graham, C. (2010). Psychological strengths and health of people over 65 years living in the community, (p. 27) Coping Resilience and Hope Building, Asia Pacific Regional Conference, 9-11 July 2010 Abstracts.

Fekadu, T. (2012). *No One's Son.* Falmouth, UK: Leapfrog Press.

Folkman, S. & Lazarus, R. S. (1990). Coping and Emotion. In Nancy Stein, N. L., Leventhal, B. & Trabasso, T. (eds.), *Psychological and Biological Approaches to Emotion.* New Jersey: Lawrence Erlbaum Associates.

Hargreaves, D., (2010). Insider view of promoting resilience and hope building in times of natural disasters: the Australian bushfires, floods and droughts, (p.7) Coping Resilience and Hope Building, Asia Pacific Regional Conference, 9-11 July 2010 Abstracts.

Hill, R. (2012). Trauma—Creating Beneficial Change. In Pulla, V., Shatté, A., Warren, S. (Eds.), *Perspectives on Coping and Resilience*, Authors Press, New Delhi.

Jaffee, S. R., Caspi, A., Moffitt, T. E., Polo-Tomás, M., & Taylor, A. (2007). Individual, family, and neighborhood factors distinguish resilient from non-resilient maltreated children: A cumulative stressors model. *Child Abuse & Neglect, 31*(3), 231-253. doi: 10.1016/j.chiabu.2006.03.011.

Kataria, M, Laughter Yoga International. (2012). What is laughter yoga? Retrieved from: http://laughteryoga.org/index.php?option=com_content&view=article&id=180:what-is-laughter-yoga&catid=85:about-laughter-yoga&Itemid=265

Kokonyange, Jacques Kikuni, & Syfia International. (2012). Straddling the Congo-Uganda border with two nationalities—best of both lives. Worldcrunch: all the news is global, 2012(28 August). http://www.worldcrunch.com/culture-society/straddling-the-congo-uganda-border-with-two-nationalities-best-of-both-lives/drc-uganda-border-identification-african-economy/c3s9431/#.UI2yx2flbj1

Lazarus, R. S., & Folkman, S. (1984). *Stress, Appraisal, and Coping*. New York, NY: Springer Publishing.

Leadbeater, B., Dodgen, D. & Solarz, A. (2005). The resilience revolution: A paradigm shift for research and policy. In R.D. Peters, B. Leadbeater & R.J. McMahon (eds.), *Resilience in children, families, and communities: Linking context to practice and policy*, (pp. 47-63). New York: Kluwer.

Leskošek, V. (2005). Globalne neenakosti. *Socialno delo*, letnik 44 (2005), št. 4-5. [*Global inequalities. Social Work*, year 44 (2005), number 4-5].

Luthar, S. S., & Cicchetti, D. (2000). "The Construct of Resilience: A Critical Evaluation and Guidelines for Future Work". [Article]. *Child Development, 71*(3), 543.

_____, & Zelazo, L. B. (2003). Research on Resilience: An Integrative Review. In S. S. Luthar (Ed.), *Resilience and Vulnerability: Adaptation in the Context of Childhood Adversitites* (pp. 510-549). New York: Cambridge Univ Press.

Masten, A.S., & Coatsworth, J.D. (1998). The development of competence in favourable and unfavourable environments: lessons from research on successful children. *American Psychologist, 53* (2). 205-220.

_____. (2001). Ordinary magic: Resilience processes in development. *American Psychologist*, 56(3), 227-238.

_____ (2009). Ordinary Magic: Lessons from research on resilience in human development. *Education Canada* 49 (3): 28-32. Retrieved from: http://www.cea-ace.ca/sites/default/files/EdCan-2009-v49-n3-Masten.pdf.

_____, Obradovic, J. (2006). "Competence and resilience in development". Annals of the New York Academy of Sciences 1094: 13-27. doi:10.1196/annals.1376.003. PMID 17347338.

Murray, K., (2010). Resilience among Sudanese in Australia (p.33) Coping Resilience and Hope Building, Asia Pacific Regional Conference, 9-11 July 2010 Abstracts.

Nirui, M., (2010). Resilience and health in homeless families with acompnaying children, (p.34) Coping Resilience and Hope Building, Asia Pacific Regional Conference, 9-11 July 2010 Abstracts.

Panchanatham, N. (2011) Surviving the Harsher Economic Times—The Indian Mantra of Remaining Alive and Kicking, Strengths Based Management of Social Change with Special Focus on Transition Countries, International Conference, Sarajevo: 2011.

Pulla, V., (2010) Presidential Speech at the International Conference (p.!V-V) Coping Resilience and Hope Building, Asia Pacific Regional Conference, 9-11 July 2010 Abstracts.

_____, Bharadwaj, S., (2010). Is resilience a renewable resource? Case of Mumbaites and mendicants of Varanasi, (p.44) Coping Resilience and Hope Building, Asia Pacific Regional Conference, 9-11 July 2010. Abstracts.

Revich, K. & Shatté, A. (2002). *The Resilience factor.* New York: Broadway Books.

Riggs, A. (2010) In the shadows… Art that reveals, transforms and restores(p.13) Coping Resilience and Hope Building, Asia Pacific Regional Conference, 9-11 July 2010 Abstracts.

Rutter, M. (2008). Developing concepts in developmental psychopathology. In J.J. Hudziak (ed.), *Developmental psychopathology and wellness: Genetic and environmental influences* (pp.3-22). Washington, DC: American Psychiatric Publishing.

Schneider, S. (2001), In search of realistic optimism. *American Psychologist,* 56 (3). 250-261.

Siegel, D.(1999). *The Developing Mind.* New York: Guilford Press.

Smark, T. (2009) Resilience and spirituality—A chapter review: 'Mental health across cultures: A practical guide for primary care' by J. Benson and J. Thistlethwaite (2008; Sydney: Radcliffe), *Australian Journal of Pastoral Care and Health,* Vol.3, No.1, June.

Snyder, C.R. (ed.) (1999) *Coping: The Psychology of What Works.* New York: Oxford University Press.

Stoeber J. & Janssen D.P. (2011). Perfectionism and coping with daily failures: positive reframing helps achieve satisfaction at the end of the day. *Anxiety Stress Coping.* 24(5):477-97.

Trotman, P., & and Townson, L. (2012). The role of language in promoting trauma recovery and resilience. In Pulla, V., Shatté, A., Warren, S. (Eds.), *Perspectives on Coping and Resilience,* Authors Press, New Delhi.

Ungar, M. (2004). A constructionist discourse on resilience: Multiple contexts, multiple realities among at-risk children and youth. *Youth and Society,* 35(3), 341-365.

_____. (2010). Families as navigators and negotiators: facilitating culturally and contextually specific expressions of resilience. *Family Process, 49*(3), 421-435. doi: 10.1111/j.1545-5300.2010.01331.x

_____ (2011). The Social Ecology of Resilience: Addressing Contextual and Cultural Ambiguity of a Nascent Construct. *American Journal of Orthopsychiatry, 81*(1), 1-17. doi: 10.1111/j.1939-0025.2010.01067.x

_____ (2012). Resilience Research Centre Retrieved 18 May 2012, 2012, from http://resilience.socialwork.dal.ca/

Walsh, F. (2006). *Strengthening Family Resilience*. New York: Guilford Press.

Wang, J., Korczykowski, M., Rao, H., Fan, Y. & Pluta, J. (2007). Gender difference in neural response to psychological stress. *SCAN* 2, 227-239.

Weiten, W. & Lloyd, M.A. (2008) *Psychology Applied to Modern Life (9th ed.)*. Wadsworth: Cengage Learning.

Zolli, A. and Healy, A,M. (2012). *Resilience: Why Things Bounce Back*, Free Press

Zeidner, M. & Endler, N.S. (eds.) (1996) *Handbook of Coping: Theory, Research, Applications*. New York: John Wiley.

1 March 18.

Hmm... Sure thought-provoking ideas but not that helpful.

CHAPTER 2

Toward a Philosophy of Resilience

Thomas W. Dukes

Abstract

The study of resilience has captured the attention of researchers and laity alike due to the fact that it addresses and seeks to elucidate aspects of the human experience that include, but move beyond, the practical and into the spiritual or transcendent dimension. It is this dimension that is made the focus of study in the subjective psychology tradition. While the work done to date in the field of resilience has been significant, it can also be said that it is based primarily on a *practical psychology* perspective, or what has been termed *objective psychology*. In contrast, *subjective psychology* has been largely ignored. From the perspective afforded by this tradition, and by employing certain specific systems of philosophical thought, we may find it possible to better and more fully describe and understand the "magic" (Masten 2001) that is resilience.

To enhance, or enlarge, our understanding of resilience, it seems necessary to place the resilience literature in dialogue with another body of work that may serve to move the conversation in productive new directions. This is not meant to be a systematic analysis; rather, it is an attempt to bring a philosophical system into the discussion with the hope that a more complete understanding of the topic of resilience may emerge.

Key Words

Resilience, adversity, existentialism, will, boundary situations, transcendence, dynamic contextualism

While it is understood that the primary focus of interest for resilience researchers is the clinical, it is nevertheless important to provide a broader context and foundation for this generically important area of intellectual and clinical inquiry. Overton (1998) has noted that "philosophy's traditional function has been *conceptual clarification*—exploring conceptual foundations and ensuring that they can carry the intended load" (p. 108). This study represents an initial foray into what might be designated the *philosophy of resilience*. Such an effort is necessary if the field of resilience studies is to continue to evolve, mature, and contribute from a solid intellectual base both theoretically in the field of developmental psychology and clinically in the form of prevention and intervention efforts.

The following remarks are aimed at exploring the potential for mutually enlightening dialogue between developmental psychology and existential philosophy. In a sense, this study represents a return to the origins of psychology when strict divisions between academic disciplines were not observed. Miller (2004) has recently argued that such a return is warranted in the realm of the clinical practice of psychology because it is ultimately a moral endeavor. It is moral, Miller noted, because at its very core, psychology is concerned with facing human suffering, as the title of his book proclaims. No less can be said of the true focus of resilience research. The aim is, and has always been, to better understand those examples of unusually healthy adaptation and growth that occur in the midst of terrible adversity, and to pass on the lessons learned to those for whom the exigencies of life are more difficult to surmount. Essentially, resilience is studied in order that human suffering may be minimized, while achievement of the so-called good life, as variously defined, is realized. Therefore the study of resilience and the emergent clinical applications and interventions may similarly be termed moral endeavors.

Before progressing further, however, attention must be given to defining some fundamental terms. According to Miller (2004), "the basic feature of being moral or ethical is a concern with how one ought to live—how does one define and create the 'good life?'" (p. 22). A close look at the assorted definitions ascribed to the term *resilience* in recent years reveals that a similar question is implicitly imbedded in this area of study. Rutter (1987) has suggested that resilience is "the term used to describe the positive pole of individual differences in people's response to stress and adversity" (p. 316). Luthar (1991) has defined resilience as remaining "competent despite exposure to stressful life experiences" (p. 600). Masten (1994) has asserted that resilience relates to "how effectiveness in the environment is achieved, sustained or recovered despite adversity" (p. 4). More recently, Masten and Coatsworth (1998) characterized the study of resilience as an investigation into "how children overcome adversity to achieve good developmental outcomes" (p. 205). Garmezy (1993) suggested, "The central element in the study of resilience lies in the power of recovery and in the ability to return once again to those patterns of adaptation and competence that characterized the individual prior to the prestress period" (p. 129). O'Connell Higgins (1994) broadly defined resilience as "the ability to function psychologically at a far greater level than expected given a person's earlier developmental experiences" (p. 17). While similar to some extent, these various definitions have led to both confusion and criticism with regard to the growing field of study known as resilience (Bartelt 1994; Tarter & Vanyukov 1999).

Taking Miller's (2004) point to heart, to speak of definitions of resilience is to imply or assume an understanding of adaptation and health that, in turn, implies an accepted broad conclusion about what comprises the good life. In the absence of an explicit discussion or rationale for such conclusions, however, this is simply too far reaching an assumption to make. Or, if the intellectual effort has not been put forth by researchers of resilience, then implied agreement on what constitutes the good life may merely be borrowed from our particular culture at this particular time in history. According to Miller (2004), "one's culture or subculture defines for one a picture of how life ought to be, what optimal or less than optimal functioning is, and what should be done if one is not up to par" (p. 5). Neither of these options is suitable for providing the intellectual basis of a serious field of inquiry. To properly support the weight of resilience as a topic for study, it is first necessary to examine and, if need be, construct an intellectual foundation that addresses these fundamental issues.

Returning for the moment to the question of whether moral philosophy is relevant to clinical understanding and research, Miller (2004) noted:

> Moral concern expressed abstractly in philosophical—theological explorations of the nature of the "good life" is not, as a set of goals we strive for, about finding out what is the case but rather what ought to be the case. It is concerned with reducing human suffering and maximizing human well-being or flourishing. (p. 24)

Certainly as much is true for developmental psychologists concerned with understanding and promoting resilience. As Masten (1994) has asserted, "The rationale for examining resilience phenomena rests on the fundamental assumption that understanding how individuals overcome challenges to development and recover from trauma will reveal processes of adaptation that can guide intervention efforts with others at risk" (p. 3). Any assessment of positive adaptation presumes an implicit broad conceptualization of the good life, health, well-being, and of desired developmental achievements. It is important to ground a commonly accepted definition and an understanding of resilience as a discreet and empirically verifiable phenomenon. Only in this way can the field move forward at both theoretical and applied levels.

An Existential Perspective

Generally, the area of philosophy that will be employed here is known as *existentialism*. Specifically, the work that will be examined is that of Jaspers (1932), a German philosopher credited as one of the founders of existentialism (Flew 1979). Before moving into a discussion of Jaspers's work, it is first prudent to return to the issue of "what psychology can learn from the Existentialists," as Maslow (1968, p. 11) put it. As noted, Maslow began by suggesting, "the existentialists may supply psychology with the underlying philosophy which it now lacks" (p. 10). This is accomplished through an emphasis on two main points. First of these is a "radical stress on the concept of identity and the experience of identity as a *sine qua non* of human nature and of any philosophy or science of human nature" (p. 9). The second key point of existential philosophy is that

> it lays great stress on starting from experiential knowledge rather than from systems of concepts or abstract categories or a prioris. Existentialism rests on phenomenology, i.e., it uses personal, subjective experience as the foundation upon which abstract knowledge is built. (p. 9)

This last point is relevant for the present discussion and is in keeping with the earlier point regarding the subjective psychological viewpoint defined by Jaspers (1932). Much of the resilience literature has sought to measure both adversity and adaptation in empirical terms as a sort of balance sheet of risks and protective factors that can be mathematically compared and calculated to derive a ratio indicating probable coping. However, as Maslow (1968) has suggested, it may be that the European phenomenologists "can reteach us that the best way of understanding another human being, or at least *a* way necessary for some purposes, is to get into *his* weltanschauung and to be able to see *his* world through *his* eyes" (p. 14). This seems especially important in investigations of resilience, in which attempts at objective quantification are specious given the lack of a suitable and comprehensive definition. This is a field of study in which any investigation of component parts that loses sight of the whole winds up missing the point altogether. Like the study of resilience, existential psychology brings "a concern with the ideal, authentic, or perfect or godlike human being, a study of human potentialities as *now* existing in a certain sense, as current knowable reality" (p. 11). By turning attention to the lived experience of the individual who exemplifies an instance or pattern of such ideal or authentic living, we hope to learn something of the process that leads to a resilient outcome. To do this, however, we must first establish the parameters within which such attention may be focused.

In the second volume of his three-volume set titled *Philosophy*, Jaspers (1932) observes that we always find ourselves in situations that he defines as "a reality for an existing subject who has a stake in it" (p. 177). However, this is not simply an objective, concrete reality; rather, "it is a sense-related reality—neither psychological nor physical, but both in one" (p. 177). We might say that modern psychological theory and practice has been developed to aid in our negotiation of such situations. As Jaspers implies, "I have to put up with them as given, but not as definitively given; there remains a chance of transforming them" (p. 178). Were this not the case, there would be no point in attempting to influence a person's ability or approach to dealing with the situations within which he or she is embedded. However, it is important to note that our influence is not necessarily direct, and is certainly not absolute: "We do not proceed directly toward a goal; we bring about the situation from which it will arise" (p. 178). The process that ensues is a reciprocal one in which one's actions affect the situation, which then is a new reality that must be perceived, evaluated, and responded to yet again: "The consequences of whatever I do will confront me as a new situation which I have helped to bring about, and which is now given" (p. 178). The natural result of this dynamic is that "any understanding of situations means that I proceed toward ways of transforming them" (p. 178). The implication here is that the individual self takes center-stage in the ongoing effort to transform the situation to suit its own needs and preferences. With our necessarily finite knowledge of any particular situation in which we find ourselves, we make use of the limited means at our disposal to make that situation more accommodating to our purposes. We seek to change circumstances to facilitate, or at least to allow for the possibility of, achieving our desired ends. Alternatively, if our goals are not achievable given our particular situations, we may work toward accepting the limitations being imposed on us and reformulate our goals, i.e., adapt or cope. However, this adaptive coping does not seem to adequately describe the phenomenon of resilience as it has been reported. The topic of resilience holds our attention, indeed, captures our imaginations, because it is clearly more than mere coping. As will be discussed here, the human capacity to thrive in the midst of adversity, in contrast to succumbing or merely surviving adverse circumstances, indicates something more than these terms imply.

In the writings of Jaspers (1932), existentialism is seen "as an attempt to deal with the problem of 'Existenz' (a special sense of 'existence') through reason" (Flew 1979, p. 184). This special sense of existence is facilitated by certain kinds of situations that an individual experiences in his or her lifetime. What Jaspers (1932) provides is a way to conceptualize the varying types or levels of existence and the impact of each on the situations with which we are faced. Grabau (1971) instructed that "according to this view, consciousness is always awareness of something. Every act of awareness is therefore analyzable according to a model in which a subject is related to an object" (p. xvi). This subject-object differentiation provides the context for apprehending Jaspers's conceptualization of our modes of being in the world:

> The general relation of subject to object, therefore, is the horizon or encompassing background of all awareness, and the particular ways that a subject may be related to an object can be called modes of this encompassing. The analysis of the encompassing is thus an elucidation of the main ways a subject is related to an object. (Grabau 1971, p. xvi)

What follows is a brief description of the *immanent* and *transcendent modes* of both the subjective and objective encompassing.

Jaspers's (1932) first immanent mode is *existence*, the consciousness of the subjective, everyday experience of being "rooted in *my* landscape" (Latzel 1957, p. 179), in historically defined situations. Grabau (1971) described this as follows: "Man is first an organic being who is there, who exists in a practical life-world in space and time" (pp. xvii-xviii). The second immanent mode of subjectivity, *consciousness in general*, is achieved by separating from the subjective experience of the world and taking an objective, scientific view: "I must leave behind my unique, concrete existence, with its fullness of life, and my personal consciousness and become mere 'consciousness-as-such' which can be the same in every human being" (Latzel 1957, p. 179). Here is found the consciousness that affords the opportunity for objective scientific inquiry. The third immanent mode is referred to as *spirit*. Grabau (1971) explained, "Jaspers often talks of spirit as a kind of synthesis of existence and abstract consciousness in general" (p. xix). The result of this synthesis is "a concrete universal which Jaspers calls 'idea'" (p. xix). In this mode, men are viewed as *members of totalities*, or *historic unities* formed by an idea, rather than as individuals. These three represent the "basic possibilities of my being as a man" (Latzel 1957, p. 180). However, it is important to understand that this is not a hierarchy or developmental-stage model of human being, but rather a conceptualization of three distinct, yet interrelated levels of consciousness. Latzel (1957) explained:

> As mere existence, I would be confined to the biological realm, I would not be essentially human. As mere consciousness-as-such, I should be replaceable at will, and wholly without individual reality. As mere spirit, I should be "rarified"; I would deny my finiteness and thus become false. Each of these kinds of being requires the other two, if their expression is to be pure. Only as a whole man, a human being who continually lives all three of these kinds of

being—all of which reciprocally condition, support, and enhance one another—can I become authentically myself. (p. 181)

[handwritten annotation: The Trinity!]

These, then, represent the three immanent modes of the subject-object relationship.

Equally important to an understanding of Jaspers's (1932) work is the transcendent mode: "Remembering that the general structure is that of the subject-object relation, we get a transcendent mode of subjectivity (Existenz) and of objectivity (Transcendence) " (Grabau 1971, p. xvi). On the subjective side, "man as *Existenz* completely transcends all that he is, knows or does. *Existenz* is the primordial, spontaneous depth of each self. Never given, it must be actualized by each person" (p. xx). As such, Existenz appears to be the force, or source, out of which creativity and spontaneity emerge:

> It is man as *Existenz* who continually breaks out of established patterns to create new historical organizations at the level of existence, new knowledge and understanding at the level of consciousness in general, and new ideas in the realm of spirit, as in morals, art, religion. (p. xx)

On the objective side of the equation, the transcendent mode is merely labeled *transcendence*: "Transcendence is the representation of being itself beyond all objectivity" (Grabau 1971, p. xxi). According to Grabau's interpretation of Jaspers's (1971) work, "neither Existenz nor transcendence are objects. They are sources from which everything else springs" (p. xxi). The transcendent modes make possible a being that is not limited to the immanent modes. For, "if there were no transcendence, if the world were all there were to being, Existenz would not be possible. Man would be a mundane being, describable in the concepts of the various immanent modes of the encompassing" (p. xxi). For the sake of clarity, Jaspers's conceptualization of the encompassing can be depicted in the adaptation of Grabau's (1971) analysis shown in Table 1. While brief, this introduction to Jaspers's

(1971) conceptualizations is provided as the general basis for applying his analytical model to the phenomenon of resilience.

Table 1. The Encompassing

	Immanent Modes	Transcendent Modes
The encompassing of subjectivity	Existence; consciousness in general; spirit	Existenz
The encompassing of objectivity	World	Transcendence

Boundary Situations

Turning attention to the specific types of situation that hold the most relevance and potential value with respect to resilience, Jaspers (1932) identifies certain kinds of situations as *boundary situations* or *ultimate situations*. Whereas situations, as discussed by Jaspers, "exist by changing" (p. 178), what he calls boundary situations "never change, except in appearance" (p. 178). This special class of situations includes "that I am always in situations; that I cannot live without struggling and suffering; that I cannot avoid guilt; that I must die" (p. 178). Essentially, Jaspers is directing our attention to the existential dilemmas years later to be outlined and made clinically relevant by, among others, Yalom (1980).

One unique and certainly important aspect of boundary situations is the fact that they cannot be influenced in the same way as other situations. Whereas situations are open to being transformed, boundary situations are not: "We cannot modify them; all that we can do is to make them lucid, but without explaining or deducing them from something else. They go with existence itself" (Jaspers 1932, p. 178). What purpose does this lucidity serve? What is to be gained from a clearer awareness of such existential dilemmas?

The meaningful way for us to react to boundary situations is therefore not by planning and calculating to overcome them but by the very different activity of becoming the Existenz we potentially are; we become ourselves by entering with open eyes into the boundary situations. (p. 179)

This very image of "entering with open eyes" implies a deliberateness and intentionality that merits further consideration.

Grabau (1971) pointed out that Jaspers (1971), in his writings, "speaks of *Existenz* as doing or willing something" (p. xx). To "become ourselves," it seems that Jaspers is suggesting that we must consciously, through an act of will, enter into and experience the boundary situation. But what sort of *doing* is involved in entering a situation that cannot be changed? What does the entering entail? One answer to questions such as these can be pursued through an exploration of the nature and effect of *will*.

Will

James (1890) has characterized will as *mental effort*. More specifically, "effort of attention is... the essential phenomenon of will" (p. 562). For James, then, will is a conscious, intrapsychic doing of sorts: "The immediate point of application of the volitional effort lies exclusively in the mental world. The whole drama is a mental drama. The whole difficulty is a mental difficulty, a difficulty with an object of our thought" (p. 564). The particular form and direction of this mental effort, the doing, we might say, and the object to which this effort is directed are of particular relevance to our discussion of resilience: "The essential achievement of the will, in short, when it is most 'voluntary,' is to *attend* to a difficult object and hold it fast before the mind" (p. 561). If we conceive of the difficult object as a representation of an adversity faced, we may begin to see the parallel between entering with open eyes into the boundary situations and holding it fast before the mind. The conscious leap required to achieve Existenz, the entering with open eyes, may be analogous to the conscious choice and ensuing effort involved in initiating and maintaining attention on a difficult object.

However, it is not simply effort of attention that constitutes will for James (1890): "The effort to *attend* is therefore only a part of what the word 'will' covers; it covers also the effort to *consent* to something to which our attention is not quite complete" (p. 568). Will, therefore, involves not only the effort to attend, but also consenting to the reality of that to which one attends, "so that although attention is the first and fundamental thing in volition, *express consent to the reality of what is attended to* is often an additional and quite distinct phenomenon involved" (p. 568). James is pointing here to acceptance of the reality to which one's attention is now fixed. First, will comprises the effort of attention, and second, it is made up of consenting to the reality of what has been held in focus.

With reference to the adversities of life, it would seem that James (1890) distinguished the resilient, or, in his words, the *hero*, based on the force and effectiveness of his or her will. What follows is a beautifully written passage that captures the relevance and applicability of James's view of will to the conceptualization and study of resilience:

> The huge world that girdles us about puts all sorts of questions to us, and tests us in all sorts of ways. Some of the tests we meet by actions that are easy, and some of the questions we answer in articulately formulated words. But the deepest question that is ever asked admits of no reply but the dumb turning of will and tightening of our heartstrings as we say, "*Yes, I will even have it so!*" When a dreadful object is presented, or when life as a whole turns up its dark abysses to our view, then the worthless ones among us lose their hold on the situation altogether, and either escape from its difficulties by averting their attention, or if they cannot do that, collapse into yielding masses of plaintiveness and fear. The effort required for facing and consenting to such objects is beyond their power to make. But the heroic mind does differently. To it, too, the objects are sinister and dreadful, unwelcome, incompatible with wished-for things. But it can face them if necessary, without for that losing its hold upon the rest of life. The world thus finds in the heroic man its worthy match and mate; and the effort which he is able to put forth to hold himself

erect and keep his heart unshaken is the direct measure of his worth and function in the game of human life. He can *stand* this Universe. He can meet it and keep up his faith in it in presence of those same features which lay his weaker brethren low. He can still find zest in it, not by "ostrich-like forgetfulness," but by pure inward willingness to face the world with those deterrent objects there. And hereby he becomes one of the masters and the lords of life. (pp. 578-579)

Existential Thought in Clinical Practice

It may be helpful, for the sake of clarity, to refer to the work of those who have applied this philosophical viewpoint more directly in clinical practice. Rogers (1961), in describing his view of the good life based on decades of clinical experience, concluded,

> It involves the stretching and growing of becoming more and more of one's potentialities. It involves the courage to be. It means launching oneself fully into the stream of life. Yet the deeply exciting thing about human beings is that when the individual is inwardly free, he chooses as the good life this process of becoming. (p. 196)

Frankl (1969) has suggested that

> one must recognize that being human profoundly means being engaged and entangled in a situation, and confronted with a world whose objectivity and reality is in no way detracted from by the subjectivity of that "being" who is "in the world." (p. 51)

In fact, it is the subjective viewpoint that is of most interest in this case. The boundary situation provides an opportunity for the fullest and deepest expression of individual consciousness. For "when we are ourselves, they [boundary situations] can make us aware of being" (Jaspers 1932, p. 179).

Defining Adversity

The first side of the resilience equation in need of a commonly accepted definition has to do with the risk or adversity impinging on a given individual. Where should the line be drawn differentiating annoyance or moderate difficulty from real adversity? How might we define and quantify sufficient trauma to warrant consideration for the resilient designation? Perhaps Jaspers (1932) has provided the criteria by which such questions might be addressed:

> There are indeed situations I cannot get out of, situations I cannot see through as a whole. It is only where situations are wholly transparent to me that knowledge gets me out of them. The ones I cannot knowingly control I can only grasp existentially. (p. 180)

Here Jaspers makes clear a key distinction between situations and boundary situations. As an active participant in situations, we bring to bear our knowledge, skills, talents, and will to alter and transform them toward our goals and purposes. However, when faced with boundary situations, our efforts at producing change through these usual modes of action are ineffectual. The boundary situation is, by definition, outside of our influence.

The boundary situation thus pushes individual meaning making, or at least attention and consent, the activity and purview of the individual self, to its limit. Peripheral concerns fade away when one is confronted with the fundamental existential questions introduced by the boundary situation as long as one is able to keep that "difficult object" in mind. Or as Maslow (1968) has described it, "it is when the shallow life doesn't work that it is questioned and that there occurs a call to fundamentals" (p. 14). This is the opportunity that presents itself or that may be forced on an individual who is experiencing a boundary situation (Jaspers 1932). It is an opportunity to exercise attention, consent, and perhaps reflection, interpretation, and evaluation. Ultimately, however, it is an opportunity for authentic being: "In ultimate situations I accomplish in three stages—by a conscious inner act—the leap from existence to *Existenz*, and hence the birth of my authentic self" (Latzel 1957, p. 189). The manifest adversity that is a boundary situation for a given individual provides an opportunity not just for coping, but for authentic being: "I am no longer an individual finitely concerned with particular situations; I grasp the boundary situations of existence as infinitely concerned Existenz" (Latzel 1957, p. 181). Grabau (1971) has similarly noted, "Corresponding to Existenz is transcendence. Transcendence is the representation of being itself beyond all objectivity" (p. xxi). In concert with these, Frankl (1969) has asserted, "Human beings are transcending themselves toward meanings which are something other than themselves, which are more than mere expressions of themselves, more than mere projections of themselves" (p. 60). Boundary situations, those adversities that inevitably occur in life for each of us, bring us to the very clear awareness of our finiteness and consequently point us in the direction, or beg the question, of a meaning outside of ourselves. Direct experiencing of existential dilemmas moves us toward the transcendent, toward finding this meaning outside of ourselves. Nozick (1989) has also noted, "Typically, people worry about the meaning of their lives when they see their existences as limited, perhaps because death will end them and so mark their final limit. To seek to give life meaning is to seek to transcend the limits of one's individual life" (p. 166). This would seem to correlate with Jaspers's (1932) contention that Existenz occurs only in boundary situations: those situations where we can only simply "be," when one is no longer "an individual finitely concerned with particular situations" (p. 181), but rather, one aware of, and concerned with, Existenz.

Most important, then, "the boundary thus plays its proper role of something immanent which already points to transcendence" (Jaspers 1932 p. 179). It is argued here that transcendence is at the core of the resilience process. The boundary situation represents an opportunity to leap from existence to Existenz. The potential gift of adversity is transcendence. Resilience, then, might best be understood as referring to the uniquely human capacity to transcend both environmental factors of context and the self. As Frankl (1969) suggested, "self-transcendence is the essence of existence. Being human is directed to something other than itself" (p. 50). Maslow (1968) also pointed to transcendence as an important component of the human experience: "Adequacy, adjustment, adaptation, competence, mastery, coping, these are all environment-oriented words and are therefore inadequate to describe the *whole* psyche, part of which has nothing to do with the environment" (p. 203). In this sense, transcendence of both the self and one's environment, or context, is potentially a part of the human experience. With regard to resilience, it may be a central component. Again, Frankl (1969) emphasized this point, suggesting, "Human existence is not authentic unless it is lived in terms of self-transcendence" (p. 52).

Dynamic Contextualism

For the purpose of connecting the preceding material more directly to the study of resilience within the context of life span development, the work of Lerner (1998 1999), among others, may now be incorporated within the present discussion. While Lerner did not address resilience per se, it will be shown that the concept of dynamic contextualism he outlined in his writings is congruent with the view of humans espoused by the existentialists. In concert, it is hoped that these diverse bodies of work will shape an understanding of resilience that is profitable for researchers and clinicians alike.

In explaining this perspective, Lerner (1998) noted:

> A developmental systems perspective involves the study of active people providing a source, across the life span, of their individual developmental trajectories; this development occurs through the dynamic interactions people experience with the specific characteristics of the changing contexts within which they are embedded. (p. 16)

The parallels to Jaspers's (1932) philosophical work as discussed are apparent. We are always in situations, and we have a role in shaping those situations. The self is again seen as the mediator or, to a certain extent, the author, within biological and environmental limits, of its own development; that is to say, "individuals are both the products and active producers of their ontogeny and personal development over the life span" (Brandtstadter & Lerner 1999, p. ix). More specifically,

> through action, and through experiencing the effects and limitations of goal-related activities, we construe representations and internal working models of ourselves and of the physical, social, and symbolic environments in which we are situated. These representations in turn guide and motivate activities through which we shape the further course of personal development. (Brandtstadter & Lerner 1999, p. ix)

This construction is compatible with Jaspers's (1932) contention that we continually seek to have an impact on the situations in which we find ourselves. The process is a bidirectional one. We shape the situation to facilitate movement toward our goals, at the same time shaping ourselves in response to the feedback we receive from the environment in this continual and recursive process of our own development. In the words of Lerner and Walls (1999), "our goal must be to understand how the individually different actions of diverse people, and the actions of their similarly diverse contexts on them, combine—coact—to foster the unique developmental trajectories involved in human life" (p. 26).

This same mandate echoes in the resilience literature. The degree to which we will our own transcendence (are resilient) can be seen to be a function of our awareness of being at the center of multiple dynamics and relationships to which we ascribe meaning and on which we base our activity: "The individual, in dynamic interactions on and by his or her context, is at the core of the relations of the developmental system during ontogenetic change" (Lerner & Walls 1999, p. 13). In the same way that Jaspers (1932) highlights the place of the self in the situation,

Lerner and his colleagues also appear to place the individual at the center of the enterprise. This centrality is not to be confused with omnipotence. However, it does indicate a degree of agency. There is always choice and, with it, an amount of will that may be exercised, awareness brought to attend. From the perspective proposed by Lerner and others, "the causes of development are the *relationships* among components, and not the components themselves" (Lerner & Walls 1999, p. 16). Again, such a perspective places the active individual at the center of his or her own development; according to Brandtstadter (1999),

> the individual, and the adult in particular, takes an active and creative stance toward his or her personal development. In the course of their ontogeny, individuals form mental representations of what they can or should be or become, and these representations feed into the ways in which they interpret, organize, and evaluate their actual and future development. (pp. 37-38)

Perhaps yet another way of describing this overlap between the two disciplines of psychology and philosophy is a similar dynamic proposed by Kegan (1982), who spoke of the function of meaning making:

> What an organism does is organize; and what the human organism organizes is meaning. Thus it is not that a person makes meaning, as much as that the activity of being a person is the activity of meaning-making. There is thus no feeling, no experience, no thought, no perception, independent of a meaning-making context in which it *becomes* a feeling, an experience, a thought, a perception, because we *are* the meaning-making context. (p. 11)

Each of these characterizations, while emerging from disparate disciplines, appears to be describing components of the same human potential or capacity: the potential for attending, evaluating, meaning making, and transcendent living.

These views are also congruent with several important contributions to the study of resilience. Anthony and Cohler (1987) have likewise suggested that development is an interactive process between the individual and his or her environment throughout the entire lifespan:

> If this interactional viewpoint is accepted, not only does growing up become an active, constructive, and increasingly autonomous process of getting to know oneself and one's milieu; the phenomena of risk, vulnerability, and resilience also become active and ever-changing constructions. (p. 33)

The philosophy of Jaspers (1932) provides a philosophical and intellectual foundation for these psychological understandings. Current developmental theory, as noted by reference to Lerner's (1998) work, is also consistent with this position. In both, however, it must be emphasized that our decision-making processes and the actions that follow need not be thought of as having direct influence. As Brandtstadter (1999) noted, "although humans may not be free throughout to choose or change their wants, beliefs, or desires, they have evolved the unique capacity to take an evaluative, critical stance toward them, and to form metaintentions or 'second-order volitions'" (p. 40). According to Brandtstadter (1999), this type of metacognitive activity parallels the deliberate leaps described by Jaspers (1932) that lead from the consciousness of existence to *Existenz*:

> The capacity to enact such secondary volitions, and to empower them with sufficient strength to override "primary" action tendencies, is addressed in such traditional virtue concepts as "willpower" and "self-discipline" as well as in psychological concepts of self-regulation and self-management. (p. 40)

Concepts such as these can also be seen as key ingredients in resilient lives and are attitudinal or evaluative as much or more than physically directive.

Works Cited

Ansbacher, H. L., & Ansbacher, R. R. (1956). *The Individual Psychology of Alfred Adler*. New York: Harper & Row.

Anthony, E. J., & Cohler, B. J. (1987). *The Invulnerable Child*. New York: Guilford Press.

Bartelt, D. W. (1994). On resilience: Questions of validity. In M. C. Wang & E. W. Gordon (Eds.), *Educational Resilience in Inner-city America* (pp. 97-108). Hillsdale, NJ: Lawrence Erlbaum.

Brandtstadter, J. L. (1999). The self in action and development: Cultural, biosocial, and ontogenetic bases of intentional self-development. In J. L. Brandtstadter & R. M. Lerner (Eds.), *Action and Self-development: Theory and Research through the Life Span* (pp. 37-55). Thousand Oaks, CA: Sage.

_____, & Lerner, R. M. (1999). Introduction: Development, action, and intentionality. In J. L. Brandtstadter & R. M. Lerner (Eds.), *Action and Self-development: Theory and Research through the Life Span* (pp. ix-xx). Thousand Oaks, CA: Sage.

Flew, A. (1979). *A Dictionary of Philosophy*. New York: St. Martin's Press.

Frankl, V. E. (1969). *The Will to Meaning*. New York: Penguin Books.

Garmezy, N. (1993). Children in poverty: Resilience despite risk. *Psychiatry, 56*(1), 127-136.

Grabau, R. F. (1971). Preface. In K. Jaspers (Ed.), *Philosophy of Existence*. Philadelphia: University of Pennsylvania Press.

James, W. (1890). *The Principles of Psychology*. New York: Dover.

Jaspers, K. (1932). *Philosophy* (Vol. 2, E. B. Ashton, Trans.). Chicago: University of Chicago Press.

_____ (1971). *Philosophy of Existence*. Philadelphia: University of Pennsylvania Press.

Kegan, R. (1982). *The Evolving Self: Problem and Process in Human Development*. Cambridge, MA: Harvard University Press.

Latzel, E. (1957). The concept of "ultimate situation" in Jaspers' philosophy (G. L. Kline, Trans.). In P. A. Schilpp (Ed.), *The Philosophy of Karl Jaspers* (pp. 177-209). New York: Tudor.

Lerner, R. M. (1998). Theories of human development: Contemporary perspectives. In R. M. Lerner (Ed.), *Handbook of Child Psychology* (Vol. 1, pp. 1-24). New York: John Wiley.

_____, & Walls, T. (1999). Revisiting individuals as producers of their development: From dynamic interactionism to developmental systems. In J. L. Brandtstadter & R. M. Lerner (Ed.), *Action and Self-development: Theory and Research through the Life Span* (pp. 3-36). Thousand Oaks, CA: Sage.

Luthar, S. S. (1991). Vulnerability and resilience: A study of high-risk adolescents. *Child Development, 62,* 600-616.

Maslow, A. H. (1968). *Toward a Psychology of Being*. New York: John Wiley.

Masten, A. S. (1994). Resilience in individual development: Successful adaptation despite risk and anxiety. In M. C. Wang & E. W. Gordon (Eds.), *Educational Resilience in Inner-city America* (pp. 3-25). Hillsdale, NJ: Lawrence Erlbaum.

_____, (2001). Ordinary magic: Resilience processes in development. *American Psychologist, 56,* 227-238.

_____, & Coatsworth, J. D. (1998). The development of competence in favorable and unfavorable environments: Lessons from research on successful children. *American Psychologist, 53,* 205-220.

Miller, R. B. (2004). *Facing Human Suffering: Psychology and Psychotherapy as Moral Engagement*. Washington, DC: American Psychological Association.

Nozick, R. (1989). *The Examined Life: Philosophical Meditations*. New York: Simon & Schuster.

O'Connell Higgins, G. (1994). *Resilient Adults*. San Francisco: Jossey-Bass.

Overton, W. F. (1998). Developmental psychology: Philosophy, concepts, and methodology. In R. M. Lerner (Ed.), *Handbook of child psychology* (Vol. 1, pp. 107-188). New York: John Wiley.

Rogers, C. R. (1961). *On Becoming a Person*. New York: Houghton Mifflin.

Rutter, M. (1987). Psychosocial resilience and protective mechanisms. *American Journal of Orthopsychiatry, 57,* 316-331.

Tarter, R. E., & Vanyukov, M. (1999). Re-visiting the validity of the construct of resilience. In M. D. Galantz & J. L. Johnson (Eds.), *Resilience and development: Positive life adaptations* (pp. 85-100). New York: Kluwer Academic/Plenum.

Yalom, I. D. (1980). *Existential Psychotherapy*. New York: Basic Books.

Chapter 3

Using Metaphors to Develop Resilience

Robin Hills and Doug Haynes

This chapter aims to provide the necessary theoretical context and background to a unique tool to support the building of resilience. The tool has been designed by the authors to use in their work in supporting leadership development and organisational change.

What is Resilience?

Most dictionaries define resilience as "the ability to recover quickly from stress". The idea of resilience originates from material science where it describes the property of a material to resume its original shape after distortion.

Toughness is an associated word that, in the same context, means the ability of a material to absorb energy and plastically deform without rupture or the resistance to fracture when stressed.

Certainly the concepts of "resilience" and "toughness" share certain attributes, like the ability to cope with and handle the stresses and strains encountered in the day to day work environment, associated with stamina, a power of endurance and an unyielding spirit.

High levels of resilience are considered to be exemplary traits that should be encouraged and fostered. In times of continuous pressure and change, resilience is often referred to as one of the key attributes of a successful leader.

The antonyms of resilience; words like "fragility", "inflexibility" and "weakness", are not regarded as useful in the work setting leading to long-term problems for the individual and the organisation.

Traditionally, we have thought of resilience as something to be admired: a resilient individual, organisation or community is one that is able to withstand the stresses of radical change to the status quo, one that does not give into pressure.

We all strive for more resilience to stave off the effects of living with adversity yet an excess of resilience is almost never considered.

What if resilience is also the thing that inhibits the necessary change? In other words, too much resilience can lead to a withstanding of the forces that are necessary to lead to change or a lack of motivation to overcome these challenges.

Also, some people may appear to have too much resilience. Richard J. Davidson writes in his 2012 book *The Emotional Life of Your Brain* about his research in this area. He has shown that people who recover too quickly from adversity show a higher activity in their left prefrontal cortex. He infers that this activity sends inhibitory signals to the amygdala, instructing this emotional gateway of the brain to quieten down. He, also, goes on to suggest that by rebounding too quickly, especially in relation to the emotions of others, people with too much resilience can, lack empathy by not comprehending the anxieties of others and by not understanding their inability to respond in the same way. True resilience may, therefore, be a balance between a rapid response and a depth-of-processing response.

In building up appropriate levels of resilience, individuals describe this in increasing stages:

— Those who have an ability to bounce back, but who have a limited ability to describe what they went through and how they did it.

— Those who describe their ability to bounce back and who learn from the setback.

— Those who describe what they have learnt and recover quicker from the setback and at reduced cost.

(Campbell: 2009)

There is a further level of resilience, whereby an extreme challenge is transformed into an opportunity and achieves good outcomes even in the face of loss—often referred to as post-traumatic growth (Tedeshi, Calhoun 1995; Tedeshi, Calhoun 2004; Linley, Joseph 2004).

Leaders who use their resilience well have the ability to analyse problems, discover root causes, make changes, implement plans and manage the consequences of decisions. Being resilient enables them to quickly recover and move on from difficult situations but not at the expense of necessary change, other people and their emotions.

Resilience is closely linked to emotional intelligence yet it is not considered as a distinct component or competence of emotional intelligence.

Resilience and Emotional Intelligence

Emotional intelligence is a relatively recent behavioural model, rising to prominence with Daniel Goleman's 1995 book *Emotional Intelligence—Why it can matter more than IQ*.

Emotional Intelligence theory was originally developed during the 1980s by Howard Gardner who introduced the concept of multiple intelligences and the work and writings of psychologists Peter Salovey and John Mayer.

Emotional intelligence is increasingly relevant to organisational development and developing people, because the principles provide a new way to understand and assess people's behaviours, management styles, attitudes, interpersonal skills, and potential.

Goleman identified the five key elements of emotional intelligence as:

1. *Self-awareness*: Knowing your emotions.
2. *Self-regulation*: Managing your own emotions.
3. *Motivation*: Motivating yourself.
4. *Empathy*: Recognising and understanding other people's emotions.
5. *Social skills*: Managing relationships through managing the emotions of others.

The process and outcomes of emotional intelligence development contain many fundamentals important in the development of resilience within individuals and organisations. These are being motivated to use self-awareness around resilience to regulate emotions and to use empathy appropriately leading to reduced conflict, improvement in relationships and understanding. This, in turn, supports increasing stability, continuity and harmony.

Personality and Resilience

Some researchers believe that individuals have a resilience profile within their personality evidenced in the way that their personality traits are expressed (Friborg 2005; Ahangar 2010; Robertson, Cooper 2011). These traits naturally equip them to cope with situations effectively and can be measured by using well-constructed, highly valid and reliable psychometrics.

There is a very large, diverse and commercial market of psychometric testing. Some questionnaires are designed to look at an individual's ability to cope with pressures and stress and demands, etc. and, using these, it is possible to have some measure of resilience.

Windle, Bennett and Noyes (2011) conducted a meta-analysis of 19 resilience measures reported as reliable and valid. They concluded that there is no gold standard measure of resilience. A number of interesting scales are in the early stages of development; however, all require further validation work.

A 360-degree assessments can help identify an individual's ability to deal with the different aspects relating to resilience at work. They can help with development and growth and can be applied across whole organisations. The methodology is important but needs to be handled very carefully. As with all measures of personal performance, individuals will be concerned about what will happen with the outputs; are they to form part of an appraisal, could they affect jobs, or is the assessment, uniquely, a learning and development tool?

Well-defined assessments can be used as a basis for individual or departmental coaching. However, there are other approaches for developing resilience as well as psychometrics. It can be helpful to use contexts, references and past experiences as a measure which can give deep awareness leading to insights and long-term learning, which grows individual resilience, particularly when supported by the right level of coaching support.

A recent review of the literature shows that resilience can be developed, widened and deepened (Lewis, Donaldson-Feilder, Pangallo 2011). Within organisations, executive coaching is a good intervention that can be deployed to support the development of resilience (Spence, Cavanagh, Grant 2008; Grant, Curtayne, Burton 2009).

Resilience can be very context specific (Windle 2011) and to address this there is a tool developed by EI4Change Ltd., which can help.

Images of Resilience is a coaching tool that contains multiple copies of 16 carefully designed images drawn in an attractive cartoon style. The images represent metaphors, depicting a range of experiences and emotions linked with the theme of resilience. All 16 images are presented below.

Metaphors

A metaphor is a figure of speech that describes a subject by comparing it to and describing it in terms of another, otherwise, unrelated topic. This definition of metaphor includes similes, parables, analogies, parallels, literary metaphors, etc.

This is often important in one or two dynamic ways that have deep, significant meaning to the person using the metaphor.

Wendy Sullivan and Judy Rees in their 2008 book *Clean Language: Revealing Metaphors and Opening Minds* suggest that paying attention and working with metaphor may enhance the results you get from communication because:

- Metaphors can represent experience more fully than abstract concepts and so enable more effective communication.
- Metaphors condense information, making things more tangible and easier to work with.
- The metaphor for an experience has a similar structure to the experience that it represents.
- Metaphors provide an important route into the deeper, more profound levels of a person's thinking.
- When people experience change, both the metaphor and real-life experience generally change in tandem.

The word *metaphor* comes from the Greek word *amphora*, which is a storage container used for transporting valuable goods. As we use metaphor—as a means to transport meaning from one subject to another—the word *metaphor* is itself a metaphor.

As human beings, we appear to be hardwired to think in metaphor and we are also hardwired to respond to metaphor through storytelling, anecdotes, etc. Sue Knight in her 2009 book *NLP at Work* states that "metaphors permeate our lives. They are symbols for what our unconscious mind is saying. The more we can learn to listen to the metaphors in our life, the more we can draw on the power of the unconscious mind."

Any kind of experience can act as a metaphor. Whenever there is a need to describe abstract, complex or emotional situations, we are likely to use a more concrete metaphor to pass on information to others, often bypassing the more conscious, critical faculties.

Images of Resilience

Of course, to be at all persuasive, the metaphor must have some resonance with a person's experience. All 16 images in the *Images of Resilience* toolbox are drawn in a cartoon style that people at all levels in organisations find appealing and can immediately relate to. Using the images depicted, they describe their experiences through their own metaphors, understanding and meaning. The images seem to facilitate the exploration of different facets of resilience and its connections with stress, change, challenge and the potential for learning.

The dialogue that opens might otherwise be too risky or challenging to be tackled directly. Questions can be introduced that allows for exploration of meaning promoting discussion around how strategies can be developed to build resilience and ways to cope with stress more effectively.

The set of images and the associated questions explore some of the components of resilience introducing the challenge to think about what it means and how resilience can be developed. They support discussions around how resilience can be used to enhance experiences rather than leading to ineffective or damaging behaviour.

The cards are designed to be used to stimulate thought and discussion in individual coaching or in group-work—whenever the learning objectives relate to personal, team and leadership development. They give focus to motivation, change management, stress management and an exploration of the balance of work as a part of life.

Using Images of Resilience

The picture cards are accompanied with supporting notes and questions which explain the original thinking behind the choice of image. Of course, they are open to individual interpretation and as a stimulus for ideas which can lead to new insights. In working with the toolbox, people respond positively to some images whilst other images have little significance for them. Often recognition can simply be of a remembered experience. It has been observed that this is predominately related to overcoming difficulty in some context. Sometimes the connections are very obvious to a person and sometimes there is confusion as they cannot make any connections at all.

Images of Resilience can be used with individuals or in small groups. A revealing technique used by two people working together was to take a set of the 16 images and to look at each image individually discussing its inferences, the messages that it contained and what it meant for them personally. They put aside any images that they could not make sense any of and returned to them later.

If any strong emotions are shown, then investigating what those emotions are and why the person feels them may elicit some very valuable information about resilience.

Challenging people to think deeper about these images and the metaphors has given rise to insights far beyond those expected. On many occasions, these were not even considered within the design of the toolbox.

The focus of the images is on three aspects of resilience designed to prompt ideas about.

1. What resilience is and what it means for the individual.
2. When resilience is needed.
3. What qualities and skills can be developed to enhance the use of resilience.

1. What resilience is and what it means for the individual

The images *Bouncing Back* and *New Growth* are intended to symbolise resilience itself—the ability to take knocks and rebound, and the ability to grow and thrive in difficult, unfavorable conditions. These specific images are widely used and popular representations of resilience.

Bouncing Back

The roly-poly toys wobble when pushed and have the ability to right themselves or regain their original position after being pushed around. No matter what happens to them, they are able to bounce back to an upright position as if nothing has happened to them. They have something inside them to withstand being pushed around. Balls and space hoppers bounce yet return back to their original shape. Springs are elastic objects that store energy and add bounce to the toy.

New Growth

Despite a barren parched environment, life continues to flourish. There is new growth and there are new prospects. Out of adversity comes opportunity and a new plant grows where others would fail to flourish. The old is replaced by the new, that will eventually grow to full maturity and the new plant will be an integral part of a new landscape and new environment.

2. When resilience is needed

Six images symbolise the pressures, challenges and situations that require most resilience—these are titled *Ambiguity and Uncertainty, Keeping Focus, Barriers to Progress, Limited Challenges, Risk* and *Overcoming Fear*.

Ambiguity and Uncertainty

The ultimate goal may be clear but the way ahead is set with a number of different challenges that are unknown. There will be many changes of direction with many turns and, even the need to reverse direction and go backwards at times before the end point is reached. The goal is worth the effort but it is unclear how long it will take to achieve as the nature of the way forward is uncertain. Once the goal is achieved, there may be further uncertainty of the way ahead as the challenge of the maze continues to hide the way out.

Keeping Focus

The ultimate goal is clear but the way ahead is set with a number of different challenges and risks. However, these are known and can be planned for and will each need attention before the end point is reached. The goal is worth the effort but it is unclear how long it will take to achieve it as each risk needs to be assessed and each challenge needs to be faced head on and dealt with.

Barriers to Progress

Despite the willingness to make progress, individuals find themselves up against a series of external obstacles that appear to be insurmountable and are beyond their control. It is difficult to understand why they are there. There are many rivers to cross and many mountains to climb, and at times, it is like banging your head against a brick wall. This excessive regulation or rigid conformity to formal rules hinders or prevents action or decision making.

Limited Challenges

Individuals are ascending or descending a never-ending staircase that means they are going nowhere fast. They are going through the motions, moving forward but are not making any progress. There appears to be no escape. It doesn't matter if the individual goes up or down the staircase, as the situation does not change over time. Over time this can lead to boredom or frustration through lack of challenge.

Risk

The individual is working in circumstances in which the personal outcomes are unknown and where there are significant personal risks. In this image, a person is going into a toxic environment aware of the risks to themselves even though they will not know the long-term effect of this action. There is the willingness and determination to continue despite the dangers or risks involved. There is an element of fear but this is suppressed in order achieve an outcome. An alternative viewpoint is that this image might represent foolhardiness. This image has often lead to discussions around perceived good and bad risk.

Overcoming Fear

With a roller coaster, or a bungee jump, individuals face a major personal challenge that may require them to overcome their fears. The risk is perceived rather than actual, as the activity is assessed, safety checked and proven. However, individuals may tell themselves and others that they can't do it so there is a mental barrier to overcome. Once achieved there is a sense of exhilaration and achievement and people enjoy the ride.

3. What qualities and skills can be developed to enhance the use of resilience

Endurance, Self-Management, Tolerance, Determination, Feeling in Control, Drive and Motivation, Guidance and *Flexibility* are all purported dimensions of resilience and the images below are designed to help the participant experience these within the moment.

Endurance

The individuals are in a race to get to an endpoint but are being held back. At times it feels like they take three steps forward and two back. They have to jump over many hurdles and jump through a number of hoops. This seems to involve doing more things than are strictly necessary. These obstacles require the necessary stamina to tackle them in the correct sequence and in the right way to finish the course.

Self-management

The individual has the tenacity and persistence to focus and concentrate on the task at hand—to continue studying—despite many tempting distractions. The long-term achievement or outcome of the task is considered more important than short-term gratification.

Tolerance

Tolerating a certain amount of stress is a normal part of everyday work and presents a challenge that everyone must cope with. There should be sufficient challenge for people to feel stretched in order to develop and balanced so that they can cope. Levels of stress will vary from individual to individual. Too much stress leads to health issues and burn out, whilst too little leads to frustration and boredom.

Determination

These people have overcome major adversity and are doing something that is fun, competitive and that they enjoy. They have faced life-changing physical events and have taken up new challenges to ensure that they can still enjoy life and the contributions that they can make despite major setbacks. There is a determination not to let setbacks get in the way of ambition.

Whatever life throws at them, these people will carry on enjoying the challenge of life with optimism and a positive outlook.

Feeling in Control

Close hauled ?

Sailing a small yacht means knowing the capabilities of the craft and utilising all available resources to sail skillfully across the sea. Being in control means the yacht can be maneouvred quickly and easily. Clever harnessing of resources allows for the yacht to be sailed by adapting to subtle changes in the use of the sailor's body, the boat and the elements. The direction of sail can be changed frequently according to the speed and direction of the wind. Changing the direction of a large vessel is not as easy as it takes a lot of time and energy.

Drive and Motivation

Motivation is the driving force that leads towards the achievement of goals. Animals have an internal compass that drives them to make journeys of many thousands of miles across unfamiliar terrains to breed, for food or to live in more favourable environments. Migration takes place in teams, with a sociability factor, that ensures that the group works towards its ultimate goal successfully.

Guidance

This picture shows a light that acts as guidance for the person on the road by illuminating a way forward. The road twists and turns with many branches. People are travelling along various routes. There are choices on the route with the light shining to provide a clear direction.

Flexibility

The tree in this situation can withstand the elements and changes in the weather. It has the flexibility to bend in high wind and to flourish. Others have different reactions. Some find the situation uncomfortable and huddle together, whilst some people are ignoring the reality of the situation. The ostriches bury their heads in the sand.

Each of the 16 images is supplied three times within the toolbox and comes with the supporting facilitator notes along with a series of carefully crafted questions. These probing coaching questions allow for an exploration of the metaphor depicted to investigate what resilience means for the individual, the situations when resilience is needed and the qualities and skills that can be developed to enhance the use of resilience. It is intended that the images are used in close dialogue with a coach / facilitator as part of a development programme to gain maximum benefit.

The toolbox *Images of Resilience* was developed to give a supportive framework for personal development, training and coaching. The images have been widely tested in management training and coaching workshops across a range of sectors, where they have stimulated consistent discussion of the issues intended within their design.

The authors do not claim that the images relate to the development of resilience in any scientifically proven way held as gold standard. Indeed, as already noted, Windle, Bennett and Noyes (2011) concluded that there is no gold standard measure of resilience. To rigorously test the impact of *Images of Resilience* on a person's development of resilience would require sophisticated, longitudinal studies that identify specific criteria and predictive validity.

The toolbox *Images of Resilience* has been designed to add a different dimension and depth to coaching and training around resilience.

Described below are a series of techniques that are intended for anyone wishing to explore resilience with another person that can be used with or without the toolbox.

Using metaphors prompts context, references and past experiences that are personal. They make possible an awareness that leads to insights which may grow individual resilience. This awareness can lead to long-term learning, especially when supported by the right method of coaching.

The following instructions are a guide to using metaphor and the series *Image of Resilience* as a facilitator within a coaching or training intervention.

Developing Skills and Qualities

As the facilitator, explain that the images represent a range of aspects of resilience: some of the skills, behaviours and attitudes that are required to develop personal resilience and deal with challenges, pressures and stress in both personal and professional environments.

Explain that this process is intended to help individuals to think about the responsibilities and pressures that they are currently facing and to consider their own strategies and approaches to managing themselves.

Begin by giving an example. Select the image called *Drive and Motivation*—the picture of migrating animals and birds. Describe how this image may symbolise an internal drive that motivates the animals to undertake long, demanding and potentially dangerous journeys.

Ask the questions:

"What is it that motivates you?"

"What is the internal drive that makes you want to commit to something that might be difficult and stressful?"

Listen to the answers, then show the card called *Risk*—the person entering the radioactive environment. Describe how a challenging management role has risks attached—for both the manager and the people being managed.

Ask, "What are those risks and what do you think you can do to prevent or overcome them?"

When you have worked with these two examples, spread the remaining cards (with supporting notes) randomly on a table and ask the coachee to choose two or three further cards. Each of these cards should represent an aspect of resilience that the coachee feels is important to demonstrate and strengthen. (Allow enough time for the coachee to consider the cards and think about what they might mean—a minimum of five minutes of reflection time.)

When the cards have been selected, ask the coachee what the cards mean to him/her.

Explore two aspects:

i) Why the coachee selected this card and why it is an important skill or quality.

ii) The extent to which the coachee feels that they have, and can rely upon, this quality.

Can they give examples of how and when they use it?

For example, if the coachee selected the image entitled *Bouncing Back*—the wobbly toys, can he/she describe situations in which he/she has taken knocks or criticism and been able to bounce back in a positive way?

Finally, ask the coachee to select two cards (these may include a card or cards that have already been discussed).

i) The first card should represent what they feel is their own most valuable ability in relation to resilience (i.e., what they think they do best and find most useful). For example, this might be *endurance*—a willingness to work with uncertainty and ambiguity or an ability to find creative ways of dealing with barriers to progress.

ii) The second card should represent what they believe they would find most difficult. For example, keeping focus when there are many distractions and being flexible about a process when under pressure to deliver results or overcoming their fears.

Explore the coachee's choice of cards and then ask them to summarise their thoughts and discussions through effective questioning.

This process will explore various dimensions of personal resilience within the working environment leading to a depth that may have taken many hours within an ordinary coaching session.

Exploring Change in Resilience

Spread the cards at random on a table and ask the coachee to choose the card or cards that, for them, depicts when they did not feel resilient—felt vulnerable, susceptible, tense, unyielding or inflexible. Here are some questions to explore with them.

- What did you do?
- What did it feel like?
- What were you thinking?
- What needs were being met or not met?
- What characteristics were you demonstrating?
- What was important for you?

Ask them to select a card or cards that illustrates when they felt they were at their most resilient. Focusing on the metaphor, ask

- What did you do?
- What did it feel like?
- What were you thinking?
- What needs were being met?
- What characteristics were you demonstrating?
- What was important for you?

Finally ask them to select a card or cards that illustrate how they want to develop their resilience within their current situation. If this card is different from the first card chosen, explore the differences, what they are and what they mean. Exploring the metaphor in detail, ask:

- How is this important today?
- What are you doing?
- What does it feel like?
- What are you thinking?
- What lies outside of you that concerns you?
- What unique contribution do you want to make towards this?
- What is important for you?
- What does this tell you about your resilience?

This activity investigates a coachee's understanding of what resilience means and how it can be applied. It looks at what aspects of resilience are necessary and important for them to apply within various situations and what the implications are for enhancing its use in the most appropriate way.

Exploring Relationships

This exercise is useful to give insights into connections between people through their relationships and how this affects resilience. It can be used in a work context to look at how the relationship with an organisation, a manager, their direct reports or with colleagues can impact upon resilience. It can also be used to explore relationships with partners, family members, neighbours or friends.

Spread the cards at random on a table and ask the coachee to choose the card or cards that they feel show their connection to their current situation, environment or to focus on the relationship.

Once the image has been chosen, get the person to consider:
- What happens when they step into the image / metaphor?
- What do they notice?
- Where is the energy?
- Where does it flow or stop?
- What catches their attention, in particular?
- What makes them curious?
- What is out of sight?
- What might be confusing?

Ask them to consider what part of the image represents their contribution and what part is beyond their ability to control.
- What do they notice about this?
- What happens when these contributions alter?

Explore with them different ways of changing the connection and notice which choices make things better or make things worse.
- How does the image form and grow?
- How might it become something else?
- What is it like being on the outside looking onto or into the image?
- What lies beyond the picture?
- What are the different ways of getting into the metaphor, or out of it?

Take some time to explore how this might happen.

Consider the relative contributions and how they are connected.
- What happens when the contributions change significantly?
- Which contribution takes the lead?
- How can the contributions be made more harmonious?

Take time to investigate how this changes their resilience through the learning that becomes available and that the exploration uncovers.

Planning for the Future

Ask the coach to think of a situation that is coming up when they would like to be more resilient.

As they think of this event, ask them how much resilience they have in this situation using a scale of 1 to 10 (1 low-10 high).

Get them to select an image from the cards that represents a time when they were operating with the resilience that they are looking for.

Ask them to describe the image or to select a metaphor that the image suggests in terms of... it is like X. Encourage them to work instinctively.

The interpretation of the question, the image selected and the answer given is very personal and the person should not be directed in any way.

For example, if the card *Feeling in Control* is selected then X may represent the person sailing the small yacht. This person is in control, knows their capabilities and can use the resources available to them.

Another example is if the card *Ambiguity and Uncertainty* is selected then X may represent the challenge of working towards a defined goal but the challenges ahead are uncertain.

Taking this metaphor, ask the coachee to answer each of the following statements with at least three responses.

- An X can be ... it can be ... it can be ...
- An X can't be ... it can't be ... it can't be ...
- An X doesn't have to be ... it doesn't have to be ... it doesn't have to be ...
- An X does have to be ... it has to be ... it has to be ...

The answers given are very specific to the person being coached and the discussion may open up in many different ways.

Now get the coach to think about what allows the metaphor to work.

In the example of the person sailing the yacht this could be the skills or dexterity needed to manoeuvre the craft.

In the example of the trophy in the maze it could be the challenge of the maze itself or the focus on the ultimate prize.

Thinking of what enables or allows the metaphor to work, answer the questions again.

- An X can be … it can be … it can be …
- An X can't be … it can't be … it can't be …
- An X doesn't have to be … it doesn't have to be … it doesn't have to be …
- An X does have to be … it has to be … it has to be …

Step into the image/metaphor and hear the answers again.

Get the coach to imagine being in the situation once more.

- What are they doing?
- What are others seeing and experiencing?
- What is your level of resilience now?

Get the coach to think of the situation that is coming up and ask them how much resilience they have now using a scale of 1 to 10 (1 low-10 high).

Developing Inner Resilience

Ask the coach to select the card that they associate with inner resilience. Ask them to consider the question "When you have inner resilience you are like what?"

Encourage them to let their minds freely roam and allow them to select freely so that whatever comes up to come up. The coachee may have a unique handle on how this is expressed and there is no right answer.

Ask them how much resilience they have in this situation using a scale of 1 to 10 (1 low-10 high).

Encourage them to answer the following questions as they are being asked without the need to rationalize.

- When you have inner resilience you are like what? (We will call this metaphor X)
- What is X like?
- What else is there about X?
- Where is X? Whereabouts is X?
- Is anything connected to X? How are they connected? What is the relationship between them?
- What was before X? And what was before that?
- Where is the source of X? What is it like?
- How does this connect with the present?
- What would you rather have as X?
- What has to happen for this to happen? What else?
- Can it? (If no, go back to the previous question.)

Get the coachee to select a further image that calls for inner resilience and link the images together.

- How is this situation different or similar to situations in the past?

Finally, ask them how much inner resilience they have in this situation using a scale of 1 to 10 (1 low-10 high).

This section uses some Clean Language questioning techniques founded by David Grove who drew on his bicultural (Mâori/Pâkeha) roots when designing a therapeutic and coaching communication process.

Clean Language questioning techniques are explored in a purer form in the next section.

Clean Language

Coaching using Clean Language questions is the practice of listening and observing with full attention on the words being used (and non-verbal signals) without giving advice, sharing opinions or adding in any assumptions around the metaphors used.

Everyone's way of experiencing the world is different yet all communication directs attention in some way. Clean questions have been perfected over the years to reduce the direction, assumptions and inferences that they contain. This minimizes the amount of contamination from the questioner to free up the resources of the person being questioned so that they can think effectively for themselves. This is important so that the person can do their very best thinking, can explore their inner world and take responsibility for their own choices.

Using *Images of Resilience* pose the question, "When you are most resilient you are like what?"

Spread the cards at random on a table and ask the coachee to choose the card or cards that they feel helps to answer the question. Get them to explore the image(s) and the ideas they have generated describing the metaphor for themselves.

The basic Clean Language questions when exploring metaphors are:

- (And) what kind of X (is that X)?
- (And) is there anything else about X?

where X refers to one or more words the person has used in describing the metaphor.

Using a coachee's own words within these questions indicates that the person has been listened to in a non-judgmental way, which helps them feel respected and acknowledged.

Use the Clean Language questions in any order and a few times. The questions can be asked several times in any order about any aspect of the metaphor. Allow the coachee to explore the metaphor(s) around this dimension of resilience in their own way.

To develop the coaching session further, ask the coachee to select a card or cards that focuses on a future state: how they could develop their resilience.

This time, ask some or all of these Clean Language questions:

- What would you like to have happen?

and/or

- What needs to happen?

and/or

- Is there anything else that needs to happen?
- (And) what needs to happen for X?
- (And) can X (happen)?

Again, use the Clean language questions in any order and a few times about any aspect of the metaphor. Allow the coachee to explore the metaphor(s) around developing their resilience in their own way.

This should allow the person to describe some specific examples of situations or contexts in which this would be useful and give them some insights as to what they can do for themselves to work better with their resilience.

Clean Language questions were originally designed for exploring people's metaphors. As mentioned earlier, they were devised by a New Zealand-born psychotherapist, David Grove (1950-2008). While David Grove did not publish widely, his methods achieved outstanding results, which attracted worldwide attention in the therapeutic community. During the 1990s Penny Tompkins and James Lawley codified and developed David Grove's work. Through their research, they found that Clean Language questions encouraged the metaphor to come to life and become more real for the coachee, often uncovering new and surprising information and leading to positive change. (Lawley, Tomkins: 2000)

Clean Language recognises the profound significance of the metaphor. The questions contain as few assumptions and direction as possible, so that there is space for the coachee's metaphors to grow and develop. Building upon their internal metaphorical landscapes enables them to reach ever-deeper levels of rapport with their unconscious minds to transcend limiting beliefs and behaviours and find resolution to issues.

The Last Word

The *Images of Resilience* toolbox was developed to give a focus and a structure to training and coaching around the subject of resilience due to the absence of any other suitable material. EI4Change has learnt much on the journey to producing this valuable resource and the feedback has been very encouraging.

The toolbox was not designed as a scientifically validated tool. In testing, the images have been shown to consistently represent aspects of resilience in a metaphorical manner. They have produced results that support learning and personal growth through workshops and coaching in keeping with the expectations of using similar types of training material.

There is an interesting opportunity for further research to empirically validate the tool using design and analysis methods adopted by researchers working with other flashcards or images that test subjective perception (such as the Rorschach Inkblot Test).

All of the methods and techniques described above can be applied to coaching with metaphor with or without the toolbox *Images of Resilience*. They are all tried and tested techniques adapted from Burgess (2011), Knight (2009), Sullivan, Rees (2008), with tremendous learning potential for both coach and coachee.

The techniques can be customized to accommodate the coachee's structure and desired outcomes and can, also, be incorporated into training programmes.

We hope that this chapter has given you a greater insight into working with metaphor and you are able to expand your ideas about what is possible when developing resilience.

Robin Hills is a science graduate from Durham University with the Chartered Institute of Marketing diploma and holds the British Psychological Society Certificate of Competence in Occupational Testing—Ability and Personality (trait, type and behaviour). Robin is able to apply this complete range of personality assessments with pragmatic business applications in a unique way. For the last six years he has been running his own business specialising in Emotional Intelligence, recognised in 2012 by the Association of Business Psychologists.

Robin is an empathetic communicator, team player and facilitative leader with a calm and positive outlook and a special interest in emotional intelligence. He is a confident presenter using a wide variety of media working with large or small groups, and presents on a wide variety of subjects focused around emotional intelligence to national and international audiences.

Doug Haynes has a BSc in Statistics, MA in Operational Research, PGCert in Business & Executive coaching. In the last 20 years, he has held several senior roles at Liverpool Business School (Liverpool John Moores University), including Director of the School of Business Information and Chair of Quality for the Faculty of Business & Law.

Doug's primary focus is *human activity systems* and how organisational structures, processes, and people combine in an holistic way to produce viable products and services. Critically, this involves a professional understanding of how people are effectively organised, motivated, and utilise information. He is a member of several *Communities of Practice* and his Pro Bono work includes being a Trustee for the Alternative Futures Group (a large social care charity) and for Hospice Africa.

Works Cited

Ahangar, R. (2010). *Africa Journal of Business Management* Vol. 4(6), pp. 953-961.

Burgess F. (2011). *The NLP Cookbook (50 Life Enhancing NLP Techniques for Coaches, Therapists and Trainers)*: Crown House Publishing.

Campbell, J. (2009). *Resilience Personal and Organisational Life*, TimesWork: Edinburgh.

Davidson R, & Begley, S. (2012). *The Emotional Life of Your Brain*; Hodder & Stoughton.

Friborg, O et al (2005). Resilience in relation to personality and intelligence. *International Journal of Methods in Psychiatric Research*, 2005, Volume 14, Number I, pp. 29-42.

Gardiner, H. (1983). *Frames of Mind: The Theory of Multiple Intelligences*: Basic Books.

Goleman, D. (1995). *Emotional Intelligence—Why it can matter more than IQ:* Bloomsbury Publishing.

———. (1998). *Working with Emotional Intelligence:* Bloomsbury Publishing.

Grant, A. M., Curtayne, L., & Burton, G. (2009). Executive coaching enhances goal attainment, resilience and workplace well-being: a randomised controlled study. *The Journal of Positive Psychology:* Dedicated to furthering research and promoting good practice, 4(5), 396-407.

Grove D. (1989). *Resolving traumatic memories: metaphors and symbols in psychotherapy*: Irvington.

Knight S. (2009). *NLP At Work: The Essence of Excellence* (3rd Edition) (People Skills for Professionals): Nicholas Brealey Publishing.

Lawley J. & Tompkins P (2000). *Metaphors in Mind—Transformation Through Symbolic Modelling*. Developing Company Press.

Lewis R, Donaldson-Feilder E and Pangallo A. (2011). *Developing Resilience*. Report commissioned by Affinity Health at Work and CIPD.

Linley, P.A. and Joseph, S. (2004). Positive Change Following Trauma and Adversity: A Review. *Journal of Traumatic Stress*, 17, 11-21.

Roberston, R. and Cooper C. (2011). *Well-being: Productivity and Happiness at Work*: Lancaster, Palgrave Macmillan.

Salovey, P., & Mayer, J.D. (1990). *Emotional intelligence. Imagination, Cognition, and Personality*, 9, 185-211.

Spence G., Cavanagh M., and Grant A. (2008). *An International Journal of Theory, Research and Practice* Vol. 1, No. 2, 144-162.

Sullivan, W. & Rees, J. (2008) *Clean Language: Revealing Metaphors and Opening Minds*: Crown House, Carmarthen.

Tedeschi, R.G., & Calhoun, L.G. (1995). *Trauma and Transformation: Growing in the Aftermath of Suffering.* Thousand Oaks, CA: Sage.

Tedeshi, R.G., & Calhoun, L.G. (2004). *Posttraumatic Growth: Conceptual Foundation and Empirical Evidence.* Philadelphia, PA: Lawrence Erlbaum Associates.

Windle G. (2011). *Reviews in Clinical Gerontology* May 2011 21: pp. 152-169.

Windle G., Bennett K. and J. Noyes (2011). *Health and Quality of Life Outcomes,* 9:8.

CHAPTER 4

Developing Personal Resilience in Organizational Settings

Linda L. Hoopes

Abstract

Changes that take place in the workplace often have a significant impact on the well-being of individuals both at work and at home; in turn, the ability of individuals to cope with change affects organizational productivity and effectiveness. This makes the workplace a natural place to develop resilience. This chapter summarizes studies linking resilience to work performance and showing the organizational impact of resilience interventions. It provides examples of how resilience concepts and tools have been applied at individual, team, and organizational levels. It offers guidance on effective practices for planning and deploying resilience interventions in organizational settings. The overall goal of this article is to provide resilience practitioners working in a variety of organizational settings ideas and evidence that can help them increase the quality and effectiveness of their interventions.

Key Words

Personal resilience, organizations, resilient culture, performance, sponsorship, team resilience

Developing Personal Resilience in Organizational Settings

Most individuals spend a substantial part of their lives working in organizational settings. The changes that take place in the workplace often have a significant impact on the well-being of individuals both at work and at home, and, in turn, the ability of individuals to cope with change affects organizational productivity and effectiveness. This makes the workplace a natural place to discuss and nurture resilience. The overall goal of this article is to provide resilience practitioners working in a variety of organizational settings ideas and evidence that can help them increase the quality and effectiveness of their interventions.

Organizational settings are often a good place to help people strengthen their resilience. This is true for several reasons:

First, from the individual's point of view, the organization provides a rich environment for developing a capability that can benefit all aspects of life. Most workplaces have at least moderate levels of change taking place, with these changes having the potential to present disruption, challenges, and even trauma to people inside and outside the organization. Layoffs, reorganizations, new technology, new work processes, and other organizational changes call on individuals to engage their resilience and coping mechanisms on a regular basis. The ability to respond effectively to disruption is useful in the workplace, but potentially even more useful in addressing challenges in life outside of work.

Second, developing individual resilience is a desirable goal from an organizational perspective. Organizations need to periodically make significant changes to stay competitive in the marketplace, and many of these changes have major impact on the individuals involved. To the extent that individuals can recover quickly and effectively from any negative implications of organizational changes, the organization's performance and the well-being of its employees are enhanced. In addition, individuals who are affected by negative events outside the workplace often carry the stress and strain into their work environment. Increases in resilience are likely to reduce the organizational impact of non-work issues.

Third, from a pragmatic perspective, organizations often possess the resources to provide support and training that might not be as readily available in other settings. This means that individuals have the opportunity to learn perspectives and skills related to resilience that have broad applicability both inside and outside the organization.

The goal of this chapter is to provide practitioners working in organizational settings ideas and evidence that can help them increase the quality and effectiveness of resilience interventions.

A Framework for Resilience

There are multiple ways of defining and approaching resilience. Our selected approach is based on a model that articulates a set of seven resilience characteristics (ODR 1996), developed on the basis of a review of the literature and observations of individuals encountering change in organizational settings. The characteristics are briefly defined in Table 1.

In practice, these characteristics are presented as a set of elements that work together to help individuals use their energy most effectively when dealing with disruption. We often use the metaphor of "change muscles" to describe these characteristics; this implies both that there are individual differences in the extent to which people employ each characteristic, and that the characteristics can be developed through exercise and practice.

A 75-item online assessment, the Personal Resilience Questionnaire (PRQ) (ODR 1993a), allows individuals to gain an understanding of the extent to which they tend to display each of these characteristics when facing uncertainty and disruption, with scores on the resulting Personal Resilience Profile (PRP) (ODR 1993b) based on comparisons to a database of over 70,000 individuals. These characteristics are then linked to developmental activities presented in one-on-one, small-group, and classroom settings. In the next section, we will discuss some research linking the PRP to a range of performance outcomes; at this point we will also note that research to support the internal-consistency and test-retest reliability of the instrument (Bryant 1995), as well as its construct validity (ODR 1996), has been conducted.

Table 1. Summary of Personal Resilience Characteristics

Characteristic	Description	Related constructs
Positive: The World (PW)	Resilient individuals effectively identify opportunities in turbulent environments.	Optimism Positive affectivity
Positive: Yourself (PY)	Resilient individuals have the personal confidence to believe they can succeed in the face of uncertainty.	Self-esteem Self-efficacy Internal locus of control
Focused (FO)	Resilient individuals have a clear vision of what they want to achieve and use this as a guide when they become disoriented.	Value clarity Life meaning/purpose
Flexible: Thoughts (FT)	Resilient individuals generate a wide range of ideas and approaches for responding to change.	Creativity Cognitive complexity Ambiguity tolerance
Flexible: Social (FS)	Resilient individuals draw readily on others' resources for assistance and support during change.	Interpersonal comfort Extraversion Social support
Organized (OR)	Resilient individuals effectively develop and apply systems, processes, and structures when dealing with change.	Conscientiousness Self-discipline Planfulness
Proactive (PR)	Resilient individuals initiate action in the face of uncertainty, taking calculated risks rather than seeking the comfort of the status quo.	Risk-taking Sensation-seeking

Resilience development activities can certainly be accomplished without the use of an assessment tool. Informal self-evaluations are useful, and even general sessions that give people insight into how each characteristic is developed and applied—without exploring individual differences—can provide value. However, we have found that people are much more engaged in the learning process when they have information that helps them understand their own strengths and weaknesses from an objective standpoint. For this reason, most of the applications described below involve the use of this tool.

Building the Business Case

Before an organization will invest in developing employee resilience, leaders understandably want evidence that resilience is related to business outcomes, and that efforts to increase resilience will have a meaningful result. We have taken two basic paths to building an effective business case. The first approach is to use research data to link resilience characteristics to performance related outcomes, and resilience interventions to changes in performance.

To establish the relationship between resilience and business-related outcomes, we have summarized a number of studies looking at the relationship of the dimensions of the PRP to performance-related outcomes in business and other settings. Table 2 displays the source of the research, the population studied, the performance criterion employed, and relationships that were found to be statistically significant at á<.05 (indicated by +).

As an example of other literature linking resilience to business outcomes, Shin et al. (2012) recently reported that psychological resilience, mediated by positive emotions, predicts higher levels of normative and affective commitment to change.

These findings suggest that organizations going through change are likely to benefit from the presence of individuals with high levels of resilience. The next important question, of course,

Table 2. Summary of Research Linking Resilience to Performance Outcomes

Source	Population	Criterion	PW	PY	FO	FT	FS	OR	PR
Bryant (1995)	College freshmen	Adjustment to university life	+	+	+	+	+	+	+
ODR (1996)	Employees in a financial services organization	High vs. low performers	+	+	+		+		+
ODR (1996)	Employees in a financial services organization	High vs. low performers	+	+	+				
Chehrazi (2002)	Parents of children with autism	Healthy adaptation (less social isolation)			+ for composite score				
Isaacs (2003)	School principals	Transformational leadership practices	+		+	+	+	+	+
Wang (2003)	International students	Adjustment to university life	+	+	+	+	+	+	+
Sylvester (2009)	Front line sales professionals	Transformational leadership behaviors	+	+	+	+	+	+	+
Resilience Alliance (2011)	Workers in a telephone call center	Supervisors' performance ratings		+	+			+	
Fletcher (2011)	Sales force for a large organization	Sales performance	+ for composite score: Manager resilience predicted sales team performance, mediated by manager skills						

is whether interventions designed to influence resilience have the desired impact and, by extension, whether it is worthwhile for organizations to engage in efforts to develop employee resilience.

Both anecdotal evidence and preliminary investigations suggest that resilience interventions have the potential to shift individual perspectives, at least in the short-term, and that long-term practice can create deeper shifts in how individuals approach and respond to change. This is supported by neuroscience research describing the plasticity of the brain and the ways that experience and internal mental activity (thoughts) can affect the structure of the brain (emotional life) (Begley & Davidson 2012).

Table 3 summarizes findings from several interventions in organizational settings.

The second approach to developing a business case is to help organizations estimate and visualize the benefits to be gained from increased resilience in the workforce using an approach derived from utility analysis. We ask leaders to think of some of the unproductive behaviors that people have displayed when going through major change—including errors, accidents, time spent in complaining or gossiping. We then ask them to calculate the potential value of small reductions in these unproductive behaviors spread over time. For instance, if an organization has 1,000 employees being paid an average of $15/hour, and it is able to increase by five minutes per day per employee the amount of time spent in productive work due to more effective responses to disruptive change, there is a potential, over the course of a year, to reap $1250/day in benefits, or $250,000 over the course of a 200-day working year.

Experiences in Developing Resilience in Organizations

The following case examples are drawn from our experiences in working to develop resilience in organizations. They illustrate some of the approaches that can be taken, and also show some issues and challenges that can arise in this work.

Table 3. Summary of Findings from Resilience interventions

Source	Population	Criterion	Findings
Aetna & ODR (1995)	Employees of a large organization	Changes in resilience scores for participants in a computer-based tutorial vs. control group	Larger score increases for treatment group than for control group; lower within-person pre-post correlations for treatment group than for control group
Taylor (1997)	Minority medical school applicants	Stress levels during a career-threatening milestone	Resilience training minimized stress for low-resilience participants; coaching minimized stress for high-resilience participants
Fletcher & Hoopes (2010)	Employees of a large organization	Employee survey results	Larger increases in indices of "Change," "Leadership," and "Engagement" for groups that had experienced resilience training

Case 1. Individual Coaching

A coaching client was interested in learning more about his resilience and how it might affect his leadership style. He had been very successful in his career as an individual contributor. He had been identified as a high-potential young leader, and taken on new responsibilities including managing two small groups of employees. This, not surprisingly, represented a major change for him.

One of the groups had had several managers in the previous few years, and had operated very independently with little oversight. The client had been charged with designing and implementing a new compensation model for this function.

His profile indicated that his strengths were in the areas of Positive: Yourself, Flexible: Thoughts and Proactive. His greatest developmental areas were in the areas of Focused, Flexible, Social and Organized. This would suggest that in dealing with this new challenge, he would be likely to approach it with a great deal of self-confidence, creativity, and a bias toward action. The coach helped him see that while these elements were very beneficial in his role as an individual contributor, he could benefit from emphasizing additional resilience characteristics—using the Focused characteristic to help him define and articulate a clear vision, the Flexible: Social characteristic by including employees in the design process for the new model, and the Organized characteristic by applying a clear structure and implementation approach that would help the team gain a sense of predictability as the new system is put into place.

The client found the information helpful and used it to increase his likelihood of success in the new environment.

Case 2. Team Development

A team in the HR department of a large organization wanted to explore members' individual resilience and how they could leverage individual strengths as a team. The team members had previously attended a department-wide session where they received individual Personal Resilience Profiles. In a follow-up meeting with the team, we spent additional time helping them understand what resilience is, why it is important, and how each of the characteristics included in the profile plays a role in helping them use their energy more effectively to prepare for and respond to disruption. We shared a composite summary of the team's scores, which displayed the range and average for each of the seven characteristics described above. The team had a relatively wide range on most of the characteristics, with one or more individuals above the 80th percentile on each characteristic, and one or more individuals below the 30th percentile on all but one of the characteristics. The team's collective strengths (highest averages) were in the areas of Positive: Yourself and Flexible: Social, with their least-strong characteristics (lowest averages) in the areas of Positive: The World and Proactive. We discussed how these scores might affect the team's interactions with one another and with other parts of the organization. Key themes that emerged were the team's high comfort in social interactions, members' willingness to reach out to one another and to others for support during times of uncertainty, and a moderate level of caution in trying out new ideas.

Because the team had a high level of openness with one another and all were comfortable with self-disclosure, we also explored how each of the characteristics played out in the team's interactions. In a very exploratory and non-judgmental way, members of the team shared their strengths and weaknesses, revealing who had the highest and lowest scores on each characteristic and discussing how the team could make sure it was using its strengths most effectively. This led to some very interesting conversations, including a discussion of the Proactive characteristic, where the range of percentile scores was 23 to 90, but the average was a 46. The team wanted to understand more about what it looked/felt like to apply this characteristic. The person with the score of 90 shared his experience of feeling restless, moving and changing jobs frequently, and being willing to take risks that might seem extreme to others. This led to further discussion about how the characteristics balance one other, how strengths might be overused, and how one develops various characteristics.

The last part of the session involved each member of the team identifying one or more characteristics he or she wanted to develop, and one or more characteristics for which he or she would be willing to be a coach. We then conducted two rounds of discussion in which people were paired up according to their selections and worked to develop action plans, with each person serving as a coach in one round and a coachee in the other.

This session helped the team members better understand their own resilience and gain insights into how the team operated during change, and created opportunities for team members to help one another develop their resilience.

Case 3. Organization-wide Development

The Organizational Effectiveness team in a large organization had become interested in the topic of Resilience as part of their desire to build the change-related capability of the organization. After some initial workshops, they decided to introduce the core concepts of resilience to the organization's field sales leadership at a conference. The first challenge was to figure out how to simultaneously engage 800 people in a way that was engaging and delivered value. The resulting design involved simultaneous breakout sessions, each kicked off by a leader and guided by an internal facilitator who had been trained to deliver a standard program. Participants received their confidential Personal Resilience Profiles at the session, and facilitators were available for one-on-one meetings for anyone who desired one after the session. Based on the feedback from that session, we worked with the client to develop a program that included an introductory session, recorded webinars that provided guidance on developing each of the characteristics, and a module for managers that provided guidance on developing resilience at the individual, team, and organizational levels. Although the extended modules have only had limited traction, the basic program has spread somewhat virally to other parts of the organization, including a range of global locations. This led to the need to translate the tool and training material into several additional languages, and train instructors from global locations.

We have found that the program is most useful when used with intact groups, especially in conjunction with a group profile that helps group members see the range of "change muscles" present in their group. We have also worked with the client to incorporate resilience-related concepts into other leadership-development programs. The client has seen positive results in business-related outcomes that they are able to attribute, at least in part, to the resilience work that was done.

Case 4. Advanced Team Development

The Senior Leadership Team (SLT) of an organization in the health-care industry was composed of ten individuals, most of whom had worked together for several years. The organization has been nationally recognized for both the quality of its service and the strength of its leadership team. The organization had recently agreed to be acquired by a larger company, and the CEO decided that focusing on the team's resilience would be important given the challenges that lay ahead.

In addition to the PRP, team members filled out a questionnaire that looked at the effectiveness of the team's group process. This tool was based on a model of team synergy (Conner 1993), and resulted in a report that provided scores and normative comparisons on various elements of team effectiveness.

The work with the team was done over two sessions. The first session began with the CEO explaining why she decided to focus on resilience and how this work connected to previous teambuilding sessions. The basic tenets of change and resilience were reviewed and discussed; individuals also received their Personal Resilience Profile (PRP) results and developed personal action plans, the highlights of which they shared with their peers. A chart depicting the average and range of PRP scores was reviewed. The second session began with each individual reporting on their progress in implementing their action plans. The concept of synergy was reviewed, and the SLT's synergy scores were displayed and discussed. While the group's overall results were relatively strong, they had a somewhat lower score in the Integration phase of synergy (combining diverse perspectives into innovative approaches). The facilitator was able to link this potential deficit to the overall Personal Resilience strengths and weaknesses of the group. The group members decided in the meeting that they needed to improve their results in the Integration phase, brainstormed and prioritized methods for doing so in the offsite, and have returned to the topic during their regularly scheduled meetings over the past several months. The acquisition was finalized, after some stressful delays, with minimal disruption. The SLT remains intact, has had a very smooth combination process with their acquirers thus far, and is now pursuing some very exciting new opportunities.

Themes and Recommendations

As a venue for developing resilience, the organizational setting differs from educational, clinical, and community settings in several ways. While it offers an excellent opportunity to reach large numbers of individuals, this can only happen with support from organizational leaders. In addition, there is the risk that individuals will experience efforts to help them develop their resilience as manipulative and for the organization's benefit rather than their own. Based on our experience in working with multiple organizations in several countries across a range of interventions illustrated by the case examples above, we have identified several elements that are predictive of successful interventions:

Leader Support

Whether resilience interventions come in the form of classroom training, team-based sessions, or one-on-one coaching and development, they require the investment of individual time, which is one of an organization's scarcest assets. Leader support is essential to ensuring the availability of this time and to ensuring that appropriate follow-up activities take place. Key elements in gaining leader support include:

1. *Building a compelling case.* Leaders need to see the business value of building resilience. In addition to the strategies outlined above—presenting data to show the relationship of resilience to business outcomes, and focusing on the reduction of lost time and energy—it can also be useful to focus on the competitive advantage of having a resilient workforce. Most organizations in a given industry are implementing similar initiatives in the interests of staying competitive. The organization that can execute these changes most efficiently and effectively can begin reaping the benefits faster, and workforce resilience is one important ingredient in moving through change effectively.

2. *Demonstrating personal value.* Leaders are more likely to sponsor resilience development efforts if they have personally experienced value from such activities. We typically seek to identify key leaders and introduce them to resilience concepts and tools that will enable them to strengthen their own resilience before asking them to support broader organizational efforts. A second benefit of this approach is that participants in training sessions are often much more highly motivated to learn when the session is opened by a leader sharing a personal story of how he or she has gained value from developing his or her resilience.

3. *Ensuring sponsorship.* In any organizational intervention, there are multiple roles to be considered (Conner 1993).

Sponsors are those who help people sustain new behaviors through influential communication and the use of effective positive and negative consequences. Advocates are those who would like to see change take place but are not in a position to operate as sponsors. Agents are those who do the work of planning and executing interventions. In many cases, interest in developing resilience is led by agents and advocates. While they may have financial resources to bring in training and education programs, the desired changes in mindsets and behaviors will not take place unless people are supported in their efforts to increase resilience by strong sponsors.

Participant Engagement

Resilience interventions are ineffective unless individuals actively participate in their own learning and development. Ideally, they should freely choose to engage in activities (rather than attending mandatory training), and the activities should be designed to appeal to adult learners. Some elements in creating high levels of engagement include:

1. *Making strong connections.* The best way to engage individuals is to help them immediately see things they can use. This can be done by using real-life examples, relevant stories, and hands-on application to help them address specific challenges in their current situation.

2. *Keeping it simple.* It's important to help people start with small steps and simple frameworks, and apply what they are learning to the daily challenges they face, rather than focusing exclusively on dealing with significant disruptions. While it may seem that the magnitude of changes at work is relatively small compared to some of the traumatic events that can happen in other arenas of life, evidence from neuroscience research suggests that recovery from minor challenges is strongly correlated with and predictive of how someone copes with larger sources

of adversity (Begley & Davidson 2012), which suggests that practice on the small things builds capability for handling larger challenges.

3. *Following through.* Many training programs are isolated efforts. However, developing resilience is not done quickly. It involves restructuring the brain to respond differently to stressful situations. This requires that people have multiple opportunities over a period of time to be reminded of and practice new responses. Because of the competing demands on time and energy in organizational settings, individuals will be far more likely to invest time to practice new ways of thinking and behaving when the practice is supported, encouraged, and reinforced. This can be done by helping individuals incorporate resilience into their personal development goals, using a consistent, shared language to talk about resilience in multiple settings, creating specific opportunities for practice, and a range of other things that pull the thread of resilience through the day-to-day activities of the organization.

4. *Emphasizing learning rather than performance.* There is room for everyone to increase some element of his or her resilience, whether it involves changing self-talk, challenging negative beliefs, becoming clearer about personal priorities, learning to take risks, or developing some other aspect of resilience. If we imply that there is a standard of perfection, rather than meeting people where they are, affirming their strengths, and inviting them to grow, we push people toward "performance goals" rather than "learning goals" (Dweck & Leggett 1988). Keeping the focus on learning, while positively reinforcing small gains, can lead to a positive spiral of energy. To support this contention, we have numerous stories of people who believed that the way they responded to change was something that was just part of them, and were delighted to find out that they could learn and grow in this area.

Creating Trust

Because there are so many benefits to an organization for helping employees become more resilient, individuals can sometimes see organizational efforts to develop resilience as manipulative and self-serving. In addition, the work of learning to become more resilient often calls for revealing areas of weakness and vulnerability, which can be very difficult for people in situations where they feel they may be judged for doing so. Some things that can help an organization establish an environment of trust include:

1. *Guarding confidentiality.* Individuals must believe that information they share, and data they provide, will be treated confidentially. As an example, we set clear expectations with organizations that individuals are the only ones (other than administrators who have agreed to strict confidentiality guidelines) who can see their PRP scores, unless they choose to share them, and that there should be no pressure to share them. Managers and others with whom individuals share their data must be clear that the information is to be used for development purposes only, and that it is not appropriate to use this information to judge or make decisions about individuals. If this confidentiality is breached, it can cause irreparable harm to future efforts, as individuals will be motivated to share information that places them in a favorable light rather than being candid about their own concerns and issues.

2. *Sharing responsibility.* Inviting individuals to develop their resilience sends a healthy message—that individuals can take responsibility for their own responses to change. But it's very easy for people to read this as: "We are planning more change, and we don't really care about its impact on you; we just need you to get on board—here are some tools, but it's your own fault if you're not happy." To create greater trust, it's important for organizations to send

a different message: "Change is a part of life in this organization. We (leaders) have a responsibility to manage the amount of disruption in the organization, both by implementing changes as effectively as possible (including communication, involvement, and well-thought-out plans) and managing the number of changes we are seeking to execute at once. You have a part in this, too. If you are able to increase your own ability to deal effectively with change-related disruption, it will help the organization be more successful, and you will have some tools and skills you can use when facing challenges outside the workplace as well."

3. *Building resilient cultures.* An organization's culture is the set of shared norms and values that shape behavior. Organizational culture can reinforce or undermine resilient behaviors. For instance, an organization in which mistakes are harshly punished is likely to see little experimentation or risk-taking, which are both important to resilience. An organization in which people are encouraged to reach out to others for assistance is likely to see a stronger level of interpersonal support, which is also important to resilience. Leaders who wish to foster resilience should do their best to model and reinforce resilient ways of thinking and acting.

Reaching a Broad Audience

One of the advantages of using organizations as a venue to develop resilience is the number of people that can be reached. Effective practices to increase the reach of resilience interventions include:

1. *Developing internal resources.* One of the best ways to increase the number of people reached in an organization is to prepare members of the organization to serve as educators and coaches for resilience. While people who are interested in serving in this role often come from the Human Resources and/or Organization Development

areas, it's also useful to draw on people who are in other areas of the business, as they can provide practical guidance to help the people they work with apply their learning to daily challenges.
2. *Applying technology.* Although work to help people strengthen their resilience is often best done in person, there are several ways that technology can be helpful. Web-based education can be useful for the initial stages of building awareness and providing information. Simulations and other game-based learning approaches can be useful in reaching workers who are geographically dispersed or prefer to learn on their own. Web links to useful resources (books, articles, videos, etc.) can enable people to quickly find what they need.
3. *Working globally.* Although there are cultural differences in how the various elements of resilience are manifested, the human process of adapting to disruptive events is universal. Reaching people across the globe requires sensitivity to cultural differences and nuances, thoughtful work to translate tools and concepts into a range of languages (we were interested to find, for instance, that in some cultures it was difficult to find a word reflecting the conceptual equivalent of "resilience,") and ongoing exploration of effective ways to reach diverse populations.

Conclusion

Both data and practical experience suggest that it is not only possible, but also useful, to use organizational settings as a venue for helping people develop their resilience. The things individuals learn while dealing with workplace challenges can be applied in the home, the community, and the larger world. This article has described one way of conceptualizing resilience, summarized data to support its effectiveness, provided examples of various applications in organizational settings, and presented ideas for increasing the power of organizational interventions. It is our hope that this information will prove useful to people in a variety of situations and settings.

Works Cited

Aetna Health Plans and ODR, Inc. (1995). Increasing Your Resilience pilot study evaluation report. Technical report.

Begley, Sharon and Richard J. Davidson (2012). *The emotional life of your brain.* Kindle edition. Penguin Publishing.

Bryant, P.C. II (1995). Predictive validity and test-retest reliability of a measure of resilience. M.S. Thesis in Psychology, Georgia Institute of Technology.

Chehrazi, Avazeh (2002). Healthy adaptation in parents of children with autism: Implications of personality and resilience. Ph.D. Dissertation, Psychology, Alliant International University.

Conner, Daryl (1993). *Managing at the speed of change.* Random House.

Dweck, C. S.; Leggett, E. L. (1988). A social-cognitive approach to motivation and personality. *Psychological Review* 95 (2): 256-273.

Fletcher, Joseph A. (2011). Bouncing back and adapting to change: Managers' resilience, skills, and pharmaceutical sales team performance. M.S. Thesis in Organizational Effectiveness, Development, and Change, University of Delaware.

_____ & Linda Hoopes (2010). Building resilience at AstraZeneca. Presentation to the New York chapter of the HR Planning Society.

Isaacs, Albertus J. (2003). An investigation of attributes of school principals in relation to resilience and leadership practices. Ph.D. Dissertation, Department of Educational Leadership and Policy Studies, The Florida State University.

ODR (1993a). *The personal resilience questionnaire.* ODR, Inc., Atlanta, GA.

_____ (1993b). *The personal resilience profile.* ODR, Inc., Atlanta, GA.

_____ (1996). *The personal resilience profile handbook.* ODR, Inc., Atlanta, GA.

Resilience Alliance (2011). Predicting call center performance. Unpublished technical report.

Shin, Jiseon, M. Susan Taylor, & Myeong-gu Seo (2012). Resources for change: The relationships of organizational inducements and psychological resilience to employees' attitudes and behaviors toward organizational change. *Academy of Management Journal* (55)3, 727-748.

Sylvester, Mary H. (2009). Transformational leadership behaviors of frontline sales professionals: An investigation of the impact of resilience and key demographics. Ph.D. Dissertation, School of Business and Technology, Capella University.

Taylor, Lynn M. (1997). The impact of resilience training and coaching on stress and performance during a career-threatening milestone. Ph.D. Dissertation, College of Arts and Sciences, Georgia State University.

Wang, Jing (2003). A study of the adjustment of international graduate students at American universities, including both resilience characteristics and traditional background factors. Ph.D. Dissertation, Department of Educational Leadership and Policy Studies, The Florida State University.

Chapter 5

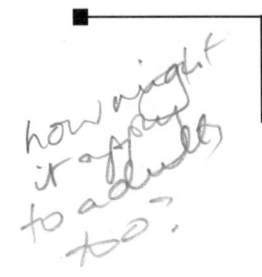

Emotion Regulation in Children: Towards a Resilience Framework

Jennifer Hudson and Venkat Pulla

This chapter explores how children aged from birth to six years old develop an ability to regulate their emotions, including issues that limit this, and discusses factors that increase their long-term resilience to life's difficulties.

The wellbeing of our children is of paramount importance, and much work is done to try to ensure their health and happiness. However, life can be complicated and difficult, and even parents with the best intentions for their children may struggle to find the right path. Most simply do the best they can, generally using the experience they have of their own upbringing, which reflects varying degrees of capacity and effectiveness.

For a variety of reasons, some children develop a range of problems, some of which relate to their ability to regulate their emotions. While all children exhibit some oppositional behaviour, for some others this is extreme, such as destroying property and aggression towards others. Sometimes children display avoidant and withdrawing behaviours, both clinging to caregivers as well as resisting their approach. Caregivers struggle to manage these children, and in some cases children and their families experience difficulties to the extent that they seek the support of specialist services, including mental health services.

About half of all children's referrals to mental health services are for oppositional or aggressive behaviours—which can also be understood as emotion regulation problems (Lewis, Granic, & Lamm 2006). Children who are unable to inhibit their emotional impulses have higher levels of aggression, and these behaviours are often linked to longer term problems, including peer relations and academic progress. In addition, aggressive problems in children often co-occur with anxiety, and children with both these issues are at higher risk for a number of negative outcomes in the longer term (Lewis, et al. 2006).

Definitions

A number of definitions of emotion regulation are found in the literature. Emotions are different from mood, in that mood has a sustained rather than fleeting duration and it does not react to life events and environment (Rossouw 2011). Emotion regulation includes being able to accurately identify your own emotions and cues of others, the ability to express your emotional experience, and the ability to return to a comfortable state of arousal after increased intensity of emotional experience (Kinniburgh, Blaustein, Spinazzola, & Bessel 2005). Emotional regulation has been defined by a number of authors as having a capacity to respond flexibly in a socially acceptable way to different environment demands, allowing for spontaneity as well as being able to inhibit behaviour (Bariola, Hughes, & Gullone 2012; Jungmeen & Cicchetti 2010). In contrast, emotion dysregulation is excessive or constricted emotional reactions, including reduced empathy and inappropriate affective responses for the context (Jungmeen & Cicchetti 2010).

For the purpose of this chapter, emotion regulation will be seen within the context of the system—in terms of children's relationships with others. It will be defined as the ability to interact with others in a socially acceptable way, which includes the capacity and flexibility to adjust intense emotions and related behaviour responses to the situation.

A definition of resilience comes from how material things are able to take up their original shape again distortion. The idea of bouncing back has subsequently been linked with how people endure after stress, and how flexible they are in resuming a state of wellbeing again (Hills & Haynes 2012). Resilience requires that the individual is able to identify and negotiate the psychological, social, cultural, and physical resources that sustain their well-being, in a way appropriate to their culture (Barnard, Morland, & Nagy 1999; Ungar 2012). Resilience will be viewed in the context of the system—how the child's quality of relationships strengthens their capacity to cope with adversity. Children's capacity to cope with ongoing trauma in their everyday lives will be explored, rather than how they respond to specific traumatic incidents. In addition, resilience is more than being able to survive a difficult experience and return as the same person, but that change and potential growth is likely through the struggle of such adversity.

Theoretical Framework—Factors that Impact Emotion Regulation

To conceptualise a child's developmental contexts and understand the interplay between individuals, groups and communities, Bronfenbrenner's 1979 model will be used, which uses a series of concentric rings, with each ring influencing each other ring (DeHart, Sroufe, & Cooper 2004). The centre circle is for the child, with his/her particular biological makeup. Surrounding this is the child's immediate environment, and depending on age, may includes caregivers, family, physical setting, peers and teachers. Next is the social and economic context, representing the next layer which is slightly more removed but still has an impact on the child, such as the school curriculum and management system or the caregivers work place. Finally, the outer ring represents the cultural context—the beliefs, attitudes, values and guidelines that people in a particular culture share.

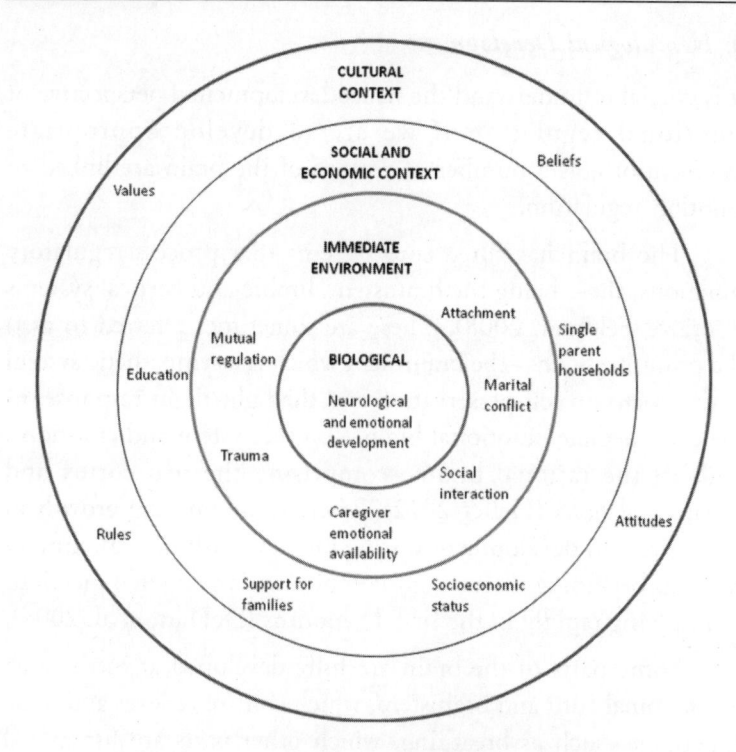

Figure 1. Factors for the Development of Children's Emotion Regulation

While it is acknowledged that the social, economic and cultural contexts are crucial to the child's emotional development, this chapter focus on the biological and the immediate environment.

Biology

A child's biological makeup is made up of three essential components, these being the evolutionally heritage shared by all humans, the child's individual genetic inheritance and the biological results of the interaction between genetics and the environment (DeHart, et al. 2004). In terms of the evolutionally heritage, children's development usually follows a number of expected stages, recognising that there will be a number of individual differences within a range.

A. Neurological Development

It is crucial to understand the neurodevelopmental perspective of emotional regulation if we are to develop appropriate interventions, as a number of regions of the brain are linked to emotion regulation.

The brain has three core systems that process regulatory functions, these being the brainstem, limbic and cortical systems (Geva & Feldman 2008). These are sometimes referred to as i) the primitive brain—the brain stem which is a sympathetic system with a focus on self-preservation and the fight/flight response; ii) the intermediate/emotional brain—limbic system and emotions; and iii) the rational brain—comprising the neo cortex and intellectual tasks (Helfer 2012). There is an amazing growth in brain size and development during infancy, with the structure of neurons becoming increasingly complex and the interconnections multiplying rapidly in the first 15 months (DeHart, et al. 2004).

Some parts of the brain are fully developed at birth, such as the spinal cord and brainstem, which control reflexes and basic functions—such as breathing, which other parts are functional at birth but develop further during childhood. A child's nervous system is dependent on its experience and the environment it develops in for all the necessary connections to develop appropriately (Helfer 2012).

A well-functioning brainstem integrated with the limbic system is crucial for the development of emotion regulation capacities (Geva & Feldman 2008). The limbic system, also known as the intermediate or emotional brain, is a collection of structures that are involved in integrating sensory information, memory formation and emotional responses (Rossouw 2011).

One of the structures in the limbic system is the Amygdala, and safety is its main function. It is activated in response to fear—such as facial signs of fear, and can be overactive in children who have experienced trauma, interpreting neutral signals as dangerous

(Davidson, Putnam, & Larson 2000). If there is chronic hyper activation then anxiety is increased and there are more worried ruminations, which can also lead to unhelpful avoidance strategies and depression (Rossouw 2011).

The limbic system also contains the Hippocampus, the role of which is to map events and put things in context of time and space (Rossouw 2011). This means that fear can be associated with environmental stimuli, meaning that children may live with chronic fear and anxiety. A good sleeping pattern for children is crucial as one of the functions that sleep performs is to process the day's events, and clear the hippocampus of insignificant details (Rossouw 2011).

The brain has a left and right hemisphere, which performs specific functions. The right hemisphere specialises in non-verbal recognition and emotional memory, reading faces, emotions and assessing the emotional significance of an incident (Rossouw 2011). In contrast, the left hemisphere specialises in verbal work, making meanings, organising information, problem solving and analysis. Interestingly, the left hemisphere also inhibits the activity of the right hemisphere, and it is on this basis that some therapeutic interventions, such as Cognitive Behaviour Therapy, aim to strengthen the left hemisphere as this may reduce intense emotions (Rossouw 2011).

The right hemisphere is very active during children's early years, and through the process of the senses being stimulated, sensory memory is stored (Australian Childhood Foundation 2010). This hemisphere registers the state of the child's body as her senses respond to touch, sound, light, warmth, hunger, comfort and rest, and forms templates that represent the most consistent responses from carers. Children are then able to develop an internal sense of predictability about having their needs met. It is from these familiar routines when needs are met, that babies learn to deal with their stress and are more settled; this occurs because memory templates act to reduce the levels of arousal that they experience as they are exposed to changes in their environment. When routines are disrupted the stress increases, however when they are re-established the memory templates are confirmed and the child settles. Ideally, a relationship develops in which children trust that their needs will be met by the caregiver through these positive experiences (Australian Childhood Foundation 2010).

The Prefrontal Cortex (PFC) is an important part of the cortical system, or "rational" brain, because it is associated with self-control and the ability to inhibit responses, which are crucial to emotion regulation (Lewis, et al. 2006). When considering the ability of children to regulate their emotions, it is helpful to understand that the PFC is not in full operation until someone is in their mid 20s (Rossouw 2011). Another part of the brain that plays a role in the regulation of mood and behaviour, personality, motivation and cognition is the Orbito Frontal Cortex (OFC) (Rossouw 2011). It has been noted by Eslinger et al. (2009) that the importance of the PFC in regards to moral behaviour, rests on its capacity to develop empathy and the ability to adapt socially.

Research indicates that children who display impulsive aggression have a low threshold for emotions, such as anger, distress and agitation, and they are often unable to regulate these negative emotions (Davidson et al. 2000). Children with aggressive behaviour show reduced neural activity related to emotion regulation, and find it more difficult to be flexible in their behaviours (Lewis, et al. 2006).

Children with an intellectual disability may have a lower threshold for the negative comments they are able to tolerate before they become distressed, and therefore will generally struggle more with emotion regulation skills than those who are developing typically (Green & Baker 2011). Research also suggests a link between hyperactivity and neuropsychological abilities, particularly attention and executive function, seen in children as young as four years old, with children often diagnosed with Attention Deficit Hyperactivity Disorder (ADHD) (Youngwirth, Harvey, Gates, Hashim, & Friedman-Weieneth 2007).

B. Emotional Development

Children initially have primary emotions and gradually develop secondary, or self-conscious, emotions over time. The primary emotions that are present from birth in animals and other humans are surprise, interest, joy, anger, sadness, fear and disgust (Santrock 2004). Erickson describes the psychosocial developmental stage during a child's first year as trust or mistrust, which depends on whether their needs are met by caregivers, and children who develop trust at this stage are likely to see the world as a safe place in the longer term (DeHart, et al. 2004).

Children aged one to three years develop autonomy versus shame and doubt, according to Erickson; this occurs when they start to assert their independence (DeHart, et al. 2004). Caregiver response to this newly developed autonomy is important because if children are too restrained or punished too harshly, they may develop shame and doubt (Santrock 2004). As children's cognitive abilities develop, self-conscious emotions emerge from about 18 months old, such as empathy, jealousy and embarrassment. From two and a half years, children start to exhibit pride, shame and guilt (Santrock 2004). Children with damage to the OFC fail to develop feelings of shame and guilt later in life, which are crucial emotions to develop for a sense of morals (Helfer 2012).

Theory of mind is the awareness that children develop about their own mental processes and the mental processes of others (Santrock 2004). Children aged two to three years are able to distinguish between positive (e.g. happy) and negative (e.g. sad), however their understanding of how their thoughts or beliefs can influence behaviour is limited, thinking that people are at the mercy of their desires (Santrock 2004). From four to five years, children start to understand that the mind may not always represent objects or events accurately—that people have false beliefs. Theory of Mind is developed through positive reciprocal interactions with caregivers where children learn to consider what others feel and adjust their behaviour accordingly.

Erickson's psychosocial stage for children aged three to five years is termed initiative versus guilt. As children are asked to assume more responsibility their initiative increases, however so does a sense of anxiety if they are irresponsible (Santrock 2004). During this stage children will commence preschool, with widening social interactions, started playing in a group, and are learning how to take turns (Hobday & Ollier 1988). Competence with peers increases and friendships endure (DeHart, et al. 2004). Their world continues to expand, they become more self-reliant with both instrumental and emotional areas, their self-control increases—including their ability to tolerate frustration, and their sense of self remains constant (Hobday & Ollier 1988). Their language and cognitive skills improve and they are better able to comprehend simple emotions, such as happy, sad and angry (DeHart, et al. 2004). Teachers play a significant role in children's development during this stage, and with caregivers can help them discover a sense of their own competence through accomplishment (Santrock 2004).

Finally, the role of children's temperament in the development of emotional regulation skills is acknowledged, being their behavioural style and characteristic way of responding. The temperament of children may also influence the type of care they receive—for example, children that are easy to interact with may attract positive reinforcement of this, while difficult children are more likely to attract negative feedback, these both being reinforcing loops (Bond & McConkey 2001).

Immediate Environment

The immediate environment for young children is their family, particularly their caregivers, and these relationships create the first opportunities for emotional interaction. As children grow this environment extends to include child care centres, school, teachers and peers.

C. Attachment

When considering how children develop the capacity to regulate their emotions, it is important to understand attachment theory, initially developed by John Bowlby in 1958. Attachment theory changed the way that the bond between caregiver and infant was viewed, emphasising the connection between the two, rather than it being a relationship based purely on survival (Fitton 2012). The caregiver's sensitivity, responsiveness and attunement to the child in the first 12 months creates a trusting, safe and secure relationship, with the subsequent secure attachment having positive long-term implications (Santrock 2004). This early, enduring and irreplaceable attachment relationship provides an environment that supports mental and emotional growth (Fitton 2012). Secure attachment is a protective system for the child, creating a foundation for positive, mutual interactions between the parent and the child and other long-term relationships (Kochanska et al. 2010).

In contrast, children who do not experience a sensitive and responsive caregiver may develop an insecure attachment type. At a neurobiological level, where a child has developed insecure attachment in the context of basic nurturing needs not being met, this can leave negative neural looping and neuro-chemical reactions in the memory system (Rossouw 2011, p. 29). There are three types of insecure attachment, these being i) avoidant—avoiding the caregiver; ii) resistant—clinging then pushing away; and iii) disorganised—dazed, confused and fearful (Santrock 2004) (see Table 1).

These types of attachment were researched by Ainsworth in 1983, using the "Strange Situation Test", which observed the nature and quality of the child's social interaction with their caregiver (Bond & McConkey 2001).

Table 1: Caregiver Attachment Types

Caregivers behaviour	Child behaviours	Attachment type
Sensitive, responsive. Able to repair mismatches in emotional interactions.	The child is upset and protests when the caregiver departs, searches for her while away and displays delight on her return.	Secure
Abusive. Limited sensitivity and responsiveness.	The child displays indifference when the caregiver departs or returns, and is reluctant to cling to her anytime.	Insecure – avoidant (also known as dismissing)
Neglectful. Caregivers are inconsistently and unpredictably available. Limited positive interactions with child.	The child often clings to the caregiver and show distress when she departs, however do not show delight or are comforted by her return.	Insecure – resistant (also known as preoccupied/ambivalent)
Caregivers often look to the child to help with their own emotion regulation and feel helpless or inadequate to protect their child.	The child appears overwhelmed, displaying frozen, confused and fearful behaviours.	Insecure – disorganised (also known as unresolved)

Caregivers who are warm and responsive elicit an eager, willing stance in the child and a mutually responsive, cooperative relationship develops (Kochanska, Barry, Stellern, & O'Bleness 2009). It is within the safety of this relationship that children develop a trust of the caregiver, and subsequently do not generally see any assertion of power as a threat. However, where attachment has not been developed securely, such as when caregivers have a harsh style of control, the relationship usually becomes more difficult after the end of the first year, and the child may enter into a dysfunctional cycle with a caregiver, becoming resentful and oppositional (Kochanska, et al. 2009, p. 1288).

D. *Mutual Regulation*

The Mutual Regulation Model is the process where the caregiver and child have interactions where they experience times of matching and mismatching emotionally, with the crucial point being the process of repairing mismatch (DiCorcia & Tronick 2011; Tronick & Beeghly 2011). Periods of child-caregiver matching is associated with a child's positive affect and engagement, whereas mismatches are associated with their negative affect and dysregulation.

This model emerged from the *Everyday Stress Resilience Hypothesis*, formulated by DiCorcia & Tronick (2011), which argues that through the process of being supported while facing daily stressors, children increase their capacity to cope with more extreme stress. This "regulatory resilience" (DiCorcia & Tronick 2011, p. 1594) emphasises the importance of the quality of the child-caregiver relationship, with the process providing a scaffolding experience where the child is able to increasingly learn to regulate their own emotions, through experiencing dysregulation and repair with their caregiver (DiCorcia & Tronick 2011). When children are deprived of this regulatory support, they show deficits in their own emotional regulation, reducing their ongoing resilience in other relationships.

Children need a certain amount of frequent low-intensity maternal negative expression to give them opportunities to learn from the experience and practice their emotion understanding (Green & Baker 2011). However, if the negative expressivity is too high, this increases children's arousal to the point where they are unable to regulate their own distress and therefore not able to learn about others distress. Sensitive caregivers find a balance between allowing a certain level of discomfort to help children learn to regulate themselves, and stepping in to support when needed (Green & Baker 2011).

The child experiences the world in a certain way, giving meaning to interactions which can shape how they engage with others in the longer term (Tronick & Reck 2009). If a child has a positive experience in one relationship of repairing misses in communication, this can help them feel more effective and trusting that they could experience this reparation after miscommunication or conflict in another relationship (Tronick 2003). Caregivers expression of positive affect with their children has been associated with increased social competence, improved adjustment, emotion understanding, socially acceptable behaviour and higher self-esteem (Green & Baker 2011).

Children find meaning in their key interactions and relationships that influence how they perceive the world and themselves—whether this be positive or negative. The emotional availability of caregivers may limit their capacity to provide appropriate care, influenced by issues such as mental health, significant substance use and conflict in caregiver relationships (Cooper 2009; Davies & Cummings 1994). Children who do not have a sensitive adult to help them learn appropriate ways to interact and repair mismatches do not have a choice but to engage the best they can with caregivers whose interactions may be negative, with frequent mismatches and ineffective processes of repair following a mismatch (Tronick & Beeghly 2011).

E. Trauma

The inability to regulate emotions is one of the most profound consequences of early neglect and abuse (Helfer 2012). Children who are often left at an escalated arousal state without regulation from the caregiver will eventually become traumatised (Helfer 2012; Jungmeen & Cicchetti 2010). Findings from neuroscience show that prolonged exposure to violence can effect emotion development, stress response and learning (Feigelson 2011). Instead of providing a calm and safe environment, caregivers may escalate interactions with their child, such as being punitive or violent, giving in to demands or oscillating between impulsiveness and submission (Weinblatt & Omer 2008, p. 75).

An experience of chronic abuse increases the risk of a range of behavioural, neuropsychological, cognitive, emotional and interpersonal disorders (Becker-Weidman & Hughes 2008). Children who have been exposed to early trauma are at higher risk for developing depression or anxiety as an adult (Heim & Nemeroff 2001). In contrast, when children have secure attachment with a caregiver, they will recover better from trauma than children without access to comfort (Foley 2012).

Research conducted by Jungmeen & Cicchetti (2010) indicate that children who experience multiple subtypes of abuse, particularly if it started early, are more likely to have difficulties with emotional regulation and will show more externalising problems. Further, because of these aggressive and disruptive behaviours, they are more likely to be rejected by their peers, and subsequently have fewer opportunities for positive social interaction. Children who have been physically abused show enhanced perceptual sensitivity to angry facial cues, whereas neglected children have difficulties differentiating between and responding to expressions of emotion. In contrast, children with internalising symptoms do not experience peer rejection in this way, and in fact peer acceptance is a protective effect of emotional regulation (Jungmeen & Cicchetti 2010).

Social and Economic Context

There are a number of protective and risk factors for the development of emotion regulation in the social and economic context, that influences a children's resilience to trauma. These include: (i) parental and wider family support; (ii) social structures—such as school, church or other community groups; and finally, (iii) economic factors—such as adequate income and housing (Barnard, et al. 1999). As noted previously, while the impact of these systems on the child is significant, these will not all be discussed in this chapter.

The relationship of families with services for children, particularly the therapeutic alliance, is more significant than any other particular intervention for a range of problems (Helfer 2012). Providing an environment where the therapist is able to manage their own negative responses to the child's negative behaviour, while encouraging positive interactions, may lead to the development of a more positive emotional state for the child (Tronick & Reck 2009). The therapeutic relationship provided by services also provides an important opportunity to support caregivers to improve their own emotion regulation and capacity to attend to their child, as illustrated by a number of the interventions discussed below.

Services and individual therapists may struggle to provide a compassionate and safe environment for caregivers who may often be dysregulated themselves. Caregivers themselves may have had an adverse developmental environment as a child, such as insecure attachment and limited experience of mutual regulation with their own caregivers, and as adults continue to experience frequent unresolved conflict throughout many relationships. Even with the best intentions, these caregivers will struggle to provide an appropriate environment for their children, as they do not have their own skills and experience of mutual regulation.

To be able to offer a compassionate and mutually regulating therapeutic relationship, the therapist requires a full and rich life of their own, to be able to have the difficult conversations, to listen rather than just waiting to speak, to be flexible to others needs, to be imperfect, to allow themselves not to know everything, to sit in the discomfort of being stuck, to have compassion, and to already be self-nourishing and self-nourished so that they don't bring their own needs into the relationship (Fuller 1998). While services can play a significant role in a child's life, the primary relationships in the child's environment is the caregiver, as this is where the majority of the child's experience of interaction occurs (Tronick & Reck 2009). The socioeconomic status has a considerable impact, with adverse economic and social factors described as "structural conditions that can create toxic levels of stress in families" making it more difficult for them to provide appropriate care for their children (Feigelson 2011, p. 6). These levels of stress may also exacerbate caregiver mental health problems (Australian Bureau of Statistics 2007), and as noted previously, this may limit a caregiver's capacity to offer positive mutual regulation experiences. Given the impact of social and economic factors on caregivers, it is vital to include broader social interventions that improve caregiver resources.

Cultural Context

The outer ring in Bronfenbrenner's model of a child's environment is the cultural context, the beliefs, attitudes and values that are held in particular cultures. Socialisation is the way that cultures pass onto children the values, beliefs, rules and attitudes, and through this process influence the way that children are encouraged to and expected to regulate their emotions. While families are the primary cultural influence when children are young, peer groups provides significant reinforcement of the values, beliefs and behaviour standards that are a part of this culture (DeHart, et al. 2004). The characteristics of a child's neighbourhood also have an impact on their development, and where children experience a number of positive role model adults monitoring them, this also is helpful.

Towards a Resilience Framework

In many ways, emotional dysregulation is a developmental problem, where the child has not learnt to manage their emotions because of a lack of nurturing and practice through mutual regulation. Emotional regulation is developed within the context of a responsive caregiver who provides the child with a safe and predictable environment, with opportunities to learn the process of becoming distressed and returning to a stable emotional state (Bariola, et al. 2012; Jungmeen & Cicchetti 2010). The sensitivity and flexibility of the emotional communication between child and caregiver is vital, with recognition of the interplay between biological, psychological and social factors (Lewis, et al. 2006; DeHart, et al. 2004).

The concept of resilience, the ability to bounce back and respond flexibly to situations, is useful to consider in the context of how a child learns emotion regulation. The experience of learning that repair can come from mismatch and miscommunication helps children build resilience. With this comes the understanding that it is not the emotion that causes the problem, but past experience of the emotion, with success of managing intense emotions building skills and breeding confidence for the longer term. Children who have effective emotional regulation skills recognise that repair is possible after conflict in relationships, and have more flexibility, enabling them to manage life struggles better.

A resilience framework is likely to include a number of positive environmental factors, some of which are included in Figure 2.

There are a number of important characteristics in children who demonstrate resilience, including a higher temperamental tolerance to distress, a caregiver who is attuned to their needs, secure attachment, opportunities to gradually practice, ability to learn and social supports (Perry 2006).

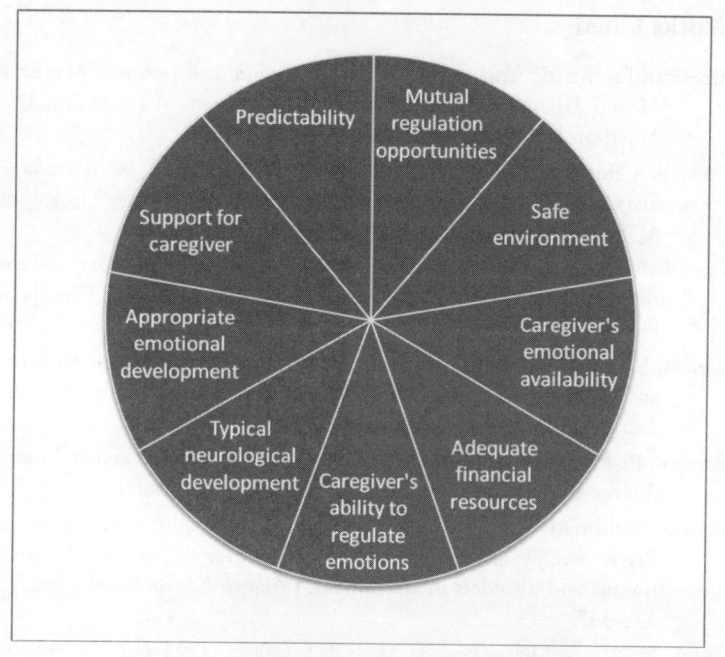

Figure 2. Towards a Resilience Framework

(Pie chart segments: Predictability; Mutual regulation opportunities; Safe environment; Caregiver's emotional availability; Adequate financial resources; Caregiver's ability to regulate emotions; Typical neurological development; Appropriate emotional development; Support for caregiver)

For caregivers to be able to provide a responsive and sensitive environment, they need the capacity, information, access to resources and necessary other supports to achieve this (Cubis 2012). As the number of positive factors in a child's life increase across the range of contexts, so does their likelihood of developing the flexibility to return to a stable emotional state after being distressed, with increased resilience to life's longer term struggles. The brain has remarkable plasticity, thus it is certainly worth investing time and effort into children with oppositional and aggressive behaviours. Any intervention aiming at increasing a child's ability to regulate their emotions should recognise these factors, and incorporate a range of strategies to assist children and their families. It is also clear that the social, economic and cultural contexts are important to these issues, and these need to be explored further to build a more comprehensive framework for resilience.

Works Cited

American Psychiatric Association. (2000). *Diagnostic and Statistical Manual of Mental Disorders, Fourth Edition, Text Revision*. Washington, DC: American Psychiatric Association.

Australian Bureau of Statistics. (2007). *Health of Children in Australia: A Snapshot, 2004-05* Canberra: Retrieved from http://www.abs.gov.au/AUSSTATS/abs@.nsf/mf/4829.0.55.001/.

Australian Childhood Foundation. (2010). *Making Space for Learning: Trauma Informed Practice in Schools*. Ringwood, VIC: Australian Childhood Foundation.

Bariola, E., Hughes, E., & Gullone, E. (2012). Relationships Between Parent and Child Emotion Regulation Strategy Use: A Brief Report. [Article]. *Journal of Child & Family Studies*, 21(3), 443-448.

Barnard, P., Morland, I., & Nagy, J. (1999). *Children, Bereavement and Trauma: Nurturing Resilience*. London: Jessica Kingsley Publishers.

Becker-Weidman, A., & Hughes, D. (2008). Dydadic Developmental Psychotherapy: an evidence-based treatment for children with complex trauma and disorders of attachment. *Child & Family Social Work*, 13, 329-337.

Bond, N. W., & McConkey, K. M. (Eds.). (2001). *Psychological science: An introduction*. Sydney: The McGraw-Hill Companies, Inc.

Bridges, L. J., Denham, S. A., & Ganiban, J. M. (2004). Definitional Issues in Emotion Regulation Research. [Article]. *Child Development*, 75(2), 340-345.

Cooper, G., Hoffman, K. & Powell, B. (2009). *Circle of Security Parenting: A Relationship Based Parenting Program. Facilitator DVD Manual 5.0.*.

Cubis, J. (2012). A Brief Review of Resilience to Traumatic Events in Children and Adolescents Retrieved 06 August, 2012

Dadds, M. R., & Hawes, D. (2006). *Integrated Family Intervention for Child Conduct Problems: A Behaviour-Attachment-Systems Intervention for Parents*. Brisbane: Australian Academic Press.

Davidson, R. J., Putnam, K. M., & Larson, C. L. (2000). Dysfunction in the Neural Circuitry of Emotion Regulation—A Possible Prelude to Violence. *Science*, 289(5479), 591.

Davies, P., & Cummings, E. M. (1994). Marital confict and child adjustment: An emotional security hypothesis. *Psychological Bulletin*, 116(3), 387-441.

DeHart, G. B., Sroufe, L. A., & Cooper, R. G. (2004). *Child development: Its nature and course*. New York: McGraw-Hill.

DiCorcia, J. A., & Tronick, E. (2011). Quotidian resilience: Exploring mechanisms that drive resilience from a perspective of everyday stress and coping. *Neuroscience & Biobehavioral Reviews*, 35(7), 1593-1602.

Eslinger, P. J., Robinson-Long, M., Realmuto, J., Moll, J., deOliveira-Souza, R., Tovar-Moll, F.,... Yang, Q. X. (2009). Developmental frontal lobe imaging in moral judgment: Arthur Benton's enduring influence 60 years later. *Journal of Clinical & Experimental Neuropsychology*, 31(2), 158-169.

Feigelson, M. J. (2011). Hidden Violence: Protecting young children at home. *Early Childhood Matters*, 116.

Fitton, V. A. (2012). Attachment Theory: History, Research, and Practice. [Article]. *Psychoanalytic Social Work*, 19(1/2), 121-143.

Foley, S. (2012). *The velcro and the buttons in working with attachment for clinicians, families and children.* Paper presented at the Child & Adolescent Mental Health Services training, Queanbeyan.

Fuller, A. (1998). *From surviving to thriving: Promoting mental health in young people.* Melbourne: ACER Press.

Geva, R., & Feldman, R. (2008). A neurobiological model for the effects of early brainstem functioning on the development of behavior and emotion regulation in infants: implications for prenatal and perinatal risk. *Journal of Child Psychology & Psychiatry*, 49(10), 1031-1041.

Green, S., & Baker, B. (2011). Parents' emotion expression as a predictor of child's social competence: children with or without intellectual disability. *Journal of Intellectual Disability Research*, 55(3), 324-338.

Gross, J. J., & Levenson, R. W. (1997). Hiding Feelings: The Acute Effects of Inhibiting Negative and Positive Emotion. *Journal of Abnormal Psychology, 1*(February 1997), 95-103.

Healy, K. (2005). *Social Work Theories in Context: Creating Frameworks for Practice.* Hampshire: Palgrave Macmillan.

Heim, C., & Nemeroff, C. B. (2001). The role of childhood trauma in the neurobiology of mood and anxiety disorders: Preclinical and clinical studies. *Biological Psychiatry, 49*(12), 1023-1039.

Helfer, S. (2012). Complex Cases: A Neurodelevopmental perspective of emotion regulation, morals and empathy. [Child & Adolescent Mental Health Services Podcast]. Sydney: MH-Kids.

Hills, R., & Haynes, D. (2012). *Perspectives on Coping and Resilience.* Sydney: IRIS.

Hobday, A., & Ollier, K. (1988). *Creative Therapy: Activities with children and adolescents.* Melbourne: ACER Press.

Jungmeen, K., & Cicchetti, D. (2010). Longitudinal pathways linking child maltreatment, emotion regulation, peer relations, and psychopathology. *Journal of Child Psychology & Psychiatry,* 51(6), 706-716.

Kinniburgh, K. J., Blaustein, M., Spinazzola, J., & Bessel, A. (2005). Attachment, Self-Regulation and Competency. *Psychiatric Annals,* 35(5), 424-430.

Kochanska, G., Barry, R. A., Stellern, S. A., & O'Bleness, J. J. (2009). Early Attachment Organization Moderates the Parent—Child Mutually Coercive Pathway to Children's Antisocial Conduct. *Child Development,* 80(4), 1288-1300.

_____, Woodard, J., Kim, S., Koenig, J. L., Jeung Eun, Y., & Barry, R. A. (2010). Positive socialization mechanisms in secure and insecure parent—child dyads: two longitudinal studies. *Journal of Child Psychology & Psychiatry,* 51(9), 998-1009.

Lenze, S. N., Pautsch, J., & Luby, J. (2011). Parent-child interaction therapy emotion development: a novel treatment for depression in preschool children. *Depression & Anxiety (1091-4269),* 28(2), 153-159.

Lewis, M. D., Granic, I., & Lamm, C. (2006). Behavioral Differences in Aggressive Children Linked with Neural Mechanisms of Emotion Regulation. *Annals of the New York Academy of Sciences,* 1094(1), 164-177.

Martini, T. S., & Busseri, M. A. (2012). Emotion regulation and relationship quality in mother-young adult child dyads. *Journal of Social & Personal Relationships,* 29(2), 185-205.

Nunn, K. (2011). Conduct Disorder. *MH-Kids Podcasts.* Sydney: NSW Health, Mental Health and Drug & Alcohol office.

Perry, B. (2006). Resilience: Where does it come from?. *Early Childhood Today*(April, Scholastics).

Relationships Australia. (2012). What about the Children? Retrieved 9 September 2012, 2012

Rossouw, P. (2011). *The Neuroscience of Depression.* Paper presented at the Mediros Clinical Solutions, Sydney.

Santrock, J. W. (2004). *Child Development* (10th ed.). New York: McGraw-Hill.

Scott, G., Ciarrochi, J., & Deane, F. P. (2004). Disadvantages of being an individualist in an individualistic culture: Idiocentrism,emotional competence, stress, and mental health. *Australian Psychologist,* 39(2), 143-153.

Tackett, J. L., Balsis, S., Oltmanns, T. F., & Krueger, R. F. (2009). A unifying perspective on personality pathology across the life span: Developmental considerations for the fifth edition of the Diagnostic and Statistical Manual of Mental Disorders. *Development & Psychopathology, 21*, 687-713.

Tronick, E. (2003). "Of course all relationships are unique": How co-creative processes generate unique mother-infant and patient-therapist relationships and change other relationships. *Psychological Inquiry, 23*(3), 473-491.

_____, & Beeghly, M. (2011). Infants' Meaning Making and the Development of Mental Health Problems. *American Psychologist, 66*(2), 107-119.

_____, & Reck, C. (2009). Infants of Depressed Mothers. *Harvard Review of Psychiatry, 17*(2), 147-156.

Ungar, M. (2012). Resilience Research Centre Retrieved 18 May 2012, 2012, from http://resilience.socialwork.dal.ca/

Weinblatt, U., & Omer, H. (2008). Nonviolent resistence: A treatment for parents of children with acute behaviour problems. *Journal of Marital and Family Therapy, 34*(1), 75-92.

Youngwirth, S. D., Harvey, E. A., Gates, E. C., Hashim, R. L., & Friedman-Weieneth, J. L. (2007). Neuropsychological Abilities of Preschool-Aged Children Who Display Hyperactivity and/or Oppositional-Defiant Behavior Problems. *Child Neuropsychology, 13*(5), 422-443.

Zastrow, C. H. (2003). *The Practice of Social Work: Applications of Generalist and Advanced Content* (Seventh ed.). Victoria: Thomson—Brooks/Cole.

CHAPTER 6

Strengthening the Capacity for Resilience in Children

Alyce White and Venkat Pulla

Introduction

Promoting resilience in children has become an important concern within contemporary research and practice. This chapter will focus on developing a theory of strengthening resilience within the generalised context of child development. Resilience is a concept which recognises that children have agency in negotiating challenges and adversity; however, children are embedded in, and are dependent upon, their place within their surrounding social ecology. There are multiple theories, understandings and approaches to strengthening resilience, either concerned with early intervention and individual abilities or providing an environment which facilitates a child's potential. Strengthening resilience as a process is concerned with prevention to ensure that children are better enabled to positively develop despite life's adversities and challenges. This chapter will examine processes that promote pathways to positive child development and wellbeing despite adversity. These processes occur across multiple systems in a child's life such as, family, community or neighbourhood, school and wider society. It is within these systems which the chapter will concentrate on integrating resilience theory and knowledge to create a supportive environment that promotes positive development, well-being and resilience in children.

Understanding Resilience in Children

Despite there being over two decades of research and literature into 'resilience', the term still exists as a highly contested and problematic concept, emphasising the need for uniformity in understanding 'resilience' across many disciplines and professions. Resilience occurs in situations of adversity and risk such as cumulative disadvantage or negative life circumstances that are known to lead to poor outcomes (Luthar & Cicchetti 2000). Resilience is a relative construct and can be conceptualised as a child experiencing better outcomes compared to expectations or similar adversity (Luthar & Cicchetti 2000; Rutter 2012). Understandings and definitions of positive and negative outcomes are embedded within a social and cultural context, and are dependent upon the interactions between this environment and the child (Rutter 2012; Ungar 2010). This chapter advocates for a proactive resilience strengthening approach that encompasses all children especially those at greater disadvantage.

For the purpose of this chapter resilience is understood as a dynamic process of interactions between a child and his or her social and physical ecology; these interventions promote adaptation and positive outcomes despite adversity or cumulative disadvantage (Sameroff & Rosenblum 2006; Ungar 2011b). Within a focus on children and development, resilience is further conceptualised as a developmental process where children learn to use internal and external resources to positively adapt despite adverse situations (Yates, Egeland, & Sroufe 2003). This chapter integrates child development and current resilience theories to propose a holistic and multisystemic approach to strengthening resilience, through building a supportive environment for children to grow and develop.

The cross-disciplinary use of resilience in research, practice and policy emphasises the need for definitions and guidelines so that future research and uses of resilience can be meaningful and applicable across varying disciplines, systems and societies. There have been numerous authors (Anthony, Alter, & Jenson 2009; Luthar & Zelazo 2003; Ungar 2011b; Windle 2011) who attempted to develop a universal understanding and approach to resilience research and interventions, through developing principles, rules, and definitions of resilience. It is beyond the limits of this chapter to review and address this issue in its entirety.

Understandings of resilience have traditionally focused on a child's individual abilities and characteristics, with resilience practice utilising interventions as ways of strengthening these individual qualities. Whilst children possess strengths and abilities, these characteristics are not necessarily the sole factors of resilience processes and outcomes, and their contributions are seen as dynamic and relational (Jaffee, Caspi, Moffitt, Polo-Tomás, & Taylor 2007; Rutter 2012; Sameroff & Rosenblum 2006; Ungar 2011b). Moreover, views of resilience as a fixed personal attribute are highly problematic, as the features that make a person 'resilient' in one situation may not necessarily aid the same person in a different context (Rutter 2012). Through concentrating on individual characteristics and abilities, children can be given the responsibility for negotiating positive and negative outcomes, when they often have little opportunity to individually develop an inventory for coping with adversity. Interventions need to focus on both the child's strengths and their environment so they can be holistically supported to develop the capacity to be resilient.

Childhood, Development and Resilience

Strengthening the capacity for resilience in children is deeply embedded within understandings of childhood and child development. Evolving understandings draw attention to the journey of childhood and the experience children derive from it (Graham 2011). Childhood is socially embedded within context and time, and children are seen as active agents who interact with their social ecology, and who make meaning and sense of the world around them. Therefore interventions should endeavour to engage children, to explore and strengthen their potential and capacity as active participants within society (Graham 2011). Promoting positive child wellbeing is at the centre of resilience. Each child is located in a context within which they interact, and interventions need to be aware of and tailored to a child's context (Camfield, Streuli, & Woodhead 2009). Thus, current understandings of childhood strongly support a social ecological, contextual and culturally relevant conception of resilience.

The theories and strategies in promoting resilience that are presented in this chapter correlate strongly with theories of contextual child development, including Bronfenbrenner's ecological systems theory and Vygotsky's sociocultural theory (cited in Hoffnung et al. 2010). These child development theories in particular inform the chapter's conceptualisation of resilience and strategies towards the strengthening of resilience in children. Bronfenbrenner's theory outlines the different interactive systems which influence a child's development: the microsystem, mesosystem, exosystem and the macrosystem (Hoffnung et al. 2010, p. 9). The microsystem includes systems such as family, peer group, school and church; systems with which a child has direct interactions and that influence the child's development. The mesosystem consists of the interactions and relationships between the microsystems in a child's life that influence their development, for example the connection between a family and their child's school. The exosystem includes the systems with which the child does not directly interact, but which indirectly affects a child with the decisions and changes it makes, for example a local government or a parent's workplace. The macrosystem refers to the defining features and characteristics of a society; for example, the cultural and social norms, traditions, ideologies, practices, beliefs, knowledge, laws and policies (Hoffnung, et al. 2010, p. 9). Vygotsky's socio-cultural theory understands child development as being embedded within the historical and cultural context in which the child lives, and dependent on the interactions, connections and relationships with representatives of the culture such as family members or the child's school and teachers (Hoffnung, et al. 2010). Resilience, grounded in contextual understandings of child development focuses on interventions that work with children and their social, cultural and physical environment.

Strengthening resilience in children is explored in this chapter as an essential process in a child's development, not exclusively for children who have experienced adversity. Promoting resilience needs to be seen as collective responsibility towards creating a social and physical context for all children that supports positive outcomes despite adversity. Thus the relationships between communities, schools and families, and the combination of resources and assets can promote resilient outcomes for children (Kia-Keating, Dowdy, Morgan, & Noam 2011). The combination and integration of resilience with child development provides an in-depth understanding of positive development and could be critical in strengthening the power of resilience-focused interventions and their relevance and effectiveness when working with children (Kia-Keating, et al. 2011). Therefore child development is a central concern in strengthening the capacity for resilience in children. This chapter addresses resilience through concentrating on interventions within various systems, including: the child's, family, community, school and society.

A social ecological understanding of resilience is emerging as an integral approach to understanding and promoting resilience in contemporary literature. Ungar (2011b), a strong advocate of this approach, reframes resilience within the context of contemporary literature drawing on understandings of environmental factors as also contributing to resilience. Social ecological understandings of resilience expand and deepen the connection between resilience and child development.

Social ecology theory argues that a child is placed and interacts within a social and physical environment, consisting of diverse forms of influence and personal agency. A child's context can either allow or limit the extent to which a child can develop and utilise individual characteristics and coping strategies (Ungar 2011b). A child's context usually embodies both negative and positive processes which are constantly interacting and changing, creating a social and physical ecology where a child's resilience is placed at its centre. This approach emphasises that resilience is not dependent exclusively on environmental factors, nor is it on individual qualities rather it is a combination, resilience "is the qualities of both the individual and the individual's environment that potentiate positive development"(Ungar & Liebenberg 2011, p. 127). The social and cultural context in which a child lives is integral to understanding coping, adversity and development however; child-centred approaches which dedicate resources into narrow streams of support tend to disregard the promotion of an environment, which may foster the potential for positive development. Individual traits are embedded within and derive meaning from the child's social and cultural context (Ungar 2011b). Furthermore culture can influence and define meaning in a child's life and what is considered positive development, adaptive coping strategies and positive outcomes.

A social ecological approach, whilst effective in consolidating holistic understandings of resilience has potential complexities in application to interventions. The theory identifies the importance of ecologically appropriate approaches to building resilience, and tailoring interventions in collaboration with the client to ensure interventions can be effective and meaningful according to a client's context. Social ecological understandings often make designing frameworks and uniform policies for interventions quite difficult, particularly in tailoring culturally appropriate interventions multicultural populations. A culturally tailored approach means there is no 'easy fix' or 'one size fits all' solution or strategy, particularly in the recognition of diversity. Theories of resilience tend to appear abstract and often times distanced from the pragmatic focus of contemporary services, organisations and policy in the context of children. This phenomenon occurs despite the rich and complex variation that social ecological theories impart to the understanding of the dynamic process of resilience.

Integrating contextual child development theories and a social ecological resilience theory acknowledges a child's agency and individual ability; however, it also acknowledges that children are essentially vulnerable and dependent upon their social and physical environment in which they are embedded. To work effectively towards strengthening the capacity for resilience in children means working with children individually and collectively, but also working within their micro-, meso-, exo- and macrosystems. Interventions need to holistically address problems and strengthen the child and their social ecology so that it can support a child's development and growth as well as their agency in society.

Risk, Protective and Promotive Factors

A large part of research regarding resilience focuses on risk and protective factors. Risk factors or vulnerability factors, as referred to by Luthar and Cicchetti (2000, p. 858), "encompass those indices that exacerbate the negative effects of the risk condition", arguing that the impacts of adversity upon individuals are not inherently determined by their exposure to negative stimuli, but rather that outcomes are negotiated by the individual. Protective factors promote positive outcomes in adverse situations, yet they do not completely shelter an individual from negative stimuli. Despite this, research into resilience continues to focus on identifying factors in situations of adversity, and translating these findings into interventions. Promotive factors are resources and processes that benefit individuals, families and communities (Rutter 2012). They are both internal and external strengths that promote positive outcomes (Kia-Keating, et al. 2011).

There is contention surrounding the use of risk, protective and promotive factors in research and interventions as people affected by severe adversity and stressors do not interact with risk factors or resources in the same way that unaffected people might (Rutter 2012). Contemporary research and understandings of resilience has shifted from focusing solely on factors, to focusing on the processes of interaction between a subject, the adversity and the environment. Increasingly, research is embodying contextual forms of discourse when viewing risk and protective factors, which is demonstrated in the complexity of contemporary literature on the concept of resilience. Rutter (2012) demonstrates through his discussion of a study on Romanian adoptees, that a focus on environmental mediation is integral to further resilience research and intervention, as it is one factor that differentiates resilience from the risk and protection research. The author argues that interventions and research must focus on studying "environmental mediation of risk effects", rather than simply quantifying a range of risk and protective factors (Rutter 2012, p. 341). Research which focuses on risk, protective and promotive factors needs to integrate perspectives which consider environmental contexts.

Contemporary Perspectives on Resilience Interventions

This chapter will outline current knowledge and approaches regarding strengthening the capacity for resilience in children across the various systems and levels in society. There are several theories and approaches that seek to address and promote resilience. Current research suggests that interventions need to address environmental influences as well as individual factors, allowing for a holistic, multi-systemic approach that incorporates strategies and supports for children, families, schools, and communities (Friesen & Brennan 2005; Jaffee, et al. 2007; Kia-Keating, et al. 2011; Luthar & Zelazo 2003; Rutter 2012; The Commission on Children at Risk 2007; Ungar 2010, 2011a, 2011b; Walsh 2006). Therefore this chapter will address resilience in the five key intervention areas: child-based, family-based, community-based, school-based and society-based, including social policy and structural change.

Child-based Interventions

Individualised resilience interventions have commonly endeavoured to collaboratively strengthen a child to resist and persist through adversity, using 'up-skilling' strategies. This type of approach tends to focus on a child's agency within a situation, rather than addressing surrounding factors. Resilience interventions concerning children should be adjusted to account for the multiple processes and resources within their contextual environment, especially because children vulnerable members of society.

Resilience interventions involve diverse forms of interactions and relationships, with some approaches utilising group work to build individual abilities and skills. Alvord and Grados (2005) provide an example of a resilience model for group interventions with children. This model is firmly grounded within a psychological perspective, and approaches the concept of resilience as a set of skills and attributes which can be developed or enhanced. The authors mention families, communities, services and religion as protective factors. However, a review of the work they conducted through their group model of resilience intervention shows that they have not utilised the efficacy of communities, services and religion in their actual work. To promote ongoing learning, the model encourages parents to discuss the program with their child's teacher; however, the involvement of the school is largely dependent on the parents and their motivation to reinforce their children's learning both at school and at home. This model appears to have a narrow approach to resilience interventions as its focus is on building on individual skills and it has limited reflection of the current holistic understandings of resilience.

Another example of an intervention that focuses on the child is an Australian intervention called the "Resilience Doughnut"

(Worsley 2006). The Resilience Doughnut is a framework and intervention centred on the child, and endeavours to strengthen temperament, social skills, and promote optimistic thinking. This intervention encompasses seven 'factors': money, parent, skill, family, education, peer group, and community factors that interact with the child and the child's internal messages of 'I have', 'I am' and 'I can' (Worsley 2006). The framework focuses on the child but incorporates parents, teachers, family, friends and the community in as much that they promote positive internal messages and create a sense of belonging. The framework encourages positive interventions and fits strongly within a holistic strengths-based perspective, embodying elements which resonate with resilience approaches.

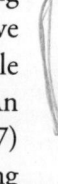

Despite ongoing support for individualised, skill building interventions there is no guarantee these interventions will have long-term effects or guarantee resilience in the face of multiple or cumulative stressors and adversity (Jaffee, et al. 2007). An American longitudinal study conducted by Jaffee et al., (2007) focuses on child maltreatment and family adversity, concentrating on identifying factors which contribute to resilient outcomes in maltreated children. The study explores whether a child's individual strengths promote resilience, despite familial and community adversity and stressors. This study found that individual strengths—such as above-average IQ or an easy-going attitude—were strong mediators and protective factors when children were exposed to few stressors; however, when children were exposed to multiple or extreme stressors, individual strengths did not serve a protective function (Jaffee, et al. 2007). The authors in the above study argue that individual strengths are difficult to change through intervention, suggesting that behaviour modification may be a more suitable approach in conjunction with family and neighbourhood interventions. The results of the study suggested that resilience is influenced by the interplay between individual, family, and neighbourhood risk and protection factors (Jaffee, et al. 2007). Furthermore, the study supports multi-systemic interventions as a holistic way of engaging with a child's ecology. The study emphasises that practitioners need to acknowledge the complexity of both understanding adversity, and in designing interventions that adequately address both the individual and their context.

A problematic aspect of resilience interventions lay in identifying what specific elements will promote resilience in different settings. Studies and programs that focus on individualised approaches seek to strengthen general skills for building resilience such as:

- Social and emotional skills including: self-efficacy, self-regulation/self-control, social competencies, stress-coping abilities, communicating feelings, making friends, relaxation techniques, conflict resolution and interpersonal skills.

- Coping mechanisms including: coping with change and loss, coping with rejection, adapting coping strategies to different situations, recognising negative emotions and developing strategies for coping with these feelings.

- Cognitive abilities including: information processing, reasoning, enquiry, evaluation, creative thinking and problem solving skills.

(Alvord & Grados 2005, p. 242; Davis et al. 2011; Froehlich-Gildhoff & Roennau-Boese 2012; MacConville 2008; Mishara & Ystgaard 2006).

The list of skills was compiled from several contemporary studies and interventions (mentioned above), each revealing a different set of skills supported by research. Whilst this complexity means there is a variety of skills and behaviours which can be tailored, many of the interventions targeted a specific group of people, making their methodology difficult to transfer to other demographics. Jaffee et al. (2007, p. 247) argue that "the protective effects of children's individual strengths must be understood within the context of children's life circumstances" and as such it is understood that skills or coping strategies will vary from situation to situation and from child to child. A child's capacity to draw on his or her own skills and resources can be limited by environmental stressors and adversities (Ungar 2011b). Jaffee et al. (2007) argue that:

> Interventions should attempt to minimize the number of family and neighbourhood stressors children experience, so that children can draw on innate personal resources or on those that are fostered through the intervention process (Jaffee, et al. 2007, p. 248).

This statement strongly emphasises a social ecological approach, viewing resilience as a child's opportunity to draw on resources, as negotiated and determined by their interactions with their surrounding environment. Environmental stressors and adversities impinge on a child's capacity to draw on his or her own skills and resources, and so it is important that interventions which seek to work on these individual skills and behaviours must also work within the child's context to, ensure it facilitates a childs capacity for resilience (Jaffee, et al. 2007; Ungar 2011b).

Family-based Interventions

Resilience processes within families are essential in creating a strong foundation and a supportive environment for children. Families are influential relationships and factors in a child's development (Sheridan, Eagle, & Dowd 2006) and therefore it is critical to promote resilience processes within families, so they can provide a supportive environment for the child to grow and develop. Interventions within the family concentrate on understanding, identifying and developing interactional processes that promote resilience and positive functioning in the face of adversity (Walsh 2006).

Family interventions should endeavour to develop positive relational processes and communication within families (Sheridan,

Eagle, et al. 2006; Walsh 2006). Walsh (2006) supports a multisystemic, strengths-based understanding of family resilience and interventions, which is embedded within the interactions and processes between the family and their social and cultural ecology. Furthermore, Walsh outlines (2006) key processes and factors in family resilience, such as: family belief systems—making meaning of adversity, positive outlook, transcendence and spirituality; organisational patterns—flexibility, connectedness, social and economic resources; and communication processes—clarity, open emotional expression, and collaborative problem solving (p. 26). Moreover, Sheridan, Eagle and Dowd (2006) argue that the family relational processes that are important in resilience practice involve promoting family cohesion and family adaptability, focusing on the interactions within the family unit.

Contemporary understandings of resilience interventions support a strong emphasis on environmental factors and stressors interacting with the child and family; therefore there is an increasing need for a structural understanding of contexts, and addressing barriers that make pro-social behaviour difficult (Ungar 2010). Rather than focusing solely on the individual and their 'anti-social' behaviour, Ungar (2010) challenges dominant forms of understanding poor behaviours, arguing that maladaptive coping strategies are deeply imbedded within a social, cultural and temporal context. The author emphasises the need for family therapists to link with other support networks and services to form a "matrix" of support that is accessible and relevant (Ungar 2010, p. 433). Ungar highlights the importance of solutions which seek change in a child's social ecology, rather than solutions that seek changes within individuals.

Interventions with families need to be culturally appropriate, tailored and meaningful for each child and family, and should promote positive relational processes within the family. Moreover, interventions should develop skills to assist the family in accessing and using resources and services within the community effectively (Sheridan, Eagle, et al. 2006; Ungar 2010). Families are central to a child's positive development and it is critical that interventions centre on the child and ensure that the child is supported to achieve his or her potential.

Community-based Interventions

Children and families are embedded within a community, irrespective of their engagement within the community or their knowledge about resources that exist within the community. Communities have a number of potential resources to promote resilience and facilitate positive interactions and collaboration between children, families and communities. Such an approach will assist in minimising or protecting against adversity and cumulative stressors that impact a child's capacity for resilience.

Community resilience is "the result of a tangled web of services, supports, and social policies", consisting of a community's informal and formal social capital and physical resources (Ungar 2011a, p. 1744). Furthermore, community resilience is dependent on the nature of the adversity: how a community experiences it, its meaning the people affected derive from it, and the ability of a community to adapt and grow from it (Ungar 2011a).

Communities can promote resilience and support children through developing healthy neighbourhood environments, providing youth programs and mentors, and supporting a child's family to enhance their capacity to create a facilitative environment for their child (Friesen & Brennan 2005). Community services can also help to build support networks between families and schools and other services, to strengthen holistic approaches to promoting resilience and a network of support for children (Luthar & Zelazo 2003; Sheridan, Eagle, et al. 2006; Ungar 2011a). Moreover, a child should be supported by a surrounding environment which allows them to draw on their own resources and external assets and to be resilient in situations of adversity.

Resilience in communities is linked with social and physical capital, such as public amenity and safety, access to education, housing, healthcare and employment; however, "the factors that predict a community's resilience are those most relevant to the individuals with the greatest need" (Ungar 2011a, p. 1744). Therefore, we need to move beyond exclusively building community resources and services, and develop a complex understanding of the processes underlying a child's context. This perspective can help build an environment that facilitates communities and families to support each child's development and wellbeing especially those at greater disadvantage.

There are a variety of interventions that endeavour to work with communities to promote resilience in children. An example of this is an out-of-school time program founded on a risk and resilience framework developed by Anthony, Alter and Jenson (2009) which they hoped would be adopted as a unified cross-system framework for policy and practice development. The authors (Anthony, et al. 2009) apply their risk and resilience framework to the development and evaluation of an out-of-school time program. The program was implemented and altered according to the needs of the community. It began by offering a scholarship program for students from three public housing estates in a large city, who intended on going to college. The authors found that this was ineffective as there were not many students to receive the benefit and they recognised that it could be more effective working with younger children to promote readiness for college (Anthony, et al. 2009). The activities within the program have a central focus on building relationships, with a mentoring component and positive role-modelling, as well as tutorials, which seek to improve literacy and enthusiasm for education and build engagement and attachment with the local community (Anthony, et al. 2009). Whilst the aim of the program intended on ensuring readiness for college, the program itself provided a supportive environment that focused on both internal and external resources and strengthening these factors, as well as tailoring the approach to suit the changes in the communities, promoting resilience within, and outside of an educational context.

Promoting a cross-system framework, Anthony, et al., (2009) support an integrated multi-disciplinary approach to resilience, utilising professions in their areas of speciality and propose that medicine and psychology can work on the internal dynamics of resilience-building; social work can focus on building protections (Anthony, et al. 2009). A multidisciplinary approach coupled with their use of both a problem and a strengths focus encourages a deeper understanding of the underlying processes, both positive and negative, and therefore a deeper understanding of a child's context.

Community resilience can be promoted through interventions focusing on a community's capacity to facilitate the mobilisation of social and physical resources, whether informal or formal, whilst acknowledging the multiple combined influences and points of interaction (Ungar 2011a). Sheridan, Eagle and Dowd (2006) suggest that family-centred, culturally appropriate services can support families to develop competencies and processes associated with resilience such as cohesion, effective parenting styles, family involvement and affective interactions (p. 170). Interventions are based on the needs and priorities identified by the family and children through collaboration with the intervening service, which should work to identify capacities and strengths, and develop skills in families to access and use resources in ways that will benefit and support them.

Applying a critical analysis of community resilience, Daro and Dodge (2009) view social ecology as an essential concept to creating and evaluating facilitative environments for community development and child protection. The authors concentrate on child abuse and child protection, and the responsibilities of communities, highlighting the need for a community approach to address negative influences which can overwhelm parents (Daro & Dodge 2009). The authors suggest the need for facilitative environments within social and cultural spaces, which emphasise interaction between and within the child, family, community and culture. The authors argue that interventions need to develop a sense of willingness and ownership within subject individuals, so they become involved and cooperative, rather than simply building social capital and resources within communities (Daro & Dodge 2009). Interventions are inherently grounded within a cultural context, and they need to be meaningful and relevant to the community, families and children involved (Ungar 2011b).

Strengthening communities can be a key strategy in promoting resilience and creating an environment that facilitates positive outcomes in children, particularly in the face of adversity. An example of a strategy to promote resilience in children through a community approach is a study conducted by Betancourt, Myers-Ohki, Stulac, Barrera, Mushashi and Beardslee (Betancourt et al. 2011) in Rwanda called, 'Abashize hamwe ntakibananira' (Nothing can defeat combined hands). The study is also an example of a culturally and contextually targeted approach to both research and interventions intending to promote resilience in children. The study concentrates on children and families affected by HIV/AIDS in a low-resource, rural 'catchment area', investigating natural sources of resilience that contribute to resilient, positive outcomes. The study was used to inform the development of a culturally appropriate family strengthening intervention service to target HIV/AIDS affected communities, families and children. The sources of resilience and positive processes that are discovered may be less relevant to dissimilar situations as the study is targeted to children and families affected by HIV/AIDS in a rural, low-resource setting. The research was conducted in collaboration with the Rwandan government and a non-government organisation which works in partnership with the Ministry of Health. The study included children and adults directly affected by HIV/AIDS, and carers and professionals who worked in the area of HIV/AIDS.

The findings identified five interdependent protective processes, including: the individual resources of patience/perseverance and self-esteem, family supports such as family unity/trust, and good parenting, and communal/social support (Betancourt, et al. 2011, p. 695). The study extrapolates on these by identifying a list of factors that might indicate the presence of each of the five protective processes.

The study was used as the foundation for a family strengthening intervention targeting children and their families affected by HIV/AIDS in Rwanda. The findings suggest that resilient outcomes may be achieved in children affected by HIV/AIDS through "apt utilisation and augmentation of resources", holistically addressing their social ecologies (Betancourt, et al. 2011, p. 699). Not only do the findings reflect current understandings of resilience, it reflects current understandings of interventions seeking to promote and strengthen resilience in children.

Through a concentration on local protective processes, Betancourt et al. (2011) acknowledge that resilience processes are dynamic and can be dependent on culture, socio-economic contexts and the specific adversity. The study delves deeply into the meaning of identified protective processes for all participants. Through research and community involvement, the study is creating meaning and relevance for family-strengthening interventions. The study targets processes at the child's individual level, the family level and the community level to create an environment for children that promotes resilience and positive outcomes in their own life and within their ecology. Whether designed for a specific context, or adapted from another context, interventions are inherently grounded within a cultural context, and they need to be meaningful and relevant to the community, families and children involved and the social and cultural environment in which they are embedded (Ungar 2011b).

Developing community resilience can work strongly towards strengthening families and building their capacity to provide and care for their children. Communities, in collaboration with families can promote positive and resilient outcomes for children and provide them with opportunities to thrive despite adversity and risk across different cultures and contexts.

School-based Interventions

Schools are important spaces for development in children, not only educational, but also social growth and learning. Sheridan et al., (2006), argues, the school environment is an "essential interacting system" for children and families (p. 172) because almost all children have connections with an educational system and therefore by proxy, families do too. Education and schools are major systems in a child's life. Using strategies and services that integrate schools with communities, families and children could be more effective in holistically addressing and strengthening resilience and creating an integrated, supportive environment for all children, especially those at greater risk. Brooks (2006) argues that schools can reach and engage vulnerable families serving as a buffer to some risks, and promoting positive development in all students. Schools have the advantage of being situated within communities and reaching a range of families and children and can therefore be used as an effective tool in strengthening resilience in children and their surrounding ecologies.

School-based interventions are often focused on individual children despite utilising classrooms and group settings. These interventions concentrate on social, emotional and coping skills of each student (Brooks 2006; Froehlich-Gildhoff & Roennau-Boese 2012; MacConville 2008; Mishara & Ystgaard 2006). Mishara and Ystgaard (2006), in their research of the implementation of a school-based universal program, called 'Zippy's Friends', found that the promotion of mental health and the improvement of coping and socio-emotional skills in children was possible. The 'Zippy's Friend' program was designed for children in kindergarten and year one. Utilising over 24 sessions, covering topics such as: recognising negative feelings and strategies for coping with these feelings, communicating their feelings, making friends and coping with rejection, conflict resolution, coping with change and loss, and adapting coping strategies in different situations (Mishara & Ystgaard 2006, p. 113). The authors found that the effectiveness of the program is determined by the quality of teaching, teacher enthusiasm and holistic understanding of the program.

Mental health promotion and coping skills are critical aspects in a child's healthy development (Mishara & Ystgaard 2006). The short-term effects of 'Zippy's Friends' included, improvements in coping abilities, social and emotional skills, a decrease in problematic behaviours, an improvement in the classroom environment and with child/teacher relationships. The authors (Mishara & Ystgaard 2006) hope that the improvement of abilities and skills will be ongoing and will develop in the long-term but had no evidence to prove that it would. The program focused almost exclusively on individual traits and skills within the school context. A program such as 'Zippy's Friends' would be more effective if interactional processes between the child and the family, community and the child's social ecology were considered and integrated into the intervention.

Another example of a school-based intervention is a program called "How to Make Friends" developed by MacConville (2008) which focuses on building resilience and promoting positive peer relationships. According to MacConville (2008) positive peer relationships are critical factors in a child's development and positive well-being, and it has a positive flow on effect for education and learning. The program claims to concentrate on emotional resilience, though MacConville does little to explore what this means and there is no clear way of discerning whether or not this program has been empirically tested or how effective it will be. Rather than promoting resilience, this program endeavours to build skills in peer relationships, with MacConville arguing that the program is not a stand-alone solution and would work effectively as part of the schooling system.

Some school interventions incorporate a framework for teaching that promotes resilience, understands risk, and develops strategies for teaching, behaviour management and parent involvement (Brooks 2006; Stormont 2007). Stormont (2007) proposes a framework for teaching when working with vulnerable children, identifying that risk and protective factors as well as resilience is embedded within interactions in a social ecology. Stormont (2007) presents strategies for the classroom to support or develop positive behaviour and concentrates on building resilience through partnerships between the family environment and the teachers The book advocates that teachers should link families with communities and family support services to assist at-risk children and families. The book is targeted for teachers and not surprisingly is very focused on the teacher and what they can do in the classroom and with a student's family. Though the framework utilises a systems approach, it is limited because it only includes systems which interact directly with the teacher. Stormont does not make it clear what resilience is, which can perpetuate misconceptions regarding resilience. The author focuses heavily on risk and understanding a child's vulnerability which, whilst necessary, appears quite dependent on a negative frame of reference rather than developing a positive approach to strengthening resilience.

A facilitative and supportive school environment that connects with the wider community has the ability to promote resilience in children. Engaging vulnerable families in partnerships with communities and services is a key role of "resilience-promoting schools" to ensure resources are accessible and used effectively for the benefit of their children (Brooks 2006, p. 72). Froehlich-Gildhoff and Reonnau-Boese (2012) argue that early childhood institutions are vital in the promotion of resilience. The authors identify early childhood as a critical time in a child's development, further emphasising the importance of early childhood institutions in resilience interventions, as they work closely with children and parents, and build extensive social networks within communities. Froehlich Gildhoff and Roennau Boese (2012) conducted a program aiming to build resilience capacity in early childhood institutions to promote resilience and positive mental health. Their program incorporated children, parents and the community. The program is based on the following factors: perception of self and others, sense of self-efficacy, self-regulation/self-control, problem solving skills, social competencies and stress-coping abilities (Froehlich-Gildhoff & Roennau-Boese 2012, p. 132). The strategies the program utilised included a ten week program concentrating on resilience factors they identified within research, weekly consultations with parents, opportunities for educational counselling and parental education courses, and developing relationships and networking between early childhood institutions and other organisations. The early-childhood educators received training to develop an understanding of the approach, and they were involved in the implementation of the program to ensure motivation for the program (Froehlich-Gildhoff & Roennau-Boese 2012). The inclusion of educators in the research and program implementation was found to be a valuable strategy that sought to ensure an ongoing and effective maintenance of the program.

In this program resilience is defined as a dynamic characteristic and an ability that allowed people to manage and cope with crises and developmental tasks. The authors acknowledge that sustainable resilience programs "need to consider the personal, social and environmental factors that influence the development of a child" (Froehlich-Gildhoff & Roennau-Boese 2012, p. 133). This demonstrates an ecological understanding of resilience. However, Froehlich-Gildhoff and Reonnau-Boese (2012) appear to imply that children are passive and environmental factors 'influence' them and their development rather than an interaction between the child and their social ecology.

Research also presents another model of resilience development within schools, utilising what is known as 'Conjoint Behavioural Consultation' (CBC) (Sheridan, Eagle, et al. 2006) This model is founded on an ecological understanding of a child and supports the need for cross-system collaboration to promote the education and wellbeing of children (Sheridan, Clarke, Knoche, & Edwards 2006). CBC focuses on creating partnerships and encouraging collaboration between parents and teachers towards "promoting assets within the child and strengthening the environments within which the child functions" (Sheridan, Clarke, et al. 2006, p. 609). Both teachers and parents work together in partnership to identify and address the needs of an individual child, acknowledging and building on strengths, developing skills in accessing resources, and promoting parenting abilities (Sheridan, Eagle, et al. 2006). Through encouraging parental participation in their child's education, schools can promote positive interactions and networks between schools and families, which can contribute towards promoting resilience and positive well-being for children.

Through collaboration between schools and communities, services and families, resilience practice shifts from a fragmented approach towards an integrated approach which creates a supportive environment providing children with a legitimate opportunity to explore their potential. Furthermore, integrated approaches in schools develop a strong network of support for children, families, teachers and community members and future interventions can be more effectively targeted and tailored for specific areas of need through communication within this network (Brooks 2006). Through engaging with families and communities, schools can be a strong force for strengthening resilience and developing a facilitative environment for children to achieve positive outcomes and wellbeing.

Society-based Interventions

Developing child-centred social policy and working within

macrosystems is integral to promoting the capacity for resilience in children and building an environment that supports children to grow and realise their potential. Seccombe (2002) argues that sound policies can increase the effectiveness of interventions that focus on individuals, families and communities, supporting the need for an integrated, research based approach to policy. Furthermore, effective social policy can facilitate and support families, communities, neighbourhoods and schools in providing a facilitative, engaging environment for children to strengthen their capacity and ability to achieve their potential.

Using an integrated approach between experts, researchers, practitioners and policy workers is one way of ensuring child-centred policies are based on evidence. The capacity of policy can be enhanced through the use of research and evidence to promote a unified, child-centred, cross-system approach to policy design and implementation (Jenson & Fraser 2011a, 2011b; Knitzer & Cohen 2007; Seccombe 2002; Walsh 2006).

A framework for child-centred social policy which incorporates a risk and resilience perspective concentrates on both reframing a prevention focus to a promotion focus, and advocating positive interactions and processes towards development and well-being for children. Jenson and Fraser (2011b) propose a framework which incorporates the following five steps:

- evaluate risk and protective factors,
- assign policy responsibility in ways that promote service integration across systems,
- use evidence to create public policy responses,
- determine the course of specific individual and social interventions, and
- implement, monitor and evaluate policies and interventions.

(Jenson & Fraser 2011b, p. 358).

The benefits of this framework are that it has both a strengths and problem focus, and it values the necessity of a strong foundation in research, and ongoing evaluation. The author's research endeavours to create a uniform integrative and collaborative approach to policy development and implementation with a greater understanding of child development, adversity and their ecological context. It focuses on creating a supportive environment for all children especially those exposed to severe adversity and disadvantage (Jenson & Fraser 2011b).

Contemporary policy making needs to expand its focus from individual factors to incorporating a structural analysis of social and economic conditions that perpetuate disadvantage and poverty. Furthermore, researchers should liaise with policy makers and ensure research is accessible, practical and easy to integrate into policy (Seccombe 2002). Resilience research needs to work on becoming more practical in a policy sense, as research and theories of resilience are often too abstract, and complex to mould into appropriate and effective policy.

Interventions and approaches towards resilience have often focused on creating children to 'beat the odds', resilience practice should endeavour to change 'the odds' against children so they can thrive (Seccombe 2002; Ungar 2011b). It is clear that despite developments in the field of resilience, social and ecological perspectives are yet to be comprehensively understood and integrated with resilience theory and interventions in order to benefit children facing adversity and cumulative disadvantage. Furthermore current interventions that continue to concentrate on individual strengths will have limited effectiveness as there appears to be a tendency to exclude social and environmental elements that affect and influence a child's life (Luthar & Zelazo 2003). Walsh (2006) advocates for resilience practice that transcends 'bandaid treatments' to more comprehensive structural interventions. If communities and governments can provide tailored and accessible resources and support to people facing adversity, they may be more likely to thrive as they have easier access to the supports they need to get through their specific hardship. In this sense resilience can be understood as the capacity of individuals to access resources they need but also the capacity of communities and society to provide tailored resources and supports for these people (Ungar 2011a).

Walsh (2006) also states, "systemic changes are needed to address larger institutional and cultural influences that breed poverty and discrimination and that severely strain families", interventions could achieve this through advocacy, in collaboration with families, promoting the development of social policies that are inherently family-centred (p. 177). Services and organisations within society are often fragmented, which can lead to services overlooking interrelated problems or concerns and therefore inadequately addressing these problems (Walsh 2006). Structural change endeavouring to build resilience in children is concerned with creating an environment that promotes child development and wellbeing, and creates opportunities for all children. Perry, Kaufmann and Knitzer (2007) use the metaphor of 'building a bridge' between services and systems. Contemporary resilience practice can go one step further and endeavour to build a bridge between communities and governments, collaboratively working towards a positive facilitative environment for all children, especially those exposed to greater risk and disadvantage.

A Way Forward

Resilience is a multifaceted, dynamic concept and there are many pathways to building resilience. Contemporary understandings of resilience are grounded in social ecology theory concentrating on environmental and contextual factors as integral in determining resilience. Interventions and research need to understand the interactional processes that occur in the cultural, temporal and socioeconomic ecology in which a child is embedded. Strategies for promoting resilience occur within multiple sectors in society including individuals, families, communities, neighbourhoods, social policy and society. Interventions must also transcend individualised approaches to attain the structural change that is necessary to challenge power distribution and cumulative disadvantage. Child-centred social policy must be implemented that effectively facilitate families, communities and schools to support all children, especially those at greater disadvantage. Promoting resilience in children means that we need to create a supportive social ecology that facilitates a child's capacity to grow and explore their potential. Strengthening the capacity for resilience in children is more than creating pathways to resilience; it is creating pathways to a brighter future.

Works Cited

Alvord, M. K., & Grados, J. J. (2005). Enhancing resilience in children: A proactive approach. *Professional Psychology—Reasearch and Practice,* 36(3), 238-245.

Anthony, E., K., Alter, C., F., & Jenson, J., M. (2009). Development of a risk and resilience-based out-of-school time program for children and youths. *Social Work,* 54(1), 45-45.

Betancourt, T. S., Meyers-Ohki, S., Stulac, S. N., Barrera, A. E., Mushashi, C., & Beardslee, W. R. (2011). Nothing can defeat combined hands (Abashize hamwe ntakibananira): Protective processes and resilience in Rwandan children and families affected by HIV/AIDS. *Social Science & Medicine,* 73(5), 693-701. doi: 10.1016/j.socscimed.2011.06.053.

Brooks, J. E. (2006). Strengthening resilience in children and youths: Maximizing opportunities through the schools. *Children & Schools,* 28(2), 69-76.

Camfield, L., Streuli, N., & Woodhead, M. (2009). What's the use of 'wellbeing' in contexts of child poverty? Approaches to research, monitoring and children's participation. *International Journal of Children's Rights,* 17(1), 65-109. doi: 10.1163/157181808x357330.

Daro, D., & Dodge, K. A. (2009). Creating community responsibility for child protection: Possibilities and challenges. *The Future of Children,* 19(2), 67-93.

Davis, E., Williamson, L., Mackinnon, A., Cook, K., Waters, E., Herman, H.,... Marshall, B. (2011). Building the capacity of family day care educators to promote children's social and emotional wellbeing: An exploratory cluster randomised controlled trial. *BMC Public Health,* 11(1), 842-848. doi: 10.1186/1471-2458-11-842.

Friesen, B. J., & Brennan, E. (2005). Strengthening families and communities: System building for resilience. In M. Ungar (Ed.), *Handbook for working with children and youth: Pathways to resilience across cultures and contexts* (pp. 295-311). Thousand Oaks: Sage Publications.

Froehlich-Gildhoff, K., & Roennau-Boese, M. (2012). Prevention of exclusion: The promotion of resilience in early childhood institutions in disadvantaged areas. *Journal of Public Health, 20*(2), 131-139. doi: 10.1007/s10389-011-0451-1.

Graham, M. (2011). Changing paradigms and conditions of childhood: Implications for the social professions and social work. *British Journal of Social Work,* 41(8), 1532-1547.

Hoffnung, M., Hoffnung, R. J., Seifert, K. L., Burton Smith, R., Hine, A., Ward, L., & Quinn, A. (2010). *Lifespan development.* Milton, Queensland: John Wiley & Sons.

Jaffee, S. R., Caspi, A., Moffitt, T. E., Polo-Tomás, M., & Taylor, A. (2007). Individual, family, and neighborhood factors distinguish resilient from non-resilient maltreated children: A cumulative stressors model. *Child Abuse & Neglect,* 31(3), 231-253. doi: 10.1016/j.chiabu.2006.03.011.

Jenson, J. M., & Fraser, M. W. (2011a). A risk and resilience framework for child, youth, and family policy. In J. M. Jenson & M. W. Fraser (Eds.), *Social policy for children and families: A risk and resilience perspective* (2nd ed., pp. 5-24). Thousand Oaks, California: Sage.

――― (2011b). Toward the integration of child, youth, and family policy. In J. M. Jenson & M. W. Fraser (Eds.), *Social policy for children & families: A risk and resilience perspective* (2nd ed., pp. 353-370). Thousand Oaks, California: Sage.

Kia-Keating, M., Dowdy, E., Morgan, M. L., & Noam, G. G. (2011). Protecting and promoting: An integrative conceptual model for healthy development of adolescents. *Journal of Adolescent Health,* 48(3), 220-228. doi: 10.1016/j.jadohealth.2010.08.006.

Knitzer, J., & Cohen, E. P. (2007). Promoting resilience in young children and families at the highest risk. In D. F. Perry, R. K. Kaufmann & J. Knitzer (Eds.), *Social & emotional health in early childhood: Building bridges between services & systems* (pp. 335-359). Baltimore: Paul H. Brookes.

Luthar, S. S., & Cicchetti, D. (2000). The construct of resilience: A critical evaluation and guidelines for future work. *Child Development,* 71(3), 543.

_____, & Zelazo, L. B. (2003). Research on resilience: An integrative review. In S. S. Luthar (Ed.), *Resilience and vulnerability: Adaptation in the context of childhood adversitites* (pp. 510-549). New York: Cambridge University Press.

MacConville, R. (2008). *How to make friends: Building resilience and supportive peer groups.* Los Angeles: Sage.

Mishara, B. L., & Ystgaard, M. (2006). Effectiveness of a mental health promotion program to improve coping skills in young children: Zippy's Friends. *Early Childhood Research Quarterly,* 21(1), 110-123. doi: 10.1016/j.ecresq.2006.01.002.

Perry, D. F., Kaufmann, R. K., & Knitzer, J. (2007). Building bridges: Linking services, strategies, and systems for young children and their families. In D. F. Perry, R. K. Kaufmann & J. Knitzer (Eds.), *Social & emotional health in early childhood: Building bridges between services & systems.* (pp. 3-11). Baltimore: Paul H. Brookes.

Rutter, M. (2012). Resilience as a dynamic concept. *Development and Psychopathology,* 24(02), 335-344. doi: 10.1017/S0954579412000028.

Sameroff, A. J., & Rosenblum, K. L. (2006). Psychosocial constraints on the development of resilience. *Annals of the New York Academy of Sciences,* 1094(1), 116-124. doi: 10.1196/annals.1376.010.

Seccombe, K. (2002). 'Beating the odds' versus 'changing the odds': Poverty, resilience, and family policy. *Journal of Marriage & Family,* 64(2), 384-394.

Sheridan, S. M., Clarke, B. L., Knoche, L. L., & Edwards, C. P. (2006). The effects of conjoint behavioral consultation in early childhood settings. *Early Education & Development,* 17(4), 593-617. doi: 10.1207/s15566935eed1704_5.

_____, Eagle, J. W., & Dowd, S. E. (2006). Families as contexts for children's adaptation. In S. Goldstein & R. B. Brooks (Eds.), *Handbook of resilience in children* (pp. 165-179). New York: Springer.

Stormont, M. (2007). *Fostering resilience in young children at risk for failure: Strategies for grades K-3.* Upper Saddle River, New Jersey: Pearson/Merrill Prentice Hall.

The Commission on Children at Risk. (2007). Hardwired to connect: The new scientific case for authoritative communities. In K. K. Kline (Ed.), *Authoritative communities: The scientific case for nurturing children.* Berlin: Springer New York.

Ungar, M. (2010). Families as navigators and negotiators: Facilitating culturally and contextually specific expressions of resilience. *Family Process,* 49(3), 421-435. doi: 10.1111/j.1545-5300.2010.01331.x.

_____. (2011a). Community resilience for youth and families: Facilitative physical and social capital in contexts of adversity. *Children and Youth Services Review*, 33(9), 1742-1748. doi: 10.1016/j.childyouth.2011.04.027.

_____. (2011b). The social ecology of resilience: Addressing contextual and cultural ambiguity of a nascent construct. *American Journal of Orthopsychiatry*, 81(1), 1-17. doi: 10.1111/j.1939-0025.2010.01067.x.

_____, & Liebenberg, L. (2011). Assessing Resilience Across Cultures Using Mixed Methods: Construction of the Child and Youth Resilience Measure. *Journal of Mixed Methods Research*, 5(2), 126-149. doi: 10.1177/1558689811400607

Walsh, F. (2006). *Strengthening family resilience*. New York: Guilford Press.

Windle, G. (2011). What is resilience? A review and concept analysis. *Reviews in Clinical Gerontology*, 21(02), 152-169. doi: 10.1017/S0959259810000420.

Worsley, L. (2006). *The resilience doughnut: The secret of strong kids*. Eastwood: Wild and Woolley.

Yates, T. M., Egeland, B. L., & Sroufe, A. (2003). Rethinking resilience: A developmental process perspective. In S. S. Luthar (Ed.), *Resilience and vulnerability: Adaptation in the context of childhood adversities* (pp. 243-266). Cambridge: Cambridge University Press.

CHAPTER 7

Resilience Building Using Art Therapy with Adolescents in Australia

Jo Kelly

Abstract

Adolescence is recognised as being a transitional time of growing autonomy and turbulence, with a number of factors inhibiting young people's capacity for learning. These factors can include poor self-esteem, emotional development, social interaction, and peer group pressure, as well as identity formation and confusion. Adolescence is also acknowledged to be the time when the early signs and symptoms of many mental health problems can develop. Schools are obvious places for promoting health, resilience and well-being in young people, if integrated within the broader curriculum. Currently, service provision in schools is inadequate for those most vulnerable of young people; the high student-to-counsellor ratio is one example of this deficiency. Art therapy is a relatively new profession in Australia. Although formally recognised and regulated in other countries, in Australia it is under-utilised as an early intervention, prevention or treatment option for a number of reasons. In terms of art therapy developing in Australia, the evidence base is small and, as a new profession, there is still a lack of empirical literature on art therapy that is Australian based. The potential exists for integrating specialist, highly qualified art therapists in schools, thus enhancing the current primarily verbally based service. Art therapists could provide a new approach to supporting the social and emotional needs of not only those most vulnerable, but also potentially all students. Therapeutic intervention using the creative process can help provide young people with the skills and resilience-building strategies that are potentially lifelong.

Key Words

Art therapy, education, young people, adolescents resilience, art making

Introduction

This chapter describes how the emergent profession of art therapy can be utilised within educational settings as a resilience-building and early intervention for young people. The chapter reviews the needs of young people by considering and discussing current developmental theories, particularly relating to adolescence, which is a transitional and liminal time when young people are vulnerable to diagnosable mental illness. The chapter defines art therapy and its theoretical influences and articulates why it can be such a powerful experiential process for this population by using available evidence, particularly from the United States and the United Kingdom where art therapy is more established. In addition, the chapter considers the current provision of counselling services in Australian schools and argues that these are inadequate. The chapter also briefly describes recent theories on resilience and on coping, in psychological and social terms, and links these theories with those art therapy qualities that differentiate it from other forms of therapy, particularly verbal therapy. In addition to drawing on select studies, the chapter discusses the life-long resilience building and coping potentialities of art therapy, particularly within educational and pastoral care curricula. Finally, the chapter concludes with recommendations for the introduction of art therapy interventions, particularly within school environments to fill the current gap in existing service provision.

Adolescence

In a few short years, adolescents must navigate a raft of changes as they transition from childhood to adulthood. Alongside physical and hormonal changes, brain and cognitive changes and psychological and emotional upheavals, they are also required to navigate increasing societal responsibilities and, at the same time, develop a robust self-concept. While most adolescents manage this successfully, and Mussen, Conger, Kagan and Huston (1984) argue that the storm and difficulty of this period is exaggerated, adolescence remains a vulnerable time for many and a period when resilience building and coping strategies could be well placed to be integrated within their daily lives.

Evidence provided by many authorities including Arden and Linford (2009) and Fall and Roberts (2012), among others, indicate that adolescence is recognised as being a transitional and confusing time that can impact on learning and future capacity. According to Greenhalgh (1994), a number of factors inhibit a young person's capacity for learning. These include poor self-esteem, the young person's emotional maturity and their degrees of social interaction, including the developmental tasks associated with identity formation as well as the early signs and symptoms of mental health problems that can develop at this time. The long-term consequences on a young person's quality of life can vary; from negatively impacting on a young person's ability to reach his or her potential capacities to being life threatening.

The most obvious changes that take place in adolescence are the physical and behavioural changes brought on by puberty during the years from about ten to eighteen. It is recognised by Caspi (1993) and others that the early onset of puberty, rather than later maturational onset, can be associated with increased problems such as delinquency. In addition, Ellis and Garber's (2000) research indicates that early onset of puberty for girls can cause stress in families. Early puberty is also often a consequence of dysfunctional environments and the presence of a non-biological male in the home can trigger early physiological maturational processes in girls. Clearly, the disruption of physical and hormonal changes alone can have profound effects and long-term implications for young people.

Alongside the profound hormonal and physical changes that adolescence experience, are the significant cognitive changes that also occur throughout this period. Cognitive developmental theorists, such as Piaget (1896-1980), argued that young people develop through a series of dynamic stages enabling adaptation and construction of reality through a process of equilibration by balancing assimilation and accommodation. This interactive process enables the adolescent to modify their understanding and assumption about the world (Burton, Westen and Kowalski 2009). According to Piaget, adolescence is a time of cognitive transition from concrete thinking towards the developing ability to think abstractly. As a result, young people in their teenage years tend to question and rethink their ideas. This rethinking can result in uncertainty and confusion as they move towards the increasing societal expectation of autonomy. In addition, integrative developmental theories such as those of Vygotsky (1896-1934) and Case (1992) include the importance of cultural and social influences. More recently, relational perspectives that focus on the internal, experiential and subjective worlds of individuals, as advanced by Stolorow and Atwood (1992), illustrate the complexity of need that accompanies young people during this transitional phase of their lives.

Adolescents must also navigate the tasks of emotional and social development at a time when their bodies are rapidly changing. In addition, as adolescents move away from their families, their peer group becomes increasingly important and valued. Walker and Irving (1998) show that, although peer groups are important for young children in providing sources of support as well as distress, during adolescence the group develops from same sex to mixed sex with increasing intimacy. This creates another potential stressful time for young people. Both group influence and commercial media also affect the way young people view themselves and, according to Riley (2001), is also the source of much identity confusion at this time. These influences can form a vicious cycle for young people who are unhappy and who elicit negative responses in their peers. In turn, this contributes towards increasing negativity and unhappiness in the young person.

The development of self-identity or self-concept is another major task that adolescents must navigate and influences social and emotional development. Self-concept evolves throughout childhood alongside their cognitive development, moving from personality qualities to more relational aspects of self. According to Burton, Western and Kowalski (2009) a young person's self-concept during adolescence becomes more complex as it becomes more abstract. Erikson's broad framework of psychosocial development holds that the teenage years to be a crisis period of identity confusion (Erikson 1968). Kahn, Zimmerman, Csikzentmihalyi and Getzels (1985) consider that the failure to develop a positive sense of self can result in poor outcomes, delinquency and disruption in later life.

Adolescence and Mental Health

In addition to the tasks of adolescence, managed with varying degrees of difficulty, is the increased vulnerability of young people to experiencing mental health problems. The Australian National Survey of Health and Wellbeing (ABS 2007) concluded that, due to many reasons including stigma, lack of knowledge, reporting and self-reporting inaccuracies, the actual percentage of children and adolescents with mental health problems in the Australian population is really unknown. The findings also indicate that the uptake of services among the 16-24 age group is among the lowest of the surveyed population. Other reasons for inaccurate estimation include a lack of empirical research as reported by Slade, Johnston, Browne, Andrews and Whiteford (2009).

Research undertaken in New Zealand by Browne, Wells, Scott and McGee (2006) suggests that most mental problems start early in life. Further, Begg, Vos, Barker, Stevenson, Stanley &

Lopez (2007) found mental ill health to be the biggest disease burden in terms of years lost to death and disability in Australia among adolescents and young adults aged between 15 and 24 years. This outcome is therefore a major health, social and economic issue in Australia and in other developed countries. There is also concern about the considerable stigma that continues to be associated with mental health as described by the Australian Human Rights and Equal Opportunities Commission (1993). Taken together, the general turbulence of adolescence combined with mental health vulnerability illustrates that mental health issues among young people need to be addressed urgently.

Neurogenesis or 'kindling' (Persaud 2001; Arden and Linford 2009), is the concept that the more mental ill health experienced by an individual the more neurological changes take place, and the more vulnerable the individual becomes to further mental problems (APA 2000). The principle of kindling suggests one reason why that resilience building, early intervention and prevention should be a priority for health and education policy makers. Mental health professionals, such as art therapists in mainstream schools, are in an ideal position to foster the resilience by building the necessary skills and strategies thus encouraging effective coping mechanisms (Seligman 1975; Doidge 2008; Persaud 2001). Duncan, Miller and Sparks (2004) argue that early intervention strategies may empower and enable young people to be better prepared for adverse life events. From this evidence, it is obvious that young people need active understanding and sensitivity from those charged with their education and care. One potential way of meeting these needs can be found in art therapy. Prior to examining what art therapy can do to foster resilience, it is necessary to briefly consider the definition of resilience and some of the factors associated with it.

Resilience

According to Masten (2001), the concept of resilience is the ability to recover and thrive in spite of adversity. The idea of resilience has been a part of philosophical discourse for thousands of years (Evans 2012) with both Cicero and Socrates referring to learning resilience skills as "care of the soul" (p. 6). Although resilience is complex by nature, studies by Rutter (1990) and others have shown that many risk factors, such as low socio-economic status, are established predictors of potential problems. Positive resources, such as good parenting for example, can offset accumulation of risk. Empirical studies in this field are complicated by value laden subjectivity regarding whether individuals can be said to have adapted to threats, thereby characterising a good outcome and being resilient (Luthar, Cicchetti and Becker 2000). Masten (2001) considers that many researchers have defined the ability to be resilient as measured by external societal and cultural expectations while other researchers have concentrated on the absence of psychopathology and impairment as measures of resilience.

Early research into resilience concluded that there was something special about individuals who thrived in the face of adversity. However, the accumulated data over time has suggested that resilience is a common characteristic (see Masten 2001) of humans' ability to adapt to circumstance. Masten suggests that the prevailing deficit models of psychopathology, with expectation that some special quality was needed to overcome adverse situations, influenced early researchers in the subject. More recently, other research has confirmed the importance of a set of global factors that contribute towards resilience, particularly as researched by Seligman and Csikszentmihalyi (2000). According to Masten, these skills include relational connectedness, the presence of caring significant adults, the need for cognitive and self-regulation skills and a belief in oneself to be motivated and competent in one's environment.

Qualitative research with 'at-risk' children undertaken by Howard and Johnson in South Australia (2000) showed that schools can be considered a protective factor and that they can engage in specific practices to assist young people to develop resilience, particularly in school Years eight and nine. In addition, they concluded that schools needed to have access to a range of "extensive resources" (Howard and Johnson 2000, p. 4) to help meet complex needs. An earlier review of data of mental health services across service sectors undertaken in the United States by Burns, Costello, Tweed Stangl, Farmer and Erkanli (1995), concluded that most children and young people's mental health needs were not being met by specialist services but often by 'ad hoc' measures in schools. The policy implication for Burns et al was that the education system could potentially be a major player in providing mental health support via resilience building strategies for young people by integrating a range of school based mental health supports. One of these resilience building strategies is found in art therapy.

What is Art Therapy?

Art therapy may be viewed as a holistic intervention that reflects on internal emotions and feelings and attempts to make meaning from them. Through self-reflection and meaning making, art therapy can encourage latent inner resources for young people to help themselves achieve resilience when adversity strikes. As a modality of psychotherapy, art therapy uses and privileges the visual creative process for psychological healing. Allen (1995), Cappacchione (2001), Malchiodi (2002, 2003) and Moon (2004) argue that art therapy promotes self-awareness, transformation and growth. In addition, art therapy can be both a verbal and non-verbal means of communication (Ballou 1995) between therapist and client, enhancing personal growth and self-understanding as well as assisting with emotional reparation.

According to Vick (2003) and Westwood (2010), art therapy originated from a hybrid of sources including art, psychology, psychoanalysis and social movements. While there are many and varied forms of art therapy with different historical influences (Rubin 2001; Kapitan 2009), a core value that unites art therapists is the belief in the inherent creativity of individuals and the power of art-making to heal. It is this core value that allows trained art therapists to deeply understand, use and value an individual's creativity through art materials towards therapeutic healing.

Lowenfeld (1987) demonstrated how art-making activities are fundamental to healthy development with perceptual sensitivity being a basis for learning. Through direct observations of young people and their art making, he showed how they develop by way of definite artistic and aesthetic developmental stages. Lowenfeld suggested that these stages tended to be enhanced or retarded, depending on the child's experience. Thus, positive experiences such as encouragement from care-givers would enrich and encourage growth and negative experiences such as neglect would impact on growth and learning. He argued that making art had deep meanings for young people and was not a trivial or diversional activity. This leading educator believed that all young people have "deeply rooted creative impulses" (Lowenfeld 1987, p. 7) and it is through this process that they learn and make meaning from their experiences.

By making art by using all five senses and which is a natural and enjoyable activity, young people learn about themselves, about their unique individuality and how they think, feel and view the world. Lowenfeld considered that the ability to think, imagine and self-direct are central tenets of art-making. In developing and using all five perceptual senses, young people learn about the world, themselves and their place in it. Riley (2001) states, "imagery taps into a person's earliest way of knowing and reacting to the world" (p. 54). Making marks as a creative impulse is an innately defining human activity as many researchers such as Bronowski (1976), Dissanayake (1992) and Lagasse (2000) have observed.

Art therapy is a relatively new profession in Australia (ABS 2011), only being recognised by the Australian and New Zealand Standard Classification of Occupations (ANZSCO) during the past six years. Although formally recognised and regulated in other countries, art therapy in Australia and New Zealand is underutilised as a prevention, early intervention, or treatment option for a number of reasons including relatively few numbers of art therapists in Australia and New Zealand. In terms of art therapy developing as a modality in Australia, there is a growing base of evidence from Australia and overseas to seriously consider the principle of incorporating art therapists in educational settings with promotional materials developed by the art therapy profession association that targets schools (ANZATA 2011).

The Art Therapy Process

According to Riley (2005), many young people do not have the verbal capacity to articulate strong emotions or to identify what has given rise to their experience of crises. This is especially so for those who have been traumatised, where art can be a way to communicate feelings and experiences without words. Riley's (2005) view is that art therapy can assist young people by reducing anxiety, by increasing memory retrieval and by helping them to give expression to their experiences and perceptions. Goleman (1996) states that art is the "medium of the unconscious" (Goleman 1996, p. 209). He believes that, through symbol and metaphor, art can encourage young people to reveal more than by verbal means.

Both Riley (2005) and Malchiodi (1997) argue that young people can gain a sense of control by working with images. The art-based therapeutic encounter uses core characteristics of participation through active involvement (by making the art work), through connectedness with both the therapist and the artwork (by engaging in self-reflection and meaning making) and through the attractive notion that young people can manage the process (Riley 2001). According to Riley, the art provides an overt representation of the issue or problem and, in addition, the art can subvert the person's defenses by accessing subconscious thoughts. Learning about oneself, one's thoughts, beliefs, motivations, desires, expectations and fantasies shape experience and develop self-agency (Knox 2011) and is at the heart of psychological growth. Oliver, Collin Burns and Nicholas (2006) argue that these core characteristics of participation, connectedness and control can be learned and can contribute towards resilience building in young people.

Art therapy requires a safe space in which to develop a therapeutic relationship. It is argued by Fenner (2010) and others, such as Hyland Moon (2001), that the art therapy space provides a particular setting that can augment the therapeutic relationship and is fundamental to it. According to Fenner, the visual aesthetic of the room can enhance the therapeutic relationship reflecting values and beliefs that are imbued with a sense of 'temenos' (Abramovitch 1997, p. 570) or sacredness. This is not however, the case with verbally based therapies. Engaging in art is first and foremost, non-threatening according to Riley (2001). The manipulation of art materials may actually be novel for a young person who has had little exposure to the freedom to make art. The artistic experience and knowledge of art media that the therapist is intimately familiar with, can facilitate, explore and influence emotions and well-being (McNiff 2004). This, too, is different to verbally-based therapies and offers a way of kinesthetically and somatically connecting with emotions.

Through this engagement with the art materials, a young person can thus explore their inner world without words, moving away from a cognitive rationalisation of feelings. By means of this experiential process, a young person creates a relationship in a non-verbal way with the therapist, with the materials and with the artwork within a particular space. In this holistic setting, the therapist accepts the artwork and, by extension, accepts the young person (Schroder 2005). This unconditional acceptance encourages the young person to respond to the therapist through the art, which is distanced from, and yet remains an expression of, the young person and is therefore. Liebmann (2003) concurs with Goleman (1996) in considering that during such a transitional phase as adolescence, the use of symbol and metaphor can be a particularly effective way for young people to indirectly express themselves and engage in therapy.

Practicing artist and art therapist McNiff (2004) writes eloquently and poignantly about the important role of artistic media that can enhance elemental processes and depth in healing. McNiff cites his own introduction to art therapy when working as an artist and sculptor while looking for work as a social worker. Throughout his career, McNiff has turned to the everyday and ordinary to connect and re-connect with art and with healing. Even the simple act of looking at a created art piece can impact and encourage understanding through seeing. "The pictures carry medicine, energies creative spirits and vitality that they will give to you freely" (McNiff 2004, p. 54). McNiff links art and healing to ancient cultural practices, spirituality and care of the soul. He argues that by accessing and liberating our inherent creativity, it will find the way to draw attention in our lives to what needs addressing. To access creativity is the first goal and then to actively use it as a coping and resilience building practice to sustain and enhance our quality of life, is another.

By active involvement in the creative process, young people actively contribute towards the developing therapeutic relationship and that focuses on the artwork and not on the 'problem' or on them. During the process of creating, choices and decisions are made, either alone or with the assistance of the therapist. If mistakes occur, these can be re-created providing symbolic messages of hope that can encourage young people to move from a deficit model of self to one of capacity and self-belief. During this process, subtle and tacit information is intuitively sensed by the therapist who empathically attunes to the young client through a heightened awareness of non-verbal clues, somatic felt senses, silences and the use of materials. In turn, the young person responds through both tacit and overt encouragement. An intimate relationship is thus co-created within the therapeutic space where new possibilities, strengths and attitudes can be enacted.

Once the artwork is completed, the young person can dialogue with, and make meaning from, the image when ready to do so. By making sense of aspects of the image, previously hidden and unknown elements such as fears and anxieties, may be revealed to the young person. With the help of the therapist, the young person can re-create new possibilities with different perspectives. These can involve the inclusion of optimism and hope or acknowledgement and acceptance of a situation. In raising awareness, the new perspectives can be integrated into the self and growth can be encouraged. In addition, the artwork is a permanent record of this overall encounter and process that can be revisited and contemplated.

Art Therapy Research

While research on art therapy in school settings has been documented, there is a call for further empirical research. For instance, Hollopeter's (2008) North American study recommends that more research needs to be achieved in art therapy programs that enhance the social and emotional literacy of students. Her research found that, not only were the social and emotional levels were improved, but the students' academic competency also improved after art therapy interventions. In the United States Jackson's (2003) research involved collaboration between school counsellors and art teachers to assist at-risk students. She found her collaborative art experiences model could be implemented in schools with existing staff. She also acknowledged that further empirical research would be valuable, particularly for identifying early intervention strategies.

In Australia, art therapy studies have been undertaken with young people, and are limited to investigations of heterogeneous populations, short duration studies (Ford 2008) or single case studies (Griffin 2008). All these studies recommend further research, particularly in the areas of mainstream education. Further, Linnell's (2009) recent accounts of her collaborative work with indigenous children in foster care commented on the appropriateness of art therapy. It is not difficult to see that further research among vulnerable children's' groups over time would considerably advance the knowledge base and continue to strengthen the argument for art therapy in educational settings.

According to Gilroy (2006) however, the evidence base for art therapy with children and young people is complicated by the typical terminology in which the diagnostic descriptors of healthcare are inappropriate for both schools and social services (Gilroy 2006, p. 139). She has also voiced concern over the limitations of research with assessment for diagnostic purposes. Thus, according to Fox and Hawton (2004), inconsistency in the terminology between disciplines may partially explain the reasons for the gaps in literature that exist when working psychotherapeutically with young people. However, as this author has discovered, the ethical considerations of implementing research over a period of time among vulnerable young people can be fraught with blocks to approval, yet further limiting the empirical research available.

Postmodernism, with its challenging assumptions of epistemology is beginning to create increasingly multidisciplinary ways of working and researching. In the United Kingdom, Gilroy (2006) argues that art therapists need to engage in the debate about what constitutes evidence and argues for evaluating and researching art therapy in a way that reflects practice. Rosenberg (2008) states that the problems of attempting to fit art based interventions into traditionally health-based methodologies or evaluation techniques, has resulted in new ways to consider the nature of evidence. Leavy's (2009) work in the emerging field of transdisciplinary research furthers this view by suggesting that appropriate arts based design can intersect disciplines, thus creating transformative and new perspectives on what constitutes evidence.

Although pinning down the language of art and affective processes to unpack and study can be complex, in recent years increasingly more research has been undertaken throughout the world in the field of creativity and emotion (Robinson 1999; Csíkszentmihályi 1996; Boden 2004; Hass-Cohen and Carr 2008). This work is directly aligned with coping, resilience and a strengths-based approach. Research undertaken by Robinson and Azzam (2009) indicate that divergent thinking, problem solving and creativity are linked and that by developing and fostering creative processes, positive mental health may well result.

Art Therapy in Schools

Ewing (2010) argues that the 'arts' should play an intrinsic and fundamental role in the lives of both children and adults because they enable a rewarding "way of human knowing and being—of imagination, aesthetic knowledge and translation and expression of ideas" (Ewing 2010, p. 5). Further, the power of the arts to transform an individual's life is widely acknowledged by the Australian National Educational and the Arts Statement (2007) released by the Ministerial Council for Education, Employment, Training and Youth Affairs (MCEETYA) and by the Cultural Ministers Council (CMC). However, Ewing comments that the government's policy statement plays lip service to this view. But in reality, low priority is given to the arts in society-at-large or through funding for school education.

In the United Kingdom, Robinson's (1999) observed that fostering creativity in education is essential. He emphasises the importance of encouraging multiple ways of knowing, creative thinking and emotional intelligence. He is critical of the low hierarchical status of the arts in the curriculum and the inequity of provision throughout Britain. More recently, Baker (2012) argues that artistic experiences are a central part of human life. Creatively impoverished individuals suffer impacts in academic learning and social competencies, including their perseverance and problem solving. Such competencies are considered in the adult learning literature (See for example, Briggs and Tang 2011) to be lifelong generic skills.

Social competencies can be adaptive and learned. These skills also contribute toward resilience and are protective (Howard and Johnson 2000). One of these competencies is problem-solving skills which involves creative thinking by the use of the imagination and openness. By being adaptive and able to solve problems one can encourage a self-belief in personal capacity to be competent. It is not hard to see the connection between encouraging these skills that can be taught and the ability to bounce back after hardship and adversity. Clearly, with the growing concern and awareness of mental health issues in young people (combined with seemingly neglected areas of the curriculum that would assist with developing resilience and coping skills), there appears to be a widening gap between teaching and educating young people, not only about their academic futures but also about life "at its best and worst" (Evans 2012).

According to Glover, Patton, Butler, DiPetro, Begg and Ollis (2002), the school community as an influential institution for young people can be an ideal place for promoting health, resilience and wellbeing. This is not only within the curriculum itself, but also within the school community in its pastoral care. The socialising environment of the school influences the emotional wellbeing of students for it is widely recognised that connectedness and positive communication with staff enhances student capabilities (NSDES 2003). Rastle (2008) and Hollopeter (2008) have both undertaken research projects on art therapy within elementary schools in the United States. Both researchers concluded that although further studies needed to be done and the numerical data was not statistically significant, integrating this form of intervention is possible with positive outcomes in both academic and social functioning of the students.

Counselling services currently offered in Australian schools widely appear to be widely inadequate with high student-to-counsellor ratios (AGCA 2008). In addition, McGorry, Parker and Purcell (2010) argue that while demand is increasing, services are currently lacking for the most vulnerable young people. This service gap, fuelled by the stigma and lack of knowledge about mental health among adolescents, indicates a clear need to build resilience training within the school context. Resilience training is a preventative as well as a potential mental health intervention. Further, it can be designed into the curriculum, rather than sitting outside it as an added extra for 'problem students' (Rastle 2008).

Counsellors using verbally based therapy are not trained in visual and creative communication unless they have had training as art therapists, or are artists committed to their artistic practice. The numbers of therapists able and sufficiently qualified to work as art therapists by holding the international minimum qualification of a postgraduate degree are few. There is greater potential in better utilising art therapists within educational settings than currently exists. It is not known how many qualified art therapists are working within educational settings in Australia but, anecdotally, the number would appear to be low.

Trained art therapists could help fill a gap in services, currently being only partially provided by trained counsellors. In most Australian states and territories, the qualifications required to work as a counsellor are a teaching degree in addition to an Australian Psychology Council (APAC) approved psychology qualification with the demand for counsellors well exceeding the supply, particularly in some rural and remote areas (Thornton 2007). Art therapists could provide a new approach by enhancing the verbally-based service (DET 2011). With provision being inadequate at the present time and with counsellors providing only verbally based services, a dimension of communicating and learning with young people is not being exploited. One practical way this can be achieved would be by closely integrating art therapy within the school curriculum in psycho-educational programs that enhance young people's learning. Another way is for art therapists to work collaboratively with verbal counsellors, pastoral carers and welfare staff. In doing so, they provide art-based enrichment experiences with small groups of appropriately assessed students that can be designed and evaluated using art based multi methods.

Conclusion

In countries where art therapy is established, such as in the United Kingdom and the United States, a greater number of therapists are employed and integrated within multidisciplinary teams in mainstream educational settings. In Australia, this is not the case due in part, to the relative newness of the profession as well as the ongoing need to develop the knowledge base through research. The issue is exacerbated by the relatively few art therapists working in Australia and by the lack of understanding even among mental health professionals as to the power and depth of the benefits. There is obviously considerable potential for using non-verbally based therapeutic interventions within schools, not only for students struggling and at risk of mental health problems, but for all students as a holistic tool to develop resilience and coping. Adolescence is acknowledged to be a period of change that many transit with few problems, but many do not. Young people need to develop their creative inner resources and skills to enable them to flourish and enrich in their lives, in spite of difficulties and adversities that they will undoubtedly experience. Building resilience through art therapy provides a substantial platform for achieving this goal in society through the school setting. With the present service provision gap that exists, the current author is undertaking doctoral research studies of art therapy interventions in a mainstream high school and is in an ideal position to practice, research and document the fostering and development of resilience through art therapy, by encouraging self-acceptance and belief, building skills and mentoring effective health promoting strategies.

Works Cited

Abramovitch, H. 1997. Temenos regained: Reflections on the absence of the analyst. *Journal of Analytical Psychology*, 42, 569-584

ABS. 2007. *National Survey of Mental Health and Wellbeing: Summary of Results.* Canberra: Australian Bureau of Statistics.

――――. 2011. *ANZSCO Australian and New Zealand Standard Classification of Occupations* 2011 [cited 5 March 2011]. Available from http://www.abs.gov.au/AUSSTATS/abs@.nsf/Lookup/173D4D67348CB91CCA2575DF002DA7A7.

AGCA. 2008. *An Australian Wide Comparison of School Counsellor/Psychologist Guidance Services.* Australian Guidance and Counselling Association.

Allen, Pat B. 1995. *Art is a Way of Knowing. A Guide to Self-Knowledge and Spiritual Fulfilment through Creativity.* Boston: Shambala, USA.

ANZATA. 2011. ANZATA's information on evidence based treatment. http://www.anzata.org/professional-info/.

APA. 2000. *Quick Reference to the Diagnostic Criteria from DSM-IV-TR*: American Psychiatric Association.

Arden, J B, and L Linford. 2009. *Brain-Based Therapy with Children and Adolescents. Evidence-Based Treatment for Everyday Practice.* New Jersey: Wiley & Sons Inc.

Baker, Bill. 2012. The Arts pale behind literacy and numeracy. *Education Review*: 28.

Ballou, M. 1995. Art Therapy. In *Psychological interventions a guide to strategies*, edited by M. Ballou. Westport CT: Praeger Publisher.

Begg, S., T. Vos, B. Barker, C. Stevenson, L. Stanley, and A.D. Lopez, 2007. *The Burden of Disease and Injury in Australia 2003.* Canberra: Australian Institute of Health and Welfare.

Boden, Margaret. 2004. *The Creative Mind: Myths And Mechanisms.* New York: Routledge.

Briggs, J.B. and Tang, C . 2011. *Teaching for Quality Learning at University (Society for Research into Higher Education).* Maidenhead, New York: Open University Press/McGraw Education.

Bronowski, J. 1976. *The Ascent of Man.* London: British Brodcasting Corporation.

Browne, M. Oakley, J. Wells, K. Scott, and M. McGee. 2006. Lifetime prevalence and protected lifetime risk of DSMIV disorders in Te Rau Hinengaro: the New Zealand Mental Health Survey (NZMHS). *Australian and New Zealand Journal of Psychiatry* (40):865-872.

Burns, B.J., E.J. Costello, D. Tweed, D. Stangl, E.M. Farmer, and A. Erkanli. 1995. Children's mental health service use across service across service sectors. *Health Affairs*, 14 (3):147-159.

Burton, Lorelle, Drew Westen, and Robin Kowalski. 2009. *Psychology* 2nd Edition Australian and New Zealand. Brisbane: John Wiley and Sons, Australia Ltd.

Capacchione, Lucia. 2001. *The Art of Emotional Healing*. Boston and London: Shambala.

Case, R. 1992. Neo-Piagetian theories of child development. In *Intellectual development*, edited by R. J. Sternberg and C. A. Berg. New York: Cambridge University Press.

Caspi, A, D. Lynam, T. Moffitt, and P. Silva. 1993. Unraveling girls' delinquency: Biological, dispositional and contextual contributions to adolescent misbehavior. *Developmental Psychology* 29:19-30.

Commission, Human Rights and Equal Opportunity. 1993. *Report of the National Inquiry into the Human Rights of People with Mental Illness*. Canberra: Australian Government Publishing Service.

Csíkszentmihályi, Mihály. 1996. *Creativity: Flow and the Psychology of Discovery and Invention*. New York: Harper Collins.

DET, NSW. 2011. *Going to a Public School. School Counselling Services*. Department of Education and Training 2011 [cited 26 August 2011]. Available from http://www.schools.nsw.edu.au/gotoschool/a-z/counselservice.php.

Dissanayake, E. 1992. *Homo Aestheticus: where art comes from and why*. New York: Free Press.

Doidge, Norman. 2008. *The Brain That Changes Itself*. Melbourne: Scribe.

Duncan, Barry L., Scott D. Miller, and Jacqueline A. Sparks. 2004. *The Heroic Client*. San Fransisco: Jossey Bass.

Ellis, B.J., and J. Garber. 2000. Psychosocial antecedents of variation in girls' pubertal timing: Maternal depression, stepfather presence and marital and family stress. *Child Development* 71:485-501.

Erikson, Eric. 1968. *Identity: Youth and Crisis*. New York: W W Norton.

Evans, J. 2012. *Philosophy for Life*. London Sydney Auckland Johannesburg: Random House Group.

Ewing, Robyn. 2010. The Arts and Australian Education: Realising Potential. *Australian Education Review* (58).

Fall, A, and G Roberts. 2012. High school dropouts: Interactions between social context, self-perceptions, school engagement and student dropout. *Journal of Adolescence* 35:787-798.

Fenner, P. 2010. *Place, matter and meaning: Extending our understanding of the art therapy encounter*, La Trobe University, Melbourne.

Fox, Claudine, and Keith Hawton. 2004. *Deliberate Self Harm in Adolescence*: Jessica Kingsley.

Gilroy, Andrea. 2006. *Art Therapy, Research and Evidence-based Practice*. London: Sage Publications.

Glover, S., G. Patton, H. Butler, G. DiPetro, B. Begg, D. Ollis, S. Chair, and J. Watson. 2002. *Gatehouse Project. Teaching Strategies for Emotional Wellbeing*. Centre for Adolescent Health, University of Melbourne, Victoria.

Goleman, D. 1996. *Emotional Intelligence. why it can matter more than IQ*. London, Berlin, New York: Bloomsbury.

Greenhalgh, Paul. 1994. *Emotional Growth and Learning*. London, New York: Routledge.

Griffin, Jane. 2008. *The experience of cross cultural art therapy with a newly arrived Conglalese refugee in a school setting*. Masters, School of Medicine, Dept of Psychiatry, Queensland, Brisbane.

Hass-Cohen, Noah, and Richard Carr. 2008. *Art Therapy and Clinical Neuroscience*. London and Philadephia: Jessica Kingsley.

Hollopeter, Anissa Ann. 2008. *Art Therapy Program Development for Elementary School Students*. Masters, Ursuline College, Ursuline College, Ohio.

Howard, S., and B. Johnson. 2000. Young Adolescents Displaying Resilient and Non-Resilent Behaviour: Insights from a Qualitative Study—Can Schools Make a Difference? In *Association for Active Educational Researchers*. Sydney: AARE.

Kahn, S., G. Zimmerman, M. Csikzentmihalyi, and J. Getzels. 1985. Relations between identity in young adulthood and intimacy in midlife. *Journal of Personality and Social Psychology* 49:1316-1322.

Kapitan, Lynn. 2009. Reauthoring the Dominant Narrative of Our Profession. *Art Therapy: Journal of the American Art Therapy Association* 26 (3):135-138.

Knox, J., 2011. *Self Agency in Psychotherapy. Attachment, Autonomy and Intimacy*. New York, London: W W norton and Company.

Lagasse, Paul. 2000. The Columbia Encyclopedia. In *The Columbia Encyclopedia*: Columbia University Press.

Leavy, Patricia. 2009. *Method Meets Art. Arts-Based Research Practice*. New York, London: The Guilford Press.

Liebmann, Marian. 2003. *Art Therapy for Groups. A Handbook of Themes, Games and Exercises*: Brookline Books USA.

Linnell, Sheridan. 2009. Becoming 'Otherwise': A Story of a Collaborative and Narrative Approach to Art Therapy with Indigenous Kids 'in care'. *Australian and New Zealand Journal of Art Therapy* 4 (1):15-26.

Lowenfeld, Viktor, and W. Lambert Brittain. 1987. *Creative and Mental Growth*. 8 ed. New York, London: Macmillan Publications

Luthar, S.S., D. Cicchetti, and B. Becker. 2000. The construct of resilience: A critical evaluation and guidelines for future work. *Child Development* 71:543-562.

Malchiodi, Cathy. 2002. *The Soul's Palette. Drawing on Art's Transformative Powers for Healing and Well-Being*. Boston: Shambhala.

_____, ed. 2003. *Handbook of Art Therapy*. New York, Guilford: Guilford Press.

Malchiodi, Cathy A. 1997. *Breaking the Silence. Art Therapy with Children from Violent Homes*. New York, Abingdon: Routledge, Taylor & Francis Group.

Masten, A. 2001. Ordinary Magic. Resilience Processes in Development. *American Psychologist* 56 (3):227-238.

McGorry, Patrick D., Alexandra Parker, and Rosemary Purcell. 2010. Youth Mental Health: A New Stream of Mental Health Care for Adolescents and YOung Adults. In *Mental Health in Australia*, edited by G. Meadows, B. Singh and M. Grigg. Oxford New York: Oxford University Press.

McNiff, Shaun. 2004. *Art Heals. How Creativity Cures the Soul*. Boston: Shambala, USA.

Ministerial Council for Education, Employment, Training and Youth Affairs (MCEETYA) and Cultural MInisters Council (CMC). 2007. *National Statement on Education and the Arts*. Edited by I. T. A. T. A. Department of Communication. Canberra: Australian Commonwealth Government.

Moon, Bruce L. 2004. *Art and Soul. Reflections on an Artistic Psychology*. Springfield, Illinois: Charles C Thomas.

Moon, C. Hyland. 2001. *Studio Art Therapy: Cultivating the Artist Identity in the Art Therapist*. London, Philadephia: Jessica Kingsley Publishers.

Mussen, Paul Henry, John Janeway Conger, Jerome Kagan, and Aletha Carol Huston. 1984. *Child Development and Personality*. Sixth Edition ed. New York: Harper International.

NSDES. 2003. *Guidelines for Pastoral Care in Catholic Schools*. Catholic Commission Sydney NSW: National Schools Drug Education Strategy.

Oliver, Kylie G., Phiippa Collin, Jane Burns, and Jonathon Nicholas. 2006. Building resilience in young people through meaningful participation. *Australian e-Journal for the Advancement of Mental Health* 5 (1).

Persaud, Raj. 2001. *Staying Sane. How to make your mind work for you.* London, New York, Toronto, Sydney, Auckland: Bantam Books.

Rastle, Margaret Ann. 2008. *Individual Art Therapy Counseling with At-Risk Children in a School Setting,* Art Therapy and Counseling Program, Ursuline College, Ohio.

Riley, Shirley. 2001. Art Therapy with Adolescents. *Western Journal of Medicine* 175 (1):54-57.

_____. 2005. *Contemporary Art Therapy with Adolescents.* London and Philadelphia: Jessica Kingsley.

Robinson, Ken. 1999. *All our futures: Creativity, Culture and Education.* London: National Advisory Committee on Creative and Cultural Education.

_____, A. M. Azzam. 2009. "Why creativity now? *Educational Leadership* 67 (1):22-26.

Rosenberg, M. 2008. The Evaluation Game: Detrmining the Benefits of Arts Engagement in Health. In *Proving the Practice. Evidencing the effects of community arts programs on mental health,* edited by A. Lewis and D. Doyle. Freemantle: Disability in the Arts Disadvantage in the Arts Australia (DADAA).

Rubin, Judith Aron, ed. 2001. *Approaches to Art Therapy. Theory and Technique.* 2nd ed. London: Brunner Routledge.

Rutter, M. 1990. Psychosocial resilienceand protective mechanisms. In *Risk and protective factors in the development of psychopathology,* edited by J. Rolf, A. S. Masten, D. Cicchetti, K. H. Nuechterlein and S. Weintraub. New York: Cambridge University Press.

Schroder, D. 2005. *Little Windows in Art Therapy. Small Openings for Beginning Therapists.* London, Phildephia: Jessica Kingsley Publishers.

Seligman, M.E.P., and M. Czikszentmihalyi. 2000. Positive psychology [Special issue]. *American Psychologist* 55 (1).

_____. 1975. *Helplessness: On Depression, Development and Death.* San Fransisco: W H Freeman.

Slade, Tim, Amy Johnston, Mark A. Oakley Browne, Gavin Andrews, and Harvey Whiteford. 2009. 2007 National Survey of Mental Health and Wellbeing: methods and key findings. *Australian and New Zealand Journal of Psychiatry* (43):594-605.

Stolorow, R. D., and C.E. Atwood. 1992. *Contexts of Being: The Intersubjective Foundations of Psychological Life.* HIllsdale NJ: Analytic Press.

Thornton, T. 2007. Remotely Interested. *AGCA Newsletter*, December.

Vick, Randy. 2003. A Brief History of Art Therapy. In *Handbook of Art Therapy*, edited by C. Malchiodi. London: The Guilford Press.

Walker, S., and K. Irving. 1998. The effecto of perceived social status on preschool children's evaluations of behaviour. *Australian Research in Early childhood Education: Journal of Australian Research in Early Childhood Education* 1:94-113.

Westwood, Jill. 2010. *Hybrid Creatures. Mapping the emerging shape of art therapy education in Australia*, Research Centre for Social Justice and Social Change, University of Western Sydney, Sydney.

CHAPTER 8

Out of the Shadows: Into the Light: Resilience and Coping Skills through Arts Practice

Anne Riggs

Abstract

This chapter explores community creative arts practice as a tool for adult women to recover from the impact of childhood trauma.

In an examination of arts recovery programs led by myself as artist in a collaborative creative engagement with women victims of childhood sexual abuse, I explore what participation contributes to an individual's well-being. The visual arts are inherently a mode of expression, and the benefits of being part of a group are known to assist recovery, when these are offered together in an arts recovery program, victims of trauma improve coping skills and develop resilience to better manage and enjoy their daily life.

Drawing on participants' reflections and artworks, as well as theories in art, psychology and neuroscience, I consider creative practice as a tool to enhance an individual's capacity to live well, better communicate and function in the world, leading to a reduction in isolation, debilitating feelings of poor self-esteem, and depression. As creativity empowered women to think, behave and relate in ways that until their participation had largely been elusive, it offered hope, belief and skills for a happier future: a remarkable shift for those who previously lived on the brink of suicide. The chapter considers how a thoughtful, creative practice can transform what hurts, disturbs and stultifies, in to art that reveals, restores and envigorates.

Introduction

Art belongs to humanity's responsive and creative capacity. An engagement with creative practice and an artist gives adult victims of childhood sexual abuse practical tools to cope with the experience and impact of their past so they may develop resilience to recover from adversity in the present and future—both are required if individuals are to lead a content life without being overwhelmed by their past. Theories and research of neuroscience, psychology and psychiatry, such as that being undertaken by the Child Trauma Academy, USA, Victorian State Government Department of Human Services help explain scientifically what artists have long been observing (Perry 2009; Dept of Human Services 2012)

The reasons arts programs are successful in building coping and resilience skills are not especially difficult understand. They work because they provide victims with a safe place in which to create, learn and be social. They have an artist as a guide and a counsellor to support them. Although many choose to refer to the programs as 'art therapy', I steadfastly assert that they are not, although they are therapeutic. Built on the principles of creative arts practice, participants learn art-making skills, about materials and artists, and how to utilize these for personal self-expression and growth. These are the inherent quality of art-making. Additionally, creative practice develops a sense of self and hope that aid recovery from the impact of their traumatic past.

The creative processes I describe here, including the sometimes intuitive interventions of the artist, assist adult victims rebuild their lives after profoundly damaging trauma experiences in childhood. When trauma, especially childhood sexual abuse (CSA) is properly understood as an experience, for its continuing affect and for what is lost because of it, art as a means to recovery can then be appreciated for its effectiveness to touch what has not be touched and to heal the wounds that have been left to weep (Perry 2001; Perry, Pollard, Blakely, Baker, & Vigilante 1995).

The journey towards working with victims of childhood sexual abuse grew out of my practice as a contemporary studio and community visual artist. Whilst living in the UK for much of my young adulthood, I noticed how often the First World War was alluded to as a watershed event and how the trauma, losses and grief resulting from it reverberated through families and communities for many generations in patterns of addiction, violence and poor mental health (Winter 1995, p. 21). Curiosity led to me explore this subject through a Masters of Fine Arts degree and the research led to an immersion into its European landscape, its domestic affect and particularly its impact upon women.

The research opened my eyes to the potential for all trauma to have a continuing legacy and adversely impose upon others whether they were directly involved or not. I witnessed through my related exhibitions that an artist-led invitation to express and grieve losses enabled communities and individuals to engage with their feelings of loss, even when these feelings had been long-ignored. Sometimes the artist can gently guide viewers towards a safe place where the unviewable and unknowable can be felt, observed and named.

Around the time when I was seeking a suitable group to study for my doctoral work researching recovery from trauma, loss and grief through an engagement with arts, I was offered an artist role at the South Eastern Centre Against Sexual Assault[1] facilitating a 12-week mosaic group with female victims of abuse. As sexual trauma is a particularly sensitive field, a counsellor was a co-participant and available to provide psychological support to participants. In most previous community arts group I had facilitated, as was the usual practice, there was no professional emotional support available to participants and I often found myself providing it. Now, with a counsellor present and available to assist individuals, group discussions regarding trauma and its impacts were few; I was able to fully focus on my role as the artist, leaving the artspace open as a venue for creative practice. The project raised some questions for the forthcoming PhD seeking to understand some of the specific benefits of arts practice to trauma recovery. The PhD was conceived using this same model and art recovery groups continue as artist-led and counsellor-supported interventions.

Rather than encourage group discussions about the issues that bring participants to a group, I now encourage thinking and feeling to be done through creative practice. Minimising talking is not silencing; participants are instead guided towards contemplating the impacts of abuse and how these can be creatively explored and expressed. Every woman has reported benefits as a result of her participation; for many, the changes have been transformational. The compelling evidence from the on-going research has encouraged sexual assault organisations to adopt more creative practices into the services being offered to clients (Riggs 2010).

The principle components discussed in this chapter are the benefits of creative practice, working with an artist and being part of a group of people who have a shared experience of childhood sexual trauma to building resilience and coping skills. Participants' words, writings and emails to me are included as contributions to understanding and I acknowledge their generosity in sharing them.

Key Concepts

Creativity and Creative Practice

Creativity is an innate human endeavour. "It is meaningful and generates positive feelings," says Therese Schmid who defines creativity as "the capacity to think and act in original ways, to be inventive and to find new and original solutions to needs, problems and forms of expression". Creativity "can be used in all activities." Schmid 2005 p. 29). In stating "Human creativity is in range as wide as the world of human encounter and its potential reaches as deep" McDonagh notes the difficulty many of us have in defining this human practice. In form, it is primarily responsive but no less free and innovative (McDonagh 2005).

For both maker and the viewer, an artistic creation is a new entity "open to fresh encounter" forming a new sense of the self and the world (McDonagh 2005).

Some, including project participants, view creative practice as a means of emancipation, as skillfully executed works speak to the social situation of the makers and liberates them from the consequences of an abusive past (Adams & Goldbard 2001, p. 21).

Mosaic making and working with clay are the primary forms of creative practice being discussed in this chapter, however, creative practice is also mode of thought, of looking at the world through different eyes and from a different perspective, it is a practice of curiosity. Creativity is an essential element of change, "always on the move, seeking to transcend current boundaries, it is imbued with a fresh mission," says McDonagh.

Schmid discusses creativity in relation to wellbeing through the practice of self-actualisation, referring to the humanist psychology theorists (Maslow 1962 1971, 1987; Rogers 1970; Runco et al. 1991 and Sheldon 1995), who observe that "the creative person is one who is fulfilled, is self-actualised and is functioning freely and fully" (Schmid 2005, p. 43). It is a thread followed by Danita Walsh who says that "creativity underpins our health and well-being" as an enabling process that helps us "learn about, relate to and evolve with life" and is therefore an essential component in keeping us connected to the self and to others (in Lewis & Doyle 2008, p. 78). As both suggest creativity is fundamental to human well-being and relationships, a discussion about building coping and resilience within individuals who have been damaged by childhood sexual abuse can only be enhanced by a discussion with creativity at its centre.

In the model of practice discussed here, the artist draws on years of professional arts practice, utilizes art materials such as clay and tiles, and develops conceptual thinking to engage participants in a process-driven and thought provoking creative journey. These are learning focused groups. The program's design and aims were developed by the author in collaboration with sexual assault service providers (South Eastern Centre Against Sexual Assault, (SECASA), a program of Southern Health, Melbourne and Connections Uniting Care, a community welfare agency of the Uniting Church's Uniting Care Network of Australia). Participants were sought through the organisations' networks.

Trauma and Childhood Sexual Abuse (CSA)

The words "trauma" and "traumatic" are widely used to describe stressful or confronting experiences and feelings such as fear, shock, loss and grief associated with these experiences. Accidents, medical emergencies and natural disasters can all be considered traumatic events; here the focus is on psychological trauma, described by Judith Lewis Herman as "an affliction of the powerless", when a person is "rendered helpless by overwhelming force which cannot be overcome, no matter what action the victim might take" (Herman 1992, p. 33) and specifically childhood sexual abuse. The circumstances of the event can include abuse of power, entrapment, witnessing the abuse of others, helplessness or threat. Those who are exposed to events that threaten their own or others' life or physical integrity are likely to be affected by the experience and will show signs of distress and disturbance at the time, but often not until years later. Trauma is characterized by its distinct imprint upon survivors, such as flashbacks, which differentiate it from other challenging or momentous experiences and indicate that the trauma experience has not been relegated to the past (Herman 1992; van der Kolk, McFarlane, & Weisaeth 1996). Neuroscience research in identifying how childhood trauma impacts upon the brain structure develops knowledge of how this also effects the victim's health, capacity to learn, engage well with others and regulate emotions (Perry 2001, 2009; Perry & Pollard 1998).

The South Eastern Centre for Sexual Assault Melbourne says "a child or young person is sexually abused when any person uses their power to involve that child in sexual activity. Abuse occurs when a person uses their authority, either by using force or not, to involve a child in activities that are for the sexual gratification of the person in authority, and may occur once or many times over a period of months or years. Exposing the child to pornography or using the child for the purposes of pornography or prostitution is childhood sexual abuse. Under Victorian Child Welfare law a child is any person under seventeen years of age, therefore the term 'child' include infants to adolescents" (SECASA 2012).

SECASA notes that adults always have more power than a child who is inherently smaller, dependent, and never in a position to give informed consent. Where the relationship between the child and the adult is close, dependency is greater and therefore the power that the adult has over the child is also the greater. CSA is known to lead to numerous adverse outcomes for victims.

Research demonstrates that a child victim of trauma is likely to experience enduring negative emotions, have increased risk of psychotic and non-psychotic disorders and develop significant other health, psychological and social problems (Boyce & Harris 2011; Briere 1992; Finkelhor & Browne 1985; Perry 2009). Mental health symptoms include anxiety, depression, disruptive behaviours, post-traumatic stress (PTS) post-traumatic stress disorder (PTSD), and dissociative behaviours. There is also evidence of cognitive, developmental and behavioural impairment. Trauma-exposed youth can have reduced abilities for sustained attention, memory and executive functioning, as well as decreased verbal abilities. Academic failure is widespread and is a serious social concern as poor work opportunities, poor housing and poor health are amongst its consequences. Feelings of guilt emerge from a misplaced belief that the victim, rather than the perpetrator, is at fault and misplaced feelings of being un-deserving of anything good or worthwhile are common (Riggs 2010).

Individual responses to CSA are described as 'effective', such as telling a trusted adult, or 'ineffective', such as avoidant or dissociative behaviours, which, whilst useful at the time, predicts poor outcomes in adulthood. Children who were be pre-occupied with circumstances surrounding their abuse very often missed opportunities to learn and develop normal coping skills, such as breaking tasks into manageable parts, negotiation, conflict resolution, self-regulation and finding solace from others. Catastrophising, or seeing things only as opposites, known as 'black and white thinking', become barriers to coping. Victims of CSA are at greater risk of revictimisation and further assault; many have non-consensual sexual experiences in adulthood and experience family violence (Overstreet & Mathews 2011; Walsh, Blaustein, Knight, Spinazzola, & Kolk 2007). Self-destructive coping, such as substance abuse, running away, suicide attempts, self-harming, and overuse of prescription medicines are amongst the consistent responses to CSA (Phanichrat & Townshend 2010). Research describes how the effect of living with constant stress changes basic neurobiology indicating that the mechanisms of CSA are "truly biopsychosocial, that is, impacting upon the individual's biology, psychology and sociology" (Boyce & Harris 2011, p. 609). One of the most challenging characteristics of CSA is that victims may not be aware of the trauma until sometimes years afterwards, when they begin to search for understanding for behaviours, feelings and experiences that have negatively impacted upon them. Often, victims of CSA do not seek help until they are well into adulthood.

Although not all victims of CSA have profound long-term psychological responses to it, enough do to warrant careful, thoughtful and innovative interventions to help guide them towards leading a meaningful adult life (Boyce and Harris 2011). Learning to understand, interpret, reconsider and reshape thoughts and behaviours through talking therapy is one way to achieve this goal. However, by its very nature, this therapy relies on a verbal dialogue, and the victim being competent in forming coherent thoughts, then putting those thoughts into words. It is challenging at best, but for those attempting to address and recover from childhood trauma, when the dynamics of it have already affected the developing brain, this an especially difficult and frustrating task, for child as well as adult. Evidence suggests a range of options should be offered as modes of recovery from the particularities of childhood trauma. The arts, yoga, interactions with animals and physical activity are amongst the options being understood and recognised for their influence in restoring high level function through first addressing the lower brain functions (Mudaly 2012; Perry & Pollard 1998; Riggs 2010)

Framework

The art recovery program reflects an arts and health model of community wellbeing; creativity, artists, and learning are at its centre. Whilst its foundation is in arts practice, its aims also find resonance in contemporary mental health practices, where recovery is described as by Alain Topor "deeply personal and unique to each individual" and that recovery unfolds within a social and interpersonal context (cited in Francis 2012). According to Abraham Francis, most of the literature describes recovery as "individuals taking control of their lives" whilst W A Anthony identifies recovery as

> "a deeply personal, unique process of changing one's attitudes, values, feelings, goals, skills and/or roles. It is a way of living a satisfying, hopeful, and contributing life even with limitations caused by the illness. Recovery involves the development of new meaning and purpose in one's life as one grows beyond the catastrophic effects of mental illness" (Anthony 1993, p. 13).

Recovery involves much more than recovery from the trauma itself, from lack of opportunities for self-determination, from the negative side effects, and from crushed dreams. Recovery is often a complex, time-consuming process (Anthony 1993). When

Anthony describes recovery as involving "the development of new meaning and purpose in one's life" (1993 p.13), it is evident why an arts program is a useful tool to achieve these goals, as these aims are also those of a creative practice. Built around the principles of strengths-based practice, the art program develops skills in coping and resiliency through a creative practice that inspires a vision of the world and the self that is revelatory and alerts participants to new possibilities. Participants find their voice, literally and metaphorically, as the artist guides them through a visual arts program that explores their interior self and offers new ways to see, feel and think.

Art-making skills are critical to a mature and sophisticated visual language through which to express with acuity; some methods used to develop this language are introducing participants to a diversity of thought and materials, and encounters with humanity through the work of artists. These feed the curiosity and nurture the desire to create. Emotional intelligence and expression is matured through developing a fluent visual language, and thereby the participants, who find when they are able to express themselves well and are heard, are less likely to sink into frustration, anger and despair. Practices such as the artist demonstrating techniques, developing group projects and discussing where a particular work might be improved, all characteristics of an arts recovery program, are useful in assisting participants achieve the goals each has set for her participation.

About the Groups

Those suffering from the residual effects of CSA seek help because they yearn to see from a new perspective; they know change is essential if they are to lead a happier life. A participant once said to me, "if I continue to do what I have always done, I will get the same results"; she understood the need for change (Riggs 2010, p. 115). By the time women engage in the art group, most have attempted, with varying degrees of success, to find strategies to cope better and achieve a sense of wellbeing. All are ready to employ a positive approach to recovery by building on their desires and love of art.

The program structure is 15 weeks mosaic-making that orients women to art, design and being in a group, after which participants are invited to join a 15 week clay group that focuses on grief and loss. Each session is three hours, up to 12 women participate. Before commencing the program, I meet each new participant so we may get to know each other a little and I might learn something of her creative interests as well as aspirations for the group and her wellbeing. Women are invited to discuss anything that may assist her feel comfortable and some use this opportunity to disclose about her abuse history. Participation in the group is voluntary and requires a significant level of commitment.

One potential group member was a woman who had been attending counselling intermittently for over ten years; her counsellor encouraged her to join in a step towards embedding the therapeutic work into her life. The woman needed to be 'in the world' more fully if she was to lead a meaningful and contented life as an adult. The young woman was a victim of CSA and found it a daily struggle to manage overwhelming feelings of sorrow and loss, but also guilt and shame. Her mother denied the impact of the abuse, which further compounded the woman's poor self-esteem, and feelings of isolation. Her life was characterised by depression and loneliness.

In a very good example of a collaborative relationship between the therapist and the artist with the individual in the centre, the woman joined the mosaic group. When counsellors recommend the program, they are recognising the valuable opportunities it offers to put therapy concepts into practice. Creative, purposeful group work can demonstrate to a victim that she is a likeable, sociable, a valued and valuable friend, a creative individual or a teacher; it can provide occasions to practice negotiation skills, and develop an appreciation of beauty; it can be the place to celebrate or share with other like minded people, or to lead. And of course it develops and nurtures creativity. These are part of an experiential practice that enhances resilience and coping skills.

In the pre-group interview this woman revealed a growing interest in art and the desire to "learn different forms of art and open up to ideas of what art is. I think it can alleviate the pain, help me feel more positive about my journey." The desire to create something of which she could be proud was another powerful reason for her participation: "I would be very proud of whatever I have created; it will help me keep looking forward and moving on." Her vexed and complex family relationships negatively mirrored her low self-view. Responding to my question "What do you hope might change as a result of your participation?" she begins by describing "my family" but immediately continues with "maybe it will help me accept myself more—knowing that I can achieve something... The sense of achievement, knowing I am a worthy person." She says "I have really bad depression" and believes that participating "will be really helpful to feel a bit better about myself, do positive things and get out of the cycle of depression." Like so many others, she believed creative practice could transform what had previously been un-transformable. Thanomjit Phanichrat and Julia M Townshend (2010) describe a link between having a positive construct, such as the high hope this participant revealed, to having better outcomes in physical and psychological wellbeing. With all that in mind, there is a very great responsibility for the artist to nurture this embryonic yet determined creative desire.

The pre-group interviews, originally a component of the PhD research, proved to be a powerful tool in minimising anxiety. With the opportunity to explain the process of the group, as well as showing the layout of the building and art room, participant uncertainty was alleviated; each joined knowing what to expect and at least one person. Post-group interview are also conducted to review the program and its outcomes (Riggs 2010).

Art groups begin with simple exercises through which participants learn about materials and fundamental techniques of art, such as using tools and working with clay. These techniques are first applied to small creative projects that can be completed in one session, such as a mosaic mirror or a coil pot (Figure 1). Projects are founded on the principle of starting at the beginning and taking small steps. As women delight in their creations, they confront their first artistic success and the beginning of a healthy self-esteem.

Figure 1. Mosaic Mirror (Participant)

> I found the first session of the art group to be fundamental in learning the basic skills required. In this session we were given the opportunity to practice what was demonstrated and sought help where required. Participation in the very first session can play a big role in grasping vital skills needed to draw on in the coming weeks. It was this first introductory session that gave me the confidence to come back again and again.—*Participant*

During the following weeks new techniques are introduced and practiced, participants master tools, learn about materials, develop ideas as well as practice social skills. Some nonetheless struggle, usually because of a sabotaging inner-voice rather than any specific difficulty with a tool or technique. But the inner-voice is real and perseverance from the participant with the support of the artist is required to overcome it. In the quote below, a participant explains her struggle with an early mosaic project:

> As you said, you could look at it as a learning process, I was accepting of that. Then when I came back this week after accepting it possibly wasn't going to look great and the gaps were like they were... too big, you gave me the option to put back the missing pieces as I have more experience now and can do it. I was so pleased with how it looked. Thanks for that.—*Participant*

Estelle B Breines explains that humans spend a lifetime acquiring new skills that can eventually be performed with some level of mastery. Once learned, they provide a foundation for creativity and new learning (in Schmid 2005, p. 63). Piaget's theories of development describe this process as one of assimilation and accommodation (Salkind 2004). Many of us learned about practice early in life and know it is necessary if we are to master skills. For some, however, it is a new concept; in the past, failures led participants to give up, many had cupboards full of unfinished projects. The artist encourages participants to work hard and practice, knowing that with time, each will acquire the skills necessary to achieve her creative desires. Eventually, all move from exercises to creating meaningful pieces of work (Figure 2).

Roberta Culbertson writes of her memory of childhood sexual abuse as being both a "known and felt truth" but fragmented and illogical and as such, the memory and complete truth seem "unreachable" (Culbertson 1995, p. 170). She refers to these memories as "fragmented" (p. 178) and "obey[ing] the logic of dreams" (p. 170). The "fleeting images" (p. 174), feelings of disquiet, profound sadness, and the inability to manage and cope well with life are among the residual effects of her abuse. She also notes that trauma memory, like art, functions on two levels, sense and thinking—consciousness, and the known and felt. Culbertson considers these feelings are "below the everyday and constructions of language" (p. 170). One participant describes her thoughts and memories as going "around and around in the tangle in my head". All the women in the groups had some difficulty forming thoughts around the impact of the childhood abuse then expressing them using words. By contrast, arts practice is formed in the material world. As art is both seen and felt, the recording of feeling, fragments, story and expression into materials, gives form is to the uncertain, incomplete, ephemeral or untested.

Figure 2. Me and my twin (Participant work)

Each piece of art is one step in a process of unknotting. I think of this creative exploration in the musical term 'adagio', happening at a slow walking pace. In three hours of relative quiet, where the only imperative is to make, a personal space opens to gently untangle those knots. One at a time, an idea, feeling, experience or relationship is examined through the materials and as participants work, they discover they are not overwhelmed by the veracity of their past. In a slow, thoughtful but gentle process of making, art reveals what previously had only been felt with great discomfort. "With explanation kind", as Emily Dickinson says, "the truth must dazzle gradually or every man be blind" (Dickinson 1929, 1995, p. 137).

> I really love the clay. It really allows you to "feel" in your body and I only got my ability to "feel" back a few years ago; hence it's big for me. Clay is also a wonderful thing because it helps me stay in the present rather than confusing memories which make you feel like you are right back in the past. With the clay you are made to acknowledge that you are alive, able-bodied, safe and no longer at risk!—*Participant*

Creativity is a free play of investigation, a process of thinking, especially intuitive thinking, which I consider, is the 'felt' aspect of making. It is a conversation between the inner self and the material. With clay, a beautifully responsive material, works appeared "from beneath my fingers exactly expressing what I wanted to say, even when I didn't know that was what I wanted to say" one participant declared. When McDonagh (2005) says that "artistic creations are not primarily useful, they enrich human living as ends in themselves" he understands the harmonious relationship between the maker and the material, each responsive to a process and neither one demanding. Many describe this process as 'flow'.

Working in a Group

Attachment theorists, such as Bowlby, Ainsworth and Harlow, describe that feeling safe, having trust in others and being able to emotionally self-regulate are amongst the long-term protective factors a child develops through secure attachment to primary caregivers, especially in the period 0-3 years (Harlow 1958;

Salkind 2004). Those who have had the benefit of a secure childhood attachment hold significant advantages over children brought up with insecure or ambivalent attachment styles. These participants as children, found themselves located on a fault-line with few protective factors available to guide them into and throughout their adult life. The personal cost of CSA is a flat existence, distinguished by many adverse outcomes including loneliness, depression and anxiety. "Sometimes I only go out when I have to. I would rather hide by myself. I don't even have any hobbies or interests", said one.

Recovery from abuse is an ongoing dynamic process across the lifespan and although for some a full recovery is unlikely, changes towards a positive and resilient functioning are possible and can be achieved through shared connections with others in the community (Phanichrat and Townshend 2010). Social support can influence an individual's reactions to stressful situations, "shape an individual's cognitive experience of a stressful situation, and potentially buffer them against negative reactions, including depression" (Powers, Ressler, & Bradley 2009, p. 47). The natural development of this crucial social support network through a shared interest in art is one reason why participation in a social art group helps participants recover. The exchanges, shared interests and challenges help build and practice their resilience and coping skills.

It is challenging and takes courage to participate in a group that nobody would ideally want to join. Although torn between the desire for company and the fear of 'the other', women are persuaded "to be part of something" by the benefits they perceived of artmaking and being in a group with others who have a shared experience of abuse. Many hope to find friends, even if only for the duration of the group. The myriad problems maltreated children confront include sensitivities to change, surprises, chaotic social situations, anxiety, ill-heath, he notes that even pleasant experiences could be overwhelming (Perry 2001, p. 8). I notice this trait has continued through to adulthood, nonetheless I am often surprised by the enthusiasm to join: "I am looking forward to it" even though "I will be a bit nervous".

> I knew it would be others like me in the group and the mosaic art aspect of it was something I always wanted to try. That was what actually made me go in the first place. Even though I started looking forward to Mondays, being around everyone gave me crazy mind for a few days.—*Participant*

Worries about making conversation, being competent, or "I judge myself too much" fall away with the desire to create and be well. Others recognize it takes time to settle in, "in the last few weeks especially I finally feel like I belong in the group. I find myself thinking how sad I will be when it's finished. I feel a real kinship with the women."

The atmosphere in the room is friendly, laughter regularly erupts, but it is also often quiet. It is warm and there is music. Most choose to have coffee whilst they work rather than stop for a break. These qualities add to the purposeful intent of the class. The focus and attention is always towards the work, thereby respecting the intention of all who come to create.

> Clay is powerful stuff for me, I don't realise how much until I get it in my hands and let my mind relax. What I was creating today could be confronting to other people. I nearly smashed it, but I am glad I did not; I don't think I have ever let myself go as much as I did with that group, powerful stuff. I needed another 3 hours to work through it all and might have ended up with another figure as well. It is still churning through my mind.—*Participant*

At first some want to withdraw. Regardless of the support in place, the anxiety of coming and being with others can be overwhelming; but for most "the desire to create overrides many of the feelings of flight", as one described it. Developing relationships with fellow participants, the artist, counsellor and the work helps strengthen the desire to participate, and builds resilience enough to withstand the frustrations and anxieties that emerge from time to time. Soon participants notice others interacting with them and responding favourably to their creativity; as work is met with acclaim and encouragement, fears fall away. Empowering aspects indeed of being part of a group built on strengths, as this participant describes:

> Another personal revelation that I gained from being a part of the art group was feeling equal to others because of my ability to finish tasks just like everyone else. If there's only one thing that the art group taught me it was that each and every person is as worthy as the next. Despite the fact that we are all unique beings; every person put on earth has a lot to contribute irrespective of their life experiences. And in coming to this realisation: I've made a promise to myself that I'll never give up on anything until I've given it a good try!—*Participant*

Art making can also be seen as a process of 'un-*not*-ing', of not accepting destructive interior and exterior voices of discrimination and belittlement. Words such as: "it was my fault", "you are hopeless" and "I am worthless" are shed as art making refocuses women towards normative activities. Un-*not*-ing happens when art reveals the truth. Un-*not*-ing allows individuals to flourish because in the art object a victim sees the past, present and their potential. Un-*not*-ing happens when women find comfort in community, or their "fictive kin", a term Jay Winter[2] uses to describe a group coming together through a shared experience. Amongst their fictive kin women talk, learn to be less fearful, build trust and relationships around a common interest then find other connections that are not wholly based on trauma.

> It also seems relatively more easy being in a group whereby you know others have been through similar things to yourself. I seem to feel safer to just let go if I need to. So often I feel SO alone with the problem; so knowing that there are others just makes it all seem so much more real if that makes any sense!—*Participant*

Working Together

The artworks I show to participants demonstrate how artists express their emotions, particularly the difficult ones, through their art. The bold, yet painfully expressive printed and charcoal works of German artist, Kathe Kollwitz[3] are a meditation on mothering and suffering. Kollwitz does not recoil from pain—her feelings are seen, felt and shared. She beautifully conveys her own suffering as well as the suffering of others in her community, and through her committed female perspective, is symbolically in conversation with other women who have also suffered (Kearns 1976; Prelinger 1992). Kollwitz's body of artwork is a helpful introduction to inexperienced viewers of art who find themselves able to understand and interpret it, then to draw on it as an inspiration for their own work. The dialogue between artist, artwork and viewer extends the invitation to victims to peer deeply into their experiences and feelings then express them in art.

In 2010 a group of women did just that when Kollwitz's print of a distraught woman became the inspiration of a collaborative work. A first step towards creating a group artwork is to invite individuals to draw ideas from artworks, nature and the imagination, then share their ideas and small works as they undertake the challenging task of finding the essence within them to create a new work which becomes a representation of the group.

One young woman found that the Kollwitz artwork helped articulate her own pain, as well as her growing coping mechanisms to self-sooth through nurturing her creativity. The artwork ignited a thoughtful group conversation: where can we find compassion and solace in suffering? Do we want to evoke feelings of kindness to ourselves, or would we rather express the anger and hurt of the trauma that brought the women to the group? As we discussed ideas for the design, a vision for compassion emerged; it seemed necessary to acknowledge that solace can be found through the kindness of others. But their vision for this collaborative work also included the desire to acknowledge the suffering of the child. Their suffering. A drawing of a small dress evoked the innocent child and was incorporated into the work to acknowledge that most present had been affected by childhood abuse (Figure 3).

Figure 3. Ironing Board (Group mosaic project)

Whilst this work allowed a generosity of spirit to prevail, and rejected any overarching belief of an inherent cruelty of others, it did not gloss over or avoid the abuse. Instead, drawing on the work of courageous artists, like Kollwitz, the women found the creative language to express and acknowledge a complex range of emotions. The final group work using the hand of every participant, honoured the past pain as well as individual creativity and kindness.

One fruitful outcome of participation is the number of friendships that grow and flourish beyond the life of the group; another is the small groups of women that form to create art after the formal group is over. "We do not talk about our problems, we chat, we work". These developments speak of the embodiment of both creativity and community.

When individuals integrate art into their 'outside life' they are demonstrating the positive value of creative practice, a developing sense of self-esteem and a growing ability to cope. I actively encourage homework and give participants materials, and sometimes a project, to pursue during the week. In this integrating stage, participants grow independent of me knowing they have the skills to make a satisfying work and importantly, knowing they have skills to cope when the artwork is not working well or they are having difficulties with technique. Women start to appreciate that creativity soothes and fills their life with purpose and meaning. Gradually art takes over and that means a trip to hardware and art shops:

> Today I shall go buy some timber for the base of a mosaic. I will see what I can come up with. I take life far too seriously at times and I hope to have fun with this.—*Participant*

Women also integrate experiences of the art group and working at home with the discussions they have with their therapists. In this exchange below the participant verbalises how art helped her achieve goals that had clearly been raised in counselling. It is an example of how different interventions but with similar ambitions, can work separately and collaboratively:

> As you know, I went to the hardware shop and bought some tile nippers and tiles for my beach mosaic. The fact that I actually cared enough to go and do that was massive for me. It said a whole lot because I am often very quick to give up or not believe I am capable like other people. My self-esteem is very low. So... Me going out and caring enough to invest in a project such as mosaic was the turning point.

> Doing this art group has been one of the best things I've ever done. It helps me focus on things other than flashbacks and gives me hope that I will lead a purposeful life. I feel very supported and thoroughly enjoy doing the group. I don't know if I will be as emotionally in control as yesterday each time but all I know is that I always try my hardest to stay in the here and now!—*Participant*

I am always delighted when women tell me that they have been making art with children and friends, or they have neglected the dishes in order to finish a mosaic! But I am especially impressed to hear that a spare bedroom or shed has been cleared to set up a studio space. "I actually feel that l can mosaic here at home and am going to re-adjust the shed for space for me this week" reveals a participant. I see it as a step towards claiming a life beyond trauma. For some, it is asking others to respect her desires; claiming personal space for her own needs is, as Virginia Woolf would argue, necessary for women (Woolf 1928 2002). These revelations usually begin with "you will be pleased to know Anne...." and I always am.

The more powerful our dreams, the more beautiful the transformations: Beautiful here is the knowledge that art empowers women victims of CSA to step out into the world with a renewed vision of herself as a creative, social and competent human being. The perfect un-*not*-ting. Each had overcome some of the indignations that brought her to the group and some lives are unrecognisable from what they were only a few months or years ago... women are creating, working, exhibiting. Women have taken up tertiary education, teach art to community groups, have moved out of unhealthy relationships whilst others have felt secure enough to leave home and become independent. Many have developed strong and meaningful relationships, and all have had to become accustomed to receiving praise for their artworks, as one said "I will continue with the mosaics as I find it calming. I don't want to go back to always watching life from behind the curtains. It's lonely."

References

1. Southern Health is the largest public health provider in Victoria, Australia.
2. Jay Winter. Arts Public Lecture I—War and Remembranceat the Shrine of Remembrance Melbourne. 21 May 2007, attended by the author.
3. Kathe Kollwitz (1867-1945) became interested in social issues when very young; after her marriage to Dr Karl Kollwitz, the artist moved to Berlinwhere she came into direct contact with the industrial poor who become the subject of her ongoing work. The death of her son in the First World War became a catalyst for questioning her country, herself and war; the memorial she created to mourn him (The Parents) and the countless others who died in the war, is located in the Vladslo German Military Cemetery, Belgium (visited by the author). It took 18 years to create—a salient reminder of how long the grieving process can take. Although a highly regarded artist and teacher for most of her life, in 1937, her work was considered "Degenerate Art"by the Nazis and it was was no longer possible to continue teaching and her studio practice became increasingly difficult under this regime (Prelinger, 1992)

Works Cited

Adams, D., & Goldbard, A. (2001). *The Art of Cultural Development*. New York: The Rockerfeller Foundation.

Anthony, W. A. (1993). Recovery from Mental Illness: The guiding vision of the mental health service system in the 1990s. *Psychosocial Rehabilitation Journal,* 16(4), 11-23.

Boyce, P., & Harris, A. (2011). Childhood adversity, trauma and abuse: context and consequences. *Australian and New Zealand Journal of Psychiatry,* 45, 608-610.

Briere, J. N. (1992). *Child Abuse Trauma. Theory and treatment of the lasting effects.* London, New Delhi: Sage Publications.

Culbertson, R. (1995). Embodied Memory, Transcendence and Telling: Recounting Trauma, Re-establishing the Self. *New Literary History, 26*(No.1 Winter), 169-195.

Dickinson, E. (1929, 1995). The Pocket Emily Dickinson. In B. Hillman (Ed.), *Shambhala Pocket Classics.* Boston: Shambhala Publications.

Finkelhor, D., & Browne, A. (1985). The Traumatic Impact of Child Sexual Abuse: A conceptualization. *American Journal of Orthopsychiatry,* 55 (4), 530-541.

Francis, A. (2012). *Journey towards Recovery in Mental Health.*

Harlow, H. F. (1958). The Nature of Love. *American Psychologist,* 13, 673-685. Retrieved from http://psychclassics.yorku.ca website:

Herman, J. (1992). *Trauma and Recovery. The aftermath of violence—from domestic abuse to political terror.* New York: Basic Books.

Kearns, M. (1976). *Kathe Kollwitz: Woman and Artist.* New York: The Feminist Press and The City University.

Lewis, A., & Doyle, D. (Eds.). (2008). *Proving the Practice: Evidencing the Effects of Community Arts Programs on Mental Health.* Fremantle: Disability in the Arts Disadvantage in the Arts Australia (DADAA).

McDonagh, E. (2005). Give beauty back: art, morality and mission: for Vincent MacNamara. This article is an extract from Enda McDonagh's Immersed in Mystery: en route to Theology, published by Veritas Publications. 2008. Retrieved from http://www.catholicireland.net website:

Mudaly, N. (2012). It takes me a little longer to get angry now. Animal assisted education and therapy group. A preliminary evaluation. *Child Abuse Prevention Research Australia*: WAYSS Limited.

Overstreet, S., & Mathews, T. (2011). Challenges associated with exposure to chronic trauma: using a public health framework to foster resilient outcomes among youth. *Psychology in the Schools,* 48(7), 738-754.

Perry, B. D. (2001). Bonding and Attachment in Maltreated Children. Consequences of Emotional Neglect in Childhood. Retrieved from http://www.ChildTrauma.org website:

_____. (2009). Examining Child Maltreatment Through a Neurodevelopmental Lens: Clinical Applications of the Neurosequential Model of Therapeutics. *Journal of Loss and Trauma, 14,* 240-255.

_____, & Pollard, R. (1998). Homeostasis, Stress, Trauma, and Adaption. A Neurodevelopmental View of Childhood Trauma. *Child and Adolescent Psychiatric Clinics of North America,* 7(1), 33-51.

_____, Blakely, T. L., Baker, W. L., & Vigilante, D. (1995). Childhood Trauma, the Neurobiology of Adaption, and "Use-dependent" Development of the Brain: How "States" Become "Traits". *Infant Mental Health Journal,* 16(4), 271-291.

Phanichrat, T., & Townshend, J. M. (2010). Coping Strategies Used by Survivors of Childhood Sexual Abuse on the Journey to Recovery. *Journal of Child Sexual Abuse,* 19, 62-78.

Powers, A., Ressler, K. J., & Bradley, R. G. (2009). The protective role of friendship on the effects of childhood abuse and depression. *Depression and Anxiety,* 26, 46-53.

Prelinger, E. (1992). *Kathe Kollwitz. National Gallery of Art, Washington.* New Haven, London: Yale University Press.

Riggs, A. (2010). *The Creative Space. Art and Wellbeing in the Shadow of Trauma, Loss and Grief.* (PhD), Victoria University.

Salkind, N. J. (2004). *An Introduction to Theories of Human Development.* Thousand Oaks, London and New Delhi: Sage Publication.

Schmid, T. (Ed.). (2005). *Promoting Health Through Creativity. For professionals in health, arts and education.* London and Philadelphia: Whurr Publishers.

Services, D. o. H. (2012). *Good Practice: A Statewide Snapshot, 2012.* Melbourne: Victorian Government

van der Kolk, B. A., McFarlane, A. C., & Weisaeth, L. (1996). *Traumatic Street. The Effects of Overwhelming Experience of Mind, Body and Society.* New York: Guildford Press.

Walsh, K., Blaustein, M., Knight, W. G., Spinazzola, J., & Kolk, B. A. v. d. (2007). Resiliency Factors in the Relation Between Childhood Sexual Abuse and Adult Sexual Assault in College-Age Women. *Journal of Child Sexual Abuse,* 16(1).

Winter, J. (1995). *Sites of Memory, Sites of Mourning. the Treat War in European cultural history.* Cambridge: Cambridge University Press.

Woolf, V. (1928, 2002). *A Room of One's Own.* London: Penguin Classics.

CHAPTER 9

Resiliency and Recovery from Intimate Partner Violence

Linda A. Douglas

Abstract

The cumulative effects of long-term abuse at the hands of a caretaker or intimate partner can often be devastating and lead to ongoing problems in relationships, daily living, and planning for the future. Gender specific trauma responsive services enhance the capacity to assist survivors and recognize the intrinsic resiliency factors that contribute to recovery. This chapter will introduce the reader to current literature on gender specific trauma responsive services, and how trauma affects the brain and worldview of victim/survivors, followed by a discussion of how resiliency factors into a person's ability to recover from the trauma of childhood abuse and domestic violence. The author will use anecdotal examples to illustrate how and why some victims of abuse are able to recover and thrive after years of abuse. Theories of attachment and resiliency models along with an understanding of the spiritual aspects of a survivor's recovery will be discussed. The author will also look at how the development of gender-specific trauma responsive services specifically for persons presenting with substance abuse and mental health issues has led to a new paradigm that supports and develops resiliency while meeting the challenges of recovery.

Key Words

Trauma, recovery, substance abuse, resiliency, spirituality, attachment, trauma-responsive services, meaning-making, brain response to trauma.

In speaking with women in long-term recovery from alcohol abuse, I often ask why one might refer to herself as a "grateful recovering alcoholic" rather than as an "alcoholic" as so many others do in the 12-Step meetings she attends. The usual reply is, "because I truly am grateful. I am not grateful for being in recovery. I am grateful for having had the experiences that led me to be in recovery. I am grateful for the all the reasons that I was led to drink in the first place, for it is because of those things that I have been given the gift of being in recovery and a part of a 12-Step program. I am a better person for being an alcoholic and finding recovery than I would be if I had never had a drink at all."

This personal reflection upon life and its path to recovery illustrates resiliency in its truest form. In one of its definitions, resiliency is defined as the power or ability to return to the original form (IAC Corp, n.d.). For someone who has experienced intimate partner violence and possibly used drugs or alcohol to cope with the effects of the traumatic experiences, resiliency is more of a journey to one's true self, the person that lies beneath the years of trauma. It is through coming to terms with the abuse via a new understanding of how trauma affects the brain, making meaning of one's experience, and the ability to forgive one's self and possibly others that a person can find the ability to be resilient in the face of adversity.

Normal Reaction to Abnormal Experiences

Recent developments in understanding how the brain functions during traumatic events give us a broader understanding as to how intimate partner violence rewires the brain, causing long-term effects. The brain has a built-in stress response that releases hormones, including norepinephrine and cortisol, during times of increased stress and danger. Norepinephrine prepares the body for fight or flight by focusing attention, increasing heart rate and blood pressure, and raising the level of fear. This occurs in the amygdala, the area of the brain responsible for survival and emotions. However, this response also significantly decreases brain efficiency in terms of being able to process information and make logical decisions if the system has been flooded with the epinephrine and cortisol too often and for long periods of time. Other areas of the brain experience changes in neural processes during and after traumatic events that can affect the brain's ability to integrate and retrieve memories. These responses to trauma also affect emotional responses in social situations and the ability to relate to others (Bremner 2004).

In *Wounds That Time Won't Heal: The Neurobiology of Child Abuse*, Martin H. Teicher (2000) discusses the long-term impact of abuse. Children who are exposed to long-term and severe abuse, either emotional or physical/sexual, develop responses such as a persistent fear response, hyperarousal, dissociation and disrupted attachment (inability to form relationships). Neural pathways have formed to enable these responses as a means of surviving the impact of the trauma. However, these responses also result in increased susceptibility to stress, excessive help-seeking and dependency or excessive social isolation, and the inability to regulate emotions. The effects are cumulative and can lead to life-long difficulties in interpersonal relationships.

Some of the specific long-term effects of abuse and neglect on the developing brain can include (Teicher 2000): diminished growth in the left hemisphere, which may increase the risk for depression; irritability in the limbic system, setting the stage for the emergence of panic disorder or post-traumatic stress disorder; smaller growth in the hippocampus and limbic abnormalities (areas of emotions and memories in the brain), which can increase the risk for dissociative disorders and memory impairments; and in the connection between the two brain hemispheres, which has been linked to symptoms of attention-deficit/hyperactivity disorder.

The obvious behavioral response to danger is to get away from it, to stop it, to find a way to protect oneself or others. The signals from our body combine with past memories of danger, current choices, long-standing habits of behavior, and the influence of others around us. Because fear conditioning is so potent, even one experience with danger can result in the development of habits that may or may not be effective under circumstances that are different from the original danger (Bloom 1997).

Complex trauma, the multiple traumatic episodes that occurred over a long period of time, can reduce a person's ability to respond to perceived danger in a productive way. In addition, how the trauma is perceived by one's culture can impact the victim's resiliency. If a person receives consistent validation of the emotional and physical results of abuse and has family, community, and cultural support she is more than likely able to engage in activities that reduce the impact of the stress hormones that were engaged during the traumatic events. However, if there is little support to stop the ongoing sexual, physical and emotional violence that is being perpetrated against her, she will continue to be under the influence of the activity that is occurring in her neural processes and will respond as if she is in constant danger.

Neural pathways are continuously being reformed in response to the environment. As a person continues to experience trauma, more neural pathways that respond to the trauma are formed. This occurs to the detriment of the parts of the brain that regulate logic and reason. Survival is dependent on being able to react to violence in the moment without taking time to logically process. If we "thought" about braking when we saw danger in the middle of the road, we would more than likely hit the obstacle. Our brain is designed for acting when in danger and thinking when safety is assured. However, if the stress is constant, cognitive processes become secondary to survival even when danger is not actually present. The brain is working under the assumption that danger is constantly imminent (Bremner 2004).

Covington and Kohen (1984) stated research shows that a vast majority of addicted women have suffered violence and others forms of abuse. Furthermore, a history of being abused drastically increases the likelihood that a woman will abuse alcohol and other drugs. One of the most important developments in health care over the past several decades is the recognition that a history of serious traumatic experience plays an often-unrecognized role in a woman's physical and mental health (Messina & Grella 2006; Fellitti et al. 1998 as cited by Covington 2008). Given the amount of arousal that is occurring in the brain as part of the ongoing reaction to previous trauma, it is not surprising many survivors identify with this statement of a childhood abuse survivor with whom I met in 2008, "I am not addicted to heroin. I am addicted to *not* feeling my feelings" (personal client notes: used with permission). Survivors of trauma are often ridiculed for their use of alcohol and drugs as a means of controlling their hyper-aroused state. Resiliency, at this point, is the survivor's ability to find a means of surviving the emotions, even if it is non-productive in the long-term. Without access to safety, trustworthy relationships and an opportunity to tell their story in a validating and supportive environment, alcohol and drugs may remain the survivor's only means of relief.

The Roots of Resiliency—Attachment and Safety

Bunce and Rickards (2004) discuss the importance of early attachment and safety in the development of resiliency. Not just a matter of constitutional strength, resilience is a product of how people meet stresses and challenges. Secure attachments, absence of early loss and trauma, and easy temperament are factors that are associated with resilience. A child's ability to cope with his own emotions and those of others is impacted by early abuse or other traumas. However, if a strong attachment can develop to a responsive figure that is not a part of the traumatic situation, he or she may be able to develop the ability to manage relationships in positive and productive ways.

Often, when meeting with a survivor who is using a number of productive coping skills and is internally directed to create a new life free from further abuse, I will ask about previous relationships that were not abusive and controlling in nature. One young woman, a survivor of childhood abuse perpetrated by her mother and adult intimate partner violence, expressed gratitude for having spent the first thirteen years of her life with her grandmother, a woman who is also a survivor. The woman and her grandmother are in regular contact although separated by many miles. This young woman is able to see that her strengths have been identified and nurtured in this relationship even though her adolescence was turbulent and she participated in drug use with her mother. Now, a parent herself, the woman is able to draw on the strength she receives from her grandmother and uses her grandmother as a moral compass, a north star as she navigates her way into adulthood (personal client notes: used with permission).

Another woman, a childhood sexual assault survivor who is managing the ongoing turmoil resulting from her own daughter's sexual assault, often speaks of her anger towards her mother for not acknowledging the abuse that was perpetrated by another family member. However, when asked about the relationship that has been most positive in her life, the survivor immediately responds that it is her mother. "It wasn't all bad," she states. "My mother taught me a lot about gardening and we did a lot together. Just because she didn't acknowledge the abuse then or now, does not mean she is all bad" (personal client notes: used with permission). The survivor is not giving her mother a free pass. She is able to move out of her own pain and recognize that there are aspects of their relationship that were nurturing and productive. As she is working to forgive herself for her perceived failure to protect her own daughter she is able to expand that capacity to others, if only partially. In her book *Enhancing Resiliency in Survivors of Family Violence* (2010) Anderson states the practice of compassion and unconditional love needs to begin with the survivors themselves as they work toward embracing their "broken places" with love and gentleness rather than judgment.

Self-forgiveness for many survivors, includes choosing to not be destructive to self or others while moving beyond attaching their worth and identity to their victimization.

In their chapter on Resilience over the Lifespan in the *Handbook of Adult Resilience* (2010) Masten and Wright state that research also documents that one-fourth to one half of children exposed parental abuse and neglect show positive psychosocial functioning upon follow-up. In their longitudinal study of children born on the Isle of Wight, Collishaw and colleagues (2007) found that although intelligence and gender were not associated with later resilience in children who had experienced maltreatment, a number of critical interpersonal relationships were predictive of later resilience. Having a least one caring parent, positive peer relation and stable adult love relationships were important in developing resilience. Severity, duration, and context of the abuse were also associated with increased risk of later difficulty.

Judith Herman, in *Trauma and Recovery* (1992), states that the core experiences of psychological trauma are disempowerment and disconnection from others. Recovery, therefore, is based upon the empowerment of the survivor and the creation of new connections. Recovery can take place only within the context of relationships; it cannot occur in isolation. In her renewed connections with other people, the survivor re-creates the psychological faculties that were damaged or deformed by the traumatic experience. These faculties include the basic capacities for trust, autonomy, initiative, competence, identity and intimacy. Just as these capabilities are originally formed in relationships with other people they must be reformed in such relationships.

By engaging in safe relationships with providers such as therapists, doctors, social workers, domestic violence and sexual assault program advocates, a survivor can learn that she can be safe in relationships and will eventually be empowered to expand her network to include other people with whom she feels safe.

Having knowledge of the impact of trauma on a survivor provides the groundwork for those working with a survivor to be able to empower her to make safe choices. It is difficult, if not impossible, for a survivor to make safe and productive choices when she is engaged in ongoing neurological trauma responses. However, nurturance of innate resiliency within trusting relationships provides the survivor with a means of developing new and productive responses to the trauma.

Judith Herman describes the journey to recovery from trauma as occurring in three stages. Not to be taken too literally, Dr. Herman describes the first stage as the establishment of safety and the second stage as remembrance of the event and mourning the loss of the person the trauma survivor was before it occurred. In Herman's third stage of recovery from trauma, the survivor has regained some capacity for appropriate trust. She is able to determine when a person is worthy of her trust and when they are not. She is able to feel autonomous while remaining connected to others and can maintain her own point of view and boundaries while respecting those of others. She is able to take more initiative and creates a new identity to replace the one she lost. Her relationships contain more intimacy and depth.

Spiritual Resiliency and Finding Meaning

Reclaiming an identity of strength, courage and resilience requires analyzing survivors' stories for moments of triumph in an attempt to encourage the person to "reauthor" her life emphasizing these positive experiences. Just as trauma shatters assumptions about being invulnerable and self-determining, it also alters individuals' beliefs in a Higher Power and notions about a safe, orderly, and just world. Spiritual concerns such as the sources of faith and doubt, hope and despair, belonging and isolation are relevant in many survivors' lives (Gotterer 2001).

When survivors grasp meaning and see one's life as purposeful, their perceptions of esteem and control are likely to increase allowing for a sense of well-being (Tedeschi & Calhoun 1996). People are harmed by violence and one does not have to endure being choked, beaten, or raped to find meaning and purpose in life. Yet even under these ominous conditions, life still holds meaning (Frankl 1984; Kushner 1981).

The following story relates the movement from victim to survivor and beyond that took place in a woman, Tamara (a pseudonym), who experienced extreme abuse as a child.

> There really is no secret to who I am and why. Yes, I had some rather awful experiences. Sexually assaulted from ages 6 to 11 and then having the violent home that prevented me from even voicing what was happening to me was almost an ending for me. I struggled in my teens and tried to kill myself twice. My first marriage was to a man I barely knew. He asked and I saw it as a means of escape since it meant moving to another city. Marriage was not a great idea but it was the first stepping stone to get me on the right path.
>
> I didn't turn it around until I got pregnant two years after getting married. Having another little person that was depending on me had me take a good hard look at myself and realize I had choices that needed to be made. During all of my growing up years I was powerless and had choices made for me. Bad ones. I wasn't going to let that happen to my daughter. So...I made a choice. I could either let the abuse define me in a way that continued to make me a victim to it, or I could let it define me as a survivor. I chose the latter. It was around this time that I found my personal relationship with God to which also gave me the strength and perseverance for the changes and choices to be made. Many of those choices began with pruning certain relationships out of my life. I didn't want to be stuck in the rut of dysfunction that was blanketing my life for so many years. Turning off the tapes that ran in my head about how I was worthless and would never amount to anything had to be erased and replaced with life affirming messages. I had to learn and believe in my own self-worth. Being the genuine me and seeing what people responded favorably to was how I developed new relationships. No more chameleon existence. I used what happened to me to help others. I have started a couple of support groups within my church and I am also a part of a recovery community called Celebrate Recovery

(a Christ-centered recovery program). I could go on and on about all the different changes and choices that had to be made. There was no magic pill but just a dogged determination that the bad cycle would end with me and that my children would know and do better. And praise God my kids are doing GREAT and there isn't a soul out there that doesn't sing their praises once they meet them. I consider my life a success in that way.

Anyone that knows me knows that I am the glass half-full to over flowing kind of person. I don't like the word 'can't' and won't tell anyone why they can't do something but will always help them find ways they can. Sometimes that annoys the hell out of people.

The road has been bumpy but it has also been worthwhile. I am a strong woman because of what I endured. I am also compassionate because of it. Hey, I am able to say good things about my self....how cool is that?

So...I guess the first choice was to not be a victim anymore. I was one for a while even after the abuses stopped simply because I felt sorry for myself and wanted the world to feel sorry for me too. I love the day I picked myself up off of the dirt and brushed myself off and decided that no one...ever...was going to have me feeling low as dirt ever again. I used what happened to me as an empowering tool. And I was the kind of parent to my children that I never had. My daughter and I were chatting this morning and she said to me that growing up we may not have had a lot materially but we never realized it because we were loved so much. That made me cry. She is going to be a great mom to my grandbaby. So the other big choice—love with all my heart and being those important in my life and try to show love to all others as well."

In addition to making the conscious decision to move beyond victimhood to survivor, Tamara chose to embark on a spiritual journey and relationship with her God that led to the ability to make meaning out of her childhood abuse and become of help to others who have also experienced trauma and tragedy. Park and Folkman (1997) stated that non-religious people might question the survivor's belief in a just world when it appears that innocent people suffer. They go on to suggest that resiliency is related to the person's ability to reappraise the negative event positively. In the religious context, this might be achieved by concluding that God has a purpose for allowing the suffering to occur.

This appears to depend on how the relationship with God is established. Yangarger-Hicks's study (2004) of individuals diagnosed with serious mental illness revealed that those who lent more importance to religion also reported greater feelings of empowerments as long as they were not 'waiting for God to solve problems and asking for a miracle.' However, working *with* God toward recovery was associated with greater empowerment.

Making meaning out of one's suffering is also a pathway to supporting other's in their recovery from abuse. It is the recognition of other's pain that decreases the loneliness and despair associated with loss. This is illustrated in Phillip Moffitt's (2012) description of the Buddhist parable of the mustard seed in his book, *Emotional Chaos to Clarity* (pp. 253-254).

When a life has been lost or great physical or mental damage done, there is no going back; there is only going forward. I you hold on to a personal claim because of what you lost, you assume the identity of the victim. It may see right and proper, but oftentimes it is just another form of self-imprisonment. In the parable of the mustard seed, a distraught mother comes to the Buddha with her dead child in her arms, pleading with him to bring her child back to life.

The Buddha says he will do so if she can bring him a mustard seed from a household that has not known death. The woman frantically goes from house to house, asking if they have not known death, until finally she realizes that all households have known death, and she is able to accept that great loss is a part of life.

Enhancing Resiliency with Trauma-Responsive Services

Stephanie Covington (2008) states that as the understanding of traumatic experiences increases among clinicians, mental health theories and practices are changing, it is important for service providers to understand trauma theory as a conceptual framework for clinical practice and to provide trauma-informed services for their clients.

According to Harris & Fallot (2001), trauma-informed services do the following:

- Take the trauma into account.
- Avoid triggering trauma reactions or re-traumatizing person.
- Adjust the behavior of counselors and staff members to support the woman's coping capacity.
- Allow survivors to manage their trauma symptoms successfully so that they are able to access, retain, and benefit from the services (cited by Covington 2008).

Susan Reider, when interviewed by *UnCensored*, states that "trauma-informed care starts with the premise that clients have had some form of trauma in their lives and that the trauma often impacts the way they access or respond to services. It impacts the way people make sense of their surroundings, and it influences how they form relationships. Trauma-informed care provides services and sets up systems to help trauma survivors regain a sense of safety and stability in the world (p. 4)."

Uncensored quotes Chrys Ballerano as saying "by helping people distinguish between the patterns that helped them survive during the time of traumatic experience and the present, we can help them see their strength and success in having survived. We can acknowledge their ability to survive painful, sometimes brutal experiences and honor them by thanking them for sharing their story, acknowledging the privilege of being trusted with their story, and helping them see their dignity in the present time. For some, this is a huge contradiction of anything they have ever been told or shown. Simple saying to the person, 'I am sorry this happened to you. It was not your fault,' and thanking them for telling you about it can be incredibly healing for the survivor (p. 5)."

It is often through assisting the survivor in understanding that it is not what is wrong with them but what was done to them that opens up their willingness to explore their own resiliency. Focusing on the survivor's resourcefulness draws on her resilience and allows for alternative ways to work with clients that honors their strengths as opposed to their deficits (Anderson, p. 88). Anderson goes on to say that the answer differs for each individual; however, some commonalities include an improved evaluation of self (e.g., stronger, more compassionate), a more profound understanding of the world (e.g., life is not easy thus to be human is to suffer), and a great life purpose (e.g., breaking the cycle of violence, helping other survivors) (p. 119).

Conclusion

In discussing resiliency and providing trauma-responsive services it is important to remember that resiliency is not a tool to be taught or endowed upon the person who has suffered from the trauma of violence perpetrated by another. Resiliency is an innate trait that exists within the individual as a tree nut contains the full capacity of the tree. It is through the nurturance and support of others that the person can eventually come to recognize their own self-worth, resilient nature, and ability to engage with and support others who are also recovering from extreme loss and suffering. The goal of the counselor, advocate, or facilitator is to provide the fertile soil within which to nurture that innate resiliency, allowing the person's roots to take firm hold on their recovery and join with others to create a bond of strength and trust.

Works Cited

Anderson, Kim M. (2010) *Enhancing Resilience in Survivors of Family Violence.* New York: Springer.

Bloom, Sandra L. (1997). *Creating Sanctuary: Toward the Evolution of Sane Societies*. New York: Routledge,

Bremner, J. D. (2004). "Does Stress Damage the Brain? Understanding Trauma-related Disorders from a Mind-body Perspective." *Directions In Psychiatry* 24.15, 167-76.

Bunce, Maureen, & Rickards, A. (2004), *Working with Bereaved Children: A Guide*.,, Essex, U.K., University of Essex, Children's Legal Centre.

Collishaw, S., Pickles, A., Messer, J., Rutter, M., Shearer, C., & Maugham, B. (2007). "Resilience to adult psychopathology following childhood maltreatment: Evidence from a community sample," *Child Abuse & Neglect, 31,* 211-229.

Covington, Stephanie S. (2008) "Women and Addiction: A Trauma-Informed Approached." *Journal of Psychoactive Drugs*. 377-85.

Covington, Stephanie S., & Kohen J.(1984). "Women, Alcohol and sexuality." *Advances in Alcohol and Substance Abuse* (1984): 4(1), 41-56.

Felitti, V.J.; Anda, R.F.; Nordenberg, D.; Williamson, D.F.; Spitz, A.M.; Edwards, V.; Koss, M.P. & Marks, J.S. (1998). Relationship of childhood abuse and household dysfunction to many of the leading causes of death in adults: The adverse childhood experiences (ACE) study. *American Journal of Preventive Medicine* 14 (4): 245-58.

Frankl, V.E. (1984). *Man's Search for Meaning*. New York: Pocket Books.

Gotterer, R. (2001). The spiritual dimension in clinical social work practice: A client perspective. *Families in Society*, 82(3), 187-193.

Herman, Judith Lewis. *Trauma and Recovery*. (1992), New York, Harper Collins.

IAC Corporation (n.d.) Resilience definition. Retrieved from http://dictionary.reference.com/browse/resilience June, 2012.

Kushner, H.S. (1981). *When bad things happen to good people*. New York: HarperCollins.

Masten, Ann S., and Margaret O. Write. (2010) "Resilience over the Lifespan." *Handbook of Adult Resilience*. New York: Guilford, 213-37.

Messina, N. & Grella, C. (2006). Childhood trauma and women's health outcomes: A California prison population. *American Journal of Public Health,* 96 (10): 1842-48.

Moffitt, Phillip. (2012) *Emotional Chaos to Clarity: How to Live More Skillfully, Make Better Decisions, and Find Purpose in Life*. New York: Hudson Street.

Park, C.L., & Folkman, S. (1997). Meaning in the context of stress and coping. *Review of General Psychology,* 1(2), 115-144.

Reich, John W., Alex Zautra, and John Stuart Hall. (2010). *Handbook of Adult Resilience*. New York: Guilford.

Tedeschi, R.G., & Calhoun, L.G. (1995). *Trauma & Transformation: Growing in the aftermath of suffering*. Newbury Park, CA: SAGE Publications.

Teicher, M. D. (2000). "Wounds That Time Won't Heal: The Neurobiology of Child Abuse." *Cerebrum: He Dana Forum on Brain Science* 2.4, 50-67.

"Trauma-informed Care: Services That Heal." *Uncensored* Journal 3.1 (2012): 4. Print.

Yangarber-Hicks, N. (2004). Religious coping styles and recovery from serious mental illnesses. *Journal of Psychology and Theology, 32*(4), 305-317.

CHAPTER 10

Resistance to Resilience: Addiction, Co-dependency and Doing Life Differently

Sharalyn Drayton

Abstract

Addiction and co-dependence are destructive and potentially devastating diseases. They are diseases which ultimately lead to a sense of powerlessness and place of hopelessness. When the ability to cope is gone the addict or co-dependent is generally left with two choices: continue to try and manage the addiction or relationship (which is ultimately not possible), or give up and seek change. Either way it is a difficult situation. It has been hypothesised that addiction starts and ends in the brain (Allen 2008, p.15) and this paper will seek to explore the power of the brain and the body to change a negative, self defeating behaviour and belief system into an opportunity for growth and healing. It will look at how the negative experiences of the past can provide valuable clues which help to develop resilience and lead to a life where the ability to cope is increased and a sense of hope restored. As such it will use the metaphor of 'stretching', which the Collins dictionary (1987) defines as "to be drawn out or extended...to be capable of expanding" to describe how this psychological and physiological stretching increases resilience builds hope and increases the ability to cope.

For people in recovery from addiction and co-dependence learning to embrace the uncomfortable stretch which comes from reprogramming neural pathways, using both mind and body, is a vital tool which helps with positive long term outcomes. (Rothschild 2000, p. xiii-xiv). However, one doesn't need to be or have been an addict, or be caught in the grip of some life denying experience to appreciate that there are things which stop us from moving forward and from achieving our goals and dreams. Learning to change our thinking and behaviour can be challenging and uncomfortable. It requires an elasticity of mind and the willingness to be stretched beyond that which is familiar and feels safe, but which is ultimately limiting and self defeating. The possibilities are enormous when we learn to see and embrace our potential rather than our shortcomings.

Key Words

Addiction, brain, change, resilience, healing, stretch, co-dependence

Introduction

Addiction and co-dependence are destructive and potentially devastating diseases. They are diseases which ultimately lead to a sense of powerlessness and place of hopelessness. When the ability to cope is gone the addict or co-dependent is generally left with two choices; continue to try and manage the addiction or relationship (which is ultimately not possible), or give up and seek change. Either way it is a difficult situation. It has been hypothesised that addiction starts and ends in the brain (Allen 2008, p.15) and this paper will seek to explore the power of the brain and the body to change a negative, self-defeating behaviour and belief system into an opportunity for growth and healing. It will look at how the negative experiences of the past which create resistance to change can provide valuable clues which help to develop resilience and lead to a life where the ability to cope is increased and a sense of hope restored. As such it will use the metaphor of 'stretching', which the Collins dictionary (1987) defines as "to be drawn out or extended…to be capable of expanding" to describe how this psychological and physiological stretching increases resilience.

Research shows that athletes seeking to improve muscle strength train at various degrees of intensity, working (or stretching) the muscle to the point of soreness and then allowing time for the muscle to recover. In this process the muscle can "withstand higher loads and is more resistant to injury". (Mirkin www.drmirkin.com) Similarly for people in recovery from addiction and co-dependence learning to embrace the uncomfortable stretch which comes from reprogramming neural pathways, using both mind and body as vital tools will help with positive long-term outcomes. (Rothschild 2000, p.xiii-xiv). Stretching the mental, emotional and spiritual muscles to a level that is uncomfortable helps this reprogramming, improves the ability to cope and develops greater resilience.

Addiction is defined as a disease with "spiritual, emotional and physical components...which is characterised by an inability to consistently abstain, impairment in behavioural control, craving, diminished recognition of significant problems with ones behaviours and interpersonal relationships, and a dysfunctional emotional response. Addiction is progressive and can result in disability or premature death". (South Pacific Private Hospital (SPP), 2012, p.23). Co-dependence is defined as "a chronic condition impacting family systems across generations and is characterised by unhealthy family and personal relationships." (SPP. 2012, p.12). Addiction can also be described as anything over which we are powerless. It is the thing we are unwilling to give up and that we may feel we need to lie about, cover up or deny (Schaef 1987, p.18). Addiction and co-dependence often work together. It could be said, therefore, that to some degree or another we are all either co-dependant or addicted and the world in which we live is itself an addictive system which exhibits all the characteristics and symptoms of the individual addict (Wilson Schaef 1987, p.4). Changing our beliefs and learning to live in a way which enables us to be more conscious of the choices we make, and decide whether they will help or hinder us, will therefore be empowering on a number of different levels.

One doesn't need to be or have been an addict or be caught in the grip of some life denying experience to appreciate that there are things which stop us from moving forward and from achieving our goals and dreams. Learning to change our thinking and behaviour can be challenging and uncomfortable. It requires an elasticity of mind and the willingness to be stretched beyond that which is familiar and feels safe, but which is ultimately limiting and self-defeating. For many this brings the same fear which is experienced when entering any unknown territory. Like learning any new skill it takes time, commitment, practice, guidance and support. The things that have kept us back and held us in our painful spaces need to be reappraised, and life as we knew it needs to be looked at from an entirely different perspective. Work carried out in the field of co-dependence helps us understand that the things that brought us to the point of collapse can be turned around and can in fact become our allies. These negative beliefs or experiences can in turn become the clues that lead us into a healthy and whole understanding of how we have been and who we can become. The possibilities expand significantly when we learn to see and embrace our potential rather than our shortcomings.

Understanding Ourselves

For many people, living in a fast-paced media-driven world can feel unpredictable and uncontrollable and this can create a level of fear and uncertainty which can be difficult to live with. We are all, to some extent or another, intent on keeping ourselves safe, however when we become controlled by fear our lives are governed by the need to protect ourselves at all cost. In the effort to keep ourselves safe we often avoid facing our fear, and can become so focused on avoiding what we fear that we ultimately abandon ourselves and cease to believe in the reality of our own abilities and desires. Instead, we become caught up in the (often subconscious) belief that we are not 'worth it' and that we don't really deserve the happiness or success we think we see around us. When we envy others because we believe that they have more than we do, or that it is easier for others than it is for us, the belief that we are disadvantaged and not really worthy of success or happiness is reinforced and the cycle of self-abandonment continues. From this inaccurate thinking comes pain, anger, resentment and a sense of hopelessness leading to a life which must, by necessity, become smaller in order to make it more manageable and controllable. In this process it is easy to shut out the things that make us happy and the people we love. The result is often emotional and spiritual bankruptcy, as the belief that we are unworthy and unlovable keeps us in isolation. Connection with the 'other' is difficult and indeed we often sabotage this connection. The sabotage results from this distorted thinking and leads us to seek people and situations that reinforce our negative beliefs about ourselves as some sort of misguided justification of our self-abandonment. Subsequently we are held in this dark place where it can be all but impossible to find a way forward, and where it feels that the only way of coping is to seek to control the pain by using substances or actions which make us feel better, at least temporarily.

Addiction and co-dependence are both diseases which could be said to develop through a need to control. For many this need is developed early in life as defence mechanisms designed to help us cope with difficult family situations. These defence mechanisms in turn became survival skills which kept us safe in what we may have felt was an unsafe environment. Pia Mellody in her book *Facing Co-dependence* (Mellody 1998, pp. 78-79) has identified five natural attributes of a child. These are to be valuable, vulnerable, imperfect, dependant and immature. When these needs are not recognised or supported, children will absorb responsibility for the things which appear to be wrong and come to believe that they are inadequate, flawed and somehow to blame for their parent's failings. This in turn can lead to an intense experience of shame which distorts contact with the true self and inhibits the development of healthy self-esteem. As we mature these defence mechanisms which may have helped us to survive in a dysfunctional environment give rise to faulty thinking. This distorts our sense of reality and eventually starts to work against us and stops us from growing and moving forward in a positive way. The need to control our immediate environment (such as strong feelings or difficult people and situations) can grow to a level where tension and anxiety result in overwhelming feelings of unmanageability. The use of substances such as alcohol or drugs, or distracting ourselves with processes like gambling, shopping, work or sex, often seems to provide a sort of temporary relief. Over time, the use of mood altering substances and behaviour which seemed such an effective way to lift us out of our distress, becomes much more of a problem than the feelings which created it in the first instance. The preferred drug of choice ultimately becomes the controlling factor as the brain and body develops tolerance to the mood altering action and more and more of the substance or activity is required to keep the painful or distressing feelings at bay.

Understanding Our Feelings

The messages our brain receives affects our central nervous system which "controls almost every organ system in our body through a series of positive and negative feedback loops" (Allen 2008, p. 10). Therefore what we feel is interpreted by the brain and a behaviour is prompted based on whether the brain perceives this message as positive or negative. Feelings on their own have no context so when a strong feeling is experienced research suggests that the brain seeks to make sense of it by searching the data base of memories and experiences held in both our brains and at a cellular level in our bodies, to find a context which seems to fit with the feeling being experienced (Allen 2008, p.43-46., Rothschild 2000, p.56). Subsequently a feeling which is interpreted as negative can generate a strong sense of pain, anger, shame etc. This in turn can feel so uncomfortable that some sort of remedy is sought to suppress the feeling or change it to one which is manageable and familiar. For the addict, and co-dependant who support the addict, it is the thought processes and delusional beliefs held about the self that need to be challenged. These core beliefs and thought processes affect the way reality is perceived and for addicts who generally do not see themselves in a positive light, nor do they believe that anyone else will (Carnes 1994, pp.16-17), this is particularly difficult. The cycle of addiction is such that this faulty or impaired thinking creates a tension which becomes unbearable and needs to be soothed.

Our brains are wired for survival and as such produce chemicals such as dopamine and serotonin which make us feel good. These are the body's natural reward response to recognising our basic needs which are survival, safety and security. (Allen 2008, p.33). Understandably we like it when it feels good and in a healthy person, when we have achieved something or behaved in a way which benefits and protects us, good feelings are produced by natural means with the release of these chemicals. When mood altering substances or behaviours are used to trigger or mimic the feel good chemicals in the brain, the release brought about may appear to work, but eventually tolerance is developed and over time the brains natural reward pathways are altered. In this process, although a sense of relief may be achieved temporarily, thinking continues to be distorted and negative beliefs amplified as perceptions of reality are altered and tolerance to the body's natural feel good chemicals occur. Over time more and more effort or substance is required to bring a sense of relief. This creates a 'merry-go-round', or spiral, which in turn drives the need for more of the drug of choice to feel good, which numbs the pain and distracts us from our problems, and so the cycle of addiction grows and continues.

Understanding Denial and Fear

One of the main problems with addiction is denial or, as Allen would put it, "the problem with addiction is that it is a disease which tells us it isn't one" (2008, p.27), therefore overcoming this self-defeating thinking and behaviour, and finding the courage to become willing to change, generally requires a catalyst. This catalyst is often presented in the guise of some sort of disaster or level of distress where one is forced to confront the reality of the situation. We don't generally just wake up one morning and decide that today we will become a healthy, fully functional adult who will seek our own greater good. Even when we know that we have a significant problem denial kicks in to tell us that we can manage the situation or that our drinking, drugging, gambling, working, shopping etc., is a consequence of external factors rather than a personal responsibility. Or we may choose to believe that our behaviour is ok because it is really not as bad as someone else we know whose behaviour seems worse than our own. Consequently it is likely that the moment of awareness of the severity of the problem will be due to an issue with significant consequences such as a relationship break-up, a job loss or a serious health issue. That moment, when it comes, is always going to be a blessing in disguise and it will always be painful (Melody 1998, p.208).

To begin to live our lives with authenticity and freedom from our self-defeating thinking and behaviours is to recognise our environment for what it is, and to accept that life has become unmanageable and seek change. The choice to change and live a life based on what we want, rather than what we have been taught to believe we need, begins with that moment when we realise that in fact we no longer have a choice. It is that moment when we realise that this is not how we thought our lives would be, and that controlling our environment is exhausting and ultimately unfulfilling. Unfortunately many of us are able to continue to function adequately dragging along with us our fears and self-set limitations, and for many this results in a life of quiet desperation. It is hardly surprising therefore that "chemical dependency has reached epidemic proportions in our society" (VanVonderen 1995, p.15) and that the misuse of prescription drugs such as pain killers and medication to address sleeping, stress and anxiety issues is out of control (Armitage, 28/5/12). The addict is not just someone who falls down drunk or drugged in a gutter somewhere, but is also the person struggling to work every day, overwhelmed with feelings of pain, futility, inadequacy and hopelessness, and who uses whatever their drug of choice is as the quickest means of calming the unquiet mind. Whether we have an addiction issue or simply want to improve our quality of life, learning to look honestly at ourselves and recognise our fears and how we respond to them will help to develop awareness around how we operate in our daily lives. This awareness is the key to empowering ourselves to go to the next level and it is essential if one is to step out of the fog of survival into the clarity of a bright new day where one can consciously choose to thrive in life, rather than merely survive.

For many, fear is a significant issue which has often evolved from living or growing up in an environment where speaking out or expressing feelings resulted in harmful or humiliating consequences. As adults, we often become trapped in silence through this fear of being shamed. Richard Rhor, in his book *The Naked Now* (2009, p.17), points out that surrendering to fear "provides you with the illusion that you are in the driver's seat, navigating on safe, small roads, and usually in a single, predetermined direction that can take you only where you have already been". This metaphor of being in the driver's seat but travelling the same roads over and over is an appropriate one to describe the journey of addiction. Each time the driver gets in the car he hopes to go somewhere different, but he always ends up on the same road, in the same place and then feels shame and anger that yet again the road did not lead somewhere different.

Change requires us to "succumb to the danger of growth" (O'Donahue 1999, p.50) if we are to move forward into a new healthy way of being, and embarking on this journey into the unknown can certainly feel dangerous at times. To do this we must start to listen to the critical voice that lives within each of us. This voice whispers in our ear that we can't, won't, aren't smart enough, don't deserve it etc. Learning to outsmart this inner critic is an integral aspect of the journey towards healing and growth. The skill of hearing this negative inner voice and learning the ability to challenge it, along with the old belief systems which created it in the first place, is not easy but it is possible and it is life changing. To feel safe one must learn that it is safe to feel. Learning to trust the feelings that arise during the process of change requires determination and resilience. Each step of the journey builds hope and increases resilience. With time, determination and support the ability to cope increases also. As we start to experience the positives that come from doing life differently we are motivated to stay on the journey. Learning to embrace the uncomfortable sensations and feelings of being 'stretched' which comes with this process of change enables us to trust that we are on the right path and will enable us to continue the process of change. Connecting with others on a similar journey, and with the spiritual part of ourselves, can also provide us with the support we need to undertake and maintain this process of change. Alcoholics Anonymous, a 12-step program developed in 1935 to help those seeking recovery from alcoholism, and which has now become one of the most successful self-help programs worldwide, talks about the possibility of change which occurs much more quickly when "members find that they have tapped an unsuspected inner resource which they presently identify as their own conception of a Power greater than themselves. …. Members call it "God-Consciousness"(*Alcoholics Anonymous Big Book* 2001, pp.567-568). Connection with a power greater than ourselves helps us to recognise that we are much more than our dysfunctional thoughts and behaviours. In this process we are given permission to begin to see ourselves from another, more hopeful perspective.

Understanding Our Family Story

Understanding our histories, who we are and where we come from, is an important step into the journey of self-discovery. Along with our own stories, understanding our family histories can also be extremely helpful in gaining an insight into why we think and behave the way we do. The beliefs we have about ourselves are generated by our life experiences and relationship dynamics within our family of origin. These beliefs about ourselves are often formed early in life and understanding the belief system within the family helps to shed light on the way that we perceive ourselves (Carnes 1994, p.15). Gaining an insight into our multi-generational, and, particularly in Australia, our often multi-cultural backgrounds, can reveal many clues as to how our belief patterns have been established. What happened in our families in previous generations has a 'knock on' effect where the result of unresolved trauma or conflict is passed down generationally. The negative patterns are passed from parent to child and the pattern is continued as the child grows and becomes a parent who then passes the same behaviour and belief systems on to their own children (Mellody 1998, p.112). This can be a particular problem for those from multi-cultural families who are often trying to fit within different cultural experiences. Often it is difficult to reconcile beliefs inherent in the family of origin but which appear to have no apparent relevance or, in some cases, actually contradict the values and beliefs held in the community in which they now find themselves. It is vital to take these cultural implications into consideration when reviewing family systems, recognising that what may be true for someone from one cultural background may not be so for someone from a different background. However, it is safe to say that even as a generalisation, "traumatisation occurring as a result of less-than-nurturing parenting skills, interrupts the child's psychosocial and emotional maturing process and causes developmental immaturity in adulthood" (SPP. 2012, p.12).

The daughter of a family who immigrated to Australia, Sally (not her real name) was driving home from work one evening when the panic attack hit. This time it was so strong that she had to pull over. Eventually she had to call someone to help her as she was unable to drive home. Sally was a successful business woman who had been using sugar, work and antidepressants to keep her functioning. Therapy helped Sally connect with her feelings of fear and inadequacy stemming from beliefs she had learned in her family of origin. Sally had grown up in a family where addiction was an issue and where she was taught to believe that being female made her less important than her brothers. She learnt early that her role in the family was to be the rescuer. This meant keeping her father from being angry and her mother and brothers comforted. Subsequently her core beliefs around her ability to succeed professionally were extremely negative and work addiction developed in an endeavour to keep these negative beliefs at bay and not fail in her career. Ultimately her health and her personal relationships suffered and she recognised that she needed help. During therapy it was revealed that her grandmother had been an addict and her father had been the victim of child abuse. This helped her to understand how the roles within her family of origin, along with her cultural heritage, impacted her. This in turn enabled her to recognise how she perceived herself both within her family and within her cultural context, and gave her an awareness of how she responded professionally when her self doubt and fear crept in.

Studies of the way that families operate have been carried out by a number of professionals over many years. This has contributed significantly to our understanding of the way that the family operates as a system. Our connection and experience of our family dictates the core beliefs that we have about ourselves and this, in turn, impacts the way we function and the decisions we make. The Bowen Theory of family systems demonstrates how the family operates as an emotionally connected unit. Bowen points out that it is the nature of a family to be emotionally connected and even when there is division or distance this emotional connection is still highly active and influential over the way we respond to people and situations. (www.bowencentre.org/pages/theory.html). How we are socialised within our family systems is reflected in the way that we interact with our families and with the wider community. Our position and role within the family, our sense of self within and as separate from the family, our core relationships within the family and the community within which the family operates are all factors which influence our world view and how we function in the world. This work on family systems has led to an understanding of the power of the family to collude with addictive behaviour in an attempt to keep the family operating on a functional level, albeit superficially (Carnes 1994, p.95). Even in dysfunctional families there is a powerful ability to maintain balance which enables each member to feel safe. This feeling of safety, however, is an illusion as each member of the family pays a price in terms of their own emotional health and wellbeing. In the effort to support the addicted person shame becomes the by-product created by carrying the family problems and secrets. Shame is a powerful form of control and this dysfunctional behaviour is passed down through families and continues until someone recognises the limitations this ultimately imposes and steps out of the pattern by seeking change.

Working with an objective 'other', such as a suitably qualified therapist or counsellor can provide a safe place to start to unpack our personal history. Good experiences and bad experiences are all vital sources of information which need to be examined in order to learn about our current response patterns. These experiences are the things that have taught us how to respond. They have shown us how to protect ourselves and enabled our survival but as they now no longer serve us, they eventually become the triggers that send us into some level of distressing, and often inappropriate, response. For example, sitting in a staff training seminar Adam (a pseudonym) was singled out to perform a role play in front of his colleagues. His palms started to sweat, his heart started racing, he felt flustered and confused and felt himself starting to 'shut down' and dissociate. Afterwards he felt that he had performed poorly and was embarrassed at the idea that his colleagues had seen him as a failure. The reality of the situation was that he had actually performed quite well, particularly given his high distress levels. However, his history of school yard bullying and humiliation by a teacher set him up to respond to any situation where he felt singled out and vulnerable with the fear he had been subjected to as a child. Taking this to the next level, Adam used drugs and alcohol to medicate the feelings of shame and inadequacy he experienced. By learning to recognise his responses and understand where they came from, he was able to reprocess his thinking and teach himself that he was no longer a child in a dangerous situation, but that as an adult he had a choice over how he responded and what he would agree to do or not do. He learnt that the skills he had used to get him through the difficult aspects of his life actually demonstrated that he had great resilience and coping skills and these could now be turned around and used as stepping stones to build the hope for a less fearful and more fulfilling life.

Understanding Change

In her work on the psychophysiology of trauma and trauma treatment, Babette Rothschild points out the importance of working with memories originating from traumatic experiences which are held in the brain and at a cellular level in the body (Rothschild,2000, p.5). Often therapy will help reprogram the neural pathways by challenging unhelpful ideas and beliefs, and while this can indeed be beneficial, Rothschild demonstrates that the somatic response is powerful and releasing these body memories as well is much more effective in developing longer term mental and emotional health.

Research done on amputees who experience sensation in limbs which are no longer present has revealed the way that the brain stores information received while the limb was attached. This information is later 'replayed' even though the limb is no longer present because the absent limb is no longer able to feed new information to the brain to change its response pattern (Doidge 2007, p.185). Similarly, for those who experience difficult or traumatic experiences early in life, the information stored in the brain from these early experiences governs the responses of the adult experiencing similar situations. It is understandable, therefore, that retraining the brain, or reprogramming the neural pathways, with new information will enable different and more appropriate adult responses to old stimuli. The release of the feel good chemicals, such as dopamine, triggered during our addictive actions is also responsible for "consolidating the neuronal connections responsible for the behaviours that led us to accomplish our goal"(Doidge 2007, p.107). Therefore, as we learn that acting differently brings the reward of a positive outcome, the new programming is cemented and the ability to make better decisions reinforced. This reinforcement is repeated each time we respond in a productive or positive way.

Learning to let go of our self-defeating behaviours is at the core of all healing and growth. Being involved with a community of like-minded people often helps to support us in this process of change. Twelve Step programs, such as Alcoholics Anonymous mentioned earlier, are particularly powerful and indeed have been so effective that "250 other kinds of 12 step groups…have sprung up in conscious mimicry of its technique" (Yancey 1998, p.50). These are fellowships of like-minded men and women who are able to support each other in the journey of recovery, and they have been designed to help the addict or co-dependent take responsibility for themselves and their behaviour, recognise that a power greater than themselves can bring sanity into the craziness, and help develop awareness around the things that have led to this point.

I have heard it said that if you want to feel better then it is necessary to get better at feeling. For the addict who has done everything in their power to avoid feeling this can be a challenging situation. However feelings are the clues which will tell us what is really going on. The way that we live in the world is governed by our understanding and experience of the world in which we live. For example, if as a child we were taught to doubt our reality, that is our insights (the things we see) and perceptions (the things we think), we grow to be adults who are unsure about what is real and what is trustworthy. As adults we learn ways to adjust for this doubt so that we can function in the wider world, but we do so at a price. As in the cases mentioned earlier, Adam's experience of the world was one which taught him that to be vulnerable was to be unsafe and shameful. This caused him feelings of great pain and distress which he in turn medicated with substances in order to cope. Sally developed a work and sugar addiction along with a dependence on antidepressants to help her cope with a subconscious belief that she was betraying her family by working outside of the home, and that she wasn't really capable of doing the job she was actually doing.

By learning to access our cognitions and feelings correctly, that is recognising how the body is responding rather than just listening to what the head is telling us, we are able to identify core beliefs and old programming. From this we can change our thinking and behaviour and in so doing reprogram neural pathways in the brain so that we are no longer acting in ways which are inappropriate or irrelevant. Staying grounded in the reality of what is real rather than being caught up in the fantasy of what our damaged thinking tells us is real is essential. This helps us to remain in the present and respond in a mature and considered way, rather than reacting in a way which limits or hurts us or those we love. Learning to trust that we are supported by a Higher Power makes this all the more possible because as long as we believe we can go it alone we act as our own higher power and end up functioning in ways which are not in line with our own greater good. Indeed connecting with that spiritual part of ourselves is an essential component in the process of change. Accepting that we are loved and supported by a power greater than ourselves provides a platform from which we are able to experience the possibility of hope. When it is difficult to see or believe positive things about ourselves, learning to accept the presence of a Higher Power who supports us regardless of our beliefs and behaviour enables us to start to forgive ourselves and trust that there is hope for a new way of being. As we get better at establishing our spiritual connection through such means as attending 12-step meetings, meditation, caring for ourselves physically and emotionally and staying in reality through functional thinking, we discover that living differently is indeed possible. Being involved in support groups links us to others on the same journey and helps us to step out of a sense of isolation and self-abandonment. Connecting with others who are also in a process of change empowers us to stay connected to both our Higher Power and our own journey, and reminds us that we are supported when the stretch becomes particularly difficult or challenging.

To change the way we live from destructive to constructive is to recognise that although everything may seem alright, in actual fact nothing is as it seems! If addiction is a disease caused by control, it is also a disease of denial. The addict will often fiercely defend their behaviour, denying the seriousness of the problem. Those family members who believe they are maintaining the family's ability to function by supporting the addict also need to name the problem for what it is and stop colluding with the addict's behaviour. The path to recovery and wholeness can only be achieved by the painful action of embracing the truth, naming it for what it is and then walking through it. There is no other way around it and even when we stumble it is vital to accept that we are human and as such we are fallible. As two time Para Olympian Kurt Fearnley put it in a television interview "…it's not failure…it's just something you've got to get over" (Denton, ABC 2008). The same is true for any of us wishing to live more fulfilling lives exploring our potential rather than being held back by our fears. Developing the resilience to walk this path is achieved by consciously choosing to embrace the emotional 'stretch' which comes from the uncomfortable feelings that arise when challenging old beliefs, and from facing the things that create fear and that feel like failure, but seeking support and choosing to act differently. This can often mean enduring strong feelings that may seem unmanageable, hearing the inner critical voice which tells us that something is wrong with us, and recognising that we have a choice over what we believe and how we behave. The ability to feel the 'stretch' and trust that this is where the learning happens increases our resilience. Each time we stay with the experience we learn that more positive outcomes can be achieved. Each time we experience that positive outcome we reprogram neural pathways in our brain and learn to trust the process, and we get better at choosing to think and act differently.

Works Cited

Alcoholics Anonymous Big Book. Fourth edition. Alcoholics Anonymous World Services Inc. New York City. 2001.

Allen, J. *The Secret Disease of Addiction*. Affinity Lodge. London. 2008.

Armitage, C. "Misuse of Medicines the New Danger" in *Sydney Morning Herald*. 28/5/12. Retrieved from http://www.smh.com.au/misuse-of-medicines-the-new-danger

Bowen, M. http://www.thebowencentre.org/pages/theory.html

Carnes, P. *Out of the Shadows. Understanding Sexual Addiction*. Hazelden. Minnesota. 1983.

Collins Dictionary. London. 1987.

Doidge, N. *The Brain That Changes Itself*. Scribe. Melbourne, Australia. 2007.

Fearnly, K. on *Enough Rope with Andrew Denton*. ABC television. Australia. 25/8/08.

Mellody, P. *Facing CoDependance*. HarperCollins. SanFrancisco. 1989, 2003.

Mirkin, G. "*How Muscles Get Stronger*" http://www.drmirkin.com

O'Donahue, J. "A Blessing" in *Eternal Echoes: Exploring Our Hunger to Belong*. HarperCollins. New York. 1999.

Rhor, R. *The Naked Now*. The Crossroad Publishing Company. New York. 2009.

Rothschild, B. *The Body Remembers; The Psychophysiology of Trauma and Trauma Treatment*. WW Norton & Company. New York. 2000.

South Pacific Private. Sydney, Australia. Professional Training: Module 1. 2012.

VanVonderen, J. *Good News for the Chemically Dependant and those who Love Them*. Minneapolis. Bethany House. 2004.

Wilson Schaef, A. *When Society Becomes an Addict*. HarperCollins. New York. 1987.

Yancey, P. *Church: Why Bother?* Zondervan. Grand Rapids, Michigan. 1998.

Chapter 11

Trauma–Creating Beneficial Change

Richard Hill

> Character cannot be developed in ease and quiet. Only through experience of trial and suffering can the soul be strengthened, ambition inspired, and success achieved.
>
> —Helen Keller (1880-1968)

A traumatic experience or a traumatic episode can be the beginning of a difficult period in anyone's life. Trauma, whether acute or over time, can leave the sufferer plagued with any variety of disabling affective disturbances. Phobias, irrational fears, aversions, prejudices and personality disorders are some of the after effects that can disrupt a person's life well after the trauma has passed (Tedeschi & Calhoun 2004). Trauma comes in many different forms. It can be a trauma to the person, such as assault; mortal danger such as a plane or car accident; sexual assault; and other such direct affronts to the individual. It can be from loss: the death of a loved one, spouse or child; relationship breakdown and separation; changes in political or social support systems; and other such indirect affronts to the individual. In a different type of personal stressful experience it can be in the form of insecure attachment experiences; psychobiological deficits and disabilities; and other such challenges imposed on an individual by misfortune of family or birth. Each of these forms of trauma has different issues to deal with and different hurdles to overcome.

Assumptions that have been the foundation of safety and security can be challenged and often completely overturned leaving the sufferer floundering in an unfamiliar and unsafe psychosocial environment. Traumas challenge our sense of safety; our belief in capacity; our view of reality; our belief in what is fair; our assumptions about the world, its stability and the fragility of our mortality within it. Finding some meaning in a traumatic event can be very difficult for someone who has lost a child, especially through a sudden and unexpected cause, where some type of positive meaning is rarely found (Lehman et al. 1987; Murphy et al. 2003). Loss of spouse at a later age, however, can more often lead to positive changes in their belief they had grown stronger as they learnt how to manage their lives without a partner, albeit that men seem to find it more difficult than women (Wortman et al 1993; Lieberman 1996). Many cancer patients find they gain psychological growth (Cordova et al. 2001), people who have an unexpected close call with death also mostly find psychological growth, whereas if the near death experience was only witnessed, rather than experienced, the post-traumatic psychological growth was much less (McMillan 1997).

Recovering from the disruption and disturbance of trauma can be a long and arduous endeavour. It is, however, possible to recover and many people do. The pathway to recovery is as unique as the individual involved. The courage and strength that is often masked by the difficulties a sufferer experiences, can not only be the instigator of survival, but also the inspirer of personal growth. Adaptation to life experience is a natural aspect of being human. Brain plasticity is dependent on experience to determine what changes will be made to the neuronal architecture (Grossman et al. 2002). Positive adaptation is both experientially preferred and biologically rewarded as can be seen in beneficial responses in our immune system (Segerstrom & Sephton 2010), calming of stress systems and engagement of social systems (Carter 1998). Trauma, in its harshness, is isolating and disconnecting within self and from others. At its best, it inspires engagement with others and insight into meaning and purpose. Growth in response to experience is a natural process. Trauma is an experience.

The term "post-traumatic growth" was first presented in the literature by Tedeschi and Calhoun (1995; 1996) in the mid 1990's, although they and others had been discussing the possibility of benefits following traumatic experiences for some years before. Most notable was the work of Victor Frankl who survived the Nazi concentration camps to write the seminal work, *Man's Search for Meaning* (1959) which was first published in 1946 under the title (English translation) *From Death-Camp to Existentialism*. The philosophical comment, "What does not kill me, makes me stronger" came from Nietzsche (1990) in 1888, but tales of the hero arising from struggle, trauma and challenge can be seen in mythological stories as ancient as the tales of Hercules from Greece more than 2,500 years ago. Some trauma practitioners divide the concepts of PTG from post-traumatic adaptive change, but for the purposes of this chapter, I will include both concepts as part of broader scope which we will call, 'creating beneficial change'.

Although it may seem impossible to find any redeeming factor in the experience and the after-effects of trauma, it can be highly beneficial to try and do so. Once an event has occurred, it can never be erased from a person's life. Some minor events are not remembered and have no lasting impact on personal growth and development. The likelihood of an event being remembered either explicitly or implicitly is often directly proportional to the emotional impact at the time (Cahill & McGaugh 1995). It is, therefore, likely that most traumatic events remain in some form of memory somewhere in the brain and the body. How can we harness something that seems to be abhorrent to create strength, build resilience and find new capacities for coping? Post-traumatic Growth (PTG) and the broader scope of creating beneficial change, is an attempt to address that question.

PTG and positive adaptive change is evident in anecdote and folklore throughout many cultures and is something that nearly everyone has either witnessed in others or experienced in themselves to some degree. Stories of people who suffer great difficulty and trauma and then rise from it with new strength, stronger resolve and deepened humanity pervade literature, both fiction and non-fiction. Tedeschi and Cameron (2004) open their paper with just such stories: a cancer patient, the survivor of a plane crash and an athlete who found a new awareness to the joys of life in relationships with family and friends, the richness of nature and elevated belief in what they were capable of doing and being.

As wonderful and encouraging as these stories are, it is necessary to remember the balancing stories of people who suffer debilitation and diminishment as a result of traumatic experience. Sometimes the damaging effects can slowly be reversed, but sometimes not. Suicide is, unfortunately, a final outcome for many trauma survivors. In England in 2000, 27 per cent of female suicides were victims of childhood sexual abuse (Meltzer et al. 2000). It is reasonable to imagine that many of these women suffered PTSD, which remained unresolved. That said, I am acquainted with a sufferer of childhood sexual abuse who has become a vigorous campaigner for justice and actively helps others overcome their feeling of low self-esteem and self-disgust. She has created strength, purpose and has found some meaning for this experience in her life. Having said that, she continues to be in our concerns as a risk of suicide, although not a high risk.

Trauma can come from a wide range of events and can suffer the limitations of definition. For the purposes of this chapter and to enable a broad discussion, we shall look at traumatic experiences as those that present significant challenges to the individual's adaptive resources and also significant challenges to an individual's understanding of the world and their place in it (Janoff-Bulman 1992). The sudden impact on beliefs about the world and the individual's place in it is described by Tedeschi and Calhoun (2004) as a "psychologically seismic event that can severely shake, threaten, or reduce to rubble many of the schematic structures that have guided understanding, decision making, and meaningfulness" (p.5). Like an earthquake, a trauma can dramatically challenge our belief in safety and the fragility of our survival in many things, even to the very foundations upon which we stand.

The concept of PTG is that it can be these very challenges to our foundational elements that provide an opportunity to discover a new view of the world and the possibility that this new view can lead to positive development. It is not suggested that post-traumatic experiences are all one way or the other. Tedeschi and Calhoun (2004) make it clear that most people exhibit a combination of responses following trauma, but, the more growth that is engendered, the better it will be for the individual. In light of this positive possibility, it can be helpful to see how others have found some benefit emerging out of the disturbances of trauma.

From Trauma to Life Skill

The idea for this chapter began to emerge on hearing the story of JP (name disguised for privacy) who suffered sexual abuse as a child from an older relative. Sadly, abuse by someone who is known and trusted is all too common in sexual abuse (Finkelhor 1994). In the case of JP, the abuse took place in the relative's home and one of the distinctive features he remembers was how untidy and disordered his home was. JP found that in his own life he became very fastidious with orderliness and tidiness. He recalls how this was bordering on obsessive compulsive disorder (OCD) and certainly may have become something very debilitating in his life.

Fortunately, the abuse became known and great efforts were made to help JP find resolution and regain his self-confidence and trust. What JP found interesting was that even though he was recovering well from the damage of the traumatic events, his preference for order and tidiness continued. Instead of becoming a debilitating post-traumatic problem like OCD, it became a part of his personality and became attached to his temperament, rather than his fears.

JP found that this 'quality' began to express itself in his professional life. Rather than a burden from the past, his preference for order led to the development of the valuable skills of being able to not only see *dis*order, but to create order. As a teacher, his classes were always well structured, following a clear line that gave his students a positive advantage. He began to write and found that he could see the structure and layout of his ideas before he had even written a word. He describes writing as merely filling in the information between the heading and subheading that he sees so clearly in his mind's eye.

Of course, it's not that JP was 'grateful' for the sexual abuse. He may well have developed his sense of order from other much less malevolent stimuli. But the fact is that he did suffer the abuse and it is from this experience that he was able to generate a positive way of living. We must remember that our biology, especially in the development of synaptic connections, neuronal pathways and the production of hormones, peptides and neuropeptides, responds to experience and creates itself accordingly. It is from experience that we create character and competence and the biology that both supports and sustains those 'personal' developments (Erikson 1968). How he was able to allow his aversion to disorder to emerge as a strength is the practical aspect of post-traumatic growth. It may well be different for each person, but is there an underlying principle(s) that can be adapted for generalised use? Let us consider some more examples.

The exact truth of horror writer, Stephen King's childhood experiences are difficult to know, but he openly admits in interviews to being afraid as a child and continues to hold seemingly irrational fears about the safety of his children. He is also known to have witnessed the death of a childhood playmate in a train accident when he was four years old. In his seminal story of young boys growing up, *The Body* (King 1983) which was later made into a film, *Stand By Me* (Reiner 1986) he included no less than three accidents involving trains (Terr 1989).

These portrayals of train accidents might be considered, on one hand, to be post-traumatic stress being expressed through his writing, or the utilisation of life experience to bring truth and reality to his story. When asked by Leslie Stahl (1997) on *60 Minutes* whether he has ever seen a psychiatrist about his fears he replied, " (you go to a psychiatrist to) ... get rid of your fears, whereas if I write 'em down ... people pay me—it's good."

Scilla Elsworthy, creator of Peace Direct, has a special mantra—"my fear grows fat on the energy I feed it"(2012). Stephen King does not feed his fear, but dissipates it into the external space of the written page. It is then something that can be managed and even utilised to advantage. King shifts his initial concerns into his own imaginative creativity. It is this creative state that transforms an inner trauma into something that can be expansive. The issue for an individual is whether the expansion is beneficial or amplifies the detrimental effects of the trauma. Here we see one of the fundamental differences between post-traumatic growth and post-traumatic stress and, perhaps, the fine line on which they are balanced.

The comedian, Robin Williams, is an example of someone who has experienced the trauma of insecure attachment. We now know that although ambivalent attachment may not be a specific, damaging or terrifying trauma, it can have serious effects on later happiness and how we form relationships with others (Cassidy & Shaver 2008). His relationship with his mother may well be described as classic insecure-ambivalent attachment where the child was often left alone to fend for himself. Parents sometimes do this in order to build strength and independence. In Robin Williams's case he found himself alone much of the time in a very large house and so created imaginary friends to keep him company. The family was reasonably wealthy and he admits himself that his childhood was not unhappy, but the telltale signs of an insecure attachment can be seen in his own comments, such as how he would use comedy to try and get a reaction or response from his mother (Lipton 2001). Later, in his TV show, *Mork and*

Mindy (Storm 1981) he appeared as himself and expressed publicly that he had intimacy and engagement issues in his childhood. In an example of finding some benefit in difficulty Williams says:

> So then I got to the point where I realised that my characters could say and do things that I was afraid to do myself and, after a little while—here I am.

The Transformative Impact of Trauma

That which does not kill *can* make me stronger, although, as we have seen, not necessarily. It can also leave you chronically more vulnerable, stressed and unsafe. Either change may be considered a transformation. Trying to push for the dominant correctness of one case over the other seems to create an argument in academic literature. Perhaps the question should not be about the veracity of positive or negative changes, but rather the possibility, and even the likelihood, of a combination of effects. It is how this combination can be beneficial, rather than how it might set off a spiral into suffering and even self-destruction.

It is important to note that the theory underlying PTG does not try to suggest that there is no suffering as wisdom builds, but rather that growth occurs within the context of pain and loss. It can be that a significant experience of distress may even be necessary for growth to occur. This may well be the Catch-22 of the process of PTG: just how much distress is necessary to stimulate change, but when does this stimulus exceed a level which may impair the sufferer and render them unable to engage in the growth process (Butler et al. 2005)?

There are numerous contradictions in the research on growth after trauma, which can cloud the issue. A surprising example is concerning the general understanding that we are, innately, a meaning-making species that responds to new experiences with a natural inclination to find a meaning or purpose in order to be able to move on with a wiser and more consciously capable disposition (Marsen 2008). When new meaning is incorporated into the person's life, then the event ceases to be the central focus and the new meaning initiates a fresh set of conditions upon which to engage with the future. On the other hand, when it is hard to find meaning, then the event can become fixed in time and therefore persist in present experience. It is, in part, this fixation on the trauma, regardless of the passage of time that creates the ongoing presence of psychological barriers, stumbling blocks and distressed recall that we often describe as post-traumatic stress disorder (PTSD).

Davis et al. (2008) conducted research into the impact of making meaning after the loss of a loved one. Their results were surprising. People who had made no attempt to find any meaning to the loss reported fewer ongoing symptoms, a higher sense of well-being and rated themselves as more recovered from the loss than those who had searched for meaning. This is supported by other research that shows that minimising the event or avoiding processing the loss resulted in fewer grief symptoms (Wortman 2004). This is, indeed, a seemingly counter-intuitive result, but this conundrum shows us that the best way to process a traumatic event is not as straightforward and universal as might be expected.

The Individual Nature of Trauma

> Growth, however, does not occur as a direct result of trauma. It is the individual's struggle with the new reality in the aftermath of the trauma that is crucial in determining the extent to which posttraumatic growth occurs. (Teseschi & Calhoun 2004, p.5)

Calhoun and Tedeschi (2006), having pioneered the concept of Post-Traumatic Growth (PTG), try to construct the processes of positive psychological change that can occur as the result of the personal struggle that follows challenging, stressful, and traumatic events. Five areas are highlighted within the PTG framework: relating to others, where a new sense of connection and engagement is experienced; new possibilities, where people find that the traumatic event pushed them forward in what they do; personal strength or feeling personally stronger, which is felt in a greater sense of self-efficacy and heightened resilience; spiritual change, where people feel more closely connected to a God figure or being more connected spiritually; and a deeper appreciation of life, which is often stimulated by radical changes in prior assumptions about life (Tedeschi & Calhoun 2004).

This highlights the individual nature of response to trauma. The best approach to helping a trauma victim is to be open and responsive to their individual needs and capacities. This is very much in line with the Ericksonian practice of utilisation. Utilisation is the practice of, rather than following a prescribed or manualised form of therapy, following indicators from the client as to the best therapy to implement at any given time. It is a more creative and responsive approach to therapy and does require the therapist to have wide knowledge and experience, but it is much more inclusive of the individual nature of the client.

Milton Erickson was approached by a client suffering from post-traumatic stress. Over the course of the interview the client was desperate and truly hoped that Erickson, as one of the great therapists of the time, would be able to help and show her how to manage. Erickson took a surprising stance by telling the woman that the most expert person in the room in surviving and managing trauma was not him, but her. He praised her extraordinary capacity to be sitting in his room as a survivor. Clearly she had utilised some excellent techniques to help herself manage. Erickson asked her to teach him how she did it and, together, they would work out how to do it better (Gilligan 2011).

This level of utilisation goes deeply into the principle that therapy is a process that occurs both within and in response to a relationship—an interpersonal experience. Personal growth is certainly to do with changes within a person, but an essential aspect of personal growth is the way it changes and enhances the way in which we relate to and with others. Many of the issues in post-traumatic stress are feelings of shame, loss of self-worth, loss of belief in personal capacity and the resultant feeling of being a burden on others. On the other hand, PTSD can also be expressed in an excessive concern for and connection with others. Personal boundaries become blurred and people can live their lives vicariously through others. Both ends of this pendulum swing, however, are concerned with the intrapersonal and the interpersonal.

As has already been stated, PTG can be a very individual process because of the many variables that make up both the trauma and the subsequent disruptions to the 'world' as it was before the trauma. The last section in this chapter will discuss a novel approach, developed by the author, that incorporates both the intra- and inter-personal worlds and embraces most of the five areas of PTG highlighted by Tedeschi and Calhoun (2004). Rather than a therapy, this is a perspective, an approach—a curiosity-oriented approach. In the same vein as a strengths-based approach or a solution oriented approach, the curiosity approach is not a definitive therapy, but a perspective or viewpoint that can be applied to any therapeutic technique.

A Curiosity Approach

When Barbara Fredrickson published her research on what she called the Broaden and Build Theory (2001), she reported the benefits of positive emotion not only in the context of Positive Psychology (Seligman & Csikszentmihalyi 2000; Linley et al. 2006), but also the nature of a positive focus of attention. Rather than eliciting specific behaviours, positive emotions were more ambiguous and interactive leading to a broadening of the mental state towards a constructive state that might also be described as a creative state. Generating this creative, broadening and building state of mind is what the curiosity approach seeks to enhance and amplify (Hill 2006).

Fredrickson refers to the importance of play and wonder as triggers the Broaden and Build mindset. She incorporates the work of Jaak Panksepp (1998) and other play researchers. Ernest Rossi, one of Milton Erickson's primary protégés, also professes the importance of an expansive mental state. Among other things, he sees wonder, amazement and a sense of the tremendous beyond the limitations of oneself as a key factor in brain plasticity and positive creativity (Rossi 2004). Common threads in the works of these researchers and theorists is the benefit of looking toward future possibilities rather than ruminate on past events; of seeing oneself as the central reference point of their life, but within the context of a much larger, inter-related experience; and of seeking to creatively participate in personal growth. The curiosity approach harnesses these concepts and suggests three principle approaches to therapeutic practice. As this is an approach or a lens through which to approach a client, it is not a therapy in itself and so can be used in conjunction with any therapy. These approaches are intended to give the client and also the relationship between the client and practitioner the greatest opportunity to engender a creative, broadening and building mindset that will be inclined toward the growth that is being called post-traumatic growth, but is certainly, creating beneficial change.

1. Priming the brain toward future possibility—wonder, interest, curiosity

The brain operates within patterns that become predictable over time. The more a neuron, or a pathway of neurons, are activated, or 'fire', the stronger the connection becomes and the more likely that neuron or neuronal pathway will activate. This was expressed famously by psychologist, Donald Hebb (1949), who said that, "neurons that fire together, wire together" and is commonly known as Hebb's Law. This does not, however, mean that our brains become fixed or rigid. The flexibility of brain structure and the capacity to change the way that neurons fire together is the process that is now known as 'brain plasticity' (Doige 2007; Arden

2010), which is one of the major breakthroughs in neuroscience of the past decade. It overrides the 'old thinking' that brains become fixed sometime in the teenage years and no major change or development was possible after that. We now know that everyone is capable of learning, making changes and even growing new neurons in the brain for our entire lives. In order to take maximum advantage of this capacity of neuroplasticity it is best to have your mind interested in creating new pathways and connections. The opposite to focusing on the past and pre-existing thoughts is to be curious about as yet unknown things or novel pathways of thought. The best way to trigger that state of mind is to be creatively interested in what is happening to you and around you.

Being interested is more than just a mindful acceptance of the present moment. Interested and curious is the mindset of openness to what might come next. Curiosity is about what we do not know, what might be discovered, what is novel and what elicits change or development. That can be very difficult for people sometimes because we have the Catch-22 of having a preference for stability and predictability. Curiosity and an interest in novel possibility require a number of developmental steps that are too much to expand on here, but are certainly possible with the appropriate therapeutic process. Assuming it has been possible to engender a curious and interested intention, the next step of the curiosity oriented approach is to investigate below the surface of the problem, behaviour or struggle.

2. Opening the mind to investigation and discovery—looking for implicit messages in explicit problems

What we are able to see on the surface has often been stimulated by something more complex from our inner self. To give a benign example, there are dozens of psychobiological processes that occur regularly every day at particular times which eventually come into our conscious awareness—become explicit—as the very simplistic message, "I'm hungry". We take a series of actions in response to that message, but we certainly have no explicit awareness of whether it is just because of circadian habits, issues with digestion and stomach integrity (Houpt 1982), insulin resistance (Elliott et al. 2002), leptin receptors (Dubuc et al. 1998), excess of endocanbinoids (Pertwee 2006) or a host of other specifics. Over evolutionary time it has been sufficient for us to eat what is available and, more often than not, we survive.

In a similar way, our behaviours, moods, personality swings and affective disorders may not tell the whole story and may even be distracting from the real story that the body is trying to communicate. When someone tells us that they cannot do something, it is often seen as a problem that requires us to help them learn to do or overcome the barriers in doing this particular thing. When looking at this as a message, it may also be that, rather than a problem to fix, the thing they cannot do is, indeed something they cannot do and the fruitless effort to solve the problem is distracting them from doing the things they can do. In the area of trauma, it is not uncommon for people to lament that they cannot get over the trauma and move on. Although that concern needs to be considered appropriately, the message might be that it is not possible to 'get over' and 'move on' from the trauma. In fact, very little can be done about the trauma itself, the trauma has happened and that cannot be changed. What may be needed to 'get over' is the inertia of processing how the trauma has changed their world, what these changes now mean and what are the alternatives available. The very 'problem' that the trauma cannot be overcome is a message that the focus of attention is on the wrong place. The problem becomes a message that the person is actually seeking a way to change direction and focus. That is a fairly simplistic example, but it conveys the concept without having to recount an entire case.

The final piece in the process of the curiosity approach is to discover what to do with the interest and the message.

3. Engaging creative expansion—broadening and building

Curiosity sets up the intention of seeking something new. Amongst other things that might emerge from the therapeutic process, finding some hidden messages in the problem provides new information and/or new perspectives. The final stage is to engage with the new information and ask, "What can I create with this?" When you bring disparate elements together it is most likely that something new will emerge that will be different, a change, a fresh start. Again, using a simple example, if you were to see on a table a black cup of coffee, a white cup of coffee and a half empty milk jug what might you deduce?

Without taxing the brain too much, it would be reasonable to assume that milk had been added to one of the cups to create white coffee. That means that at some stage there were two cups of black coffee and a full jug of milk on the table. Somehow, most likely the intervention of a person, the milk was added to the black coffee and a change ensued creating the scene of one black and one white coffee. No matter how much intention, discussion, desire, potential, possibility or time is taken, if the milk is not added to the black coffee there will be no change. If the black coffee is the problem, the message is that there is a lack of engagement with the new possibilities that the milk presents. Rigidity survives when there is a lack of curiosity.

The frustration of creating something new in your life is that it is very difficult to predict whether what you create will be what you want, whether it will succeed or fail, whether it will make things better or worse. It is not a totally unreasonable argument to stay in an unpleasant state rather than risk change which might make it worse. Rigidity, however, leads to a slow decay and is not productive for a positive life experience. If you can create the white cup of coffee, then you have already proven that change is possible. If the change you acquire is not desirable, then it is a matter of spurring the curiosity again and asking the questions: what is the message in this problem of the white coffee and what can I create with that? Curiosity leaves the door always open, even if just a little. Rigidity closes the doors and often boards them up, making change, growth and renewal harder and harder to achieve.

Conclusion

The concept of post-traumatic growth is not new and may well stretch back to the dawn of humankind or even before. The modern discussion of PTG shows that it is not a cut-and-dried process. It is neither a guaranteed outcome to trauma, nor is it the same for every case. Human beings will always struggle in life to some degree. Finding points of growth out of trauma must not be a measure of a person's success or failure. Each of us has our personal journey. Some have a harder road than others. I would think that most people would hope that through life we enhance our strengths and capacities to not only cope, but thrive. It may be that modern society itself is part of the problem and part of the rigidity.

If nothing else, the concept of post-traumatic growth encourages us to imagine the possibility that life gets better. Theories like Broaden and Build; concepts like the Curiosity Oriented Approach; therapeutic developments like Positive Psychology and Strengths-Based Practice are all examples of what is possible. Every person who suffers trauma, high levels of stress or even just the struggles of day-to-day life warrants our care and attention. As a profession of therapists, social workers and counsellors we are well advised to guide who we can toward growth and hold to our hearts those who struggle, as best we can and for as long as we can.

Works Cited

Arden, J. B. (2010) *Rewire your brain: Think your way to a better life.* Hoboken, NJ: Wiley.

Butler, L.D. Blasey, C.M., Garlan, R.W., McCaslin, S.E., Azarow, J., Chen, X.H., Spiegel, D. (2005). Posttraumatic growth following the terrorist attacks of September 11, 2001: Cognitive, coping, and trauma symptom prediction in an Internet convenience sample. *Traumatology*, 11, 247-267.

Cahill, L. & McGaugh, J. L. (1995). A novel demonstration of enhanced memory associated with emotional arousal. *Consciousness and Cognition* 4(4): 410-421.

Calhoun, L. G. & Tedeschi, R.G. (2006). *Handbook of Posttraumatic Growth: Research and Practice.* New York: Erlbaum.

Carter, C. S. (1998) Neuroendocrine perspectives on social attachment and love. *Psychomeuroimmunology*, 23(8): 779-818.

Cassidy J. & Shaver P. R. (2008) *Handbook of Attachment: Theory, Research and Clinical Applications.* New York and London: Guilford Press.

Cordova, M. J., Cunningham, L. L. C., Carlson, C. R., & Andrykowski, M. A. (2001). Posttraumatic growth following breast cancer: A controlled comparison study. *Health Psychology*, 20: 176-185.

Davis,C. G., Wortman, C. B., Lehman, D. R. & Silver, R. C. (2000) Searching for meaning in loss: Are clinical assumptions correct? *Death Studies*, 24: 497-540.

Doige, N. (2007) *The brain that changes itself.* New York, NY: Viking.

Dubuc, G., Phinney, S., Stern, J., & Havel, P. (1998). Changes of serum leptin and endocrine and metabolic parameters after 7 days of energy restriction in men and women. *Metabolism: Clinical Experimental*, 47 (4): 429-34.

Elliott, S. S., Keim, N. L., Stern, J. S., Teff, K., & Havel, P. J. (2002) Fructose, weight gain, and the insulin resistance syndrome. *American Journal of Clinical Nutrition* 76 (5): 911-922

Elsworthy, S. (2012) Fighting with non-violence. Presentation to TED April, 2012. Retrieved from www.ted.com/talks/scilla_elworthy_fighting_with _non_violence.html August 2012

Erikson, E.H. (1968). *Identity: Youth and Crisis.* New York: Norton

Finkelhor, D. (1994). Current information on the scope and nature of child sexual abuse to children. *The Future of Children*, 4(2), 31-53.

Frankl, V. (1946) Ein psycholog erlebt das konzentrationslager (From death-camp to existentialism). Germany: Verlag fur Jugend und Volk

_____ . (1959) Man's search for meaning: an introduction to logotherapy. Boston: Beacon Press.

Fredrickson, B. L. (2001) The Role of Positive Emotions in Positive Psychology. *American Psychologist* 56 (3): 218-226.

Friedrich Nietzsche, F. (1990) *Twilight of the idols and the anti-christ.* English translation. London: Penguin Books.

Gilligan, S. (2011) Presentation at the 11th International Erickson Congress, Phoenix, Arizona, December, 2011. Milton H Erickson Foundation.

Grossman, A. W., Churchill, A. D., Bates, K. E., Kleim, J. A. & Greenough, W. T. (2002) A brain adaptation view of plasticity: is synaptic plasticity and overly limited concept? *Progress in Brain Research,* 138: 91-108.

Hebb, D. O. (1949) *The organization of behaviour.* New York, NY: Wiley.

Hill, R. (2006) *How the 'real world' is driving us crazy!* Sydney, Australia: Hill & Hill p/l.

Houpt, K. A. (1982) Gastrointestinal factors in hunger and satiety. *Neuroscience and Biobehavioral Reviews,* 6 (2): 145-164.

Janoff-Bulman, R. (1992) *Shattered assumptions: Towards a new psychology of trauma.* New York, NY: Free Press.

King, S. (1983) The body. In *Different Seasons,* New York, NY: Signet.

Lehman, D. R., Wortman, C. B., & Williams, A. F. (1987). Long-term effects of losing a spouse or child in a motor vehicle crash. *Journal of Personality and Social Psychology,* 52: 218-231.

Lieberman, M. (1996). Perspectives on adult life crises. In V. Bengston (Ed.), *Aging and adulthood* (pp. 146-167). NewYork: Springer.

Linley, P. A., Joseph, S., Harrington, S. & Wood, A. M. (2006) Positive psychology: Past, present and (possible) future. *Journal of Positive Psychology,* 1(1): 3-16.

Lipton, J. (2001) Inside the actors studio—Robin Williams. Video. Retrieved from: http://www.youtube.com/watch?v=owGMZ6yJ57o Aug, 2012

Marsen, S. (2008) The role of meaning in human thinking. *Journal of Evolution and Technology,* 17(1): 45-58.

McMillen, C., Smith, E. M., & Fisher, R. H. (1997). Perceived benefit and mental health after three types of disaster. *Journal of Consulting and Clinical Psychology,* 65: 733-739.

Meltzer, H., Singleton, N., Lee, A, Bebbington, B., Brugha, T. & Jenkins, R. (2000) *The social and economic circumstances of adults with mental disorders.* Office of National Statistics, London. Retrieved from: http://www.dh.gov.uk/prod_consum_dh/groups/dh_digitalassets/@dh/@en/documents/digitalasset/dh_4060765.pdf, August, 2012.

Murphy, S. A., Johnson, L. C., & Lohan, J. (2003). Finding meaning in a child's violent death: A five-year prospective analysis of parents' personal narratives and empirical data. *Death Studies,* 27: 381-404.

Panksepp, J. (1998) *Affective neuroscience: The foundations of human and animal emotions.* New York, NY: Oxford University Press.

Pertwee, R. G. (2006). The pharmacology of cannabinoid receptors and their ligands: An overview. *International Journal of Obesity* 30: S13-S18.

Reiner, R (director) (1986) Stand by me. Film, prod. *Columbia Pictures,* USA.

Rossi, E. L. (2004) Art, truth and beauty: The psychosocial genomics of consciousness, dreams, and brain growth in psychotherapy and mind-body medicine. *American Psychotherapy Association, Annals,* Fall, 2004.

Segerstrom, S. C. & Sephton S. E. (2010) Optimistic expectancies and cell-mediated immunity: The role of positive affect. *Psychological Science,* 21(3): 448-455.

Seligman, M. E. P. & Csikszentmihalyi, M. (2000) Positive psychology: An introduction. *American Psychologist,* 55(1): 5-14.

Storm, H. (1981) Mork meets Robin Williams. *Mork & Mindy,* Episode 14, Series 3. Retrieved from: Inside the Actors' Studio http://www.youtube.com/watch?v=owGMZ6yJ57o Aug, 2012.

Terr, L. C. (1989) Terror writing by the formerly terrorised: a look at Stephen King. *Psychoanalytic Study of the Child,* 44: 369-390.

Teseschi, R.G. & Calhoun, L. (1995) *Trauma and Transformation.* CA: Sage Publications.

_____ (1996) The post-traumatic growth inventory: measuring the positive legacy of trauma. *Journal of Traumatic Stress,* 9: 455-471.

Tedeschi, R. G. & Calhoun, L.G. (2004). The foundations of posttraumatic growth: new considerations. *Psychological Inquiry,* 15, 93-102.

Stahl, L. (1997) Stephen King. *60 Minutes,* Interview February 16th 1997. Retrieved from: http://www.youtube.com/watch?v=XCI3oFn50z8 August, 2012.

Wortman, C. B., Silver, R. C., & Kessler, R. C. (1993). The meaning of loss and adjustment to bereavement. In M. S. Stroebe, W. Stroebe, & R.O. Hansson (Eds.), *Bereavement:A sourcebook of research and interventions* (pp. 349-366). London: Cambridge University Press.

_____ , (2004) Posttraumatic growth: progress and problems. *Psychological Inquiry,* 15(1): 81-89.

CHAPTER 12

Trusting One's Emotional Guidance Builds Resilience

Jeanine Broderick

Abstract

Research from several fields is applied to demonstrate the connection between positive emotions, resilience and human thriving. New research demonstrating that emotions are a guidance from a sensory system designed to guide us to optimal well-being (Peil 2012) is presented together with methodologies of developing positive emotions and cultivating hope. To foster acceptance of the emotional guidance system (EGS) in people holding defined religious beliefs, indications of various religions may point to inner guidance.

Understanding the output from the emotional guidance system is easily taught and can be used to increase resilience before and after negative life events. The low cost, ease, accuracy, and effectiveness of utilizing inner guidance makes it readily applicable for widespread use. The recommended best practice for increasing resilience is to teach an understanding of emotional guidance as globally as possible beginning in early years of age and development.

Key Words

Resilience, emotional guidance, thriving, education, expectation, positivity, optimism, pessimism, hope, quantum physics, positive psychology

This chapter explores how positive emotions increase resilience while providing background on new research that suggests emotions provide guidance to better feeling emotions. I touch upon biochemical indications that even the most basic organisms are guided in appropriate responses to their environment by a guidance system in which beneficial environments feel better than less beneficial environments. While no attempt is made to prove the existence of God, I delve into religion because some religious worldviews resist or reject what others see as beneficial actions when the actions seem unsupported (or prohibited) by their worldview (BMJ 2010; Gyamfi, Byamfi, & Berkowitz 2003; & Sire 2009).

My goals are to help everyone understand their emotional guidance systems (EGS) and to make it easier for interested individuals with definitive religious beliefs to find a perspective that facilitates accepting the guidance into their existing belief structure(s) by showing it is possible to interpret religious texts as suggesting such guidance comes from God. I am not suggesting whether or not one believes in God has an impact upon whether guidance is provided, nor that the benefits of such guidance are limited to those with specific beliefs.

In this model, the EGS works regardless of behaviors or beliefs (Peil 2012). For those who rely on science, it is my opinion that the paper by Peil (2012) makes a plausible argument that the function of emotions is to provide guidance. Furthermore, experience has shown that experimenting with the concept on a personal level demonstrates the benefit of guidance rather well.

Emotions are output from our sensory system. By heeding the guidance emotions provide, one can find resilience (Cohn, Fredrickson, Brown, Mikels, & Conway 2009). The EGS can be used to understand when the environment is perceived in a less than optimal way and to identify better feeling perspectives (Peil 2012).

While people have labeled emotions that feel bad as "negative" and those that feel good as "positive," all emotions are good because they are providing guidance, whether the receiver understands the message or the appropriate response to the message, or not (Peil 2012). Emotions that do not feel good indicate that action should be taken to feel better. Action can be physical or may consist of changing the perception that is leading to the emotion that does not feel good (Peil 2012).

Peil utilizes biochemistry to support her theory that emotions are output from a sensory system (Peil 2012). In her theory, appropriate responses to negative emotion are expanded to include Right Responses. She states that Right Responses should be the first response to most of the negative emotion experienced in modern life, and involve changing the personal mindscape, deliberately, to invoke belief structures that lead to optimal emotional responses. Right Responses do not suppress emotion but change the perspective in a mature and adaptive manner.

There is a plethora of growing evidence suggesting that social ills including crime (McCarthy & Cassey 2010), teen pregnancy (Barnet et al 2008), drug and alcohol abuse (Economic and Social Research Council 2012), and more are casually related to long-term emotional pain. There is also mounting evidence that indicates improved desirable behaviors are linked to increased positive emotion including better corporate citizenship, altruism, kindness to strangers without expectation of reward, better relationships of all types, and much more (Achor 2010; Fredrickson 2009). Peil (2012) suggests the true nature of humans: we are all good at our core. Seligman echoes this argument in *Flourish* and Dacher Keltner reinforces it in *Born to be Good*. However, only when emotional guidance is followed consistently is our true nature demonstrated. Prolonged negative emotions that result when the EGS is ignored often lead to undesirable behaviors (Peil 2012). We feel emotions in response to thoughts (Seligman 2011).

Each thought elicits an emotional response (Ekmund 1992; Fredrickson 2009; & Rubenstein 1999). Emotional guidance is unique to the individual thinking the thought. Unique goals, beliefs, expectations, emotional stances and focuses cause differences in the emotional responses individuals receive. When we move away from our goals, our emotions feel worse. By deliberately choosing a different perspective, our thoughts change and better-feeling emotions can be deliberately cultivated (Rubenstein 1999). Thoughts actually create meaning for events in life (Rubenstein 1999). Our minds fill in missing details to help us make sense of the world. The details our minds supply are based less on reality than on our beliefs, expectations and emotional stance. These details, sometimes referred to as "back stories," are as unique as fingerprints. Based on the "back story" chosen, the event will be experienced (felt emotionally) as if the assigned reason is accurate (Seligman 2006).

It is really as simple as understanding that better-feeling thoughts are guiding us toward our desires. Thoughts that feel worse indicate we are moving away from our desires. Some clarity regarding desires is required. In our opinion, there is a difference between short-term and long-term desires. Although all desires contain the characteristic that we believe we will feel better by attaining them, some desires relate to immediate gratification, a response to current conditions without consideration for the long-term. Desires for some foods, drugs, alcohol, and other addictions are fueled by these types of desires. Short-term desires often conflict with longer term desires. For example, a desire to feel better right now may be satisfied by enjoyment of a cookie but a long-term desire to maintain a comfortable weight may be in direct conflict with the desire for a cookie.

Generally, the desire that feels better in the moment will win. If there is little belief that a comfortable weight will be achieved or maintained, the desire for the cookie will usually win over the long-term but unbelievable desire to maintain a comfortable weight. On the other hand, an individual with a high degree of confidence (which might be interpreted as determination or will power) may forgo the cookie now because she is able to achieve the same (or higher) degree of positive emotion through focus on and belief in the possibility of achieving the long-term goal. Note that the greater belief in the ability to succeed in this (or anything) is the better feeling thought which can be deliberately cultivated using the EGS to identify RRs.

Peil describes our emotional sense as "a feedback loop in a circular stimulate-response relationship where the output of a system is fed back into itself serving as stimulus for a subsequent round of output responses. It provides feedback in perfect accordance with harmful or environmental stimulus. In doing so, it accomplishes an optimizing developmental adaption—saying 'yes' to beneficial changes—or a self-preservationary intervention, saying 'no' to potentially self-destructive harms." There is an inherent desire to feel better. Some "desires" are not effective or beneficial in the long-term although they do provide short-term emotional relief. Without knowledge of techniques to change thoughts, endless loops can result—sugary foods, alcohol, drugs, shopping and more can temporarily improve mood but do not build long-term resilience. To build long-term resilience one must reach for better-feeling thoughts (RRs).

The EGS will guide one to feeling better, which is healthier—but it will not strongly consider long-term desires unless we have, ourselves, given deliberate focus to long-term goals.

While the feedback loop is always guiding us to better feelings and does so whether we are aware of it or not, there are significant ways that resilience can be enhanced with a little knowledge and deliberate attention to matters that impact the guidance being received. Goal setting is a well-documented and accepted business and personal growth strategy (Hill, Napoleon 1994). Establishing defined goals makes it easier to recognize the larger goals when faced with a decision where the short and long-term desires are in conflict. The individual whose friends are going to a fun party who stays home to finish a project, if focused on the short-term goals, feels left out and dissatisfied. The same individual, with a clarified desire to meet a larger goal, could feel satisfied with the decision. The greater the focus on long-term desires, the easier it is to avoid contradictory short-term desires and still feel good. The EGS of an individual who has not given any deliberate thought to long-term goals will provide different emotional responses than the EGS of an individual who has intentionally set priorities.

"Right Responses" do not indicate that there is a specific right (or wrong) answer to any question. A "Right Response" is a mindset that feels better. When in an upsetting situation the EGS can be used to obtain immediate feedback about better ways to perceive the situation. An individual can ask himself, "Is there another way to view this situation?" and as a thought occurs he can compare how that thought feels to the current interpretation. If the new thought feels better, consider adopting it as the "back story" through which the situation is perceived. This process can be utilized repeatedly. It is not normal to move from feeling awful about a situation to feeling good with one attempt but a concerted effort, over 20 minutes or days or weeks or months—depending on the severity and complexity of the situation—can result in much better feeling perspectives.

For example, at the time of the initial separation a divorce may seem like the worst possible outcome but as time and a desire to feel better about the situation are combined, it can even be perceived as the best thing that ever happened.

Short-term desires may be beneficial (i.e. socializing) but if choosing them sidetracks a longer-term desire (finishing a project and staying on-track at school or work) the long-term effect may fully negate the short-term benefits due to subsequent negative "self-talk" arising from guilt, frustration, or self-directed anger for not staying on track. A rich social life can be a long-term goal and guidance could then lead to solutions that might allow both. Framing desires in advance is a powerful tool in increasing the benefits of the EGS (Broderick 2012c).

While the EGS always provides guidance, a practice of setting balanced, long-term, big picture goals and reinforcing them with frequent attention helps ensure that our guidance gives adequate consideration to the long-term desires.

For example, in an upsetting situation it is not uncommon for individuals to reach for alcohol to provide relief from their negative emotions. Unfortunately, alcohol provides only a temporary dulling of the pain (or lessening of the focus on the painful thoughts) and can lead to even greater problems.

A more permanent and healthier method of approaching an upsetting situation is to reframe one's perception of the event in a way that feels better (Ricard 2003). With practice, finding better-feeling thoughts becomes easier in many adverse situations.

There are opportunities to practice choosing RRs in many situations, for example, during a time-constrained 2,000 mile automobile journey our vehicle broke down. We could have focused on the inconvenience of the situation, on concerns that we might not be able to finish within the required time-frame, or even paint it with a broader brush and link the situation to a "why me" attitude about life in general not going well. Or, we could focus on the helpful people we encountered who went beyond expectations to help us. All the above thoughts reflect aspects of the reality that existed. A deliberate choice was to focus on the thoughts that feel best (a "Right Response") which made the experience part of a fun adventure versus less appealing thoughts which could have made the journey seem frightening and unpredictable.

There is a children's game that is a good analogy for the way emotional guidance works. The game involves hiding an object and a child searching for it. The person who knows the location gives hints, "You're getting warmer" when the searcher is getting closer to the objective and, "You're getting colder," when she is moving away.

While it does feel different to move from despair to anger than from anger to frustration, or from hope to passion, each of these is a step in the right direction, each is "getting warmer." The common element of each step in the better-feeing direction is a feeling of relief (a releasing of tension or stress). The emotion that is in the "warmer" direction always feels better than emotions that are "getting colder" (Peil 2012).

When individuals know they have this guidance, and have practiced using it, they also know that no matter how bad their current circumstances may seem, they can find ways to feel better. Hope, a belief that a positive or desired outcome is possible, is a key emotional state for resilience. Just knowing that guidance exists builds a firm foundation for hopefulness (Peil 2012). Without this knowledge, it is easier to feel hopeless, which can lead to inertia or giving up (Seligman 2006).

The beauty of emotional guidance is that everyone has it. It is personal to everyone's unique goals and desires. It is simple to understand and follow. It does not tell anyone what others should do or not do; it is specific to a person's unique perspective and incorporates personal values (Peil 2012).

The brilliance of this guidance is in its simplicity. Anyone, even children, can understand the guidance. It does not require expensive, labor-intensive programs to oversee the guidance. No tools are required. Widespread understanding of the EGS could create resilience that will work for individuals even when the infrastructure of a country has been torn apart by war or natural disaster.

Benefits of Positive Emotions

Several branches of science have been studying human thriving. The results, when compiled, point to the fact that people thrive when they feel emotionally good and suffer when they do not (Achor 2010; Fredrickson 2003 & 2009; Seligman 2006 & 2011).

Negative life events can include, but are not limited to, events that happen to you or loved ones that cause emotional upheaval, such as death of loved ones, serious illness, disability, job loss, hospitalizations, physical and mental abuse, divorce, physical trauma, and failures (Seligman 2006). Why does one individual who endures a negative life event experience post-adversarial growth when another who suffers a similar event develops post-traumatic stress disorder (PTSD) or begins a downward spiral? A resilient person bounces back. Someone who has not developed resilience stagnates (Fredrickson 2009). The individual's skill at managing her emotional state is the difference (Peil 2012).

What are the principle components of resilience? Two factors—positivity and optimism—make the difference between whether an individual is resilient or not (Brooks & Goldstein 2004; Fredrickson 2009; Rubenstein 1999; and Seligman 2006).

Positivity

Barbara L. Fredrickson, Ph.D. states, "Positivity is perhaps the best kept secret of people who, against all odds, keep on bouncing back" (Fredrickson 2009, pg 97).[1] In her research, subjects who had more positive mindsets demonstrated greater resilience. The role positivity plays in resilience is significant. According to Fredrickson, "The most pivotal difference, though, between those with and without resilient personality styles was their positivity. It was the secret of their success. It was the mechanism behind their lesser depression and their greater psychological growth. In short, we discovered that resilience and positivity go hand-in hand. Without positivity, there is no rebound" (Fredrickson 2009, p. 102).

Often, negatively focused individuals will discount the notion that positive emotion can be present when facing negative life events. While this is probably true for them, due to their current mindsets and beliefs, it is not true for everyone (Ricard 2003).

The good news is their experiences in the future can be different from those in their past. A primary finding emerging from research with older adults is that "a significant portion manage to experience positive emotions, even in the midst of overwhelming loss. Despite variation in the types of stressors experienced, the results are remarkably consistent: Positive emotions have demonstrably beneficial effects when present during times of stress" (Ong, Bergeman, Bisconti & Wallace 2006).

One common criticism of positivity is the belief that negative emotions are being repressed. This is not based on empirical evidence, "On the contrary, resilience is marked by exquisite emotional agility" (Fredrickson 2009, pp. 109).

Some protest that positive emotions are not always good because anxiety can be a call to action. The goal of positivity is not to always be joyful. The goal is for an individual to know, no matter what happens, how to move to a better-feeling emotional state. The accomplishment of a goal is not necessary to feel happy. Progress made toward the goal will bring emotional relief.

Optimism

Optimism is the second key factor that contributes to resilience. Seligman states, "The optimistic individual perseveres. In the face of routine setbacks, and even major failures, he persists. When he comes to the wall at work, he keeps going" (Seligman 2006, pp. 255)

Optimists and pessimists alike are often adamant about the correctness of their stance. Looking deeper, it becomes apparent that they are both right because of the impact of expectation on outcome. This sums it up well:

> The optimist is right. The pessimist is right. The one differs from the other as the light differs from dark. Yet both are right. Each is

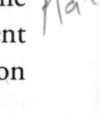

right from his own particular point of view, and this point of view is the determining factor in the life of each. It determines as to whether it is a life of power or of impotence, of peace or of pain, of success or failure (Trine, 1897, Chapter 3).

Upon examination, it becomes clear that positive expectations result in more desirable outcomes. While positivity and optimism are the most important characteristics of resilience, other components contribute to, or detract from, resilience. I developed this chart to show the direction thoughts need to move in order to develop greater resilience based on my reflections and also from readings from (Brooks & Goldstein 2004; Rubenstein 1999; Seligman 2006)

Thoughts Movement Towards Greater Resilience

Less Resilient	*More Resilient*
Disempowered perspective	Empowered perspective
Sees problems as permanent	Expects to bounce back
Victim thinking	Refuses victim mindset
Blames	Accepts responsibility
Feels fearful/helpless	Feels confidence/capable
Responds reactively	Consciously chooses perspective
Rigid thinking	Feels curiosity
Holds onto anger	Forgives easily
Resistance to new ideas	Welcomes new ideas & experiences
Feels hopeless	Feels hopeful
Expects the worse	Faith
Tendency to attack oneself	Belief in self & ability to learn
Holds onto guilt	Characterizes failure as learning
Feelings of shame	Self-acceptance and approval
Negative emotional bias	Positive emotional bias
Long-term worry and anxiety	Trust
Feels life "just happens"	Feels personal control
Sees obstacles as enemies	Obstacles are challenges (opportunities)
Being "right" is the highest goal	Places higher goals above "being right"

Resilience is so important, to individuals and society, because the negative impact of not having resilience can be so costly. On the individual level, negative life events increase the risk for many illnesses, including cancer and heart disease. Accepting what is now known about the benefits of increased positivity and optimism (Achor 2010; American Academy of Neurology 2001; Barnet, M.D et al 2008; Boehm & Kubzansky 2012; Broderick 2012a; Fredrickson 2009; McCarthy & Casey 2010; Peled, Carmil, Siboni-Samocha & Shoham-Vardi. 2008; Rissman, Staup, Lee, Justice, Rice, Vale, & Sawchenko 2012), the absence of these emotions in individuals who have suffered a negative life event increases their risk for many adverse situations. The protective benefits of positive emotions and optimism for health and well-being are significant and beneficial to individuals as well as society.

A lack of resilience can result in an individual having difficulty remaining (or becoming) a productive member of society (Fredrickson 2009). It is not just the individual lacking resilience who suffers, their families can experience many negative consequences (Seligman 2006). When employees lack resilience, employers bear some of the burden in the form of increased health care costs, absenteeism and lost productivity (Achor 2010). On the community or business level, one individual who suffers a negative life event during a key juncture can have wide-ranging adverse implications for the business or community (Achor 2010; Mason 2011). On a broader scale, when one event such as a natural disaster or a war brings widespread negative life events, a lack of resilience in the population can delay recovery for months or years (Fredrickson, Tugade, Waugh, Christian, Larkin 2003).

Negative life events are unpredictable and can happen to anyone at any time. This increases the desirability of developing resilient mindsets before they are needed. The resilient mind may be so well tuned to thriving that even in the midst of chaos, one will demonstrate leadership and inspiration. Resilience can be increased after a negative life event by finding new perspectives that allow one to move past the deep pain (Peil 2012; Weissman 2005).

Resilience is so easy to increase and the benefits so great, it should be a core part of the curriculum in schools.

Emotional Guidance

The emotional sense is present even in simple organisms. The function of basic 'negative' emotions is to provide information necessary for the safety and well-being of the body. The function of positive emotions is to guide us toward self-development and well-being (Peil 2010).

The difference between simple organisms and most humans is that simple organisms always respond to their emotional sensory output. Simple organisms do not tolerate something that feels less than optimal any longer than necessary. Humans, on the other hand, often ignore or suppress their emotions and suffer the negative consequences of doing so by living lives that are less robust than they could be (Peil 2012).

People gain no benefit by ignoring the output from their emotional system. Ignoring negative emotional output is no different than ignoring pain from one's sense of touch. Emotional pain was designed to be responded to in the same way physical pain is managed. When emotional pain is ignored or suppressed, it can be as harmful to our well-being as leaving a burning hand on a hot stove as evidenced by the previously cited health benefits of positive emotions. There are even documented case studies of spontaneous remission of cancer when emotionally abusive relationships are severed (Hirshberg & Barasch 1995). This area seems to deserve further research.

Thinking about something pleasing (past, present, or future) will create "getting warmer" emotional guidance. Thinking about something unpleasant (past, present or future) will create "getting colder" emotional guidance. Everyone has the ability to choose to focus on attributes that feel better.

Heeding emotional guidance leads to better-feeling emotions, whether it is away from fear in a harmful environment or toward becoming the best we can imagine being in a supportive environment (Broderick 2012b).

Learning to follow the guidance from our EGS may conflict with instructions received throughout life, i.e., the opinions, expectations, and desires of others. In a world that does not currently understand the EGS it is common for others to want you to behave in ways that make them happy. On the surface, it sounds very selfish to follow ones own guidance over what others may desire from you. By setting goals that include being loving or respectful to others the EGS will provide guidance that takes those goals into consideration. The research is clear that we have more to give to others when we are happy and our EGS guides us to happier states. The increased resilience we gain from following our guidance can greatly benefit our families, employers, and communities.

It is possible to maintain a positive bias about life when circumstances are not ideal. This has been proven by many in very adverse circumstances. There are many accounts; one of the most dire is the story of Viktor Frankl, documented in his book, *Man's Search for Meaning*, about his experiences in a Nazi concentration camp. In the worst of circumstances he discovered the importance of finding meaning in all forms of existence, which made his current circumstances, even though unchanged and reprehensible, feel better and provided a reason to continue living. This is an example of a RR, where the individual found better-feeling thoughts. Although the thoughts he found were philosophical in nature, any thoughts that felt better and thus made the situation more tolerable would be considered RRs.

Likewise, there are many stories of cancer survivors who claim that being diagnosed with cancer was the best thing that ever happened to them. The reasons vary, but most of the individuals learned to live more consciously instead of being content with an "auto-pilot" life, (Oregon State University 2012) where they merely react to their circumstances without any knowledge that they can control how they respond to events. "With the cancer diagnosis, my priorities changed in an instant. The list of what was truly important got real short, real quick. Decision-making became easier. I became more motivated to do things I had been putting off. The old phrase about not sweating the small stuff became crystal clear" (Montgomery 2012).

A change of perception changes everything. Each mind interprets the world according to factors specific to the individual (Lebrecht, Bar, Feldman, Barrett, & Tarr 2012), including beliefs, expectations, emotional stance and focus. These factors create a filtering system in the brain that determines the sensory input that is communicated to the conscious mind. People project their thoughts onto what they see and experience in the world. When one changes her thoughts, her world changes. People give thoughts power when they accept them as true. Everyone has a choice. Right Responses involve deliberately changing beliefs, expectations, and focus.

Many parents have found a perspective about the tragic death of a child that feels better and honors their child. One of the most widely supported and well-liked non-profit organizations in America, MADD (Mothers Against Drunk Drivers), was created after one such death. Another parent, Dr. Darren R. Weissman (2005), speaks of shifting his focus from his daughter's death to carrying on the legacy of her life and how much stronger he had become by making that shift in perspective.

People speak of the power of now. Being in the now, mindfulness, certainly helps one to enjoy life more. But how does one respond when the now is painful? How does one stay in the now and not be racked by debilitating emotional pain?

The fear of death keeps more people from living than any other fear. "Perfect harmony comes when your mind is subordinate to your heart, that is, when trust dissipates fear. The more you trust, the less you will be afraid of dying" (Karasu 2012).

Divorce causes some to crash and burn while others rise phoenix-like from the ashes and become much more than they ever imagined they might be. Some are so overwhelmed by fear that they build high and thick walls around their heart so that they are really no longer living. Others find ways to re-build a stable environment for their children that is full of love. Each of these behaviors is the result of how one chooses to perceive the situation.

Many are familiar with the story of Christopher Reeve, best known for his role as Superman. Although doctors told him he would never walk again he became even larger than the comic book hero he portrayed when he regained far more use of his legs than expected. He made a decision to quiet the negative self-talk. Over time he found resonance with something Abraham Lincoln said: "When I do good, I feel good. When I do bad, I feel bad. And that's my religion." In my opinion, this is a clear example of following one's EGS.

Influence of Expectation

Expectations greatly impact accomplishments. A bias toward optimism or pessimism influences assumptions individuals make about the future as do people's past experiences. An experience in the past that resembles a current situation may cause the brain to interpret it as the same even if there are significant differences. One way to ensure one's expectations are serving the highest good is to think more deeply about important matters. Emotional guidance is of great value. It contains more wisdom than the brain (Rollin & Atkinson 2004).

As an example, Daniel, whose wife was not faithful, perceives himself as a victim. He is now experiencing new situations through a lens that expects to be victimized by the new woman in his life. He is on guard and afraid to commit. He feels suspicious and acts jealously when she is merely being friendly. His underlying expectation is not serving him. He can adjust his expectations so that his filter does not misinterpret new experiences with the expectation of the old outcome. It may take some time, but once an individual is aware of the impact of old experiences on the interpretation of new experiences, he will be more aware when outdated interpretations are applied to new situations.

We never really "think clearly" because our filters distort reality, or perhaps more accurately, they create our individual realities. Fortunately, the EGS is designed to guide us to more accurate interpretations. All information is considered by our guidance system. It is not limited to the information that makes it to our conscious mind through the filtering system.

If Daniel knew to listen to his emotional guidance when he felt jealous, the negative emotion would tell him he was looking at the situation incorrectly. If he followed his emotional guidance to better-feeling thoughts, he would know the truth was better than he perceived it.

A positive and optimistic mindset is the key to resilience. We choose whether a situation is a problem or an opportunity. Being more conscious of what we believe and think, deliberately cultivating a positive bias, is the key to increasing the level of resilience. Various studies have shown that we often learn our explanatory style from our mothers and her style (Seligman 2011. See: Berkeley-Oakland Study) may or may not result in resilience. In fact, this is probably a contributing factor to the amount of truth in the saying "The Rich get richer and the poor get poorer." A conscious decision to change our perception and response to events is required to break an undesired cycle. Another study (Association For Psych. Science 2011) showed that nurturing moms from low-income families buffered children from the common health issues such children often face as adults. The individuals who did not have the benefit of a nurturing mom can still gain those health benefits by changing their own thinking. Taking responsibility for one's self rather than blaming another empowers the individual.

Almost no one sees or realizes his or her true potential. Often individuals are stymied by obstacles they could easily overcome if only they believed in themselves a little more. William James wrote, in *The Principles of Psychology*, "Most people live, whether physically, intellectually, or morally, in a very restricted circle of their potential being. They make very small use of their possible consciousness and of their soul's resources. In general, much like a man who, out of his whole body organism, should get into a habit of using and moving only his little finger." Deliberately increasing resilience helps individuals achieve more of their potential (Seligman 2006; Fredrickson 2009).

When people do experience and overcome adversity, they learn more about their capabilities. This may account for why those who have experienced some adversity are more resilient than those who have not experienced any significant negative life events (Seery 2011).

Most schools of psychology—Freudian, Jungian, Alderian, and Rogerian—acknowledge that a lack of self-awareness is a common root cause of personal disease and unrest (Holden 2008). This is because emotional guidance is ignored (Peil 2012).

The Impact of Beliefs and Expectations

Entire books have been written about situations of spontaneous healing and individuals who have been considered beyond repair who have recovered fully. There are many examples of how humans seem unable to do "impossible" things, but once one person accomplishes a feat, whether it is learning to walk again after a spinal cord injury or running the first four-minute mile, others who hear of it become able to do the same.

Our belief, or lack of belief, in our ability to accomplish something plays an important role in whether or not we succeed.

There are many techniques that can increase individual resilience. Reframing negative life experiences into lessons for greater success is one technique.

One of the first things that must be done is to quiet any existing negative internal dialog. The conversations that are most influential on our own lives are the ones we hold with ourselves in the privacy of our own minds. Our "thoughts" can also be referred to as "self-talk."

Refuting our internal negative "Self-Talk" is one method of lessening its volume and negative impact. In a study (Sbarra, Smith & Mahl 2001) of divorcing individuals, self-compassion—which would translate into less negative self-talk—was cited as the factor that uniquely predicts good outcomes.

Our thoughts create our realities. Two individuals can have exactly the same experience and their individual perspectives on life make the experience a nightmare for one while it is an exciting journey for the other. We choose our perspectives. The perspective determines how our experience feels. How our experience feels determines our responses to the experience.

Life is a combination of events and interactions that pass through filters in our brains and produce our perception, which is what our sensory system is responding to when the emotional feedback is provided. The filters our brain uses to determine which information reaches our conscious mind can be consciously adjusted. Utilizing Right Responses involves adjusting the filters that influence our perceptions.

The greatest resilience comes when an individual decides to be optimistic before an experience requires resilience. Forming an opinion that believes in one's own competence, ability to handle a variety of situations, flexibility, and intelligence will provide a firm foundation to meet life's challenges. While it is easier to develop resilience before it is needed, it is possible to adopt these beliefs after the fact and reframe situations that were traumatizing.

Al Siebert, PhD concludes, "Highly complex, resilient individuals are always curious, exploring, trying new ways of doing things, and learning. They are open to take in, examine, and process new inputs, ignore or let go of what is not of value or interest, and move to the next experience. They can react to an unexpected, life-disrupting change by welcoming it and converting it into a desirable life event" Siebert 2005, pp. 201-202). Emotions are information designed to guide us to what is best for our well-being. For many, this brings forth the question "Are Emotions Guidance from God?" From the perspective of whether or not we should follow our EGS the origin is irrelevant. Emotions provide guidance. They work. They help us thrive. Resilience is increased when emotional guidance is understood and acted on. However, the question is worth exploring. Although no researchers are saying they have proved the existence of God, quantum physics has proved the existence of a mechanism where all matter in the universe is connected by waves (Talbot 1992). If God does exist, this could provide a methodology to perform "miracles", including being everywhere at the same time.

> Miracles happen, not in opposition to Nature, but in opposition to what we know of Nature.
>
> —St. Augustine

There are passages in various holybooks that encourage following guidance. They are usually interpreted to mean following what is written in the books or the guidance from religious leaders. However, when considered in light of the clear evidence that we not only receive guidance through our EGS but that the guidance is specific to us, our goals and dreams, the passages actually make more sense, in my opinion, if the interpretation is that the guidance refers to our EGS.

From the *Bible*, Proverbs 3:5:

> Trust in the Lord with all your heart and lean not on your own understanding; In all your ways acknowledge Him, and He will make your paths straight.

Proverbs 16:9:

> A man's heart plans his way, but the Lord directs his steps" seems to indicate the guidance is specific to our unique goals.

When interpreted to mean one should read a holy book for guidance and considered in light of both the lack of literacy and access to the books at the time they were written the passages did not make sense to me. They seem to make more sense if the EGS is interpreted as the guidance rather than referring to words written long ago that can be interpreted in many different ways. When guidance from the EGS is used, there is no guesswork and the path to what is desired is straight. The shortest path to their goals feels better than a longer route.

Examples from other belief structures that suggest guidance is available are shown below or cited for reference.

From the *Bhagavad Gita*:

> The Supersoul within everyone's heart, directly gives us guidance....

From the *Koran* (Al-Qur'an):

> Others, however, understand the words of the soul, which, having attained the knowledge of the truth, rests satisfied, and relies securely thereon, undisturbed by doubts; or of the soul which is secure of its salvation, and free from fear or sorrow.

From Abraham:

> You cannot be separated from that which you are calling God… People hear us say, 'Reach for the thought that feels the best.' And they think, 'Oh no, I need to listen to what God wants.' But aren't we talking about the same thing? Aren't your emotions guiding you (to what you want)?

Similar wisdom is found in other belief structures. I would encourage anyone who feels concern about the use of emotional guidance conflicting with religious beliefs to explore the teachings of their religion for indications that suggest guidance is available. I found evidence everywhere I looked including Úrîmad-Bhâgavatam, the Tao, Buddhist teachings, and Confucius. For those who have chosen to live according to religious beliefs, I suggest the correlations are strong enough to allow room for the EGS to be incorporated into their existing religious beliefs and practices. The absolute beauty of our guidance systems, the brilliance of its design, is that a belief in God is not required for the system to work perfectly. Following the guidance of what feels better and using "Right Responses" in response to emotional guidance leads us to lives of thriving regardless of our religious or spiritual beliefs or absence thereof. As previously cited, positive emotions are so beneficial for us—increasing our resilience, reducing the risks from negative life events, decreasing the risk of all types of major illnesses and improving relationships (Seligman 2011). We have an EGS that helps us enjoy better-feeling emotions. It makes sense to use the guidance available to us.

Works Cited

Abraham (2004). [cd-rom]. Chicago, IL, Saturday, September 18th, 2004.

Achor, Shawn (2010). *The Happiness Advantage*. Crown Business, NY, NY.

Al-Qur'an (*The Koran*) (2005-02-01).

American Academy of Neurology (2001, July 13). Keeping up your overall health may keep dementia away, study suggests. *Science Daily*.

Association for Psychological Science (2011, September 24), *Pathways to Resilience: Maternal Nurturance as a Buffer Against the Effects of Childhood Poverty on Metabolic Syndrome at Midlife*.

Barnet, M.D Beth et al. (2008) *Arch Pediatric Adolescent Medicine*, 2008;162[3]:246-252.

Berkeley-Oakland Study (ongoing). Described by Seligman in *Flourish*. Unable to locate additional information on this study.

BMC Cancer 2008, Ronit Peled, Devora Carmil, Orly Siboni-Samocha and Ilana Shoham-Vardi. Breast cancer, psychological distress and life events among young women. *BMC Cancer* 8:245 doi:10.1186/1471-2407-8-245.

BMJ (2010). Mortality among contraceptive pill users: cohort evidence from *Royal College of General Practitioners' Oral Contraception Study*, 340 doi: 10.1136/bmj.c927 (Published 11 March 2010).

Boehm, J. K., & Jubzansky, L.D. (2012). The heart's content: The association between positive psychological well-being and cardiovascular health. *Psychological Bulletin*.

Bhagavad Gita (Bg. 10.11).

Broderick, Jeanine (2012a) Scientifically Proven Benefits of Happiness. *Happiness1st*. Retrieved from http://www.happiness1st.com/index.php/benefits/benefits-of-happiness/some-scientifically-proven-benefits-of-happiness

_____ (2012b) Your 6th Sense. *Happiness1st*. Retrieved from http://www.happiness1st.com/index.php/happiness-1st-the-blog/item/your-6th-sense

_____ (2012c), Presentation at PPIA2012, *Positive Psychology In Action, Inc. Positive Health Promotion Forum*, May 27-28, Houston, TX

Brooks, Robert, Ph.D., and Goldstein, Sam, Ph.D. (2004). *The Power of Resilience: Achieving Balance, Confidence, and Personal Strength in Your Life*, McGraw Hill.

Buddhist Teachings. Woodward, Frank Lee (2011-03-24). *The Buddha's Path of Virtue A Translation of the Dhammapada*.

Cohn, M. A., Fredrickson, B. L., Brown, S. L., Mikels, J. A., & Conway, A. M. (2009 June). Happiness Unpacked: Positive emotions Increase life Satisfaction by Building Resilience (Author Manuscript) published as 'Emotion', 9(3): 361-368, doi: 10.1037a0015952.

Confucius: "By three methods we may learn wisdom: first, by reflection, which is noblest."

Economic and Social Research Council (ESRC) (2012, March 2). A healthy teenager is a happy teenager. *ScienceDaily*.

Ekmund, P. (1992), An argument for basic emotions, *Cognition and Emotion* 6: 169-200.

Frankl, Viktor (2006) *Man's Search for Meaning*, Beacon Press, Originally Published 1946.

Fredrickson, B. L. (2001), The role of positive emotions in positive psychology: The broaden-and-build theory, *American Psychologist* 56: 218-26.

_____ & Losada M. F. (2005). Positive affect and the complex dynamics of human flourishing. *American Psychologist*, 60, 678-686.

_____, Tugade, M. M., Waugh, C. E., & Larkin, G. R. (2003, February). What good are positive emotions in crisis? A prospective study of resilience and emotions following the terrorist attacks on the United

States on September 11th, 2001., *Journal of Personality and Social Psychology*, Vol 84(2), 365-376. doi: 10.1037/0022-3514.84.2.365

Fredrickson, Ph.D., Barbara, (2010). *Positivity*, Three Rivers Press, North Carolina.

_____, Sotiropoulos, Ioannis, Catania, Caterina, Pinto, Lucilia G., Silva, Rui, Pollerberg, G. Elizabeth, Takashima, Akihiko, Sousa, Nuno, and Almeida, Osborne F. X. The Value of Positive Emotions. Stress Acts Cumulatively to Precipitate Alzheimer's Disease-Like Tau Pathology and Cognitive Deficits. *Journal of Neuroscience*, May 25, 2011; 31(21):7840-7847 DOI:10.1523/JNEUROSCI.0730-11.2011

Gyamfi, MD., Cynthia, Byamfi, JD, Mavis M., and Berkowitz, MD, Richard L. (July 2003). Ethical and medicolegal considerations in the obstetric care of a Jehovah's Witness, *Obstetrics & Gynecology*, Volume 102, Issue 1, pp.173-180.

Hirshberg, Caryle and Barasch, Marc Ian (1995), *Remarkable Recovery: What extraordinary healings tell us about getting and staying well*. Riverhead Books, NY, NY.

Hill, Napoleon (1994). *Keys to Success*. Penguin Group, NY, NY.

Holden, Ph.D., Robert (2008). *Success Intelligence*, Carlsbad, CA: Hay House.

James, William 1890 (2007) *The Principles of Psychology*, Vol 1, Cosimo, NY, NY.

Karasu, M.D., T. Bryan, (April 11, 2012). 'The Mystery of Happiness', Retrieved from:http://www.psychologytoday.com/blog/the-mystery-happiness/201204/dont-be-afraid-dying

Keltner, Dacher. (2009). *Born to be Good*. W. W. Norton & Company Ltd., NY, NY.

Kim, Eric S., Park, Nansook, and Peterson. Christopher, (2011). Health and Retirement Study. *Stroke*, 2011; DOI:10.1161/STROKEAHA.111.613448

Laozi (2009-10-04). The Tao Teh King, or the Tao and its Characteristics

Lebrecht, S., Bar, M., Feldman Barrett, L., & Tarr, M. J. (2012). 'Micro-Valences: Perceiving Affective Valence in Everyday Objects'. *Frontiers in Psychology*,; 3 DOI: 10.3389/fpsyg.2012.00107

McCarthy, Bill, and Casey, Teresa (August, 2010). Get Happy! Positive Emotion, Depression and Juvenile Crime, *American Sociological Association Annual Meeting*.

Montgomery, Joanna (May 2012). 'Cancer might be the best thing that ever happened to me,' Retrieved from: http://thestir.cafemom.com/healthy living/136851/cancer migh t be the best

Ong, A. D., Bergeman, C. S., Bisconti, T. L., & Wallace, K. A. (2006) 'Psychological Resilience, Positive Emotions, and Successful Adaptation to Stress in Later Life,' *Journal of Personality and Social Psychology* 91: 730-49.

Oregon State University (2012, May 23). 'Wearing two different hats. Moral decisions may depend on the situation.'

Ronit Peled, Devora Carmil, Orly Siboni-Samocha and Ilana Shoham-Vardi. "Breast cancer, psychological distress and life events among young women". *BMC Cancer BMC Cancer* 2008, 8:245 doi:10.1186/1471-2407-8-245.

Peil, K. T. (2012). Emotion: A Self-regulatory Sense. (C) EFS International, Retrieved from: http://www.emotionalsentience.com

Ricard, Matthieu (2003). *Happiness: A guide to Developing Life's Most Important Skill*, Litle, Brown and Company, "Happiness is also a way of interpreting the world, since while it may be difficult to change the world, it is always possible to change the way we look at it." and "It would be a pity to underestimate the mind's power of transformation. If we try resolutely over the course of years to master our thoughts as they come to us, to apply appropriate antidotes to negative emotion and to nourish positive ones, our efforts will undoubtedly yield results that would have seemed unattainable at first."

Reeve, Christopher (2002). *Nothing is Impossible: Reflections on a New Life*, Random House.

Rissman, Robert A., Staup, Michael A., Lee, Allyson Roe, Justice, Nicholas J., Rice, Kenner C., Vale, Wylie, and Sawchenko, Paul E. "Corticotropin-releasing factor receptor-dependent effects of repeated stress on tau phosphorylation, solubility, and aggregation". *Proceedings of the National Academy of Sciences*, 2012 DOI: 10.1073/pnas.1203140109

Rollin, M., Atkinson, M., & Bradley, R. T. (2004). "Electrophysiological Evidence of Intuition. Part 1: The Surprising Role of the Heart," *Journal of Alternative and Complementary Medicine* 10(1) pp. 133-143.

Rubenstein, Ph.D., (ed.) (1999). *An Awakening from the Trances of Everyday Life: A Journey to Empowerment*, Sages Way Press, North Carolina.

Sbarra, D. A., Smith, H. L., & Mehl, M. R. (2001, September 21). 'Advice to divorcees: Go easy on yourself'. *Association for Psychological Science.*

Seligman, Martin E. P. (2011). *Flourish: A Visionary New Understanding of Happiness and Well-Being*, Free Press, pp. 167 & 171.

_____ (2006). *Learned Optimism*. Simon & Schuster, NY, NY. Originally published 1991.

Seery, M. D. (2011, December 18). Traumatic experiences may make you tough. *Association for Psychological Science*.

Siebert, Al (2005). *The Resilience Advantage*, pp. 201-02, San Francisco, CA: Barrett-Koehler Publishers, Inc.

Sire, James W. (2009). *The Universe Next Door: A Basic World view Catalog*, pp. 15-16.

Úrîmad-Bhâgavatam (SB 1.19.36).

Stoeber, Joachim and Janssen, Dirk P. "Perfectionism and coping with daily failures: positive reframing helps achieve satisfaction at the end of the day". *Anxiety, Stress & Coping*, 2011.

Talbot, Michael (1992). *The Holographic Universe*, Harper Perennial, NY, NY.

Trine, Ralph Waldo (1897). *In Tune With The Infinite*, Retrieved from http://newthoughtlibrary.com/trineRalphWaldo/inTune/#1

Weissman, Dr. Darren R., (2005). *The Power of Infinite Love & Gratitude: An Evolutionary Journey to Awakening Your Spirit*, Hay House, Inc.

CHAPTER 13

The Role of Language in Promoting Trauma Recovery and Resilience

Pamela Trotman and Leisha Townson

Abstract

This chapter will provide an overview of the field of trauma psychotherapy, distinguishing between normal post-trauma emotional responses and Post-Traumatic Stress Disorder. It will also chart the historical context of key language constructs related to traumatology and explores their potential influences on the therapeutic process.

A crucial though often unrecognised influence on the outcome of trauma therapy is the mindset from which the therapist approaches and views the client. Whether the therapist, albeit unknowingly, sees the client as 'victim' or 'survivor' shapes the trajectory of the trauma recovery journey.

From a social work perspective the authors will explore the extent to which many linguistic concepts go largely unchallenged with their potential to 'cement' thinking as well as disrupt both the therapeutic relationship and the client's view of self. Discussion will centre on some core theoretical concepts including role of mirror neurons and empathic connections.

Using anecdotal evidence the authors will discuss how the anchoring the client and therapist to the concept of the Survivor Self triggers a shift in focus from the trauma narrative to the language of the Survivor Self. This shift in focus has been observed to generate a sense of empowerment and belief/faith in one's capacities to undertake the work of trauma recovery. Within the therapeutic dyad this shift occurs for both client and therapist alike.

In writing this chapter the authors seek to provide an overview of dominant themes identified in the trauma literature. The focus will be on the extent to which the language that underpins those themes promotes trauma recovery and the building of post-trauma resilience. The authors have chosen to use the phrase: 'people who have experienced a traumatic event" as it places the therapist's focus on the person rather than the trauma. This perspective ensures the person remains central to the therapeutic process rather than the trauma narrative overshadowing the person.

The discussion on language will explore how the nuances of the spoken, thought and written word, individually and when used in phrases, shape the therapeutic relationship and hence process. To this end we seek to take the reader beyond the literal meaning of words to explore how they influence the therapist's perception of the client in relation to his/her experience of trauma and, simultaneously influence the therapist's perception of her 'self'. 'Perception', in this context is seen as having the following meanings which can be present at any one time or over time: "awareness, insight, discernment, acuity (alertness), observation and sensitivity".

We acknowledge and value the work done by many researchers and therapists, each of whom has contributed to the collective learning on trauma and trauma recovery. We also salute the courage and determination of the many clients who have honoured us by their willingness to entrust their wounded[2] selves to our efforts to assist them reclaim their lives. What follows is an attempt to interweave that knowledge and wisdom with our concept of the *Survivor Self*, to craft a shared tapestry of understanding, that tapestry being the fabric of trauma recovery, post-trauma growth and human resilience.

Two words are prevalent in trauma literature: 'victim' and 'survivor'. Victim was in common usage before and during the early 1980's with a gradual shift to survivor by the early 1990s

(Herman 1992). As a descriptor the term victim highlights the sense of powerlessness/helplessness at its core. Versions III and IV of the Diagnostic and Statistical Manual of Mental Health Disorders Heal (DSM III & IV) identify the experience of powerlessness in the face of threat to life and safety as being a key pre-determinant to the presence of trauma in a person's life.

Survivor has more positive connotations as it affirms the reality that the person has survived the traumatic incident, albeit with serious psychological implications stemming from known trauma reactions. Herman 1992 describes these as "normal reactions to an abnormal event" (p33). This descriptor remains in common usage by trauma therapists. Despite the apparent differences in emphasis the authors have noticed that much of the literature, even when using the term survivor to describe a person who has experienced a traumatic event, often focuses on the trauma narrative. The trauma narrative is described as being when the traumatic events become the central theme of the therapeutic process. It is seen as having negative connotations because it highlights, and potentially reinforces, the sense of powerlessness experienced during the traumatic event. The authors have identified that when the literature focuses on the trauma narrative little or scant attention appears to be given to the extent to which the person has successfully engaged a range of coping strategies towards surviving the actual event.

At the other end of the victim-survivor continuum is the survivor narrative where the *Survivor Self* becomes hugely instrumental in achieving post-trauma recovery and in promoting post-trauma growth. We describe the *Survivor Self* as an integral facet of each person which exists *before, during* and *after* a traumatic event and which remains intact, (Townson, and Trotman. 2009). We coined the term *Survivor Self* as a synthesis of our extensive counselling of people who had experienced a traumatic event, our own trauma recovery journeys combined with formal knowledge of trauma and trauma reactions and the insights gained as a result of our growing understanding and mindfulness of key elements of brain functioning, particularly empathic attunement. This will be discussed more fully later.

Similar to the focus on the trauma narrative the authors have identified that much of the discussion in trauma literature focuses on ways to prevent or treat Post-Traumatic Stress Disorder (PTSD) with the implicit assumption that all trauma survivors [victims—sic] will, without intervention, develop some level of PTSD and as such are unlikely to fully recover (Engdahl et al 1997). Other authors cite research which confirms that many survivors do not go on to develop PTSD and are able to lead rich and rewarding lives without major or long-term impairment to psycho-social functioning. (McFarlane. et. al. 1998).

The first edition of the DSM, effectively DSM-I, included a "stress response syndrome" which was the forerunner of PTSD. In DSM-II the relevant category was "situational disorders. It was in the transition from DSM to DSM-II that the recognition shifted from syndrome to disorder—thus it is evident that stress reactions have been perceived as a disorder since 1968, long before DSM-IV came out in 1994.

This flowed from the growing recognition and documentation of a range of psycho-social disturbances exhibited by Vietnam War Veterans experiencing significant and recurring adjustment issues on their return to civilian life. Whilst a key psychiatric landmark in terms of the recognition and validation of the potential impact of traumatic experiences there is nothing in the descriptor that acknowledges that not all people who have experienced trauma will develop Post-Traumatic Stress Disorder.

The DSM IV's attachment of the word 'Disorder' when naming and describing Acute Stress is seen as being problematic because it fails to acknowledge or validate normal post-trauma reactions. As such it leaves no room for normalising perceptions that a person who has experienced trauma is likely to exhibit a range of psychological reactions which, albeit powerful and emotionally destabilising, are normal and predictable. The authors note that in both the DSM-III and IV the description of a 'disorder' includes a criterion which states:

> "Must not be merely an expectable and culturally sanctioned response to a particular event, for example, the death of a loved one". (DSM-III & IV para C).

The authors assert that lack of congruency between the DSM IV's definitions has the effect of skewing perceptions of normal trauma responses towards the pathological. If/when this conceptual framework underpins the therapist's view of the client there is a huge risk of perpetuating negative trauma constructs thereby 'locking' both client and therapist into the negative aspects of the trauma conceptual framework which potentially impedes the process of trauma recovery.

In critiquing the language used in the DSM III & IV with reference to acute stress the authors affirm that there is no dispute some people who have experienced a traumatic event do, in time, develop chronic mental health disturbances which are reflected in the currently accepted diagnosis of *Post-Traumatic Stress Disorder*. The authors posit however that the early and apparent unquestioning use of the word 'disorder' when referring to '*acute stress*' risks pathologising what is widely recognised as normal responses to abnormal circumstances and as such goes against the above key determinant of a clinical 'disorder' as set out in both DSM III and IV. This observation is reflected in Randal's et al (1999) conclusions:

> Longitudinal studies using acute stress disorder criteria, as well as broader considerations of the clinical and scientific functions that posttraumatic diagnoses should serve, suggest a need to re-evaluate the current DSM-IV approach to posttraumatic syndromes. (p. 1677)

Randal et al, go on to pose a diagnostic dilemma:

> 'The decision as to whether to define a disorder broadly or narrowly usually hinges on the relative consequences of doing so and has

been widely debated in psychiatry with respect to psychiatric diagnosis. For example, which is worse: failing to identify some persons with PTSD who could benefit from treatment, or mistakenly diagnosing some persons who are actually experiencing a normative reaction to a traumatic event?" (p1677)

The conceptual 'place' of the therapist's thinking on the 'victim-survivor' continuum and that position will be largely influenced by the dominant theoretical constructs which underpin that thinking. The therapist's conceptual place on that continuum will, in turn, shape how she relates to the client. For example: if the therapist thinks in terms of 'disorders' then she is likely to focus on those elements of the client's behaviour which validate the presence of a disorder. If she sees the client as having a 'disorder' then it removes, however obliquely, the known normative elements of post-trauma reactions. The authors posit that whilst not intended, the implied message of this conceptual framework is that the person remains powerlessness in the face of the traumatic event and subsequent reactions, and as such, is perennially locked into the status of victim. Conversely, if the dominant conceptual framework underpinning her thinking is on the likely presence of normal reactions to abnormal events the focus becomes the managing of those reactions so that the person can be assisted to integrate the traumatic events thereby regaining pre-trauma levels of psycho-social-physiological functioning.

It is interesting to note that in the early 1960's another group of researchers and practitioners were describing Crisis Intervention Theory (Caplin (also known as Kaplin 1964). This theoretical construct describes a crisis as:

..an acute emotional reaction to a powerful stimulus or demand......

There are three characteristics of all crises:

1. The usual balance between thinking and emotions is disturbed.

2. The usual coping mechanisms fail.
3. There is evidence of impairment in the individual or group involved in the crisis".

Jeffrey T Mitchell. (2010 p. 1)

The above definition is not too dissimilar to that used in DSM IV to describe Acute Stress Disorder. Another interesting observation is that Crisis Intervention theorists and the DSM IV identify different timeframes for the resolution of the crisis/acute stress state with Crisis Intervention theorists suggesting a longer timeframe (1-12 weeks) for the intervention process to achieve '*crisis resolution*': the resolution of the most pressing problem (Roberts 2000). Roberts, citing Golan (1978), makes the distinction between 'crisis reaction 'and 'crisis resolution' with the former, crisis reaction being marked by:

> helplessness, confusion, anxiety, disbelief, shock and anger... [and] the person may appear to be incoherent, disorganised, agitated and volatile, or calm, withdrawn, subdued and apathetic' (p. 7)

Roberts continues by citing Golan's assertion that: "it is during this period that the individual is often most willing to seek help and that crisis intervention is most effective at this time" (Roberts 2000 p7). The authors have also found this to be the case though it does require the therapist to have a range of crisis management strategies at her disposal.

The Role of 'Self', Empathic Attunement and Mirror Neurons

Schore (2005) draws on Kohut's (1978) concept of how the infant's sense of 'self' develops within the brain through the process of empathic attunement between the infant and primary caregivers (p. 435). Central to this process is the pattern of connection (empathic attunement) and disconnection between the caregiver and infant which, repeated over time, assists the infant to develop a sense of 'self' separate to that of the caregiver (self-self/object) and in turn the capacity to self-sooth (self-regulation) (p. 436)

Herman (1992) writes in depth on how traumatic events "shatter the construction of the self that is formed and sustained in relation to others". She goes on to assert that 'traumatic events have primary effects on not only the psychological structures of self but also on the systems of attachments and meaning that link individuals and community" (p. 51). This is the 'self' that the authors refer to as the 'wounded' person who first presents in counselling.

Rothschild's (2004) work, "mirror mirror: our brains are hardwired for empathy" crystalised our conceptual shift to view empathy as a dynamic feature of interactions rather than the earlier, more common, understanding of it being what the therapist showed towards the client. That newfound understanding of the function of empathy became the final piece in our naming of the *Survivor Self*. Having identified, from an empirical perspective, the existence of the *Survivor Self* and its presence within the therapeutic context we then took on the challenge of relating this concept to current trauma literature and research. Our journey took us into the realms of exploring how empathy functions to develop and sustain relationships and how the capacity for empathic attunement can be harnessed within the therapeutic relationship to promote trauma recovery as well as to 'protect' the therapist from the risks of vicarious traumatisation. Magee (2008) cites Rothschild's assertion that: "all emotions are contagious" (p.1) served to underpin the importance of the therapist having an awareness of how emotions are transmitted between the therapist and client and the client to therapist.

Rizzalotti et al.'s accidental discovery of mirror neurons in the mid 1990's has led to extensive research and widespread agreement by neuroscientists that we are naturally hard-wired to imitate others as discussed by Keyser (2009). Originally discovered in monkeys, Rizzalotti et al observed that every time a researcher reached for a piece of fruit or nut the monkeys' brain monitors beeped. From this observation they identified a specific group of brain cells which fired when the animal saw or heard an action and then mimicked that action, naming those cells 'mirror neurons'. They then applied this to an understanding of human brain function.

Subsequent research soon proved that, unlike monkeys who have a singular mirror neuron mechanism the "The human brain has multiple mirror neuron systems that specialize in carrying out and understanding not just the actions of others but their intentions, the social meaning of their behavior and their emotions". Blakesly (2006) cites Rizzalotti assertion that "We are exquisitely social creatures,... Our survival depends on understanding the actions, intentions and emotions of others."

Ramachandran in an interview with Marsh (2012) declares he is unsure of the role of mirror neurons in affective/emotional experiences but does support the thinking that "they are involved in empathy for, say, touch or a gentle caress or pain." In a recent interview with GoCognitive Rizzalotti (2011) maintains we are on safe ground by saying there is a mirror mechanism embedded in emotion centres and "this is another way we communicate.... communication is a way of understanding another [person] from the inside." An example being Iacoboni, in an interview with Lehrer (2008):

> "... if you see me choke up, in emotional distress..., mirror neurons in your brain simulate my distress. You automatically have empathy for me. You know how I feel because you literally feel what I am feeling."

In his 2011 videoed interview Rizzalotti's (2011) goes on to outline the role of the pre-frontal lobe in 'modulating' motor activity adding that there is a similar function with respect to emotions: "empathy is always present'....however the 'blocking' capacity of the parietal frontal cortex serves to modulate the intensity of the felt emotion". He then explains how the intensity of felt emotion can be further modulated through training and practice.

Later in this chapter, by way of the scenarios, the reader will be invited into the counselling room to witness the empirical evidence of the above brain functions and how they serve to elicit the *Survivor Self*. Our particular focus will be on the level of congruency between what the therapist feels towards/about the client, especially his/her perceived capacity for recovery, and the implicit meaning of language, promotes and sustains therapeutic attunement leading to trauma recovery. Once that attunement has been achieved it becomes the metaphoric 'connecting fibres' which helps the client reassemble self, including the capacity for self-regulation, thereby strengthening the client's resilience.

When a gradual reduction in the intensity of the acute stress response is achieved, within the attuned relationship, the opportunity is created for the client to reactivate previous positive self-regulatory strategies and to learn new ones. To this extent 'therapeutic language' becomes more than the actual words used as the bulk of the communication (language) is conveyed subliminally through the functioning of empathic attunement which is reinforced, in part, by the operation of mirror neurons. Thus when the therapist demonstrates willingness, and capacity to work with the process of attunement to enhance the efficacy of the *Survivor Self*, this action has the effect of reminding the client of the presence of an internal emotional 'anchor'. And, from the therapist's point of view, it helps maintain the focus on the survivor narrative thereby avoiding the 'trap' of remaining engaged in the emotional turmoil of the trauma narrative. In so doing it counteracts, for the therapist, the fear or concern that one will be vicariously traumatised. Each time the client is assisted to self-regulate powerful trauma reactions the sense of powerlessness is incrementally reduced which in turn reduces the client's adverse response to traumatic memory triggers (Van D Kolt 1994 p. 3), (Rothschild 2000, p. 35). This empirically based evidence is validated by Rizzalotti's explanation (see previous page) of the brain's capacity to modulate felt emotion which can be further 'modulated' by training and practice.

As mentioned above, at the other end of the victim-survivor continuum is the survivor narrative. It differs from the trauma narrative to the extent, that whilst acknowledging and validating the circumstances of the traumatic experience, its focus is on what the person may have done to assist/promote survival. Frequently the person is unaware of these aspects of the overall narrative, often discounting/overlooking them amid the disruptive aftermath of the experience. In the initial stages the emergence of the survivor narrative is frequently halting and misty—often shrouded by the presence of common trauma reactions. For its presence to be felt the therapist has to have some recognition of, and belief in, the person's capacity to recover. Thus where the therapist places herself, and hence her perception of the client, on the victim-survivor continuum will have direct implications for the emergence of the survivor narrative.

Our first awareness of the survivor narrative took shape as a result of two factors:

- Our understanding of and training in Narrative Therapy (White and Epstein 1990) which makes the distinction between the 'Dominant' and 'Alternate' narrative. To this context the trauma narrative is seen as being the Dominant narrative constructed and fuelled equally by the traumatic event and the post trauma reactions. The Alternate narrative, submerged under its dominant relative takes shape when the therapist begins to hear and heed its initially less powerful voice.

- The 'hearing' and 'heeding' of the Alternate narrative's voice occurs, at least initially, through the attunement process. As the therapist listens to the trauma narrative she is likely to also begin to *hear/feel* something that is at odds with that narrative. It might be a fleeting sense of awe and genuine wonderment at how the person was able to survive such horrific events. It might come when she experiences, (mirrors) subtle glimmers of emotions, embedded in the trauma narrative which are at odds with those of terror or powerlessness. Whatever their form, they shape the critical moment when the Alternate narrative can be assisted to 'come-into-the-light' of the counselling room. Mostly this happens when the therapist acknowledges to the client what she is 'sensing'. This oblique expression of 'sensing' has two key outcomes. Firstly it gives credence to the presence of something that contributed to the client's survival and; secondly, it activates the client's mirror neurons: as the therapist expresses the 'felt response' to the client's story the client is better able to begin connecting to that aspect of the story. That process, repeated within the therapeutic context becomes instrumental in promoting the emergence of the survivor narrative.

A secondary effect of the therapist focusing on the survivor narrative is the reduction in the potential for the therapist to vicariously experience the trauma. This reduction is achieved because the therapist is likely to also *'experience'* the empowered aspects of the survivor narrative. When this happens the therapist is better placed to position the trauma content of the narrative, and its associated emotions, within the broader framework of the client as a person who has a pre-trauma integrated sense of self, and as such, the therapist is more likely to stay connected to her own broader and integrated sense of self. In so doing her sense of self is less likely to be distorted or disrupted by having listened to the disturbing aspects of the trauma narrative. We posit that, when researchers comment on the extent to which therapists have identified ' awe', 'wonder' and an 'enriched sense of self and connection to others' as emanating from their work with survivors this is because they have unwittingly 'tuned in' to the survivor narrative(Herman 1992 p. 153), (Steed, & Downing 1998 p5). Rizzalotti's research on the brain's capacity to modulate the intensity of felt emotion combined with the therapist's trust in the *Survivor Self* are seen as being two inner resources, which both therapist and client can draw. Thus when the therapist enters the counselling room in full knowledge of the presence of these inner capacities she is less likely to fear the rigours of managing powerful trauma reactions or be fearful of being vicariously traumatised.

The *'Survivor Self'* and Its Language

As described above the *Survivor Self* is an integral facet of each person which remains intact despite exposure to traumatic events (Townson and Trotman 2009). Our observations suggest that it functions outside of the normal understanding of the 'self' constructs and as such is protected from injury. By remaining intact it provides the bedrock upon which the reconstruction of the 'trauma disrupted self' can commence.

Its place in human psycho-neurological functioning requires research however we assert that it is more than the summation of key functional elements of the brain and as such is perhaps the fabric of each person's unique personality. Readers are reminded that the 'self' research discussed above pertains to the 'self' construct developed in infancy and that it is this aspect of 'self' disrupted by traumatic experiences. The authors have observed that the *Survivor Self's* presence is 'felt' empathically with the assistance of the mirror neurons AND when the therapist is actively mindful of this potential within the therapeutic process. Trotman, (2006) describes this thus:

> I have often used this to help the client tune in to the survivor self[5] by consciously 'feeling' that sense of self before asking if the client would like me to describe what I am hearing/sensing. It is not uncommon, for the client, on listening to my description of the survivor (empowered) self, to take a deep breath, shift posture and to show mild surprise before acknowledging the accuracy of the observation. This is then frequently followed by a flood of examples of remembered successful survival strategies. The telling of survival strategies has the effect of honouring the wise, courageous and integrated part of the person which commences the reconnection process by identifying hitherto obscured inner resources. (p.8)

The *Survivor Self* is felt as a sense of 'dissonance' or incongruence within the therapeutic encounter whilst hearing the trauma narrative. That dissonance is felt by the therapist when an aspect of the trauma narrative is being discussed yet the therapist's 'felt experience' of the client at that moment is at odds with common emotions associated with trauma. An example: Client (female) was recounting being tied up and repeatedly threatened with a machete as it was brought down inches from her face and at times touching her skin as part of her assailant's threats to kill her. Despite the graphic account of those horrific moments the therapist 'felt' a different emotion—not the expected sense of terror and powerlessness. She 'felt' a powerful sense that the client was not cowered which prompted her to ask the question: "what were you thinking when he was doing this to you"? The reply, instant and unequivocal: "you're nothing but a f..king wanker?' Clearly common sense told the woman that to actually voice this opinion at the time would have probably tipped him over the edge resulting in her death yet spoken within the respectful safety of the counselling session it formed the turning point for all future sessions.

The above question, born of the therapist's decision to trust what she was sensing, resulted in the client's *Survivor Self* assuming precedence within the counselling process. As the client 'tuned in/mirrored' the therapist's sense of awe and wonderment at her presence of mind and sheer determination to survive she began to experience for herself what she had done so that this 'wanker' would not 'get the better of her'. In short she had demonstrated to herself an inescapable reality: that despite the odds being against her, and at repeated moments critical to her survival she had retained the capacity (power) to shape the outcome. This gave her the inner knowledge and strength to survive the perilous vicissitudes of a prolonged assault. A chilling footnote is that in the midst of this macabre dance of life and death, calm and terror, her assailant told her that if she had pleaded for her life he would have killed her!

Lessons from This Account

If the therapist had remained solely focused on the content based on the spoken language of the above trauma narrative, the moment for the bringing of a potentially powerful force into the counselling room would have been lost forever. It would have been lost because if the therapist had, in her own mind, used the 'victim' descriptor, the woman would have sensed this and thus she it is unlikely to have given much credence to subsequent reflections of the therapist's felt 'power', if indeed the therapist had been able to 'tune in to' this herself. Nor would they have begun the process of harnessing that power thereby enabling them both to begin shaping the survivor narrative. Instead she would have 'read/seen' the therapist's reflection of herself as being powerless in the face of such a threat. In so doing the therapist would have unwittingly re-enforced any post-trauma perceptions of powerlessness and hopelessness. The words the client later gave to what she felt when she was thinking 'you're nothing but a f.cking wanker' were 'disdain' and 'defiance'

Pivotal to the therapist's capacity to sense the powerful energy of the unspoken words of 'disdain and defiance' was her repeated practice of placing her thinking and hence perception of her clients as being towards or at the survivor end of the 'victim-survivor' continuum. Linked with this was her active use of the empathic connection as a key therapeutic tool. Thus, coming from these two conceptual viewpoints, it was a short step for her to tune-in, and give credence to, the voice of the survivor, even though, logically she would be expecting to sense *fear*, even *terror* and undoubtedly *helplessness*. Now, five years later she can recall this story with chilling accuracy. When she looks at that picture (trauma) and 'sees' the client she can still feel what she later learnt were disdain and defiance and, when she recalls asking that critical question, she is transported from the scene to the safety of counselling room in the awesome presence of the survivor. Such was the power of the encounter with the woman's

Survivor Self the therapist has not been vicariously traumatised despite retaining vivid memories of the trauma narrative.

The words 'disdain' and 'defiance' marked the key language constructs of this survival story as they embodied, and became the foundation for the woman's post-trauma recovery and integration of the traumatic experience with her larger sense of self. They represented that part of herself which she was not, even in the face of death, prepared to sacrifice. In her own words: 'I had to remain true to myself'. Having connected to the essence of what it meant to be 'her' she was then able to access and harness the powerful (stabilising) energy of those words as she grappled with the flood of common post-trauma reactions and the reality that the ongoing threat to her and her child safe was beyond her control. She used that energy to help her manage the times when despair and self-loathing (for her perceived inability to protect herself and son) threatened her emotional stability. In the subsequent court hearings she was not intimidated by the defence barrister, known for his bully of witnesses, which meant that those hearings became tangible evidence of her capacities to function under extreme duress and threat and to remain 'true to herself'. This served to shield her from the potential of being re-traumatised by the court experience.

- *Postscript 1*: The woman wishes it to be known that she was not in an intimate (domestic) relationship with her assailant.

- *Postscript 2*: She later learnt that her assailant had warned his barrister that "she was not a woman to be messed with".

- *Postscript 3:* When she read the above she experienced a similar sense of awe as that felt by her therapist during the counselling sessions. This consolidated her sense of reclaimed post trauma self—a long way from the feelings of self-loathing that had prevailed in the immediate post trauma period. She also realised that her reading of the account did not take her back into the trauma despite vividly recalling the traumatic events. She realises that she is the living proof of the brain's capacity to integrate traumatic experiences with the whole of self so that the memory remains but not as a traumatic memory. This affirms that she had recovered from the trauma and has reclaimed her life, as exemplified by her capacity to use her own experiences as the empirical evidence of the presence and capacity of the *Survivor Self*.

Illuminating the *Survivor Self* in the Counselling Room

Case I

We're in our 5th session. Paula, 25, and I are exploring further the extent to which her previous experience of emotional, sexual, physical and financial abuse within an intimate relationship was impacting on her current Depression and difficulty in engaging with her 13 month old child Lily, born to her new partner. It has taken this long to venture anywhere near the trauma narrative as Paula had initially presented with the counselling goal of wanting to 'get back on top of things', including losing weight, before her partner returned home after working interstate. We had an 8-10 week timeframe to achieve these goals.

Initially Paula's presentation was of flat emotional affect with monotone and cryptic responses to my efforts to engage with her. Too large for the chair and often mildly dishevelled she sat awkwardly with Lily playing at our feet. Lily's presence highlighted Paula's social isolation as she had no-one who could mind Lily during counselling sessions and she could not afford a baby-sitter. Frequently in the initial sessions she would remind me that she had 'difficulty feeling safe talking about her problems' though insisted she wanted to continue with me as her counsellor. Superficially she exuded a pervading sense of lethargy and of being 'stuck'. Highly intelligent she spoke of her frustration and dislike of herself because she filled her days by doing only the bare minimum of caring for Lily and of housework. To cope she often retreated into reading novels and, increasingly, avoided going to places where she may be required to socialise—fearing that she had nothing to contribute. She castigated herself for her apparent powerlessness to break this cycle. Such was the extent of her lethargy the possibility of her being clinically Depressed was raised with a subsequent referral for formal assessment, and if necessary, the provision of medication. She attended the appointment with the doctor who confirmed her Depression though she elected to defer taking medication as she wanted to try to sort this out in her own strength first.

The trauma narrative only surfaced when, in about the 3rd session, she asserted that she 'was not like this before' and was adamant that it had nothing to do with her current relationship or having become a mother. Slowly, over the next couple of sessions, we pieced together a word picture of who she was 'before' and what had occurred to cause this profound shift. She described her 'before' self as being: slim with an interest in dressing well, confident, outgoing, creative—especially interested in becoming a writer. She had been able to hold onto the last element of her former self by using writing, even contributing to a domestic violence abuse blog via a pseudonym, to alert others to the signs of abuse in relationships.

At first haltingly she described how, five years previously, she had become involved with the man who repeatedly abused and debased her over a five month period with much of the narrative emphasising, from her point of view, how stupid she had been to have 'allowed' this to happen. That self-blaming was re-enforced by her perception that she had done nothing to escape the situation. The more she felt safe enough to tell her story without being judged the more she was able to place herself beyond the trauma narrative to begin the process of exploring how and why it was still impacting on her capacity to enjoy life and relationships, including her relationship with Lily.

At our last session we had agreed that we would attempt to construct a time-line documenting key events relating to the abuse which had eroded her sense of self. This marked the first time, since the abuse, where she purposefully chose to revisit the trauma experiences. The time-line was recorded on a two page electronic whiteboard so that visually she could chart different elements of the abuse and her gradual movement towards finding and actioning an escape. Attention to the subtle indicators of her gradual movement towards finding a way to escape resulted in her identifying, for the first time, what she had successfully done to protect herself from even worse abasement and violence. This gave her insight into how the moment of her escape was not coincidental as she had previously thought. As she took in the profundity of this newfound insight I felt myself discerning a sense of her 'wholeness' which had not been crushed or disabled by the months of degradation and despair. Spoken with genuine incredulity I asked the question: "after all the dreadful things he did to you why didn't you give in?" Her response, unequivocal and immediate: "Because then he would have won"! Written in bold, over/under the record on the timeline, these words became the indelible watermark to the time-line as they aptly demonstrated the reality that "he had not won" As she 'felt' my awesome incredulity embodied in the question and the power of her words when she uttered them she needed no convincing of the rightness of what she had just connected with. This marked a knowingness that came from the very core of herself as a person: what we, as authors have describe above as her *Survivor Self*

Once spoken these words served to reconnect her to her 'former sense of self' which until that moment, she believed had been irretrievably lost. Overnight her whole demeanour changed as did her attention to her child, personal grooming and home. Gone was the lethargic young woman and in her place was someone who was able to action all the self-improvement plans she had outlined at our first counselling session.

Case II

I first met Carmel when she rang the organisation where I was working because she was struggling with life: the kids were overwhelming her; her emotions were overwhelming her and that basically life was overwhelming her. In our conversation her voice was flat and for a young person it seemed to have no life, but I could sense something powerful: frustration? anger?—there was something there. Over the next couple of months she rarely attended our scheduled appointments. Most weeks she would ring with some excuse and then make another appointment for the following week. If she didn't ring to cancel I initiated contact. Each phone call became a counselling session.

When we finally got to have face to face counselling she disclosed that she had been sexually abused as a child but there was no indication of what had caused *this* state of mind *now*. Many sessions were saturated with the words; angry, out of control, depressed, destabilised. They were expressed verbally, non-verbally and heart-felt. Whatever the catalyst she decided she wanted to lay charges against her stepfather for the abuse that had occurred 18 years previously. She had already had conversations with the police who she said were reluctant to take action.

We spent a lot of time doing work around the legal process...the interviews with police; all which could potentially make her feel increasingly devalued and exposed. What if the court didn't find him guilty? What did we need to do to counteract these? We talked about the gamut of conflicting feelings, especially of being torn between powerful forces—anger and concern, especially for her stepdad as he was both the perpetrator who had abused her and was also the person who had shown her the most thoughtfulness, affection and attention she had ever experienced. She was torn between love and concern for the impact of her allegations on family and stepdad and expressed anger, hatred and deep hurt. She was mercurial: one minute one thing, the next, something different in her demeanour and tone.

How does she hold onto a sense of herself when she didn't recognise herself? Couldn't predict herself? Often, especially in the beginning then occasionally throughout the twelve months of counselling she asked the question: "Do you believe me."

She increasingly felt as if she were in a dark hole and that apart from when she was in counselling, when she felt better about herself, she "couldn't get out". She rarely attempted any of the strategies we had agreed upon: giving one excuse after another, most of which we both knew were untrue. I challenged her: she needed to "step up to the plate"...that at the end of the day the only outcome making her feel better had to come from her rather than waiting for me to fix her up. Despite the fact that she acknowledged this as a truth, the downhill spiral continued, as did the lack of commitment to strategies, until she hit rock bottom and was talking about suicide. We both could not understand why this was the case as it was at odds with both our perceptions that I was helping her and that some shifts had occurred in how she felt about herself. From my part I felt that I was a bit at loss as to "what else...?" which I acknowledged to her. I raised the idea that it was HER journey of recovery and that like in many things other individuals can have other and different things to contribute to learning. I raised the question of whether she would consider the idea that another counsellor would be able to assist her in the rest of her journey. I made it very clear that I wasn't giving up on her; that my role would just shift more into being an advocate and witness support person. She understood the potentially positive aspects of changing counsellors and agreed.

As a last attempt it was agreed that we would use the therapeutic technique of interviewing an emotion (anger). We had spoken about using this technique for months but Carmel had been resistant. As we progressed through the interview it was like watching a flame flare up inside her. What came out was the word 'caring': if she didn't care about the perpetrator it wouldn't be so hard; if she didn't care about the fact that her mother was probably going to testify against her it wouldn't hurt so much; if she didn't care about herself ... She finally realised after 30-odd years of living that she actually did care for herself.

It's at this time that I introduced the *Survivor Self* to her as a concept; what it looks like, what others had said how it feels. She already knew I was going to Croatia to present a workshop. Our conversation was interspersed with questions such as: "from that side of the room do you think we're on the right track", "do you recognise that in yourself?". This cemented some of the positivity she had experienced towards herself and her situation during the interview.

It was a fortnight before she came back to see me. When I first saw her my heart sank. I thought 'it just wasn't happening'. Her outward demeanour remained more or less as it was when we first met. We sat down and I asked her 'what's been happening?' In response to the question she just 'lit up within'. With an air of surprised excitement she talked of a shift in the way she thought: of herself, of the abuse, of the dark hole, her own sense of value. What had changed was her reality of herself as expressed in her own words:

"If I had not seen the faith you have in me I would not have been able to have faith in myself now". AND "I can't ever see myself going back into that dark hole".

Postscript: Recently, when speaking with Carmel to get permission to tell her story, we spoke about the strengths she has built on in her recovery journey and how it was "hard work" and painful. Within the recounting and remembering she asked: "In the beginning, did you believe me...I wasn't sure if you did then?" My immediate answer was "Did I believe in all your excuses for not turning up...for not doing the things we spoke about...NO...I didn't but you already know that. Did I ever doubt your story of abuse? NEVER, but you already know that, too or you would have told me to f*ck off and left".

Conclusion

We now invite you as the reader, when reflecting on the above two scenarios, whether as therapist or in another role, to ponder on the following questions:

1. Where would you most likely place your thinking on the Victim—Survivor continuum if you had Paula and Carmel as your clients?
2. What are the dominant concepts/theoretical constructs in your thinking?
3. To what extent might the conceptual framework or language you use serve to skew or assist your capacity to fully engage with Carmel and Paula?
4. What would most challenge you if you had either of these young women as your client?

We have endeavoured to highlight apparent unchallenged thinking around the use of language and its implied meaning either in literature or within the counselling context. In particular we have made a distinction between the words, 'victim' and 'survivor'. By making this distinction we sought to encourage readers to begin their own process of critical reflection of how the language of literature and their own use of language shapes their perceptions and responses to people who have experienced trauma.

The concept of the *Survivor Self* has been introduced with an explanation of how its presence is first identified within the therapeutic process and how its particular language validates and affirms the person's enduring capacity to survive traumatic events and to endure the rigours of post-trauma recovery.

Two aspects of brain functioning relating to the role of empathy and mirror neurons in the shaping one's sense of self, capacity for self-regulation and interpersonal attunement and assessment of intention have been identified. Together they provide the theoretical 'scaffolding' for the concept of the *Survivor Self.*

By inviting you, the reader, into the counselling room through the scenarios we have attempted to introduce you to the *Survivor Self* as a 'lived' experience. It is hoped that by doing this you could observe and experience the shifts in thinking and language that can take place when the *Survivor Self* comes to the fore.

We now invite you to further explore the *Survivor Self's* journey towards the reclamation of those aspects of 'self' damaged by the trauma in the belief that the capacity for post-trauma growth and human resilience is boundless.

References

1. The term *Survivor Self* is a registered trademark.
2. This word is used here to acknowledge the reality that most clients present in counselling bearing the emotional, physical, spiritual and social impact of psychological trauma.
3. At this stage the notion of the *Survivor Self* had not been fully articulated—hence the lower case.

Works Cited

A.R. Roberts (2005). *Crisis Intervention Handbook: Assessment, Treatment, and Research.* Oxford University Press.

Anechiarico, B. (date unknown) Vicarious Trauma: What are the protective measures? *Perspectives Newsletter*—Californian Coalition On Sexual Offending.

Bell H., Kulkarni S., & Dalton L., Organizational Prevention of Vicarious Trauma *Families in Society*, 2003, v. 84, no. 4, pp. 463-470.

Blakeslee, S (2006). "Cells That Read Minds". http://www.nytimes.com/2006/01/10/science/10mirr.html?pagewanted=all

Friedman, M.J., PTSD History and Overview. Date Created: 01/31/2007 United States Dept. of Veterans Affairs, National Ceter for PTSD.

Herman, J. (1992 &1997). *Trauma and Recovery: The Aftermath of Violence—from Domestic Abuse to Political Terror.* Basic Books.

Hoyt, T. J. (April, 2011). *An Overview of Heinz Kohut's Self Psychology and Object Relations Theory*. Practical Philosophy. http://www.practical philosophy.net/?page_id=426

Izzo, E. and Carpel Miller,V. Vicarious Trauma: The Impact of Controlled Empathy. http://www.selfgrowth.com/articles/Vicarious_Trauma_The_Impact_of_Controlled_Empathy.html

Kagan J., (2005) "Temperament". In: Tremblay RE, Barr RG, Peters RDeV, eds. *Encyclopedia on Early Childhood Development* [online]. Montreal, Quebec: Centre of Excellence for Early Childhood Development. http://www.child encyclopedia.com/documents/KaganANGxp.pdf.

Keyser, C. (2011). *The Emphatic Brain Social*. Brain Press

Kramer, P. (2007). "Empathy". *The Infinite Mind*. Online. Google. [http://www.kmedia.com].

Lehrer J., (2008). Interview with Marco Iacoboni The Mirror Neuron Revolution: Explaining What Makes Humans Social Scientific American http://www.scientificamerican.com/article.cfm?id=the-mirror-neuron-revolut

Linden, Paul. (2002) *Winning Is Healing: Body Awareness and Empowerment for Abuse Survivors Being In Movement Article Summary*. Article originally published in the proceedings of the 2002 conference of the United States Association for Body Psychotherapy. Unpublished.

Marsh, Ramachandran, V.S., "Greater Good—The Science of a Meaningful Life Do Mirror Neurons Give Us Empathy?". 2012 Interview. http://greater good.berkeley.edu/article/item/do_mirror_neurons_give_empathy

McFarlane, A., Shalev A., Yehuda, R. (15 December 1998). Predicting the development of posttraumatic disorder from the acute response to a traumatic event. *Biological Psychiatry*. Volume 44, Issue 12, pp. 1305-1313.

McGee, S 2008 in www.humanresilience.com/.../blog/44-vicarious-traumatisation.html

Mitchell, Jeffrey T Ph.D. Important Crisis Intervention Background and Terminology Clinical Professor Emergency Health Services University of Maryland. President Emeritus International Critical Incident Stress Foundation 2010.

Ochberg, Frank M, (1991). Gift From Within—PTSD Resources for Survivors and Caregivers Department of Psychiatry, Michigan State University, East Lansing, Michigan 48824. The material addressed in this chapter was previously published, in a slightly different format, in Psychotherapy, Volume 28, No. 1, Spring, 1991.

Pullen, C., & Pullen, S. (1996). Secondary Trauma Associated with Managing Sex Offenders. In K. English, S. Pullen, & L. Jones (Eds.), *Managing Adult Sex Offenders on Probation and Parole: A Containment Approach.* Lexington, KY: American Probation and Parole Association, 10-1-10-11.

Randall D. M.,, Spitzer, R., Liebowitz M.R., *Psychotherapy: Theory, Research, Practice, Training,* Vol 31(3), 1994, 415-423. Special Article | November 01, 1999. Review and Critique of the New DSM-IV Diagnosis of Acute Stress Disorder. *Am J Psychiatry.* 1999;156:1677-1685.

Rizzolatti, G. (2011). "Mirror Neurons" GoCognitive. gocognitive.net/interviews/giacomo-rizzolatti-mirror-neurons

Rogers, A. G. (2006) *The Unsayable.* Ballantine Books, New York

Rothschild, B. (2000). *The Body Remembers. The Psychophysiology of Trauma and Trauma Treatment.* W.W. Norton & Company. New York and London.

Rothschild, B. (Sept/Oct 2004) Mirror Mirror: our brains are hardwired for empathy. Psychotherapy Networker

Schore, A. N. (2002) Advances in neuropsychoanalysis, attachment theory, and trauma research: implications for self psychology. *Psychoanalytic Inquiry,* 22 (3): 433-484.

Society For Neuroscience (2007, November 7). Mirror, Mirror in The Brain: Mirror Neurons, Self-understanding And Autism Research.' ScienceDaily. http://www.sciencedaily.com/releases/2007/11/071106123725.htm

Steed, L.G., & Downing, R. (1998): *A phenomenological Study of Vicarious Truamatisation Amongst Psychologists and Professional Counsellors Working in the Field of Sexual Abuse/Assault.* The Australasian Journal of Disaster and Trauma Studies. Vol: 1998-2.

Townson, L & Trotman, P. (Oct 2009). *Recognising, Nurturing & Protecting the Survivor Self.* Workshop presented at the Coping and Resilience International Conference Dubrovnik, Croatia.

Trotman, P. (2006). Walking With the Spirit Self. Unpublished paper. Presented Continuing Professional Education Conference "Out of bounds and borders: A Trans-Tasman collaboration". Auckland, New Zealand.

Van der Kolk, B. (1994). The Body keeps the score: Memory and the evolving psychobiology of post traumatic stress. *Trauma Information Pages,* Articles: van der Kolk.

White, M. & Epston, D. (1990). *Narrative Means to Therapeutic Ends.* W. New York.

Widgren, J., (1994). Narrative Completion in the Treatment of Trauma. *Psychotherapy: Theory, Research, Practice, Training*, Vol. 31(3), 415-423.

Wilson J. P., and Raphael B., *International Handbook of Traumatic Stress Syndromes*, edited by John P. Plenum Press, New York, 1993.

Wilson, J. & Thomas, R. (2004). *Empathy and the Treatment of Trauma and PTSD*. NY: Brunner Mazel.

Winerman, L. "The mind's mirror". October 2005, Vol 36, No. 9 page 48 http://www.apa.org/monitor/oct05/mirror.aspx

CHAPTER 14

The Community Resilience Profile: A Framework for Assessing Community Development Efforts

Lynn Varagona and Linda Hoopes

Abstract

Much is known about the characteristics of resilient individuals, but less has been said about the characteristics of resilient organizations, communities and nations. Combining an individual framework of resilience with a framework for transformational change offers just such a lens. A transformational change framework of resilience was applied to four international community development projects. In this chapter, case studies of these community development efforts are presented and their Community Resilience Profiles depicted to illustrate how a community-level resilience framework can serve as a diagnostic tool to aid action planning. Based on each case study's Community Resilience Profiles, recommendations to increase the community's resilience and improve the likelihood of successful realization of its development efforts are presented. Implications for practice and recommendations for future research are then discussed.

A great deal of research has been done on personal resilience—the combination of attributes that enables individuals to move through the disruption of change quickly while maximizing performance and minimizing dysfunctional reactions. One stream of research in this area has identified five characteristics that describe resilient individuals: being Positive, Focused, Flexible, Organized, and Proactive (Conner Partners 1993).

At any given time, each individual has a limited supply of attentional capacity and energy, which can be used as "adaptation resources"—the cognitive, physical, and emotional assets that enable a person to adapt when he or she encounters disruption. When this supply is depleted, increased levels of unproductive behavior and reduced adaptation result. Resilience characteristics appear to enable individuals to use their adaptation resources more efficiently, both by conserving them from waste and increasing their available quantity.

We can extrapolate this definition of individual resilience to the community, defining community resilience as a community's ability, when it encounters or initiates major change, to achieve effective outcomes with minimal waste of resources. The two constructs are related but separate. While a community made up of resilient individuals will be better positioned to quickly and effectively adapt to change, a collection of resilient people does not necessarily ensure that a community as a whole will be able to respond well to challenges in its environment—there is a systems element to the equation that must be considered.

Community Resilience Framework and Profile

The Community Resilience Framework is based on a model of organizational resilience developed by the second author (Conner Partners 1996a) and adapted to community settings by the first author. The organizational resilience model integrates the earlier-mentioned Personal Resilience framework with a model of transformational variables in organizations.

Burke and Litwin's (1992) work with organizations revealed three components that shape the course of transformation: leadership, context (vision, mission, and strategies), and culture. These "transformational variables" interact with one another to yield dramatic shifts in an organization's functioning.

When a community is faced with transformational change, its leadership, context, and culture can be examined as well. Adapting the Burke-Litwin model to a community setting, we can characterize these transformational variables as follows:

Table 1: Leadership, Context and Culture Definitions

Leadership	Executive behavior that provides direction and encourages others to take needed action during change; how leaders are perceived to behave and what they value in relation to supporting a resilient culture.
Context	The community's vision, mission, and strategy—what leaders and members believe is the central purpose of the community and how the community intends to achieve that purpose during uncertain times.
Culture	The interrelationship of shared beliefs, behaviors, and assumptions that are acquired over time by members in a community.

According to the organizational resilience model cited above, an organization will be more resilient when its leadership, context, and culture are positive, focused, flexible, organized, and proactive at various times to meet changing situational demands. Adapted to the community setting, the resilience characteristics can be thought of as follows:

Table 2: Community Resilience Characteristic Definitions

Positive: External	Recognizing the community's environment as challenging yet filled with opportunity
Positive: Internal	Cultivating strong internal resources that promote confidence in the community's ability to capitalize on opportunities during change
Focused	Adhering to goals that are clear and appropriate to changing circumstances, as well as the strategies to achieve them
Flexible: Internal	The ability to reconfigure structures and processes to meet changing environmental demands
Flexible: External	Drawing on resources outside the community to generate new ideas and approaches during change
Organized	Detecting patterns amid chaos; applying order to complex information
Proactive	Engaging change; willingness to take action in ambiguous circumstances and to test and experiment with new approaches

Every situation calling for transformation is unique and draws on resilience and transformational variables in different ways. Thus, each of the above resilience characteristics must exist in a dynamic balance to be optimally effective. For example, a strong emphasis on structuring information (Organized) may result in an overly rigid adherence to existing structures that interferes with seeking new and better ways to achieve goals (Flexible). The most resilient communities will have a well-rounded set of strengths to draw from, allowing them to succeed in any change endeavor.

The Community Resilience Questionnaire is an assessment of the constructs outlined above. Adapted from the Organizational Resilience Questionnaire (Conner Partners 1996b, 1996c), it contains 66 items, three for each combination of transformational variable and resilience characteristic (e.g. Leadership/Proactive) and three additional items. Responses are made on a seven-point scale with anchors ranging from "Strongly Agree" to "Strongly Disagree." The resulting Community Resilience Profile provides scores on each of the various elements assessed.

Community Development Case Studies

This chapter presents case studies of four international community development efforts. It depicts four sets of scores for each—Leadership, Context, Culture, and a composite Community Resilience Profile that averages the other three. Each is based on a single evaluation of the community from an individual familiar with that situation. In each case we have briefly summarized some insights from the profile and identified recommendations that were made to participants in the research. The study was designed as an exploratory inquiry into the value of the CRP as a tool to help improve the effectiveness of community development efforts.

Community A

Situated near the border of Northern Ireland, Community A has been severely affected by over thirty years of conflict in the area.

As a consequence, Community A has experienced little inward investment and little local business investment over the years, resulting in a lagging commercial environment and dilapidated town center. The conflict has impacted the quality of life in the community and created a culture of avoidance, silence, and strong inherited attitudes and mindsets. Unemployment and poverty are higher than the national average, educational attainment among adults is lower than the national average, and early school leaving has been a particular problem.

The local economy of Community A is diverse and characterized by expansion in some sub-sectors and decline in others. Historically, the local economy was based on agriculture and a number of traditional local manufacturing industries such as textiles and primary food processing. Over the years, manufacturing declined with the closure of a shirt factory and other smaller businesses. Changing economic trends have seen an increase in commercial services in the area.

Community A consists of three major religious groups (Presbyterian, Church of Ireland and Catholic) with very little interaction. Lack of social integration has worsened in recent years due to an increase in the number of new residents as a result of the community being adjacent to two larger urban centers. The area has a large proportion of minority religious groups (19.3 per cent compared to 6 per cent nationally). The population increase has been associated with a high level of commuting out of the area for work and a resulting loss of revenue to local businesses. Future population trends indicate that the population will continue to rise sharply. That said, population trends point towards continued out migration of younger people and increasing dependency ratios.

Regarding infrastructure, only one national primary road serves the region and secondary roads are of variable quality. Formerly a vibrant commercial and trading center, a bypass was constructed during the early 1990s that led to large volumes of traffic bypassing the town. This, combined with changes in the local and national economy, accelerated the decline of Community A. In addition, lack of broadband telecommunication services in the community represents a significant disadvantage to business. Limited electricity supply does not enable the community to serve industries that require high power inputs. The absence of banking facilities in the area (except for a local credit union) has contributed to poor investment in the retail sector.

Never having benefitted from EU Peace Programme funding as neighboring villages had, and given the existence of community tensions, Community A received development funding through the International Fund for Ireland and Atlantic Philanthropies. Subsequently, an overall development organization was formed to plan, implement and coordinate local and community development. As part of the development initiative, a survey was conducted with 65 local businesses to seek their views on the local economy and to assist in development of a community strategic plan. Arising from research undertaken in a socioeconomic audit—along with consultations held with the local community, business interests, the development initiative's management, statutory agencies and funders—a strategic community action plan was prepared that identified projects and actions geared toward developing economic, social and community infrastructure and services. Actions were designed to encourage and promote cross-community participation and ensure that the community is an open and equal society for all.

As a participant of the 2009 Social Capital and Community Resilience conference held in New Lanark, Scotland, one of Community A's volunteer development workers was given an opportunity to complete the *Community Resilience Questionnaire* and subsequently agreed to allow Community A to be written up as a case study. The community development representative had been working with the development initiative for a while and was responsible for overseeing implementation of the development plans, serving the various working groups and community/agency forum, and implementing peace and reconciliation building initiatives. As a result of the assessment, the following Community Resilience Profile emerged. One chart depicts the resilience characteristics of the community's leaders, one depicts the resilience characteristics of the development initiative's context (vision, mission and strategies), one depicts the resilience characteristics of the community's culture, and an overall resilience profile that consists of an average of these.

The first author reviewed the profile with the community development representative, leading to greater clarity regarding how the development initiatives were unfolding and revealing actions that could be taken to increase the likelihood of success of the development efforts. Interpretation of the profiles involves looking at the overall level of the scores, the balance of the various characteristics, and the potential impact of the relative highs and lows, which can indicate characteristics that are over- or underutilized. A relatively balanced resilience profile is preferable because it increases the likelihood that all resilience characteristics will be employed.

Leadership: The Positive characteristics suggest that Community A's leaders view the environment as posing both potential challenges and potential opportunities, but have relative confidence in their ability to respond. The leadership profile also suggests that this community's leaders may overemphasize adopting changes that other communities have made (Flexible: External) vs. looking at changes that might be made to the community's internal structures or processes (Flexible: Internal). In addition, the community's leadership may also have a tendency to take action (Proactive) before ensuring that adequate time has been spent planning the change initiatives (Organized).

Context: This shows even more pronounced relative high and low characteristics. In contrast to the community's leaders, those

Figure 1: Community A's Leadership Resilience Profile

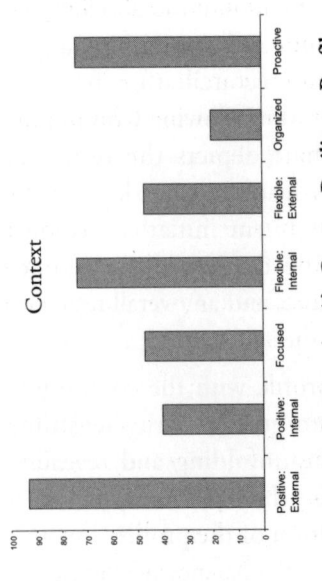

Figure 2: Community A's Context Resilience Profile

Figure 3: Community A's Culture Resilience Profile

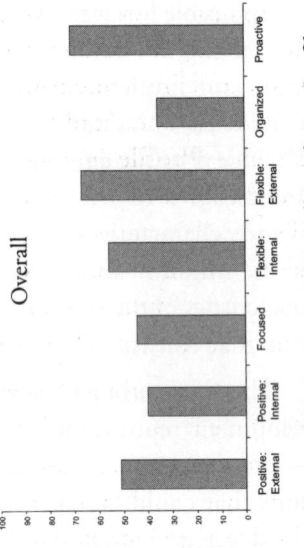

Figure 4: Community A's Overall Resilience Profile

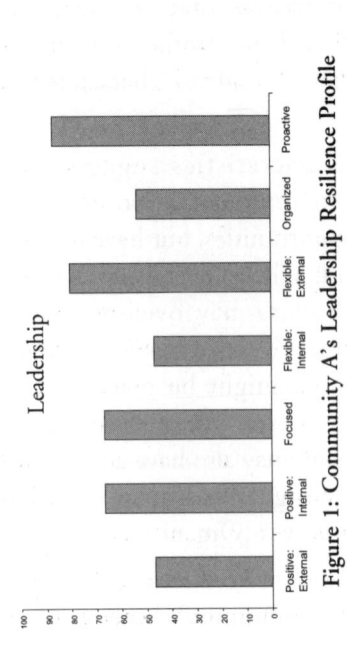

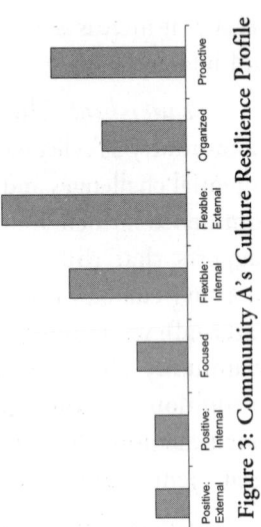

involved in strategic planning envision many opportunities (Positive: External) yet have relatively lower confidence in the ability to carry them out (Positive: Internal). Another contrast is seen with the Flexible characteristics. Those involved in strategic planning looked less at what other communities had done (Flexible: External) and more at what changes could be made to the community's structures or processes (Flexible: Internal). Similar to the leaders but even more pronounced, those involved in strategic planning were likely to take action (Proactive) without ensuring that adequate planning had taken place (Organized).

Culture: These data suggest that members of this community view changes in the environment as threatening and lack confidence in their ability to respond (Positive: External and Internal). In addition, the culture profile suggests that members are not focused on the community's goals, and perhaps view them as being inconsistent with their personal goals (Focused). Similar to the community's leaders, members run the risk of placing too much emphasis on what other communities have done (Flexible: External) rather than looking at changes that the community might make among itself (Flexible: Internal). Finally, the culture profile reveals a similar propensity to take action before adequate planning has taken place.

Overall: The overall resilience profile has fewer relative highs and lows, indicating that relatively well-developed characteristics in particular subgroups can be leveraged to offset relatively less-developed characteristics in other subgroups (e.g., Positive: External, Flexible: Internal).

The above insights that emerged from the resilience profiles were confirmed by the community development representative, who added the following information to further assist in interpreting the profiles. Given the long history of segregation in the area, three versions of community resources were common (e.g., youth groups, sports clubs, social clubs, and cultural societies). Integration among the religious groups had occurred within the community's leadership—who tended to be relatively new to the area, more educated, and relatively affluent, and who sought such integration for the larger population. However, integration had not occurred among community members—who tended to come from rural, working class backgrounds, were less educated, and had been in the area for many years. The majority of those who made up the community viewed the changes as threatening (e.g., "they're coming to take our jobs") and lacked confidence in their ability to capitalize on the development initiatives. Consequently, they didn't embrace the change efforts.

While the community leaders thought they were being representative during the strategic planning process, they didn't adequately include the elderly population who had historically been the community and continued to represent the majority of its members. This, coupled with the tendency to look at what other communities had done (vs. looking at the internal challenges that had been ingrained in the community for so many years), highlighted the development initiative's under-emphasis on the community's deep-rooted issue of religious segregation. Leaders had been able to bridge the religious divides, but the community had not.

Given Community A's across-the-board tendency to take action without adequate planning, it runs the risk of not making as much progress toward creating an open and equal society for all as it could conceivably make. Much greater emphasis could be placed on working closely with long-standing community members to understand what is important to them and include them in the action planning process. More actively engaging the community to overcome its years of divisiveness can increase the likelihood of creating a true sense of common unity.

Since interpreting Community A's resilience profiles with the community development representative, huge progress has been made as a result of internal and external relationship building. For example, cultural groups began working together on joint projects with the development group, including opening a housing shelter for elderly residents with heavy involvement from all three religious groups. A marked difference in local community relations now exists, and progress can be attributed to the dedication, forward thinking, and risk taking of the local community leaders.

Community B

Community B consists of a small school in Lanarkshire, Scotland whose town of Pather suffered more than most from a number of the problems caused by relative poverty (e.g., addiction, lowered expectations, broken families, and ill-health). It was the fourth most deprived school in North Lanarkshire, as measured by free meals and clothing grants. From 2003-2005, the school had the highest suspension/exclusion rate per child in Scotland, was ranked in the bottom ten schools in the nation, had one of the poorest attendance rates in North Lanarkshire, and experienced almost weekly vandalism to the building—often caused by ex-pupils. Nearly a fifth of the students made requests to be placed at schools that were perceived as 'better.' Needless to say, morale was low.

In 2007, the children of the P7/6 class faced a number of challenges. A tailor-made program of psychological services was undertaken to alleviate some of its problems with fall-outs, anger, and lack of teamwork, respect and empathy—but was met with limited success. The P7/6 teacher and the school's Head Teacher believed that the common factor in all the signs of a 'great' school was *relationships*. Thus, they were on the alert for a project that would foster relationships and lead to personal, social and leadership development of the children.

As a result of one of their 'what's in the news' sessions, the students of P7/6 became interested in Georgia when news of the Russian invasion hit the headlines. They subsequently began to research, investigate and fact-find about the country. After doing so, they decided to create links with a Georgian village and orphanage, raise money for the orphanage, and learn about Georgian culture, music and history—which they later shared with the larger school community.

As a participant in the 2009 Social Capital and Community Resilience conference held in New Lanark, Scotland, Community B's Head Teacher was given an opportunity to complete the *Community Resilience Questionnaire* and subsequently agreed to allow Community B to be written up as a case study. As a result of the assessment, the following Community Resilience Profile emerged.

All of the graphs for this community reflect mixed scores, suggesting that some resilience characteristics may be under-utilized compared to others. The culture profile, which we are interpreting as representing the characteristics exhibited by the P7/six students, shows the most variation among resilience characteristics.

The Positive: Internal characteristic is highest in the culture profile, suggesting a strong degree of confidence among the P7/six students. Upon debriefing the profiles with the Head Teacher, it was learned that the students exhibited more of a brash (vs. calm) confidence.

Regarding the Positive: External characteristic, the leadership profile suggests that the school leaders view a lot of opportunities and believe that they can be capitalized on. In contrast, the students view the outside world as relatively more threatening, although they also believe that they can meet the challenges they face. The school believes that this might have been a self-cultivated 'siege' mentality—defining oneself against the bigger 'other' as Scotland has often done against England—as a way of strengthening identity and bonds within and as a foundation for a more 'mature' future direction.

The Focused characteristic was relatively high on all of the profiles. In addition, all of the profiles suggest that the leaders and students may be less likely to examine changes they can make

Figure 5: Community B's Leadership Resilience Profile

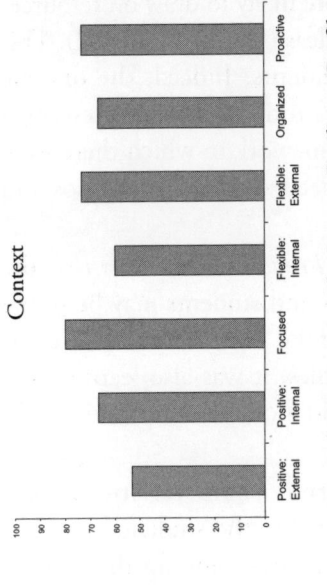

Figure 6: Community B's Context Resilience Profile

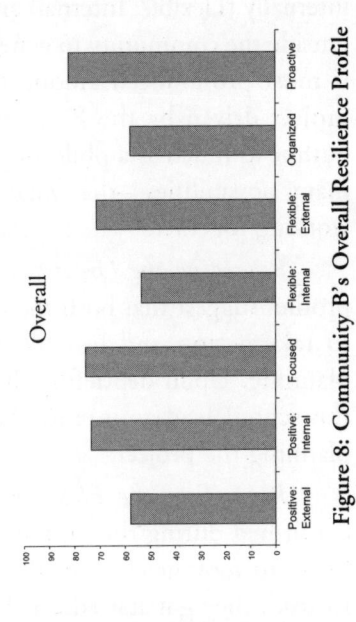

Figure 7: Community B's Culture Resilience Profile

Figure 8: Community B's Overall Resilience Profile

internally (Flexible: Internal) and more likely to draw on resources outside the community to generate ideas (Flexible: External). This is most pronounced among the students. Indeed, the organic project driven by the P7/6 students did not have a prescribed outline as much as a philosophic framework in which there were many possibilities—that what was needed was relationships and working together.

Regarding the Organized and Proactive characteristics, the profiles suggest that both the leaders and students may be prone to take action and less likely to take considerable time for planning. Upon debriefing the profiles, it was also learned that the school leaders intentionally did not become involved in planning the project.

Regarding the Flexible: Internal characteristic, it was confirmed during the profile debrief that the students were less likely to look at changes they could make among themselves. Instead, they got started, made themselves available, and looked externally for ideas, learning about Georgia and its villages and orphanages, food, traditional clothing, song and culture from class visitors.

The main theme that stood out when reviewing the profiles with the Head Teacher was that—while the project was viewed as a big success—the students may not have internalized their learning. The students fulfilled the expectations placed upon them to create a project, and readily took action—turning to outside resources for ideas, then implementing them whole-heartedly. While these are characteristics that foster resilience, the opportunity exists to help the students reflect on their success and learn about the internal changes they made. Doing so would help generate insights that the students could leverage going forward in life, thereby strengthening their resilience even further.

Community C

Primarily a mountainous region with settlements separated by an extensive coastline and sea lochs, Community C is an area of outstanding natural beauty in the Scottish Highlands. Although agriculture and fishing make up a small proportion of the community's employment, they hold a significantly higher percentage than the Highland and national average and are reflective of the community's rural and coastal setting. The economy of Community C is dependent on the tourist industry, and the proportion of part time jobs is well above the Highland average. The unemployment rate fluctuates around the Highland average as people take up seasonal jobs, but has risen recently. The long-term unemployment rate is above the Highland average and has increased slightly. Average household incomes are well below the Highland average.

Although Community C is the largest Ward in the Scottish Highlands, it has the second lowest population density. The overall age profile of Community C is older than the Highland average, with a below-average proportion in the under-50 age groups. The total population has increased moderately as a result of inward migration; over half of the homes sold in some west coast settlements were to buyers from outside Scotland. Overseas migrant workers have been moving into the area—mostly from Eastern Europe. While the population of Community C has been growing, it has also been aging due to an outward migration of youth.

The number of new homes built in Community C in the last few years was slightly below the Highland average. That said, Community C experiences a high rate of "windfall" planning applications for small developments. Around half of the sites cannot be started until Scottish Water improves the community's infrastructure, however. This could lead to a general shortage of viable sites.

As part of the Scottish Rural Development Programme aimed at promoting economic and community development within rural areas, a community Alliance was formed. A recipient of European development funding, the Alliance's aim is to bring together community residents and organizations to address the community's challenges (e.g., low employment, lack of infrastructure, relative impoverishment compared to the rest of the nation) and to promote sustainable development of the area so that all may enjoy a high quality of life. There is a strong tradition of self-help and community organization in the villages of Community C.

As a participant in the 2009 Social Capital and Community Resilience conference held in New Lanark, Scotland, the Alliance's Project Officer was given an opportunity to complete the *Community Resilience Questionnaire* and subsequently agreed to allow Community C to be written up as a case study. The following Community Resilience Profile emerged from the assessment.

The overall scores for this community are low and relatively balanced, while the three components show mixed scores. This suggests that Community C is in a position to call upon the resilience characteristics relevant to a given situation if it leverages the strengths of its leaders, strategic planners, and members. Given that the overall profile is low, however, the opportunity exists for the community to strengthen its resilience across factors.

Regarding the Positive characteristics, the community's leaders view the environment as threatening (Positive: External) but believe they can take on the challenges they face (Positive: Internal). In contrast, members of the community perceive opportunities as a result of receiving development funding (Positive: External), but are relatively less confident in their ability to capitalize on them (Positive: Internal). The same holds true for those involved in the strategic planning process.

Returning to the leadership profile, leaders of this community may have a tendency to be overconfident in their ability to address the changes they face. The leadership profile suggests that the community's leaders may have difficulty focusing on clear goals (Focused), may not be exploring as many options

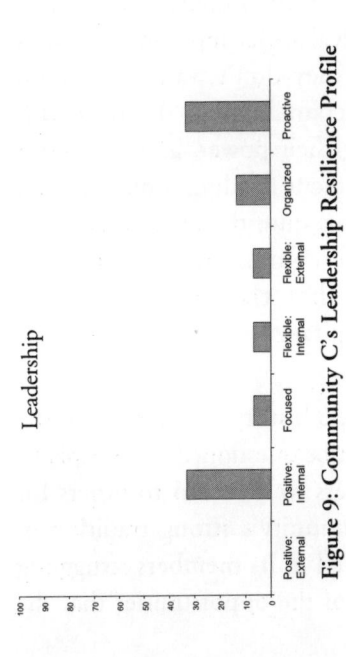

Leadership

Figure 9: Community C's Leadership Resilience Profile

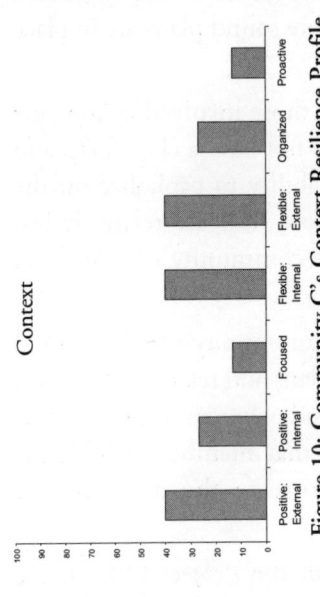

Context

Figure 10: Community C's Context Resilience Profile

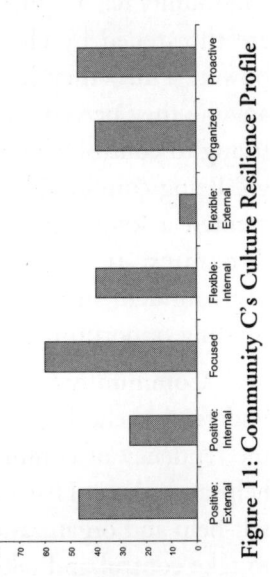

Culture

Figure 11: Community C's Culture Resilience Profile

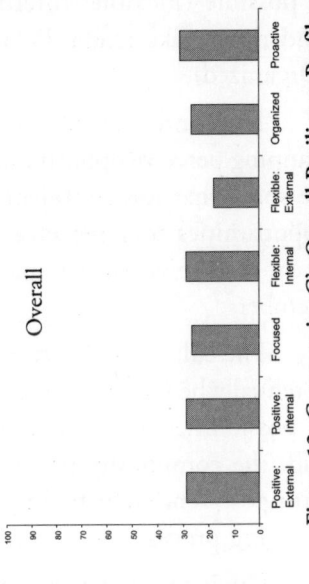

Overall

Figure 12: Community C's Overall Resilience Profile

as possible (Flexible: Internal and External), and may have a tendency to take action (Proactive) before sound plans are in place (Organized).

The context profile suggests that those involved in strategic planning perceive opportunities but do not have a clear focus and are somewhat less confident in their ability to capitalize on the opportunities they perceive. In addition, they are relatively less likely to take action compared to the community's leaders and members.

The culture profile suggests that community members could potentially be too focused on existing plans and relatively less open to possibilities, particularly from outside the community. That said, the community profile suggests that members exhibit the strongest tendency to impart structure to the development planning process and take action.

Upon reviewing the profiles with the Project Officer, the following information was obtained and further aided understanding of Community C's development efforts. The community has a history of hierarchical leadership power. Leaders are threatened by change because they don't want to give up power. Thus, they have been reluctant in their dealings with anyone they perceive as threatening their power, and have been trying to control where the development funding money should go. Being comfortable with the status quo, the leaders have not created a long-term vision for the community. Given these dynamics, it is not surprising that the leaders may be overconfident in their ability to capitalize on the development funding opportunity.

Community C's members have a history of deferring to the leaders and believing that they cannot be questioned. This explains the tendency of community members to not turn to others for help and ideas. That said, the community's strong tradition of self-help and organization has resulted in its members struggling to take control and take advantage of the opportunities that the development funding presents. Grass root projects have sprung up and informal leadership has emerged. For example, a community cooperative was formed that plants and farms organic produce for local consumption. As a result of successful grass root community efforts, a culture shift has been going on very quietly. People are learning that cooperation is working and that they don't need the hierarchal leadership.

While the Project Officer knew that the leaders did not have a long-term vision for the community, she received push-back when she tried to get the community's leaders to generate long-term plans. Upon reviewing the resilience profiles and reflecting upon the facts that informal leadership had emerged in the community and grass root efforts were proving successful, the Project Officer realized that a community development action plan needed to be put in place. Doing so would enable Community C to leverage the resilience characteristics of its members. Working with the community's members to explore what other communities have done in terms of revitalization would further build the community's resilience and enable it to realize even greater benefits from the development funding efforts.

Community D

Community D is a predominantly working-class and lower-class neighborhood in a mid-sized southern city in the United States. The neighborhood is in transition and includes those in the middle to upper classes as well. Sixty percent of residents are African-American, 37 per cent are Caucasian, and 3 per cent represent other ethnicities. The community was experiencing higher crime rates than the national average—particularly in the areas of burglary, motor vehicle theft, aggravated assault, and vandalism. Properties were run down and substance abuse was higher than in other parts of the nation.

To address the high crime rates, abuse, and deteriorated conditions, residents of Community D decided to take collective action and form a neighborhood association. Unlike associations in higher income areas that focus on maintaining the status quo, Community D's association focused on social change. The main goal of the association was to empower community members and build their capacity. Community D had a vision of what it wanted to be, and vowed not to allow drug dealers and poverty to bring down its neighborhood.

Association leaders were mostly older African-Americans who actively looked at new models outside the community and examined changes that the community could make internally. People took a proactive approach to solving the community's problems. Through the work of the association, Community D embraced education and found out what its options were (e.g., regarding government codes, regarding laws not allowing property to go to waste). People took time to put plans in place, then took action (e.g., calling the police on drug dealers even though doing so was risky and frightening).

As a participant of the 2009 Social Capital and Community Resilience conference held in New Lanark, Scotland, a researcher who spent two years as a participant observer in Community D's neighborhood association meetings and other community events (Gaynote 2004)—and whose study provided the data on which Community D's analysis was based—was given an opportunity to complete the *Community Resilience Questionnaire* and subsequently agreed to allow Community D to be written up as a case study. As a result of the assessment, the following Community Resilience Profile emerged.

All of the scores for Community D are relatively flat and high, except for the culture profile which shows somewhat greater variation among resilience characteristics. This suggests that, by and large, the community is able to call upon all of the characteristics of resilience.

Regarding the Positive characteristics, the community's leaders and those involved in strategic planning view the

Figure 13: Community D's Leadership Resilience Profile

Figure 14: Community D's Context Resilience Profile

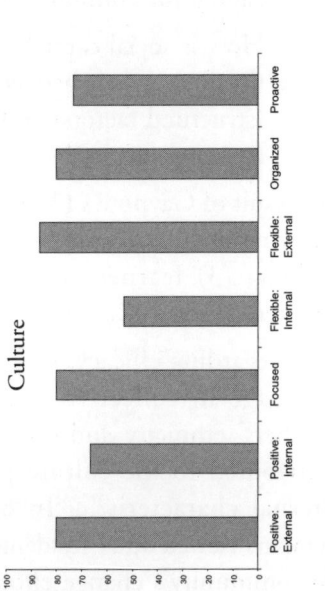

Figure 15: Community D's Culture Resilience Profile

Figure 16: Community D's Overall Resilience Profile

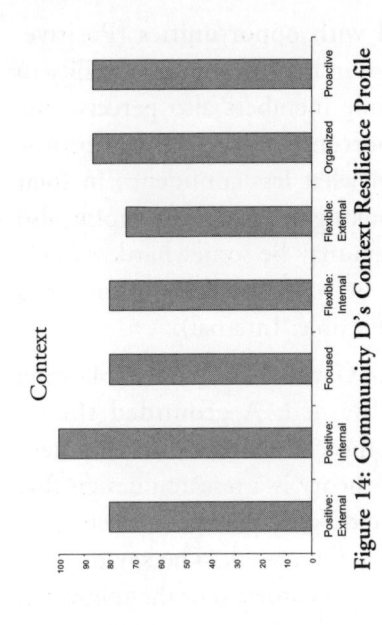

environment as primarily filled with opportunities (Positive: External) and believe even more so in the community's ability to respond (Positive: Internal). While members also perceive the environment as possessing opportunities, the culture profile suggests that members have somewhat less confidence in their ability to make them happen. Looking at the culture profile also suggests that community members may be somewhat less likely to examine changes that could be made to the community's existing structures or processes (Flexible: Internal).

Upon reviewing the data with Gaynote (2004), the following additional information was obtained. A grounded theory analytical approach to studying the community's development efforts was employed. Grounded theory is a research design that enables important concepts and findings to emerge on their own, without the influence of an existing framework. The key research questions examined in Community D consisted of the following.

1. How do cultural factors such as values, attitudes, and beliefs influence how and why people mobilize social capital for community benefit?
2. How is social capital use and mobilization influenced by the interaction between individuals' access to resources (structural factors) and their values, attitudes, and beliefs (cultural factors)?

As a result of Gaynote's (2004) research with Community D, the following main concepts emerged: (1) self-efficacy, (2) collective efficacy, (3) learned helplessness, (4) resourcefulness, (5) persistence, and (6) courage.

Regarding efficacy, Gaynote (2004) found that propensity to engage in collective action varied based on community members' ethnicity and socio-economic status. This may have contributed to the culture profile's relatively lower Positive: Internal characteristic. In other words, not all community members viewed other residents as resources to assist in addressing the community's change efforts. Specifically, middle and upper middle class Caucasian residents were likely to feel efficacious when addressing neighborhood problems, but felt they did not need to do so in a collective context. Instead, they did so individually (e.g., by making a call). In contrast, working class, middle class and upper middle class African-Americans were most likely to feel efficacious when addressing neighborhood problems either individually or collectively, and working class and middle class African-American residents were most likely to address problems collectively (e.g., by leveraging one another's contacts). The neighborhood association's leaders—who were primarily African-American—believed the community could achieve its goals together and leveraged members' connections. A third manifestation of efficacy was exhibited by lower-class residents, who tended not to address social problems in any format—collectively or individually.

Regarding learned helplessness, Gaynote (2004) found that lower class African-American and Caucasian residents were most likely to experience learned helplessness (i.e., apathy and submission) in response to the neighborhood's problems.

Similar to efficacy, resourcefulness, persistence and courage also varied based on community members' ethnicity and socio-economic status, although in different ways (Gaynote 2004). This may have contributed to the culture profile's relatively lower Positive: Internal and Flexible: Internal characteristics. In other words, some but not all community members expressed strong beliefs that they could influence positive changes in systems and processes. Specifically, working, middle and upper middle class African-Americans frequently spoke of cultural trends from their youth and from the Civil Rights Movement that shaped how they thought of their possibilities and responsibilities. In contrast, lower class African-American residents did not speak of cultural trends from their youth and from the Civil Rights Movement—these possibilities seemed absent from their thinking. Similarly, no such narratives seemed to shape the thinking of Caucasian residents.

The main themes that emerged from Gaynote's (2004) research—excluding learned helplessness which was only evident among lower class residents—seem to align with several of the resilience characteristics. Efficacy seems associated with the Positive: Internal characteristic, resourcefulness may relate to the Positive: Internal and Flexible: External characteristics, and persistence and courage may relate to the Proactive characteristic. Given the strong resilience profiles of Community D, Gaynote's (2004) research findings suggest construct validation evidence of some of the characteristics associated with the community resilience framework.

Summary

The exploratory nature of these data does not yet allow us to draw strong conclusions about the validity of the instrument as a measure of the resilience of a community. However, it is worth noting that Community D, which showed a particularly high level of effectiveness in moving their efforts forward, also showed the strongest Community Resilience Profile scores.

As an additional validation point, we found that people closely involved in the community development efforts found the Community Resilience Profiles to depict very valid assessments, and gained much clarity and insight into the strengths and challenges of the projects. Particular recommendations to increase resilience—and thereby increase the likelihood of successful change execution—were well received.

Implications for Practice

The above four case studies illustrate the potential utility of the Community Resilience Framework for assessing and strengthening community development efforts. Understanding the resilience characteristics of a community's leadership, context (vision, mission and strategies) and culture at the start of a community development effort can help identify a community's strengths and potential challenges. In turn, actions can be taken to address less-developed characteristics and, in so doing, increase the likelihood that the community's change efforts can succeed. In addition, increasing a community's resilience characteristics will aid the community in building its overall resilience capabilities and, in so doing, increase the likelihood that the community can effectively adapt to future changes as well. Thus, using the community level resilience framework to increase a community's resilience can have long-term as well as short-term benefits.

Recommendations for Future Research

For each of the four international community development case studies presented, only one representative completed the *Community Resilience Questionnaire*. To get a more comprehensive perspective of a community's resilience, we would recommend that representatives from all key constituencies (e.g., community leaders, community members, strategic planners) complete the assessment. Any notable differences in responses between constituency groups could be examined to shed light on how and why such groups might differ in their perceptions of the community's resilience.

To ascertain the benefits of implementing action plans based on the community resilience lens, community development projects could be randomly assigned to treatment and control groups. Action plans based on the Community Resilience Profile data could then be put in place for the treatment group. Success indicators for community development efforts that did and did not apply action plans based on the community level resilience framework could then be compared. In addition, action plans to increase particular resilience characteristics can be evaluated for their effectiveness—initially via case studies, then over time via experimental research.

Conclusion

Community development efforts aim to assist communities in not only adapting well to the circumstances in which they find themselves, but in capitalizing on opportunities to improve various aspects of their community's life. What is known about resilience—the process of effective coping that leads to successful adaptation—can aid community development efforts. In addition, examining the resilience profiles of a community's leaders, context (vision, mission and strategies) and culture can shed light on resilience characteristics that are well-developed and less-developed. In so doing, community resilience profiles can guide action planning to increase resilience and, ultimately, increase the success of a community's development efforts.

Works Cited

Burke, W.W. and Litwin, G. H. (1992), A Causal Model of Organizational Performance and Change, *Journal of Management*, 18 (3), 523-545.

Conner Partners (1993). *Human Resilience During Change*. Atlanta, Conner Partners (formerly ODR).

_____ (1996). *Organizational Resilience*. Atlanta, Conner Partners (formerly ODR).

_____ (1996). *Organizational Resilience Questionnaire*. Atlanta, Conner Partners (formerly ODR).

_____ (1996). *Organizational Resilience Profile*. Atlanta, Conner Partners (formerly ODR).

Gaynote, C. M. (2004). *Hopeful Action: The Role of Social Capital in Neighborhood Mobilization*. Dissertation, Vanderbilt University. Ann Arbor: ProQuest/UMI, 2004. (Publication No. [3154865]).

Chapter 15

What World Bank Metrics Don't Tell Us About Per Capita GDP: How a Nation's Resilience Affects Its Prosperity

Lynn Varagona

Abstract

> While a number of factors have been identified that predict economic growth among developing nations, development economists do not fully understand what differentiates nations that substantially improve their economic status from those that do not. As the field of development economics evolved, economists increasingly looked to human and social factors as differentiators of economic growth. Resilience is explored as a possible theoretical framework for understanding and measuring the human and social aspects of economic development. Conner Partners' organizational level resilience framework was modified to the nation level, then applied to a random sample of 50 developing nations. The findings revealed that the resilience characteristics of a nation's leaders, citizens, and context (i.e., vision, mission and strategies) predicted per capita GDP above and beyond World Bank metrics, thereby differentiating developing nations that went on to improve their economic status from those that did not. Implications for theory and practice are discussed, along with recommendations for future research.

The field of development economics arose after WWII to foster understanding of how economies and societies grow and change (Stern 2001). Over the next 50 years, factors related to economic growth among developing nations such as high levels of personal savings and educational attainment were identified. However, macroeconomists have not fully identified what differentiates developing nations that substantially improve their economic status from those that do not. The need remains to further understand total productivity's *unexplained residual* that Abramovitz (1956) spoke of so long ago.

As the field of development economics evolved, increasing attention was paid to social factors. Given that economic behavior is socially conditioned, many economists now add social capital to tangible, human and knowledge capital as sources of economic growth. Human capital consists of assets that people possess that enable then to perform labor—such as competencies, knowledge, and social and personality attributes. Social capital involves accessing assets that others possess. Originally viewed as the networks to which people belong, the notion of social capital has broadened over time to include cognitive, relational and political factors that enable people to act collectively (Wallis & Killerby 2004). The more comprehensive definitions of social capital include multiple dimensions and incorporate different levels and units of analysis (Woolcock & Narayan 2000). For example, there is growing consensus that social capital includes civic and governmental components (Wallis & Killerby 2004). Examples of civic social capital include trust, reciprocity, interpersonal networks, cooperation and coordination; examples of government social capital include the benefits of law, order, property rights, education, health and a "good environment" (Meier 2001).

A theoretical framework that captures multiple components of human and social capital has been absent from the development economics literature. The need exists for a relevant theoretical framework to more comprehensively understand and measure the human and social dimensions of economic growth. Resilience—defined here as the process of effective coping that leads to successful adaptation—may offer such a framework. This chapter will apply the coping process to the nation level to illustrate both the presence and absence of attributes and exchanges associated with resilience.

The main components of the process of coping are depicted in Figure 1. Situational characteristics refer to the characteristics of one's environment, situation or circumstances such as the presence or absence of the rule of law. Personal resources consist of relatively stable personality and attitudinal factors (Moos & Schaefer 1993) as well as an individual's knowledge, skills and abilities. Environmental resources consist of resources outside of personal resources, and can include social resources, money and political power. Cognitive appraisal represents assessment of oneself, others and events; for example, having confidence in one's abilities, perceiving someone to be trustworthy, or interpreting a situation as stressful. Affective response consists of emotions tied to appraised meanings (Lazarus & Folkman 1984), and can exhibit powerful influences on cognitions, behaviors and social relationships (Lazarus 1993).

---- Influence sometimes occurs

──── Influence always occurs, and may be subconscious

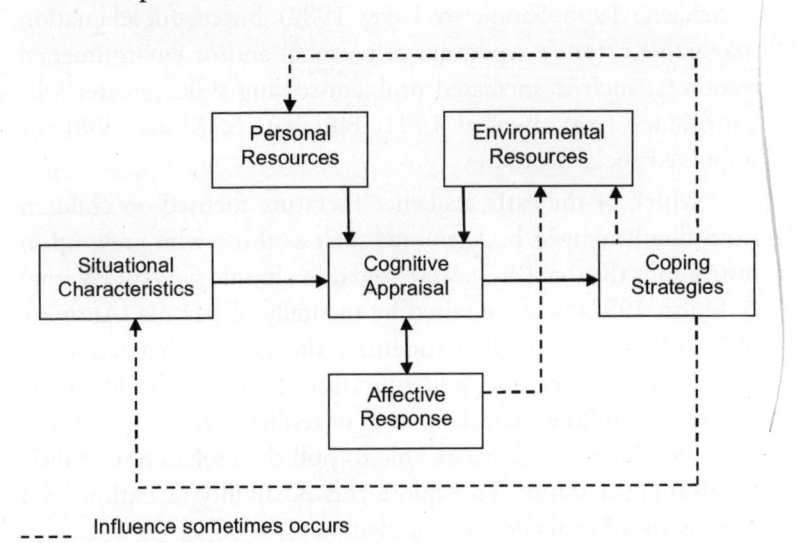

Figure 1. Process of Coping

To summarize the process of coping, personal resources, environmental resources and affective response influence the appraisal of one's ability to adapt to a particular situation and, in turn, the selection of coping strategies. Coping strategies influence the degree of successful or unsuccessful adaptation, and may influence situational characteristics. New information often results in a revision of coping strategies (Antonovsky 1987; Lazarus & Folkman 1984). Feedback can occur at various stages (Moos & Schaefer 1993), and multiple components of the model may operate concurrently.

The components of the process of coping and the process of resilience are essentially the same. The only difference is that resilience necessarily implies successful adaptation and coping does not. Individuals who use multiple resources and are flexible and appropriate in their choice of coping strategies are more likely to adapt successfully (e.g., Antonovsky 1987; Hobfoll & Leiberman 1987; Hobfoll & Walfisch 1984; Kobasa & Puccetti 1983; Moos & Schaefer 1993; Sandler & Lakey 1982). Successful adaptation may enhance one's repertoire of personal and/or environmental resources, such as increased problem-solving skills, greater self-confidence (e.g., Benard 1991; Holahan & Moos 1990) or improved social relations.

Much of the early resilience literature focused on children from disadvantaged backgrounds such as those who grew up in institutions (Rutter 1987), were reared in chronic poverty (Werner & Smith 1982) or were raised by mentally ill parents (Anthony 1987). Research sought to identify the factors that led some individuals to become well-functioning adults despite their adversity. It follows that the notion of resilience may explain why some developing nations are able to pull themselves out of their disadvantaged status. To explore this possibility, a nation level framework of resilience was needed.

Nation Level Resilience Framework

To the author's knowledge, no nation level measure of resilience existed at the time of this study. However, Conner Partners

(1996) had an organizational level measure of resilience that combined Conner's seven resilience characteristics (Positive: External, Positive: Internal, Focused, Flexible: External, Flexible: Internal, Organized, and Proactive) with Burke and Litwin's (1992) three transformational change variables (Leadership, what Conner refers to as Context, and Culture). The author had conducted research with Conner's individual level resilience instrument in the past, believes that Conner's resilience factors are relatively easy to understand and lend themselves well to development, and has used Conner's individual level assessment to foster resilience for a number of years. Thus, Conner's organizational level resilience measure was examined to see if it might be adapted to the nation level.

To achieve substantial economic development, a nation must undergo transformation (Stiglitz 2002). Conner's organizational level resilience instrument was designed to measure the ability of an organization to successfully undergo transformational change. It follows that Conner's leadership, context and culture resilience factors might differentiate developing nations that substantially improve their economic status from those that do not. Applying leadership, context and culture resilience to the nation level yields the following operational definitions.

Leadership Resilience. Nation-level leaders that (1) exhibit confidence that success in an unfamiliar and challenging environment is possible and guide the nation toward new opportunities, (2) have confidence in the capability of the nation's citizens to accomplish the nation's goals, (3) preserve the integrity of the nation's vision and mission, use them to guide strategic and tactical decisions during change and regularly stress to citizens the importance of the nation's goals, (4) draw on resources inside and outside the nation, (5) develop specific strategies to suit market conditions, creatively reconfiguring internal processes to meet the demands of changing circumstances, (6) are skilled in detecting emerging patterns, can effectively structure complex information and can effectively create structured approaches and methods to assist in managing ambiguity, and (7) are willing to take bold action in unstable environments, actively seek new challenges for the nation, build a learning environment, encourage testing of new ideas, realistically evaluate risk and accept accountability for the successes and failures of innovation.

Context Resilience. A nation (1) whose vision, mission and strategies emphasize finding opportunities, (2) whose vision, mission and strategies emphasize developing strong internal resources to effectively pursue a nation's goals, (3) that has a clear and compelling vision and mission—supported by well-communicated and explicit strategies—which provide guidance to the nation in the midst of change, (4) whose strategies emphasize adapting its structures and processes to support achievement of the vision and mission under changing conditions, (5) whose strategies emphasize drawing on the resources of other nations and non-citizens to enable it to achieve its vision and mission, (6) whose vision, mission and strategies provide a meaningful interpretation of the changing environment for all its citizens and emphasize structured approaches that assist the nation in efficiently addressing the challenges it faces, and (7) that employs strategies that actively engage change in the marketplace (e.g., experimenting with new products or markets) as a means of achieving its vision and mission.

Culture Resilience. When citizens (1) believe that the changing market offers opportunities for their nation's success, (2) understand and value their role in contributing to their nation's success during change and tend to make a personal investment in their work, (3) believe that their nation's vision, mission and strategies will provide effective guidance, assume having a relevant point of reference will lead to economic growth, and exhibit behavior that demonstrates a knowledge of and value for the vision, mission, and strategies, (4) assume there are many possible ways of achieving the nation's goals and believe difficult problems can often be resolved with creative approaches, working synergistically with other citizens and striving to develop different and better ways to achieve tasks, (5) do not assume they have all the answers and believe that learning from others can lead to success during change, typically accepting and using input from external sources, (6) believe that applying order to ambiguity and creating appropriate structures will support their nation's success during change, and (7) believe taking action during uncertainty usually leads to success, are willing to experiment during change, demonstrate appropriate risk taking (neither paralyzed by fear nor heedless of risk) and are willing to accept responsibilities for their actions.

Purpose of the Study

The purpose of this study was to determine if leadership, context and culture resilience explain economic growth among developing nations above and beyond differentiating factors already known. To this end, the following hypotheses were identified.

1. Leadership resilience will predict per capita GDP of developing nations above and beyond previously known predictors.
2. Context resilience will predict per capita GDP of developing nations above and beyond previously known predictors.
3. Culture resilience will predict per capita GDP of developing nations above and beyond previously known predictors.

Methodology

Nation Resilience Questionnaire

To measure resilience of a nation, a *Nation Resilience Questionnaire* was created by slightly modifying the wording of Conner Partners' *Organizational Resilience Questionnaire*. The instrument consisted of 63 items measuring the degree to which a nation's leadership, context and culture exhibited positive, focused, flexible, organized and proactive elements. Sample items are shown in Appendix A.

Using the *Nation Resilience Questionnaire*, nations were rated on the degree to which each item seemed characteristic of the nation since 1962—on a scale of 1 to 6, from Strongly Disagree to Strongly Agree. A nation that exhibited a particular characteristic or behavior consistently over time was more likely to be rated Strongly Agree, while a nation that exhibited a particular characteristic or behavior inconsistently over time or recently was more likely to be rated Slightly Agree. Each nation was independently rated by two people who read about the nation from The Economist Intelligence Unit's 2004 Nation Profiles and 2004 Nation Reports. In addition, Global Market Information Database reports from November 2004 to May 2005 were read for Argentina, Brazil, Chile, China, Colombia, Egypt, Greece, India, Malaysia, Mexico, Philippines, Portugal, Singapore, Spain and Venezuela. Rating pairs subsequently compared ratings, discussed their reasoning on any items rated differently, then agreed on a final rating. Five raters took part in the research and received training on resilience prior to rating the nations.

Nation Selection

A stratified random sample of 50 developing nations was drawn from the following regions: (1) Africa, (2) Central and South America and the Caribbean, (3) the Middle East and Southern Europe, and (4) South and East Asia. Nations eligible to be randomly selected had a population greater than one million in 1962 and a GNI that was reported by the World Bank.

Metrics of Developing Nations

One hundred and ninety-eight World Bank metrics of developing nations were considered for inclusion in the regression analysis. Twenty-five metrics that represented a broad range of indices were selected. For each metric chosen, 2002 or 2003 data were collected for all 50 nations. The 25 World Bank metrics selected for regression analysis are listed in Table 1.

Table 1. World Development Indicators Used in Regression Analysis

Current account balance (per cent of GDP)
Employees, industry (per cent of economically active pop)
Employees, services (per cent of economically active pop)
Employment laws index
External balance of goods and services (per cent of GDP)
Food production index (1989-91 = 100)
Fuel imports (per cent of merchandise imports)
GDP per capita, PPP (current international $)
GDP growth per capita, PPP (Real, 10 year)
GDP growth per capita, PPP (Real, 15 year)
GDP growth per capita, PPP (Real, 20 year)
General government consumption (per cent of GDP)
Gross domestic savings (per cent of GDP)
Gross foreign direct investment (per cent of GDP, PPP)
Health expenditure, total (per cent of GDP)
High-technology exports (per cent of manufactured exports)
Illiteracy rate, adult total (per cent of people 15+)
Inflation, consumer prices (annual per cent)
Interest rate spread (lending minus deposit rate)
Manufacturers exports (per cent of merchandise exports)
Physicians (per 1,000 people)
Public spending on education, total (per cent of GNP, UNESCO)
Sanitation (per cent of population with access)
Tax revenue (per cent of GDP)
Trade (per cent of GDP)

Source: World Bank *World Development Indicators* database (2004).

Data Preparation

Prior to analysis, *Nation Resilience Questionnaire* items that represented low resilience, such as "This country's leaders tend to be protective of special interest projects and functions", were reverse-scored. An inter-item correlation coefficient was computed for each scale (i.e., leadership, context, and culture resilience). Items that were not as strong measures of a particular construct were eliminated to yield a higher coefficient alpha for the scale. One out of 21 items was deleted from the leadership resilience scale resulting in a correlation coefficient of .9520, one out of 21 items was deleted from the context resilience scale resulting in a correlation coefficient of .9593 and five out of 21 items were deleted from the culture resilience scale resulting in a correlation coefficient of .9306. Leadership, context and culture resilience scores were then converted to a number from zero to one hundred.

Findings and Discussion

Rater Reliability

Rater pairs rated each item similarly 68 percent of the time and rated each item exactly the same 56 percent of the time. Ratings that differed by one were considered similar. On average, pair ratings that were not exactly the same differed by 1.4 on a six-point scale.

Descriptive Statistics

Descriptive statistics were run on the three *Nation Resilience Questionnaire* scales and 25 World Bank metrics utilized in the regression analysis. Findings are shown in Table 2. Nation rankings by leadership, context and culture resilience are presented in Table 3. Given that—aside from Singapore—the highest resilience scores were in the sixties and seventies (on a scale of 0 to 100), developing nations that are relatively resilient have the potential to become even more so.

Hypothesis Testing

To test the hypotheses, a regression model was built from the World Bank metrics using a forward/backward procedure, with

Table 2. Descriptive Statistics

	Mean	SD	Min	Max	Range
Leadership resilience	44.72	17.31	8	89	81
Context resilience	40.64	18.57	6	86	80
Culture resilience	42.76	15.78	9	80	71
Current account balance (% of GDP)	-2.04	7.79	-22.18	21.19	43.36
Employees, industry (% of economically active pop)	17.07	8.70	2	34.60	32.60
Employees, services (% of economically active pop)	40.66	21.11	4.90	76.30	71.40
Employment laws index	54.06	14.36	20	79	59
External balance of goods and services (% of GDP)	-5.25	13.49	-41.11	40.00	81.11
Food production index (1989-91 = 100)	132.68	30.14	27.40	197.60	170.20
Fuel imports (% of merchandise imports)	12.62	6.91	1.43	33.41	31.98
GDP per capita, PPP (current international $)	5554.33	5935.06	555.55	24480.49	23924.94
GDP growth per capita, PPP (Real, 10 year)	14.69	24.89	-36.21	113.89	150.09
GDP growth per capita, PPP (Real, 15 year)	19.30	40.00	-63.01	199.09	262.10
GDP growth per capita, PPP (Real, 20 year)	31.87	70.81	-63.59	404.95	468.55
General government consumption (% of GDP)	13.01	4.83	3.78	30.60	26.82
Gross domestic savings (% of GDP)	15.60	12.14	-12.33	46.69	59.02
Gross foreign direct investment (% of GDP, PPP)	3.31	2.99	0	12.23	12.23
Health expenditure, total (% of GDP)	5.49	1.88	2.60	9.50	6.90
High-technology exports (% manufactured exports)	15.96	26.31	0	100	100
Illiteracy rate, adult total (% of people 15+)	75.44	21.25	17.06	97.81	80.75
Inflation, consumer prices (annual %)	10.00	20.50	-1.88	140.08	141.96
Interest rate spread (lending minus deposit rate)	13.96	27.13	1.81	187.00	185.19
Manufacturers exports (% of merchandise exports)	36.00	30.10	0.37	92.93	92.56
Physicians (per 1,000 people)	950.68	1070.30	27.80	4400.00	4372.20
Public spending on education, total (% of GNP, UNESCO)	4.15	1.72	1.00	10.36	9.36
Sanitation (% of population with access)	71.68	25.86	8	100	92
Tax revenue (% of GDP)	15.78	7.36	0.04	36.18	36.14
Trade (% of GDP)	69.90	45.36	14.63	300.00	285.37

Table 3. Nation Rankings by Leadership, Context and Culture Resilience

score	Leadership	score	Context	score	Culture
89	Singapore	86	Singapore	80	Singapore
78	El Salvador	75	Chile	76	Chile
77	Chile	71	El Salvador	69	El Salvador
69	Costa Rica	70	Costa Rica	68	Ghana
69	Egypt, Arab Republic	70	Israel	64	Brazil
67	Brazil	68	Egypt, Arab Republic	64	Israel
66	Ghana	64	Greece	61	Costa Rica
65	Spain	63	China	59	Egypt, Arab Republic
62	Greece	63	Ghana	59	Spain
60	Israel	61	Spain	58	Greece
59	China	59	Brazil	56	Jamaica
54	Honduras	55	Malaysia	53	Malaysia
54	Malaysia	52	India	50	Mexico
53	Dominican Republic	50	Colombia	50	Peru
52	Colombia	48	Honduras	49	Cameroon
51	Mexico	46	Mexico	49	Colombia
50	Nicaragua	45	Peru	49	India
48	Argentina	44	Jamaica	48	Argentina
48	Paraguay	44	Sri Lanka	48	Honduras
48	Portugal	43	Dominican Republic	48	Portugal
47	Jamaica	43	Kenya	46	Benin
47	Kenya	42	Argentina	46	Nicaragua
47	Rwanda	42	Malawi	45	Malawi
46	Algeria	41	Thailand	44	Dominican Republic

Contd...

Contd...

46	India	39	Benin
45	Malawi	39	Ecuador
44	Cameroon	39	Portugal
43	Benin	36	Cameroon
43	Sri Lanka	36	Rwanda
42	Thailand	35	Paraguay
40	Zimbabwe	34	Algeria
38	Peru	33	Zimbabwe
37	Ecuador	31	Mauritania
37	Mauritania	31	Philippines
37	Philippines	30	Niger
34	Venezuela	29	Nicaragua
32	Papua New Guinea	29	Syrian Arab Republic
31	Morocco	27	Morocco
31	Niger	26	Cote d'Ivoire
31	Syrian Arab Republic	24	Togo
29	Chad	23	Venezuela
29	Zambia	23	Zambia
28	Sierra Leone	22	Chad
27	Mali	20	Sierra Leone
26	Cote d'Ivoire	19	Mali
26	Sudan	19	Papua New Guinea
20	Togo	17	Sudan
16	Congo, Dem. Republic	10	Burundi
10	Burundi	10	Congo Dem. Republic
8	Nepal	6	Nepal

44	Thailand	33	Cote d'Ivoire
43	China	33	Papua New Guinea
43	Kenya	30	Niger
43	Sri Lanka	30	Venezuela
41	Ecuador	30	Zimbabwe
41	Paraguay	28	Mali
36	Morocco	28	Rwanda
35	Algeria	28	Sierra Leone
34	Mauritania	28	Syrian Arab Republic
34	Philippines	28	Zambia
		21	Chad
		21	Nepal
		21	Sudan
		19	Togo
		18	Congo Dem. Republic
		9	Burundi

variables being added or deleted one at a time until a relatively parsimonious model was created that maximized adjusted R^2 and ensured t-scores greater than two and variance inflation factors between one and five. Each resilience variable was then added to and removed from the equation one at a time to determine if it predicted per capita GDP above and beyond metrics already in the equation. Appendix B shows the regression equation without resilience, the equation with culture resilience added, the equation with context resilience added and the equation with leadership resilience added. A comparison of R^2 and adjusted R^2 for the regression model without resilience constructs, with leadership resilience, with context resilience and with culture resilience is shown in Figure 2.

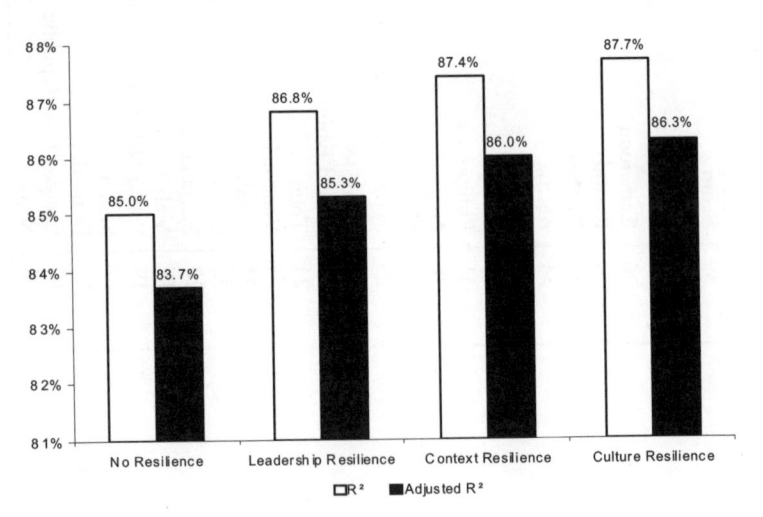

Figure 2. Regression R^2s With and Without Resilience Variables

Discussion

Interpretation of Results

Sample Characteristics

With the exception of consumer price inflation and interest rate spread, variables used in the regression analysis fell within plus or minus three standard deviations from the mean. Nations randomly selected for this study were among those first identified as developing nations by the World Bank in 1962. Forty years later, heterogeneity is notable on indices thought to be related to economic growth. Regarding scores on the leadership, context and culture resilience scales, differentiation was also evident among nations. Nation rankings were similar across resilience scales, supporting the notion that the factors represent interrelated constructs.

World Development Indicators Predictive of Per Capita GDP

Not surprisingly, many of the World Development Indicators shared considerable variance. Out of 25 indices used in the analysis, only four remained in the final regression model on per capita GDP: (1) food production index, (2) physicians, (3) gross domestic savings, and (4) trade.

Gross domestic savings is widely regarded as an economic differentiator among developing nations (e.g., Krugman & Obstfeld 2003). A high degree of savings among citizens represents an external resource and enables a nation to rely less on debt and/or equity financing to fuel economic growth. Gross domestic savings may lead citizens to have greater confidence in their ability to adapt to changing and/or challenging circumstances. If so, this relates to the Positive: Self-resilience characteristic.

Trade expressed as the sum of exports and imports of goods and services was positively related to the dependent measure, indicating that per capita GDP rose as trade increased. This implies opening one's borders to the world and may relate to the Focused, Flexible: Social, Organized, and Proactive resilience characteristics. It may be that citizens of nations with GDPs that reflect a high percentage of trade (1) possess a stronger sense of purpose and are more able to set goals to guide everyday actions and decisions, (2) are more likely to recognize their interdependence and function as a "good team player" with other nations, (3) are more likely to have citizens that possess a greater ability to plan actions for efficient use of resources, and (4) tend to take reasonable risks and are willing to try new activities more so than nations with GDPs that reflect a low percentage of trade.

Food production index was negatively predictive of per capita GDP. In other words, nations that produce a large amount of edible commodities that contain nutrients (e.g., rice) are less likely to have high per capita GDP than nations that do not produce a large amount of edible, nutritious commodities. It may be that developing nations which are not primarily agricultural in nature are more likely to engage in industrial labor and/or services—which tend to be more profitable—than nations which are more agricultural in nature. This index seems to relate to all seven of Conner Partners' resilience factors. Nations that successfully transform to industrial production and/or service delivery may tend to have citizens that (1) find opportunities in times of turmoil, (2) believe in their abilities, (3) possess a strong sense of purpose, (4) draw on environmental resources for assistance and support (which would be useful when venturing into areas where expertise is lacking), (5) are open-minded, (6) can build structure in the midst of chaos, and (7) tend to actively engage change.

The last development index that significantly predicted per capita GDP captured the number of physicians per thousand people. Interestingly, health expenditure and sanitation did not end up in the regression model. This may reflect the fact that many World Development Indicators are correlated with one another. That said, citizens of nations with a greater number of physicians per thousand people may be more likely to draw on the resources of physicians for assistance and support than citizens of nations with a lower number of physicians per thousand people. This appears to be related to the Flexible: Social resilience factor.

If the above relationships are true, they would further suggest that factors associated with economic growth of developing nations are inter-correlated. The question then becomes 'Do leadership, context and/or culture resilience constitute part of

Abramovitz's (1956; 1993) unexplained residual?' Turning to the hypothesis testing reveals the answer.

Hypothesis One

The regression analyses found support for hypothesis one. After entering leadership resilience into the best model of development indicators predictive of per capita GDP, adjusted R^2 rose from 83.7 per cent to 85.3 per cent, with $t = 2.42$, $p = .02$ and a variance inflation factor of 1.5. The degree to which a developing nation's leaders exhibit resilience seems to differentiate nations that are able to substantially improve their economic status from those that are not.

Hypothesis Two

Hypothesis two was also supported. Context resilience—the degree to which a developing nation exhibited a strong vision, mission and strategy to guide its economic growth—appears to add to the predictability of per capita GDP above and beyond previously known predictors. Upon entering the context resilience factor into the regression model, adjusted R^2 rose from 83.7 per cent to 86.0 per cent, with $t = 2.89$, $p < .01$ and a variance inflation factor of 1.8.

Hypothesis Three

The strongest support was found for hypothesis three. When the culture resilience factor was entered into the model, adjusted R^2 rose from 83.7 per cent to 86.3 per cent, with $t = 3.10$, $p < .01$ and a variance inflation factor of 1.8. Of the three resilience measures, a developing nation's degree of culture resilience appears to most strongly add to the predictability of economic growth among developing nations. This supports Landes' statement that "If we learn anything from the history of economic development, it is that culture makes all the difference" (1998; p. 516-517).

Implications for Theory and Practice

Relation Between Social Capital, Human Capital and Resilience

Resilience offers a framework for understanding and measuring the human and social aspects of economic development. When conceptualized as norms of reciprocity that enable people to act collectively, social capital relates to the situational characteristics component of the process of coping. When conceptualized as political power or social resources or networks, social capital relates to the environmental resources component of the coping process. Human capital such as knowledge, skills and abilities relates to the personal resources component of the coping process. When conceptualized as cognitive factors such as perceived trustworthiness that enable people to act collectively, social capital relates to the cognitive appraisal component of the coping process. Emotions that result from and/or influence cognitions or behaviors that enable people to act collectively relate to the affective response component of the coping process. Behaviors such as cooperation that entail people acting collectively relate to the coping strategies component of the coping process. Coping strategies can also include a choice to alter one's cognitions and/or affect.

When perceptions of and exchanges between entities in a social system lack positive, focused, flexible, organized and proactive attributes, lack of resilience is evident and successful adaptation is less likely to occur. "Poverty is about more than inadequate income or low human development; it is also about lack of voice and representation, vulnerability to abuse and corruption, violence against women, fear of crime, and lack of self-esteem" (Wolfensohn—see Holm 2004). When perceptions and interactions exhibit positive, focused, flexible, organized and proactive elements that work together in a balanced, interdependent manner, resilience is evident and successful adaptation is more likely to occur. "Culture, power and rationality play an important role in shaping developmental outcomes, but it is in and through social relations that outcomes are mediated" (Woolcock 1998). When resilience is manifested at the leadership, context and culture levels, transformational change is possible.

Support from the Literature

Evidence of Resilience. Various aspects of resilience at times influence—and at times are influenced by—other aspects of resilience. The following findings illustrate scenarios that facilitated the emergence of the Flexible: Social component of resilience. To reiterate, Flexible: Social captures the degree to which people draw on environmental resources for assistance, value the ideas of others, recognize their interdependence, and function as good team players. In his article on industrial workers in Kerala, India, Heller (1996) stated that negotiations between groups (coping strategies) made their interdependence of interests more transparent and outcomes more certain (cognitive appraisal), which increased cooperation (coping strategies). In his study of 104 peasant cooperatives in Paraguay, Molinas (1998) found that providing economic incentives to cooperate (situational characteristics) and making people more aware of their mutual interdependencies (cognitive appraisal) enhanced cooperation (coping strategies). In their analysis of community-based rural water projects, Isham & Kähkönen (2002) found that formal and informal social ties (exchanges between personal and environmental resources) deterred community members from free-riding (coping strategies) and constrained community leaders from shirking and expropriating funds (coping strategies). In his article on Irrigation Associations in Taiwan, Lam (1996) stated that having multiple arenas at different levels of the Irrigation Associations (situational characteristics) in which local farmers could work things out, communicate with one another, and resolve conflicts (coping strategies) was instrumental in facilitating good relationships (exchanges between personal and environmental resources).

The following findings illustrate outcomes resulting from the Flexible: Social component of resilience. In their study of community-based water services in Sri Lanka and India, Isham & Kähkönen (2002) found that preference for the type and level of services (cognitive appraisal) was more clearly expressed (coping strategies) when community members had a history of working together (exchanges between personal and environmental resources) and all stakeholders had a voice (situational characteristics). In speaking of the sustainability of social capital within ethnic networks, Janjuha-Jivraj (2003) stated that socialization during education and wider working experiences (exchanges between personal and environmental resources) enabled the younger Asian generation to develop greater self-confidence (personal resources) socially and in business. When women participated effectively in a Paraguayan peasant committee (exchanges between personal and environmental resources), members' perception (cognitive appraisal) of the committee's performance was more favorable (Molinas 1998).

Evidence of Varying Resilience. In analyzing the restructuring of post-communist networks in the region of Lanškroun, Czech Republic, Uhlír (1998) noted that individuals differ in the degree to which their opinions and actions are accepted by others; an individual's reputation, in turn, influences the likelihood that others will follow the person's attempt to lead. Influencing others's open-mindedness (cognitive appraisal) and guiding others toward new opportunities (coping strategies) facilitates emergence of the Flexible: Thoughts and Proactive components of resilience in others, respectively.

In comparing the growth of Argentina to the growth of Japan despite Argentina's fertile land and Japan's limited natural resources, Matsuyama (1992) highlights Japan's demonstration of the Positive: World, Positive: Self, Organized and Proactive components of resilience. Specifically, Japan (1) actively sought new challenges, (2) built a learning environment, (3) had a clear and compelling vision and mission that actively engaged change in the marketplace, and (4) had citizens that believed the changing market offered opportunities for their nation's success, and understood and valued their role in contributing to that success. It may be that nations with no substantial natural resources (situational characteristics) exercise care in their economic policies (coping strategies), while nations with an abundance of natural resources (situational characteristics) may have a false sense of security that deters economic prudence (coping strategies) (Gylfason 2001).

Dekker (2004) noted differences in coping strategies during crisis among Zimbabwean households in resettlement vs. communal areas; households in communal areas were more likely to receive assistance from their local support network (coping strategies utilizing environmental resources), while households in resettlement areas were more likely to adopt an independent coping strategy (coping strategies utilizing personal resources). This illustrates the presence of the Flexible: Social component of resilience among households in communal areas, in that they drew on environmental resources for assistance and support, and the absence of the Flexible: Social component of resilience among households in rural areas. Dekker (2004) also found that attitudes toward resettlement farmers were less favorable than attitudes toward communal farmers. Perceiving a lack of willingness on others' part to provide assistance during time of need (cognitive appraisal of lack of environmental resources) could explain resettlement farmers' choice of independent coping strategies.

Evidence of Lack of Resilience. In Collier and Gunning's (1999) explanation of African economic performance, they state that African governments behaved in ways damaging to the long-term interests of the majority of their populations by restricting trade and failing to provide adequate infrastructure and financial markets. This illustrates the absence of the Focused and Proactive components of resilience at the nation level. Specifically, African leaders (1) did not develop strategies to capitalize on market conditions or guide their nations toward new opportunities, and (2) did not actively engage change. Collier and Gunning (1999) also state that to cope with climate risks, African rural households sacrificed the gains of specialization in favor of spreading risk over multiple income-generating activities (coping strategies). This suggests under-utilization of the Proactive component of resilience at the household level given that African rural households did not exhibit a propensity to take reasonable risks or actively engage change.

In Usangu, Cleaver (2005) found that the main coping strategy of the very poor was hiring out their labor, but this limited their ability to participate in community gatherings (exchanges between personal and environmental resources). The poorest people had fewer expectations of cooperation and reciprocity (cognitive appraisal of environmental resources) and their social relations (exchanges with environmental resources) were often fragile and dependent on heavy investments of time and effort to secure very limited benefits.

It is important not to adopt a blame the victim mentality by viewing those less fortunate as the cause of their adversity. People have the ability to foster resilience in others and, one can argue, the obligation to do so. In her review of findings from the environmental protective factors literature, Benard (1991) identified the following characteristics of environments that foster resilience: (1) care and consideration (positive affective responses to, and positive exchanges with, others), (2) participation and involvement (inclusive coping strategies), and (3) high expectations (positive appraisal of others) with the provision of resources to aid goal attainment (supportive coping strategies). Fostering resilience at any level should include ensuring that environmental protective factors are in place.

Broadening Assistance to Developing Nations

The World Bank's role in recommending policies, programs and initiatives to improve a nation's economic status seems most related to the context resilience construct that captures a nation's vision, mission and strategies. Validating this assumption can help frame the theory behind the IMF's role and identify other components of context resilience that may strengthen the IMF's recommendations. To more fully address the human and social components of transformational economic growth, the World

Bank and other non-government organizations and donors may want to broaden their assistance to developing nations to include fostering leadership and culture resilience. The *Nation Resilience Questionnaire*—which measures the degree to which leaders and citizens of a nation exhibit positive, focused, flexible, organized and proactive characteristics and behaviors—can shed light on where problems of governance and social action lie. Once a nation's leadership, context and culture resilience levels are identified, efforts tailored to a nation's particular development needs can be put in place.

Limitations of the Study

No ideal measure of development exists with which to capture progress among developing nations. Per capita GDP based on purchasing power parity—the dependent measure in this study—overcomes concerns about exchange rate biases and is thus often preferable. However, once subsistence levels are reached, personal and social components of development are not adequately reflected.

Another limitation of this study concerns the fact that the *Nation Resilience Questionnaire* was adopted from a measure of organizational resilience. The inter-item correlation coefficients above .93, however, suggest that the constructs measured by the three nation-level resilience scales are strong.

Another point to mention is the need to exercise caution regarding inferring causality. For instance, it may be that once a nation moves beyond sustenance, there is more opportunity for it to be open-minded, flexible, etc.

Finally, raters learned about the nations they rated by reading various publications. While the nation information read was fairly comprehensive and included significant historical events, raters felt it was easier to deduce leaders' degree of resilience and nations' contextual resilience than to fully understand nations' cultures.

Future Research

One area for future research involves the need to further validate the *Nation Resilience Questionnaire*. It may be that the items removed in the scale reliability analyses are removed in future validation as well. In addition, adding new items may strengthen the resilience scales. If so, the instrument should be modified to reflect even stronger measures of the constructs of interest.

Another area for future research comes from the fact that this study utilized a linear regression analysis. Future research could employ non-linear analyses in the study of nation-level resilience. Yet another area for future research would be to validate the current research findings through replication of the study. Raters should be utilized who are more knowledgeable about the cultures and circumstances of the nations studied. If the research findings hold up, efforts should be made to translate resilience constructs into policies and guidelines—and to determine whether doing so significantly impacts economic growth and social well-being. Studies could be conducted to evaluate the effectiveness of interventions designed to increase the resilience of leaders and citizens. In addition, it may be that a nation's degree of leadership and culture resilience influence adherence to IMF recommendations. Ascertaining this through future research could help identify obstacles to change and facilitate the design of strategies to address resistance.

Conclusion

Leadership, context and culture resilience appear to differentiate developing nations that significantly improve their economic status from those that do not—above and beyond predictors already known—thereby explaining some of total productivity's unexplained residual. Being positive, focused, flexible, organized and proactive seems to enable leaders and citizens of developing nations to better overcome their disadvantaged status than leaders and citizens who are not collectively inherently resilient. If so, then strengthening the resilience of a nation's leadership, context and culture can aid development economists in raising the living standards of poorer countries. In turn, all nations would reap the benefits of global health, peace and prosperity.

Appendix A
Sample Nation Resilience Questionnaire Items

- Part of this country's strategy for dealing with change is to develop competencies.
- In the present market, this country is setting goals for survival, not growth.
- This country's leaders tend to be protective of special interest projects and functions.
- This country's leaders are especially skilled at planning the work, then "working the plan."
- For many citizens, this country's goals are not consistent with their personal goals.
- Most citizens generally believe that change in the environment will have positive outcomes for this country.

Appendix B
Regression Equations

Regression without Resilience Variables

Predictor	Coef	SE Coef	T	P	VIF
Constant	1956	2133	0.92	0.364	
Food production index (FPI)	-30.34	13.42	-2.26	0.029	1.4
Physicians (DOC)	4.1113	0.3469	11.85	0.000	1.2
Gross domestic savings (GDS)	79.82	34.06	2.34	0.024	1.5
Trade	35.350	9.461	3.74	0.001	1.6
S = 2396.07	R^2 = 85.0%		R^2 (adj) = 83.7%		

Regression equation: GDP = 1956—30.3 FPI + 4.11 DOC + 79.8 GDS + 35.3 TRADE

Regression with Leadership Resilience

Predictor	Coef	SE Coef	T	P	VIF
Constant	1746	2028	0.86	0.394	
Leadership Resilience (LEAD)	60.36	24.96	2.42	0.020	1.8
Food production index (FPI)	-39.79	13.33	-2.98	0.005	1.5
Physicians (DOC)	3.6080	0.3898	9.26	0.000	1.6
Gross domestic savings (GDS)	83.72	32.40	2.58	0.013	1.5
Trade	23.62	10.21	2.31	0.025	2.0

S = 2276.59 R^2 = 86.8% R^2 (adj) = 85.3%

Regression equation: 1746 + 60.4 LEAD − 39.8 FPI + 3.61 DOC + 83.7 GDS + 23.6 TRADE

Regression with Context Resilience

Predictor	Coef	SE Coef	T	P	VIF
Constant	2319	1981	1.17	0.248	
Context Resilience (CONT)	66.48	23.01	2.89	0.006	1.8
Food production index (FPI)	-42.27	13.11	-3.22	0.002	1.6
Physicians (DOC)	3.5037	0.3843	9.12	0.000	1.7
Gross domestic savings (GDS)	82.65	31.59	2.62	0.012	1.5
Trade	21.768	9.952	2.19	0.034	2.0

S = 2221.53 R^2 = 87.4% R^2 (adj) = 86.0%

Works Cited

Abramovitz, M. 1956. "Resource and Output Trends in the United States since 1870." *American Economic Review,* 46, May, 5-23.

_____ 1993. "The Search for the Sources of Growth: Areas of Ignorance, Old and New." *Journal of Economic History,* 53, June, 217-43.

Anthony, E. J. 1987. "Children at High Risk for Psychosis Growing Up Successfully." In Anthony, E. J., & Cohler, B. J. (Eds.), *The Invulnerable Child* (pp. 3-48). New York: Guildford Press.

Antonovsky, A. *Unraveling the Mystery of Health: How People Manage Stress and Stay Well.* San Francisco, CA: Jossey-Bass, 1987.

Benard, B. (1991). *Fostering Resiliency in Kids: Protective Factors in the Family, School and Community.* (Available from the Southeast Regional Center for Drug-Free Schools and Communities, Spencerian Office Plaza, University of Louisville, Louisville, KY 40292)

Burke, W.W. and Litwin, G. H. (1992), A Causal Model of Organizational Performance and Change, *Journal of Management*, 18 (3), 523-545.

Cleaver, F. 2005. The Inequality of Social Capital and the Reproduction of Chronic Poverty, *World Development*, 33(6), 893-906.

Collier, P., & Gunning, J. W. 1999. Explaining African Economic Performance, *Journal of Economic Literature*, 37(1), 64-111.

Conner Partners. 1996. *Organizational Resilience*, Atlanta, GA.

Dekker, M. 2004. Sustainability and Resourcefulness: Support Networks During Periods of Stress, *World Development*, 32(10), 1735-1751.

"2004 Nation Profile." (For each nation in study). The Economist Intelligence Unit. Retrieved 31 October 2004 <http://libcat1.cc.emory.edu:32888/2004112000322542f55ad6/index.asp?layout=countries>.

"2004 Nation Report." (For each nation in study). The Economist Intelligence Unit. Retrieved 31 October 2004 <http://libcat1.cc.emory.edu:32888/2004112000322542f55ad6 /index.asp?layout=countries>.

Global Market Information Database, *Consumer Lifestyles* reports for Argentina, Brazil, Chile, China, Colombia, Egypt, Greece, India, Malaysia, Mexico, Philippines, Portugal, Singapore, Spain and Venezuela, November 2004-May 2005.

Gylfason, T. 2001. Nature, Power, and Growth, *Scottish Journal of Political Economy*, 48(5), 558-588.

Heller, P. (1996). Social Capital as a Product of Class Mobilization and State Intervention: Industrial Workers in Kerala, India, *World Development* 24(6), 1055-1071.

Hobfall, S. E., & Leiberman, J. R. (1987). Personality and Social Resources in Immediate and Continued Stress, Resistance Among Women. *Journal of Personality and Social Psychology*, 51(1), 18-26.

_____ & Walfisch, S. (1984). Coping with a Threat to Life: A Longitudinal Study of Self-Concept, Social Support, and Psychological Distress. *American Journal of Community Psychology*, 12(1), 87-100.

Holahan, C. J., & Moos, R. H. (1990). Life Stressors, Resistance Factors, and Improved Psychological Functioning: An Extension of the Stress Resistance Paradigm. *Journal of Personality and Social Psychology*, 58(5), 909-917.

Isham, J., & Kähkönen, S. 2002. Institutional Determinants of the Impact of Community-Based Water Services: Evidence from Sri Lanka and India, *Economic Development and Cultural Change*, 50(3), 667-691.

Janjuha-Jivraj, S. 2003. The Sustainability of Social Capital within Ethnic Networks, *Journal of Business Ethics,* 47(1), 31-43.

Kobasa, S. C. O., & Puccetti, M. C. 1983. Personality and Social Resources in Stress Resistance. *Journal of Personality and Social Psychology,* 45(4), 839-850.

Krugman, P. R., & Obstfeld, M. *International Economics.* New York: Addison Wesley, 2003.

Lam, W. F. 1996. Institutional Design of Public Agencies and Coproduction: A Study of Irrigation Associations in Taiwan, *World Development,* 24(6), 1039-1054.

Landes, D. S. 1998. *The Wealth and Poverty of Nations: Why Some Are So Rich and Some So Poor.* New York: W. W. Norton.

Lazarus, R. S. 1993. Why We Should Think of Stress as a Subset of Emotion. In L. Goldberger & S. Breznitz (Eds.), *Handbook of Stress* (pp. 21-39). New York: The Free Press.

_____, & Folkman, S. *Stress, Appraisal, and Coping,* New York: Springer Publishing, 1984.

Matsuyama, K. 1992. Agricultural Productivity, Comparative Advantage, and Economic Growth, *Journal of Economic Theory,* 58, 317-334.

Meier, G. M. 2001. "Introduction: Ideas for Development". In G. M. Meier & J. E. Stiglitz (Eds.), *Frontiers of Development Economics: The Future in Perspective,* New York: Oxford University Press.

Molinas, J. R. 1998. The Impact of Inequality, Gender, External Assistance and Social Capital on Local-Level Cooperation, *World Development,* 26(3), 413-431.

Moos, R. H., & Schaefer, J. A. 1993. Coping Resources and Processes: Current Concepts and Measures. In L. Goldberger & S. Breznitz (Eds.), *Handbook of Stress* (pp. 234-257). New York: The Free Press.

Rutter, M. 1987. Psychosocial Resilience and Protective Mechanisms. *American Journal of Orthopsychiatry,* 57 (3), 316-331.

Sandler, I. N., & Lakey, B. (1982). Locus of Control as a Stress Moderator: The role of Control Perceptions and Social Support. *American Journal of Community Psychology,* 10(1), 65-80.

Stern, N. 2001. "Forward". In G. M. Meier & J. E. Stiglitz (Eds.), *Frontiers of Development Economics: The Future in Perspective,* New York: Oxford University Press.

Stiglitz, J. E. (2002). Participation and Development: Perspectives from the Comprehensive Development Paradigm, *Review of Development Economics,* 6(2), 163-182.

Uhlíø, D. 1998. Internationalization, and Institutional and Regional Change: Restructuring Post-communist Networks in the Region of Lanškroun, Czech Republic, *Regional Studies,* 32(7), 673-685.

Wallace, J., & Killerby, P. 2004. Social economics and social capital, *International Journal of Social Economics,* 31 (3).

Werner, E. E., & Smith, R. S. *Vulnerable but Invincible.* St. Louis, MO: McGraw-Hill, 1982.

Wolfensohn, J. (2004). In Holm, A., A Social Capital Idea, *Harvard International Review,* 25, Winter, 24-27.

Woolcock, M. (1998). Social Capital and Economic Development: Toward a Theoretical Synthesis and Policy Framework, *Theory and Society,* 27(2), 151-208.

_____, & Narayan, D. 2000. Social Capital: Implications for Development Theory, Research and Policy, *The World Bank Research Observer,* 15 (2), 225-249.

The World Bank. "World Development Indicators, 2003-2004." http:// devdata.worldbank.org.proxy.library.emory.edu/dataonline/ (accessed October 31, 2004).

CHAPTER 16

Building Resilience in the Next Generation and the Power of Higher Self-efficacy

Anndrea Wheatley

Abstract

Self-efficacy has been defined by Bandura (1989) as "the perception that one can achieve desired goals through one's actions" and that this also includes the mobilization of motivation and cognitive resources in order to have control over task demands. Researchers have found (Pajares 1996, Wolters, Chemers, Watson and May 2000), that self-efficacy helps determine how much effort people will expend on an activity, how long they will persevere when confronting obstacles, and how resilient they will prove to be in the face of adverse situations. Self-efficacy also has an impact on challenge/threat perceptions of tasks and adversity lowering threat when self-efficacy is higher in an individual. It would seem logical then, that to build up self-efficacy, as well as emotional regulation, and problem solving skills, in the lives of children and young people, would be one of the key and important issues in building resilience. Implementing sources of self-efficacy is important in order for this to occur and these have been stated by Joet, Bressoux, and Usher (2011) and Williams and Williams (2010), such as mastery experience which loops back into self-efficacy and builds up that person again confirming to them that they can do that task before them and take on others. Another is vicarious experience or observing the actions of others such as a close friend or peers succeeding in a challenging task or situation. Models also have an important role for those who have doubts about their skills. Another source is social persuasions and evaluative feedback from parents, teachers and peers, which can affect a young person's confidence. Providing protective processes such as these build up a child's self-efficacy and have impact right through to adulthood in facing life challenges and adversity.

Key Words

Resilience, challenge/threat perceptions, mastery, adversity, protective factors, emotional self-efficacy, emotional self-regulation, learned helplessness

Many factors make a child resilient or able to work through life difficulties. Resilience is not a static state for a child or young person, or a fixed attribute in their lives (Luthar, Cicchetti, and Becker 2000), but rather can be built by strength-building positive protective factors in their lives, or lessened by risk factors. The protective factors and risk factors balance each other like a scale. If the scale tips too far one way the child becomes extremely at risk but if more of the positive factors are loading up on the other side of the scale it will tip to resilience which will hold that child, or young person, even in adulthood, in times of extreme stress and crisis. Noted by Werner and Smith (2001) researchers have explained that children in highly adverse circumstances overcame adversity because they were exposed to protective factors that served as buffers and that furthermore, protective factors had a more profound influence on children who grew up under adverse conditions than did the specific risk factors. Making it through for those children and young people, depends on whether at the time of stress and crisis, protective factors are actually being supplied to that individual. If they are not, then the individual is going to feel inadequate, threatened and overwhelmed by their circumstances.

'At risk' youth are defined as young people whose life situations place them in danger of future negative situations. Such youth have personal characteristics or environmental conditions that predict the onset, continuity, or escalation of problematic behaviour, however, "On any given day even the most advantaged youth may be at risk for participating in or developing problematic behaviours" (Hewlett 1991 cited Smith 2006). However, even affluent youth are considered at risk because they spend much time on their own, given their parents' time-consuming careers. Hence, at risk youth come from all ethnic and socioeconomic backgrounds (Dana 2002 cited Smith 2006). "Ordinary families create high-risk environment conditions in various ways: by focusing on their jobs more than on their children; by failing to establish family rules, by heaping verbal abuse which undermines self-esteem, by neglecting to monitor with whom their children associate..."(Smith 2006). Yet, despite adverse circumstances, research has found that most children even those from highly dysfunctional or resource deprived families, manage not only to survive but also to forge decent lives for themselves. Researchers have explained that these children overcame adversity because they were exposed to protective factors that served as buffers (Werner & Smith 1992). Furthermore, protective factors had a more profound influence on children who grew up under adverse conditions than did specific risk factors. One such protective factor is self-efficacy, central to resilience and defined as "The perception that one can achieve desired goals through one's actions" (Bandura 1989). Bandura also defines perceived self-efficacy as "referring to one's capabilities to organize, and execute the course of action required achieve goals, and that this includes the mobilization of motivation and cognitive resources in order to have control over task demands. It has also been found that among the mechanisms of human agency, none is more pervasively influential than self-efficacy beliefs, namely, beliefs individuals hold about their capacity to exert control over the events that affect their lives" (Bandura 1997, 2001).

Further to this, Bandura (2001) notes that self-efficacy beliefs are not static traits, but rather dynamic constructs that can be enhanced through mastery experiences as a result of individual's capacities to reflect and learn from experience. Researchers note (Pajares 1996, Wolters 2003, Chemers, Watson and May 2000) the efficacy beliefs help determine how much effort people will expend on an activity, how long they will persevere when confronting obstacles, and how resilient they will prove in the face of adverse situations.

The self-efficacy of a child or young person can change—their self-efficacy can be built up or be lacking. According to the resources provided to them, self-efficacy can be changed in a person's life and is not set in stone.

At times an individual, when exposed to adversity, can develop strengths which may have never occurred if it were not for the stress of adversity, forcing them into new skills and areas. Cozolino (2010, p. 20) notes "Humans can be motivated to learn new skills and take on new challenges to relieve discomfit and distress." However, too much stress can be damaging unless there are protective factors to buffer that individual. Cozolino (2010, p. 250) notes that prolonged stress leads to disease, and to neuron cell death particularly in the hippocampus (involved with memory and learning) resulting in memory deficits and depression. An individual may then have less resilience and less coping ability. He further states that the human brain is well equipped to survive brief periods of stress without long-term damage, and in optimal state, stressful experiences can be quickly resolved but only with good coping skills and the help of caring others. Without, however, good coping skills or the help of caring others, the stressful experiences cannot be "quickly resolved". Cozolino further comments (2010, p.249) that sustained high levels of stress also explain in part, the powerful effect of negative experiences in parenting and attachment have on lifelong physical health, mental health, and learning.

Challenge and Threat Perceptions

It has been noted by researchers (Blascovich and Mendes 2000, Blascovich and Tomaka 1996, and Tomaka, Blascovich, Kibler, and Ernst 1997) that a challenge perception of difficult tasks and life experiences occurs when the individual experiences sufficient or nearly sufficient resources to meet situation demands. The opposite occurs if there are not sufficient resources to meet situation demands—a threat perception which brings with it all the impact of stress hormones and negative health consequences. In light of this it would seem necessary then to supply or find the resources for that person to be able to meet those situational demands—particularly in the case of children and young people. If they lack certain protective factors such as, for instance, good problem solving skills, or people that care about them, a stable home life, a good school, social support, or good self-efficacy, then it would be good to have these supplied to make up for what is lacking in those situational demands. Researchers (Caprara, Giunta, Gerbino, Pastorelli, Tramontano and Eisenberg 2008), also note that self-efficacy beliefs influence self-regulative standards adopted by people, whether they think in an enabling or a debilitating manner, the amount of effort they invest, how much they persevere in the face of difficulties, and their vulnerability to stress and depression.

When perception of a problem occurs and subsequent cognitive appraisal is made such as threat perception or challenge perception of goal relevant situations, there is also a pattern of physiological arousal that is associated with situation demands and appraisal outcome. Researchers, Blascovich and Mendes (2000) note, that threat occurs when an individual experiences *insufficient resources* to meet situational demands. These researchers also found that physiological responses such as cardiovascular functioning are attuned to challenge and threat. Emotional regulation skills are then needed in order to cope with the threat emotions and the physiological responses that come with this state. However, if self-efficacy is lower in one area for an individual it can also generalize to other areas such as emotional regulation. Caprara et al (2008) also note that self-efficacy beliefs do not operate in isolation from one another and may generalize, at least to some degree, across activities and situations, to specific domains of individual functioning. Therefore in line with this, the theory of self-efficacy has been extended to address different self-efficacy beliefs associated with the domain of emotional regulation by Bandura (2003) and Caprara (2002).

It has been found in recent studies (Wheatley 2011) that those with higher self-efficacy for self-regulated academic learning, have more of a challenge perception of problems and difficulties in facing academic tasks and difficulties, whereas those with lower self-efficacy for self-regulated learning tend to a threat perception of academic tasks. If this is so, then it is only logical to find ways to build up the self-efficacy of children and young people. This is an issue for young people, when facing challenges and difficulties, not only in academic learning, but in future major life stressors. There are sources of self-efficacy which can be provided to children and young people in order that they can become resilient in the face of adversity in their lives, and in their general academic learning challenges as school students, and in future achievements. The sources need to become available to children before the scales for them are tipped toward more risk. Without the resources and provision of buffer from stress, a sense of helplessness (Seligman 1975) can creep in the psyche of children and young people until all problems, tasks and challenges in life are perceived as an unchangeable threat.

Self-efficacy and Mastery

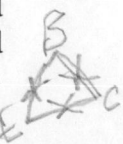

Self-efficacy is pivotal to resilience in children and young people and is defined as "The perception that one can achieve desired goals through one's own actions..." (Bandura 1989). Maddux (1995) also defines the theory of self-efficacy as concerned foremost with the role of personal cognitive factors in the triadic reciprocality model of Social Cognitive Theory by Bandura (1977,1986). Williams and Williams (2010) also state that this triadic reciprocality is how a person's behaviour, cognition and environment influence and are influenced by each other. Noted by researchers (Joet, Breussoux, and Usher 2011) that actions perceived as successful, typically raise self-efficacy, those perceived as failures lower it. Two students who have earned the same grade on an assignment might perceive the grade in different ways on the basis of difficulty of the course material, amount of help received, subjectivity of grade and how much effort was required.

Joet et al's (2011) French study of third grade students found that mastery experience was predictive of achievement over and above the children's standardized mathematics and French achievement scores. This confirmed that what is important in the construction of self-efficacy is the "phenomenological manner in which students perceive their experiences." Joel et al (2011) found support for previous research (Bandura 1997, Usher&Pajares 2008b), showing *that perceived mastery experience is a powerful source of self-efficacy across academic domains.*

Researchers Williams and Williams (2010) study of students in 33 countries, concerning mathematics achievements' of 15-year olds, suggested that there is a continuous reciprocal interaction among behavioural, cognitive, and environmental influences. They noted that mastery experience leads to feelings of self-efficacy which links to subsequent mastery of future like tasks, and after that continues to loop back into self-efficacy. When a person has gained mastery in one thing they will think that they can master the next task and most importantly have proven to themselves that they in fact can do it. This is invaluable for children and young people to gain this kind of self-efficacy which can help them in facing future challenges through into adulthood.

Model of Self-Efficacy and Mastery (Wheatley 2012)

A model of self-efficacy and how it works is illustrated well with the children's story, The Little Red Engine Story (Ross 1942)—the Little Red Engine thinks he can do it (drive up the hill) and he does and self-talks himself to the top of the hill and runs down the other side knowing that indeed he could having proven it to himself. His self-efficacy has lifted and loops back into his self-efficacy being build up enough to take on another challenge. The trick is—what made him *think he could*? Where did he get this higher self-efficacy?

A child with good or higher self-efficacy is like the Little Red Engine (Ross 1942) who comes to the foot of a big step hill and says to himself "I think I can, I think I can..." even though it looks daunting to the little steam train, he pushes himself to get up there and once reaching the top can say coming down the other side "I knew I could, I knew I could!" He has proven to himself he can do it. This is a wonderful picture of self-efficacy developing through mastery of tasks, and skills, and even life challenges and problems, in a child and young person. The most impacting time for the Little Red Engine, or any child is when they first approach the hill. At the foot of the hill they must decide to take it on—and perceive it it as a threat or a challenge. The next time is at the very steep incline of the hill near the top, when it gets very difficult to keep going on, and they must make the decision again to themselves that extra push to get to the top.

At the foot of the hill they have to decide to start saying "I think I can..." A child with low self-efficacy will say "I don't think I can..." and possibly walk away from the hill. As one student commented in a Western Sydney high school which I recently visited "That's what you do when you come to a hill like that—you turn back". This could possibly indicate a lack of good self-efficacy for that student. He saw the hill as a threat that should not be attempted. Even a student's interpretation of what they would do if they were the Little Red Engine and came to a hill, seemed to show the level of their self-efficacy. A group of Year 10 boys from a Western Sydney high school (in a lower socio-economic area) were shown a picture of The Little Red Engine sitting at the foot of the hill about to go up it and the students were asked "What did the little red engine do when he came to the bottom of the hill?" Most of the boys in this group had never heard the story before at all, and one of them said "He turned back....", I said "No, The Little Red Engine said 'I think I can, I think I can...' all the way up until he got to the top, and that is what you need to do—you push yourself and you go up the hill and talk to yourself all the way up".

There is a reason why at the bottom of the hill a child decides they will take on the challenge of the steep hill. If he has low self-efficacy he will possibly just walk away or start going up the hill and then just give up. A boy from another class of Year 12 at risk students at another Western Sydney high school, commented he thought that the Little Red Engine would keep sliding backwards again and again, until he finally gave up and went away. What makes a child or young person decide at the foot of the hill "I think I can, I think I can do it..."? This is where the work is needed on a child's life, and not just by changing their thinking. They will not even think "I can..." if they do not have self-belief or confidence in themselves. The difference is in how much self-efficacy that child or young person has—how much they believe they have ability to do anything. In fact if their self-efficacy is low, they will not take on a task even if they do have the ability to succeed.

I told the story of the Little Red Engine—to a Health class of Year 7 students in a Western Sydney high school. Most had never heard of the story, and so were asked "What do you think he did when he came to the bottom of the hill?" Their answers seemed to indicate the level of their own self-efficacy. However, one little girl immediately spoke up smiling—"He went over the hill and down the other side!" She was confident enough in herself to say he went over the hill of course—perhaps because that is what she would do.

Achieving mastery also has implications for brain plasticity, as an individual starts to move into learning or master new tasks, there is expansion of existing neurons, growth of new neurons and development of pathways in their brain (Cozolino 2010, p.17). If a child or young person perseveres and keeps mastering that area in which they are learning, this causes the pathways to become more consolidated. When people say "I feel like I am growing as a person" they literally are growing in their brain, by learning and mastering a new area or task. "Existing neurons grow through the expansion and branching of the dendrites they project to other neurons in reaction to new experiences and learning." (Purves & Voyvodic 1987 cited Cozolino 2010, p.17) Also, neurons interconnect to form neural networks, and neural networks, in turn, integrate with one another to perform increasingly complex tasks (Cozolino 2010, p.17). However, if a person will not even attempt to take on the task before them, then there is no new growth or development of their brain pathways. In short they are not coming into their full potential. "Mild to moderate stress activates neural growth hormones supportive of new learning." (Cozolino 2010, p. 20). Children and young people need to be encouraged to take the challenge, and to keep going up that hill of learning by persevering so that they can grow. They need good self-efficacy to believe in themselves enough to step up and even push themselves to take the hill.

Studies (Bandura 1977, Pintrich and Degroot 1990, Bouffard-Bouchard 1991, Maddux 1995, Pintrich 2000, Keller 2007) have concluded that self-efficacy plays a mediative or 'facilitative' role in relation to cognitive motivation, and that without positive self-perceptions there could be detrimental effects on problem solving strategies in that they might not even be used."Individuals' objective knowledge of their own cognitive processes is contaminated by their feelings of competence." (Bouffard-Bouchard 1991, p.160). A student even knowing they have the ability can still be hindered by feelings of incompetence which stop them feeling that they can do the task. Pajares (1996), Pajares and Kranzler (1995a, 1995b) note that the direct effect of self-efficacy on performance was as strong as the effect of ability. They state that the non-significant direct effect of anxiety, and the reduced effect of self-concept on performances, diminished when self-efficacy is included in the model. Self-efficacy does not necessarily reflect a rational estimation of a person's real capacity. It is rather the result of the interaction between the individual's estimation of the demands and conditions of a particular task, the resources they believe they possess, and especially their ability to use them adequately in specific this situations (Mendes 2000, Wolters 2003).

Studies by Maddux (1995) found that individuals may enter situations in which they expect success and for which they believe they possess the necessary level of skill. Their subsequent experience of success enhances their sense of efficacy, or they may avoid situations and activities in which they expect not to perform skilfully (even if they may possess the skills needed) so that they then deprive themselves of potential success experiences which would have counteracted their low sense of efficacy. Pajares and Urdan (2006) and Williams and Williams (2010), note many studies show that as one's mastery or proficiency at an activity increases, so does one's self-efficacy. Generally frequent successes lead to higher self-efficacy and consistent failures experiences usually lower it. However, accomplishments are interpreted in light of one's self-regulatory processes.

Pajares and Urdan (2006) and Joet, Bressoux, and Usher (2001) also note a source of self-efficacy in physiological reactions which can influence how an individual makes an efficacy judgement. Various studies such as those by Tomaka, Blascovich, Kibler, & Ernst (1997), Chemers, Hu and Garcia (2001), Blascovich and Mendes (2001), showed that self-efficacy has an impact on performance through its effects on attention and construal of environmental demands, and also through its effect on the ability to control and manage negative or potentially negative emotions. If a person thinks they do not have the abilities or resources to meet a task, then they will find it daunting to attempt, with a David-Goliath perception of what is required of them. They may put off taking on Goliath if they have low self-efficacy, or may not take him on at all, but if they have high self-efficacy they run to meet the challenge no matter how daunting the giant looks.

The recent study of self-efficacy by Williams and Williams (2010), further states that individuals with high self-efficacy approach difficult tasks as challenges to be mastered rather than as threats which they may avoid. They also set challenging goals for themselves, maintain a strong commitment to these goals and even heighten and sustain their efforts in the face of failure, attributing failure to insufficient effort or deficient knowledge and skills, and approach threatening situations with more assurance, exercising control over such. Whilst, in contrast, those with low self-efficacy, doubting their own capabilities, pull back from difficult tasks they view as personal threats thereby having the opposite reaction to those with higher self-efficacy.

Self-efficacy, Challenge and Threat

Chemers, Hu and Garcia (2001), Skinner and Brewer (2006), and Blascovich and Tomaka (1996) take the view, that those with self-efficacy have the ability to manage the stressors created in demanding situations due to a more positive outlook and having available coping resources so that their tendency is to see demanding situations as challenging rather than threatening. How individuals approach stressful achievement events requires consideration of both threat and challenge appraisals. Studies by Brewer and Skinner (2006) showed challenge was associated with more confident coping expectancies and experience of positive emotion. In general, it is has been noted that it is possible that intellectually competent students who have failed to acquire positive perceptions of their abilities, will avoid experiences that could provide positive evidence of their abilities. Boekaerts (1992) in particular suggests that students continuously judge whether a learning situation is benign, neutral or threatening for their well-being. Studies by Joet, Bressoux, & Usher (2011), Chemers et al

(2001), Blascovich and Tomaka (1996), Blascovich and Mendes, also note empirical work showing that challenge-threat evaluation is strongly related to affective responses and physiological reactivity.

The recent study by Joet et al (2011) of Third grade Elementary school students in France, showed gender differences in self-efficacy between boys and girls with mathematics and French, also showed mastery experience, social persuasions, physiological state and mean self-efficacy predicted self-efficacy in learning French. They noted particularly that in agreement with Bandura (1986, 1997) that individuals often interpret their physiological and emotional states, such as stress, anxiety, and fatigue, as indicators of their capabilities (Bandura 1997). Students learn to rely on their own bodily arousal as evidence of their personal competence by evaluating their arousal in diverse situations. Bandura (1997) states that strong emotional reactions can furnish useful information about one' eventual success or failure and feeling extreme stress or anxiety when undertaking a particular academic task could indicate a lack of capability thereby affecting their self-efficacy to that task.

Bandura (1997, pp.262) notes that a person's self-efficacy beliefs and self-appraisals exert significant changes in physiological status for physical and psychological health—and that strong and realistic self-efficacy beliefs appear to protect people from the deleterious bodily effects of prolonged stress. He also states that people who believe they are in control and can master even ordinarily unpredictable events maintain lower levels of blood pressure, heart rates, and stress hormone levels. "Catecholamine secretions—neurotransmitters regulating important brain activities, were shown to fundamentally mirror self-efficacy for phobic patients in the face of threat. High self-efficacy, belief that the threat is easily managed, was associated with low levels of catecholamine activity and stress hormones. Low self-efficacy beliefs were associated with elevated levels of catecholamines. When threats were removed altogether, the levels of catcheholamines and other stress hormones dropped. " (Bandura 1997, p.265)

In Chemers, Hu, and Garcia's (2001) study of 1st year college students they proposed that students high in academic self-efficacy should see themselves as more able to meet the demands of that situation and see the year ahead as a challenge rather than a threat. Chemers et al (2001) found that self-efficacy directly and indirectly showed powerful relationships to academic performance and personal adjustment of first year college students. They noted that confident and optimistic students were more likely to see the university experience as a challenge rather than a threat. They noted that the impact of self-efficacy and optimism were on the perceptions of available resources—once again, the "perception" of resources is an issue in that they may think they do not have the resources or ability when in fact they might have them!

Chemers et al (2001) notes that the effects of self-efficacy and optimism on stress, health and adjustment were totally mediated by challenge and threat (self-efficacy and optimism had no direct relationships with those variables) revealing the 'powerful role' of challenge-threat evaluations. This research may also have implications with regard to resilience and suicide amongst adolescents as shown by Orbach, Blomenson, Mikulincer, Gilboa-Schectman, Rogolsky, and Rezoni (2007), who stated that appraisals of a problem-solving task as a threat or as a challenge is an important factor in suicidal behaviour of adolescents. As noted (Wheatley 2011) in an unpublished study of University of Western Sydney students' self-efficacy and challenge/threat evaluations impacting on procrastination, results showed a positive correlation so that self-efficacy decreased, threat perception significantly increased for those students and that they had less of a challenge perception. When self-efficacy was higher, threat perception tended to be lower and students tended to more of a challenge perception. Challenge perception correlated significantly with higher self-efficacy in that as self-efficacy was higher so students tended to a more challenge perception, and when self-efficacy was lower—challenge perception was less and students tended to a more threat perception.. Lazarus and Folkman (1984) noted "appraisal of an event as threat or as a challenge depends on one's self-perception of being competent or incompetent to solve the problem at hand..." They also state that appraising a problem as a threat may potentially set in motion a negative emotional reaction, which in turn may diminish one's ability to adequately handle the problem. This then becomes a vicious cycle if their self-efficacy in emotional regulation is also low so that they are unable to calm their emotions.

Researchers (Orbach et al 2007) suggest that the appraisal of a problem-solving task as threat or as challenge affects both the actual task performance and the emotional reactions to the problem-solving task. Perceiving a problem as a challenge can elicit a sense of curiosity and mastery. This, in turn, may serve to facilitate the use of effective problem-solving strategies, as well as to increases in the sense of satisfaction in problem-solving. On the other hand, perceiving a problem-solving task as a threat can elicit tension and anxiety and a desire to avoid or get rid of the problem-solving task at hand. This, in turn, may result in the use of ineffective problem-solving strategies. Ultimately, when such distressing experiences reoccur, the perception of problems as a threat and the resulting cognitive and emotional deficits can lead to increased hopelessness and tendency to suicide.

Orbach et al (2007) note that mastery-oriented individuals are characterized by a tendency to perceive difficult problems as a challenge, and in fact as an opportunity (Orbach et al 2007) to expand their range of knowledge and abilities. They were found to adhere to or improve their problem-solving strategies even after failed attempts. Helplessness-oriented individuals, on other hand, although may not be less capable of problem-solving, are more likely to perceive problem-solving tasks as a threat. As a result, upon receiving feedback of their failure, such individuals will react with an increased withdrawal from a task and will experience decreased self-confidence, increased feelings of discouragement, self-condemnation and pessimism regarding problem solving. Studies by Boekarts and Niemivirta (2000), Dweck (1986) and Phillips (1984), note the effects of *learned helplessness* (Seligman 1975, Mickulincer 1986), which is often expressed as lack of persistence in children's learning. Helplessness (Bandura 1997) is something that can be learned from a young age, even infancy. When a child realizes that there is no benefit in anticipating consequences and when most things that happen in your world are unpredictable or unreliable, it is then he perceives his efforts as being of no use and grows apathetic and loses interest in trying to exercise personal control. Hence helplessness can begin in infancy and continue for a child if not given a chance to learn they can have some control of their world and that it can change for them.

The Little Red Engine—Model of Adversity (Wheatley 2012)

Just as children and young people treat their academic mastery as a challenge or threat, so they can also face life problems the same way and with the same helplessness if their self-efficacy has not been built up. Life adversity and problems or major stressors can come to us like the large steep hill that the Little Red Engine (Ross 1942) found himself facing. He had to say to himself once again "I think I can..." and keep going up the hill. He will only say this if he has enough self-efficacy to say he can. The learning curve here represents adversity worsening at the top until he reaches the other side and it has eased off. To get up the hill he might need some help or extra push from other engines—social support. To not be threatened by the hill and want to run away or fall into depression—he needs higher self-efficacy in order to see it as a challenge, and to tell himself to keep going on.

As stress increases near the top of the hill and the adversity reaches its peak—he needs his self-efficacy to once again keep going and not jump of the track and to tell himself to keep going. He will have to self-talk himself up there and he needs to know he is supported. He has to look after himself, emotionally, physiologically and mentally, he needs to be able to see it as a challenge and not a threat by knowing he has the resources to cope with the stressor. Having social support can help neutralize the threat and buffer him (Noddings 2006, Seligman 2006), also having the resources to go through the adversity will take away the threat because then he knows he has enough to get through. Emotional regulation is also necessary to enable the person to go through adversity and cope with stress hormones and chemicals. Once again if the person has higher self-efficacy this may also mean they have higher self-efficacy in emotional regulation. Or if the individual has lower self-efficacy they may have less self-efficacy in emotional regulation, and be likely to have a threat perception, and will have more stress hormones so that they will find it difficult to emotionally regulate themselves than someone who has a challenge perception. This then is like a vicious cycle for those with less self-efficacy.

As stated previously—good self-efficacy is the key here to turning a possible threat into a challenge and bring with this all the benefits of healthier mental well-being (Chemers, Hu, and Garcia 2001). Perceiving that he can solve the problem or even cope, is the key. If the adversity is not going to go away he may have to remove himself from the stress of the adversity if he can even briefly. If he cannot then he needs support and help solving the problem or he will lapse into helplessness and depression if he has not already jumped the cliff from stress! If he gets over the hill he has proven to himself that "I knew I could..." maybe he did not even know he could do it, but he has shown himself that indeed he did and can go through what life throws at him. Getting from the one side to the other has its toughest part at the top just before it peaks until he is on the other side. This juncture is crucial—here is where support and help is needed and the knowledge that he can do it, he is not alone, that there are resources to help him make it, in his home, in his life, in his community, and that he is cared about enough to receive those resources (Fry, Kim, Gano-Overway, Guivernau, Newton, Magyar 2011). Once again the scales tip toward risk or to resilience depending on what is supplied to that child, young person or even adult.

"A caring climate appears to help adolescents monitor, manage, and control their positive and negative emotions, and heighten their compassion for others who may be struggling. The ability to temper one's emotions, feel empathy, share with, comfort, and support is reflective of a mature and psychologically adaptive approach to life." (Noddings 2006, Seligman 2006).

Peers, Parents and Teachers

Vicarious reinforcement by close, same aged peers, is a powerful source of higher self-efficacy for young people (Joet et al,2011). Researchers have found that individuals obtain information about what they can do from the vicarious experience of observing the actions others, such as classmates, peers, and adults (Bandura 1997; Schunk 1987). They note that seeing a close friend succeed at a challenging academic task might convince a tentative student that he or she too can succeed. Models play a particularly important role in the development of self-efficacy when students have doubts about their skills or a weak experiential base in the academic area in question. The power of the media comes into play here with many young people taking their models of everyday life situations from media such as television, movies and the internet. The power of the media on shaping the minds of children and youth cannot be underestimated. Social Learning (or Cognitive) theory (Bandura 1977, 1997) states that children weigh up the results actions of others and if it is rewarded or not and take it into consideration before they will imitate or decide they will take those actions on board themselves. Bandura (1997) also states that observing another person reinforced can affect the behaviour of the observer and serves as a source of information to the person about his or her environment and the requirements for successful behaviour. In short, if children see attitudes and actions work in real life by their peers or perhaps on the screen, they will take it on board as future reference to work for themselves and this can be either positive or negative learning, therefore media needs to be monitored in their lives.

Researchers (Joet et al 2011) found that social persuasions and evaluative feedback from parents, teachers and peers can alter students' confidence. They also noted that younger students who eagerly await *evaluative judgments* from *significant others* may be most impressionable by what others tell them (Bandura 1997). What significant others say to younger students impacts them strongly and judgements and comments need to be made with careful consideration of the one they are directed at. Social persuasions and evaluative feedback from parents, teachers and peers can alter students' confidence and feedback that is catered to students' skill development can be particularly helpful in building self-efficacy (Hattie & Timperley 2007, Schunk 1983 cited Joet et al). However, disparaging comments by trusted others can leave students with a bruised sense of efficacy (Pajares, 2006). The old saying "Sticks and stones can break my bones but words can never hurt me..." obviously is not true in reality, if someone takes negative feedback on board—words can damage and affect an individual's self-efficacy. The "sticks and stones..." old English chant (The Christian Reader 1862), was made by children to counter and protect themselves from being affected by hurtful words; a kind of counter chant to break any effect on their confidence. Perhaps it was even an attempt at emotional regulation with a fight back kind of attitude that kept them from being affected by the hurtfulness of the words directed at them. In this present youth culture of mobile phone texting, and internet communication, children and young people face an onslaught of words day and night directed at them. Many of these words and sometimes images can be negative in nature that they may be being bombarded with and may eventually cause anxiety and depression. Children need to hear positive words, and know they are supported by their parents and teachers in order to have their self-efficacy built up and to be unaffected by the negative slurs of peers. Also noted from Joet et al's study (2011) that social persuasions were predictive of students' mathematics self-efficacy and that younger students are particularly apt to rely on persuasions from others because they are novices, unskilled at making independent judgements of task demands (Bandura 1997). Researchers (Williams and Williams 2010) also found on personality variables a negative association between socially prescribed perfectionism and self-efficacy which indicated that exposure to uncaring and unsupportive parents is a factor linked with low self-efficacy. As perfectionism went up from parents, self-efficacy went down for students.

It has been found that the teacher who provides routine opportunities for success and work to ensure that success is attainable for all, will have students with higher self-efficacy (Pajares 2006). Researchers (Henderlong & Lepper 2002) comment that teachers and parents who anchor verbal feedback in students' actual performances, while helping students to understand how they performed, may build students' self-efficacy more than general praise. They note that praise that focuses on effort rather than ability, conveying information on a student's competence is more likely to lift self-efficacy. Joet et al (2011) and Bandura (1997) found that students perceptions and interpretations of their mastery, and not their past standardized test scores, contribute to most of the variation of their academic self-efficacy. Therefore, they suggest that teachers and parents not only must provide students with opportunity for success but also must assist students in making adaptive interpretations of their accomplishments helping them to frame less-than-optimal performance as an opportunity for growth rather than indication that they lack ability (Dweck 2006). They also suggest that guiding young students to make healthy evaluations of their efforts will minimize their risk of prematurely giving up on their own academic accomplishments.

Williams and Williams (2010) also found, in their study of self-efficacy and maths performance in 33 countries, that the self-efficacy levels of girls are depressed by the expectations of significant others (e.g. parents, boyfriend). Perhaps this is something that needs to be addressed for girls, so that they can learn not to rely on the opinions of their significant others but rise above them. Joel et al's (2011) study notes *that girls relied primarily on social persuasions* when forming their academic self-efficacy, whereas *boys relied on mastery experience*. Researchers McKnight and Loper (2002) noted that the most prominent resilience factors in adolescent girls at risk for delinquency, were an academic motivation, a desire to go to college, absence of substance abuse, feeling loved and wanted, belief that teachers treat students fairly, parents trusting adolescent children, and religiousity.

Researchers (Roesch, Duangado, Vaughn, Aldridge and Villodas 2010) found that for low-income minority youth, hope was positively related to greater problem solving, planning, positive thinking and overall coping with stressful situations. Fry et al (2011) advocates the strengthening of adolescents hope in positive youth-development programmes and see hope as an important benefit for young. Bartol and Bartol (2008), assert that prevention and treatment programmes that are designed to foster and maintain resilience in youth are also known as *strength-based programs*. Smith (2006) emphasizes that resilience is made up of ordinary rather than extraordinary processes, and that the average child can be taught to become resilience. Strategies for developing resilience include the enhancement of a child's strengths and interests, as well as the reduction of risk or stressors and the facilitation of protective processes (Bartol and Bartol 2008).

Recently, implementing a resilience training programme for high schools in the Western Sydney area, it was found that the majority of students (mainly at risk youth), responded well to teaching on particularly mastery, planning, coping, emotional regulation, and positive self-talk or affirmations (Wheatley 2012, Hackney and Cormier 2005) which they took to almost immediately. They expressed relief when told they were not to blame for the bad things that had happened in their lives. Many had come from homes with invalidating environments. Repeating positive affirmation statements to themselves, such as 'I am a good person", "I am valuable", "I am worth something", and "everything is going to be alright..." were extremely effective in building up self-efficacy, and bringing better emotional regulation to those students who had been through or were now facing adversity in their lives.

Results of Fry et al's (2011) research with young sports people, revealed direct and indirect significant relationships between perceptions of caring climate and psychological wellbeing. They suggest that equipping adults with strategies to create a positive and caring climate can reap significant rewards for young people with regard to their overall physical and psychological wellbeing. The significance of their indirect model provides evidence that the route through which the caring climate influences youngsters' psychological wellbeing is via the strengthening of their emotional efficacy. It has also been found by researchers(Czeh, Muller-Keuker, Rygula, Abumaria, Heimke and Domenici 2007, Davidson, Jackson, & Kalin 2000 cited Cozolino 2010, p. 227) that social stress can inhibit neuron growth and plasticity, while social support, compassion and kindness support positive neural growth. In other words change is possible for children and young people even from a difficult childhood, if there is enough care and support. The effects of higher self-efficacy in a child's and young person's life is powerful and life-changing right through to adulthood, and is a key to resilience for a lifetime literally from cradle to grave.

Works Cited

Bandura, A. (1977). Self-efficacy: toward a unifying theory of behavioural change. *Psychological Review*, 84, 191-215.

_____. (1986). *Social Foundations of Thought and Action: A Social Cognitive Theory*. Englewood cliffs, NJ: Prentice-Hall.

_____. (1997*). Self-efficacy—The Exercise of Control*. W.H. Freeman and Company. United States of America.

_____. (2001). Social cognitive theory: An agentic perspective. *Annual Review of Psychology*, 52, 1-26.

Bartol, C. R. and Bartol, A. M. (2008) *Criminal Behavior—A Psychosocial Approach*. (8th Edit.) Pearson Education, Inc., Upper Saddle River, New Jersey, 07458.

Blascovich, J., & Mendes, W. B. (2000) Challenge and threat appraisals. The role of affective cues. In J. P. Forgas (Ed.), *Feeling and Thinking: the Role of Effect in Social Cognition (pp. 59-82)*. New York: Cambridge University Press.

_____, & Tomaka, J. (1996). The biopsychosocial model of arousal and regulation. In M. P. Zanna (Ed.) *Advances in experimental social psychology*. Vol. 28, 1-51. New York: Academic Press.

Boekaerts, M. & Niemivirta, M. (2000). Self-regulated learning—Finding a balance between Learning goals and ego-protective goals. *Handbook of self-regulation* (pp. 417-466). Academic Press.

Bouffard-Bouchard, T., Parent, S. & Larivee, S. (1991). Influence of self-efficacy on self-regulation and performance among Junior and Senior High-school age students. *International Journal of Behavioural Development*, 14 (2), 153-164.

Caprara, G. V., Giunta, L. D., Gerbino, M. Pastorelli, C., Tramontano, C., Eisenberg, N., (2008). Assessing Regulatory Emotional Self-efficacy in Three Countries. *Psychological Assessment*, Vol. 20, No. 3, 227-237. Doi: 10.1037/1040-3590.20.3.927

Chemers, M. M., Hu, L. & Garcia, B. F. (2001). Academic self-efficacy and First-year College student performance and adjustment. *Journal of Educational Psychology*, Vol. 93, No. 1, 55-64. doi: 10.1037//0022-0663.93.1.55

_____, Watson, C. B. & May, S. T. (2000). *Dispositional affect and leadership effectiveness: a comparison of self-esteem, optimism, and efficacy*. Society for Personality and Social Psychology, Inc. PSPB, Vol. 26, No.3, 267-277.

Cozolino, L. (2010). *The Neuroscience of Psychotherapy—Healing of the Social Brain*. (2nd Edition). W.W. Norton &Company, Inc., 500 Fifth Avenue, New York, N.Y. 10110.

Diener, C. I., & Dweck, C. S. (1978). An analysis of learned helplessness: continuous changes in performance, strategy, and achievement cognitions following failure. *Journal of Personality and Social Psychology*, 36, 451-462.

Dweck, C. S. (1986). Motivational processes affecting learning. *American Psychologist*. Vol. 41, No. 10, pp.1040-1048.

Fry, M. D., Kim, M., Gano-Overway, L. A., Guivernau, M., Newton, M., Magyar, T.M., (2011). *Sport, Exercise and Performance Psychology* (2012), Vol. 1, No. 1, 44-57. doi: 10.1037/a0025454

Hackney, H., and Cormier, S. (2005) *The Professional Counsellor*. (5th Edit.) Pearson Education, Inc.

Henderlong, J., and Lepper, M. R.(2002). The effects of praise on children's intrinsic Motivation: A review and synthesis. *Psychological Bulletin*, 128, 744-795.

Hiroto, D.S., & Seligman, M. E. P. (1975). Generality of learned helplessness in man. *Journal of Personality and Social Psychology*, 31, 311-327.

Joet, G., Bressoux, P., and Usher, E.L. (2011). Sources of Self-Efficacy: an investigation of elementary school students in France. *Journal of Educational psychology*. American Psychological Association. doi: 10.1037/a0024048.

Keller, J. (2007). When negative stereotypic expectancies turn into challenge or threat: The moderating role of regulatory focus. *Swiss Journal of Psychology* 66 (3), 163-168.

Luther, S. S., Cicchetti, D., and Becker, B. (2000). The construct of resilience: A critical Evaluation and guidelines for future work. *Child Development*, 71, 543-562.

Maddux, J. E. (1995*). Self-Efficacy, adaptation, and adjustment. Theory, Research, and Application.* Eds. Plenum Press, Plenum Publishing Corporation, New York, N.Y.10013

Martin, T. R., & Flett, G. L., Hewitt, P. L., Krames, L. & Szanto, G. (1996). Personality correlates of depression and health symptoms: a test of Self-Regulation Model. *Journal of Research in Personality*, 31, pp. 264-277, Article No. 0017.

Mikulincer, M. (1986). Attributional processes in the learned helplessness paradigm: Behavioural effects of Global attributions. *Journal of Personality and Social Psychology*, Vol. 51, No. 6, 1248-1256.

New International Bible (1985). Zondervan Bible Publishers, Grand Rapids, Michigan 49506, United States of America.

Noddings, N. (2006). *Happiness and Education.* New York, NY: Cambridge University Press.

Orbach, I., Blomenson, R., Mikulincer, M., Gilboa-Schechtman, E., Rogolsky, M., Retzoni, G. (2007). Perceiving a problem-solving task as a threat and suicidal behaviour in adolescents. *Journal of Social and Clinical Psychology*, Vol.26, No. 9, 1010-1034.

Ozer, E. M., & Bandura, A. (1990). Mechanisms governing empowerment effects: a self efficacy analysis. *Journal of Personality and Social Psychology*, Vol. 58, No. 3, p472-486.

Pajares, F.,& Kranzler, J. (1995a). Competence and confidence in mathematics: the role of Self-efficacy, self-concept, anxiety and ability. *Annual Meeting of the American Educational Research Association, San Francisco*. Review of Educational Research. Proquest Central.

_____. (1995b). Self-efficacy beliefs and general mental ability in Mathematical problem solving. *Contemporary Educational Psychology*, 26, 426-443.

_____. (1996). Self-efficacy beliefs in academic settings. *Review of Educational Research*, Vol.66, No. 4, p543-578.

_____. & Urdan, T. (2006). *Self-Efficacy Beliefs of Adolescents*. Eds. Information Age Publishing, Inc.

Phillips, D. (1984). The Illusion of Incompetence among Academically Competent Children. *Child Development*, 55, 2000-2016. Society for Research in Child Development, Inc.

Pintrich, P.R. (2000). Multiple goals, Multiple Pathways: The role of goal orientation In learning and achievement. *Journal of Educational Psychology*, Vol. 92. No. 3, 544-555. doi: 10.1037//0022-0663.92.3.544

_____. (2004). A conceptual framework for assessing motivation and self-regulated learning in college students. *Educational Psychology Review*, Vol. 16, No. 4.

_____ & De Groot, E. V. (1990). Motivational and self-regulated learning Components of classroom academic performance. *Journal of Educational Psychology*, Vol. 82, No. 1, 33-40.

Seligman, M. E. P. (2006). *Learned optimism: How to change your mind and your life*. New York, NY:Vintage

Ross, D., (1942). *The Story of the Little Red Engine*. Faber & Faber, London.

Skinner, N., & Brewer, N. (2002). The dynamics of threat and challenge appraisals prior to Stressful achievement events. *Journal of Personality and Social Psychology*, Vol.83, No. 3, 678-692.

Smith, E. J., (2006). The Strength-based counselling model. *The Counselling Psychologist* (2006) 34:13. doi 10.1177/0011000005277018

The Christian Reader (March 1862) and Miss Lindsay (1936) *Sticks and stones may break* my bones but words (names) will never hurt (harm) me...

Tomaka, J., Blascovich, J., Kibler, J., and Ernst J. M. (1997). Cognitive and Physiological, Antecedents of threat and challenge appraisal. *Journal of Personality and Social Psychology*, Vol. 73, No. 1, 63-72.

Werner, E.E., and Smith, R.S., (2001). *Journeys from childhood to midlife: risk, resilience, and recovery.* Ithaca, NY: Cornell University Press.

Wheatley, A. M. (2011). The Impact of Self-efficacy and Challenge/Threat Evaluations on Academic Procrastination. Thesis (Unpublished). Postgraduate Diploma of

Psychological Studies, University of Western Sydney, New South Wales, Australia.

Williams, T. and Williams, K. (2010). Self-efficacy and performance in mathematics: Reciprocal determinism in 33 nations. *Journal of Educational Psychology*, Vol. 102, No. 2, 453-466. doi: 10.1037/a0017271.

Wolters, C. A. (2003). Understanding procrastination from a self-regulated learning perspective. *Journal of Educational Psychology*, Vol. 95, No. 1, 179-187. doi: 10.1037/0022.0663.95.1.179.

CHAPTER 17

Revisiting Emotional Regulation: Evidence from Practice

Shane Warren

Emotions can frequently be intense and push individuals to extreme behaviour response(s). Such extreme emotions tend to change as fast as they appear as individuals find cognitive reasons to validate how they feel.

Emotional regulation is about learning to control ones emotions. It is the ability to stay calm under pressure, making a choice to control one's emotion as opposed to allowing ones emotions to control them.

The process of emotional regulation is about an individual's ability to understand and accept their emotional experience to engage in healthy strategies to manage uncomfortable emotions when necessary, and to engage in appropriate behaviour when distressed (Salters-Pedneault 2009).

Why Emotional Regulation is Important?

Society is defined by the way in which social interchanges are coordinated. Healthy societies require the individuals within them to regulate how emotions are experienced and expressed.

Individuals with good emotion regulation skills are able to control the urges to engage in impulsive behaviors, such as self-harm, recklessness, or physical aggression, during emotional distress. Emotional regulation is important for forming intimate relationships, succeeding at work, and helps us maintain physical wellbeing. People who have difficulty regulating their emotions often emotionally exhaust others and are difficult to work with (Reivich & Shatté 2002); they tend to have limited social interactions of long-term standing because the nature of their poor emotional regulation makes it hard to sustain rewarding relationship with them. Over half of the non substance related disorders of clinical disorder, and all of the personality disorders involve some form of emotion dysregulation (Gross and Levenson 1997).

Pamela presented as a very successful senior executive with more then 30 years experience in her field of which 18 had been with the same organisation. In a recent performance appraisal the feedback found that although her division always achieved targets the retention of staff was very poor. A 360 review found that a majority of her team felt isolated from the company, unappreciated by management and frightened to contribute suggestions to leaders within the company. Pamela reported that she felt she always needed to finish projects, that much of her team are lazy and that if she ever went away for too long nothing would be done. Upon close observation of Pamela's behaviour human resources supervisors noted that her communication with her staff was antagonistic, often resulting in screaming matches across the office and concluding with nasty emails revoking team members. In Executive Coaching with Pamela it was found that she rarely attended work social functions and outside of work had even less social interaction with others. Her pattern of behaviour to blame others for negative experiences and to yell aggressively had left her in a position where few people felt they could share in her life.

Emotional regulation is not about suppressing all emotion; it is about controlling what emotions we share in the moment and how much of that emotion is displayed. Pamela's assessment of the situation amongst her team may in fact be correct. The thought is was Pamela's behaviour that attributed to the outcomes might also be correct. The challenge here is that Pamela's behaviour will ensure her experience is one where 'she needs to do all the work and finish all projects' because she will have few peopled skilled enough to complete the task as they will not stay in her team for a long enough period of time to become skilled. With this in mind the anger and aggression that Pamela feels is an emotional response she has every right to experience. However, her expression of this feeling state is not effective and not working; hence the challenge is to learn better emotional regulation. To understand emotion regulation it is important to understand how it develops.

The Development of Emotion Regulation

Emotion regulation has been defined as "the ability to interact with others in a socially acceptable way, which includes the capacity and flexibility to adjust intense emotions and related behaviour responses to the situation" (Hudson and Pulla 2012). Bronfenbrenner's theory (1979; Bronfenbrenner & Morris 1998, 2006) suggests that the nature of interactions between the individual and the context in which they develop are bidirectional. Each of us during the course of our development displays a temperament as well as capacities, which, in the context of our environment, affect our developmental trajectory. Changes in life events can be imposed on the child, or arise from the child as they themselves select, create and modify their own experiences.

Bronfenbrenner's ecological framework views development as influenced by five environmental systems, ranging from proximal contexts of direct interaction with people to broad-based contexts of culture, all occurring over time. The five systems are the microsystem, mesosystem, exosystem, macrosystem and chronosystem.

1. *Microsystem.* Microsystems are any relations between a child and their immediate environment (Bronfenbrenner 1979). This includes the obvious such as child's family and

friends. But also includes peers from sporting groups, schools, religious communities and the neighbourhood.
2. *Mesosystem*. The mesosstyem refers to the interrelationships among two or more microsystems in which an individual actively participates, for example the relation of family experiences (a microsystem) to their school (another microsystem).
3. *Exosystem*. Exosystems are a social setting that affects a child but does not directly impinge on them. Exosystems include parents' place of employment, family social networks, and government and social policy.
4. *Macrosystem*. Macrosystem refers to the attitudes, beliefs and ideologies of the child's culture. For example a culture's values concerning child-rearing will have great affect on the way a child is raised hence the experience a child has of their upbring.
5. *Chronosystem*. Chronosystem refers to the pattern of the environmental events and transitions over time (Bronfenbrenner & Morris 1998, 2006).

In essence the model of Bronfenbrenner tells us that child development results from interactions between the child and their families, schools, communities and their broader society over time. In the model the historical time and place of an individual, the timing of transitions and events occurring during their lives, and historical events are all-important in determining a person's life course.

Within this ecological framework, LSAC (the Longitudinal Study of Australian Children) takes a developmental pathways approach, emphasising trajectories of development across the lifespan. This perspective seeks to identify the factors that influence pathways for good and for poor outcomes. Factors influencing trajectories, especially at crucial transition points such as entry into childcare or school, or movement out of education into the workforce, are also able to be identified and explored. The child's current circumstances and how earlier transitions have been negotiated (including the skills that children may or may not have developed through these processes) may influence subsequent transitions. By identifying early indicators of detrimental and of beneficial pathways, programs and interventions can be designed to help steer children on a healthy course through life. This is as true of the facility for emotion regulation as it is for any personality characteristic.

The Importance of Emotion Regulation

Emotions play an integral role in our behaviour; they help to tune decision-making, enhance memory for important events, and facilitate interpersonal interactions. However, this influence is a double-edged sword—emotions can hurt as well as help. Inappropriate emotional responses are implicated in many forms of psychopathology, in social difficulties, and even in physical illness. The recognition of this link between emotions and psychopathology clearly indicates a great deal hinges on our ability to successfully regulate emotions (Gross & Thompson 2006).

Research tells us that individuals who are able to regulate their emotions constructively often have better physical health. To understand why this is so it is beneficial to understand the basics of emotional responses on the body. It is also often taught to better regulate ones emotions we need to understand the physical feeling state that occurs within us to certain emotional stimuli, hence patients benefit from an awareness of their emotional feeling state and their physical response(s).

Emotional responses occur on three levels. The first involves neurophysiological and biochemical reactions to events or thoughts. Typically, this involves our bodies automatic nervous system: heart rate, blood flow, respiration, hormonal secretions and neural responses. The second response is behavioural. This is the instinctive action where emotions are expressed by physical responses such as facial expressions, crying, a natural withdrawing from others, eye glazing, or general delay in cognitive responses to ongoing stimuli. The third level of response is the cognitive which involves our thoughts and hence the words we may use to respond to the situation. It is in the third level that people name their feelings in response to an event. It tends to be at the third level of response that individual differences emerge.

Christian's team was on target to win the monthly sales competition in the office. On the last Friday of the month they where in the lead and had on the table the largest contract in the history of the company to be signed off by a long-term client. It had been a hard month but the team was consistently achieving targets and usually slightly ahead of their nearest competing team. As the clock approached close of business there was a sudden turn of events. The team who was coming in second closed their largest sale ever and Christian's team could not get their client to commit to the sale in this year's budget. The pressure was on. Christian's lead sales executive was so distracted by the anxiety she felt she flicked off her email and started to check Facebook. When Christian noticed this, his response was one of strong anger, his body trembled and in response he threw the file across the office—papers scattered everywhere. Christian's assistant responded to this action with "Settle down! There are other months to win—I guess I've got to pick all that up then…" Other members of the team did not know how to respond and just left the room; leaving Christian and his sales executive alone in the room with tears swelling in their eyes; while the administrative assistant tidied up aggressively.

This is a not uncommon scenario in many sales driven organisations around the world. In this scene we witness all levels of emotional response. Christian's trembling is a neurophysiological expression of emotion. The throwing of the file and the swelling up of tears is a behavioural response to the event; as too is the exiting of the room by other members of the team. The administrative assistant demonstrated a cognitive response by expressing her feelings with words.

The challenge we confront with the act of emotional regulation in the context of this experience is if we were to take away all the emotion from this interaction we would not have much interaction at all. Emotions represent the "wisdom of the ages", providing time-tested responses to recurrent adaptive problems (Gross 2002). The emotions raised in this interaction and the physiological responses are a list of necessary conditions for an event to qualify as a significant moment; or an emotional interaction (Gross & Thompson 2006). However, emotions do not force us to respond in certain ways, they only make it more likely we will do so. This malleability permits us to regulate our emotions (Gross 2002).

How is Emotional Regulation Achieved?

Like all skills developed over time, emotional regulation is something that is learned and can be improved. The environment provides initial emotional regulation. Individuals learn to behave in certain ways in fixed environments; take for example prayer and religious environments; when an individual walks into such a space they reflect the solemn and quietly reflective behaviour of others in the room. Compare this to standing amongst a crowd in the stadium of a major league football event—such an environment grants permission to be loud and exuberant with certain behavioural characteristics. Not all environments so strongly dictate to an individual what is the best way to behave and how one can respond to their emotional state.

The most popular tool within psychotherapy when it comes to emotional regulation is cognitive awareness and hence cognitive control of emotions. Too often practitioners have simplified this process to challenging individuals to know their emotional response is not 'working well for them' and hence they should adopt another more healthy response. The challenge with this is time and time again emotions have proven famously difficult to pin down and manage.

Effective strategies to overcome impulsive emotional responses have been to take a stop and evaluate approach:
1. Define the problem;
2. Explore all possible solutions
3. Evaluate the benefits and pitfalls of all solutions
4. Define a course of action;
5. Implement; and
6. Evaluate the results.

Such an approach is extremely powerful when an individual has the time to take each step; however, most individuals confront challenges in the moment and respond in the moment. Such situations benefit from an intentional control approach:
1. Feel the emotion;
2. Identify the source;
3. Look for a distraction;
4. Choose to change focus; and
5. Evaluate later how better to respond next time.

Walking a Patient through Emotional Regulation

To encourage a patient to move forward with an intentional control response to help them better regulate their emotion, challenge them to follow these steps. Rather then exemplify a common time when emotional regulation should be applied; such as moments of violent anger, let's explore a more subtle time when we should respond differently from how our emotions are influencing our thinking…

When they begin to notice physical signs of change within themselves take the follow actions:

- *Identify the words the best describe your feeling state and the physical.*

  For example anxiety, anger, frustrations, sadness. The patient should be encouraged to speak succinctly about their experience. Such "I am feeling anxious which is making me sweat and feel hot."

- *Encourage the patient to give that feeling a strong descriptive word.*

  I feel... For example if one is experience fear they might complete the sentence as I feel dread / apprehension / anxiety / nervous / etc.

- *Now name the event that prompts such a feeling.*

  I am …….. about …… For example "I am feeling anxious about being at home alone."

- *Find the why factor.*

  What is the reason the patient carries this feeling linked to a thought? Invite the patient to answer "I am feeling anxious about being at home alone because…."

- *How do you act?*

  Get the patient to tell you how they act in times of this feeling. For example they might cry, or run away, or scream aggressively at others, or shut down and not talk, etc.

- *Summarise the experience.*

  Invite the patient to put all the above together. For example "I know I am feeling fear and anxiety when my body triggers hot flushes and causes me to sweat. This feeling is driven by my dread of being home alone because I fear being attacked by a stranger so I tend to stay away from my house until my partner returns home."

- *How well is that working for you now?*

  Invite the patient to observe the ways the actions from this feeling are affecting their lives and get them to set the guidelines of how things need to be improved.

When allowing a patient to set out such guidelines the practitioner must ensure that they identify how their emotional state influenced their effectiveness in making decisions. Following on from our example of *not going home until the patient's partner had returned* can have a multitude of possible affects on their wellbeing and relationship. It is important to explore how the patient fills in their time—are they enhancing the emotional response and situation by partaking in behaviours that allow their fears to grow. For example, is the patient passing time having a drink in the local hotel reading the final edition newspaper, which talks of various home security and invasion issues?

Ask your patient while they process the feeling:

- What was prompting the event?
- What did you do in the situation? Did you resist or enhance?
- What factors reduced your effectiveness?
- What then do you want to do about it?

Now challenge the patient to complete the following statements:

- When I'm upset and alone first I'll .... next I'll..................... then I'll .... and finally I'll ....

It is important to help the patient to set out a number of intentional control responses so that they can better prepare for the 'what it, what next' situations.

Conclusion

Feelings are just like air you don't notice them until it's too late! With this in mind understanding how our emotions affect us and how they can work against us is as important as breathing itself…

In conclusion, ones emotions affect more then just their feeling state. They affect the way people feel, the physical responses of one body, how individuals hear and interpret a message and how people choose to act in the moment. Emotional regulation is an art that everyone should master...

Works Cited

Bronfenbrenner, U., & Morris, P. A. (1998). The ecology of developmental processes. In W. Damon & R. M. Lerner (Eds.), *Handbook of child psychology* (5th ed., Vol. 1, pp. 993-1028). New York: John Wiley & Sons.

――――, & Morris, P. A. (2006). The bioecological model of human development. In W. Damon & R. M. Lerner (Eds.), *Handbook of child psychology* (Vol. 1, pp. 793-828). New York: John Wiley & Sons.

Gross, James J. (2002). Emotion regulation: Affective, cognitive and social consequences. *Psychophysiology*, 39 (2002), pp. 281-291. Cambridge University Press, USA.

――――., and Thompson Ross A. (2006). 'Emotion Regulation: Conceptual Foundation' *The Handbook of Emotion Regulation*. Guilford Press, New York USA.

Hudson, J., & and Pulla, V. (2012). Emotion regulation in children: Towards a resilience framework. In Pulla, V., Shatté, A., Warren, S. (Eds.), *Perspectives on Coping and Resilience*, Authors Press, New Delhi

Reivich, Karen & Shatté, Andrew, (2002). *The Resileince Factor*. Broadway Books of Random House, USA.

Chapter 18

Life Narratives Mirroring the Feminization of HIV and AIDS Trauma: Zimbabwean Perspectives of Coping and Resilience

Sindiso Zhou and Nhlanhla Landa

Abstract

The conception of woman as a victim of pain and disease resonates in Zimbabwean and African societies. While HIV and AIDS trauma have affected a multitude of Zimbabweans across the gender divide, women are the most anguished. Evidence from semi-autobiographical/life narratives by women authors who have experienced the harrowing pain and consequent trauma of HIV and AIDS indicates that successful resilience and coping with HIV and AIDS begins with the woman. In this paper, the researchers examine HIV and AIDS trauma and women's responses. The inevitable feminization of the HIV and AIDS story has predominantly exposed the woman involved to a host of hardships namely poverty, stigma and discrimination as well as emotional and spiritual turmoil. While some women resort to unorthodox means of survival in the face of stressors; others have become resourceful and resolute, crafting empowering survival strategies to cope with their situations. Tendai Westerhorf, author of *Unlucky in Love* and Lutanga Shaba, author of *Secrets of a Woman's Soul* tell their stories of love, deception, disease, heartbreak and resilience. Their stories of feminized pain and trauma are representative of the Zimbabwean woman's experience. In this paper we explore the coping strategies they employ as documented in their narratives and critique the alternatives of escape from suffering available for the woman through analysis of several dimensions of coping and resilience from other existing discourses in society. The paper concludes that the strategies employed are indicative of the slim spectrum of choices that Zimbabwean women have at their disposal.

Key Words

Coping, resilience, women, trauma, semi-autobiography, life narrative, HIV and AIDS, feminization, Zimbabwe, Africana womanism

Introduction

This paper elicits and critiques coping strategies employed by Zimbabwean women in the face of HIV and AIDS trauma by exploring the nature, manifestation and implication of the pain and disease phenomenon in Zimbabwe through analysis of the semi-autobiographies (also referred to as life narratives) of Lutanga Shaba (*Secrets of a Woman's Soul* 2005) and Tendai Westerhorf (*Unlucky in Love* 2005). Yvonne Vera, an author in Zimbabwe, in an interview with Jane Bryce once said; "I'm fascinated with the individual, especially the women, especially the women in Africa, and how they are forced to endure without having a nervous breakdown—because they cannot afford it. But they collapse inside, and I'm keen to capture that collapse" (Bryce in Muponde and Taruvinga 2002: 223). In this statement, Vera, a woman herself, is making apt reference to the circumstances that surround many women and form the essence of womanhood in Zimbabwe.

The two case studies selected for this discussion are viewed as representations of the realities and experiences of Zimbabwean women and will be used as points of departure as well as references in the ensuing discussion of Zimbabwean perspectives of coping and resilience. The most fundamental and enlightening aspect about the stories of the two brave women who publicize their life narratives is that the telling itself is a form of coping with the Human Immuno Virus (HIV) and the Acquired Immuno Deficiency Syndrome (AIDS), and its attendant stressors and negative attractions. Ngoshi and Zhou (2010) have argued that autobiography or the telling of untold stories by the victims is not merely a process of remembering and telling but accords the victim speaker/narrator a speaking position that has immense healing and empowering potential. Thus autobiography is in itself and of itself a coping strategy that has been utilized by Zimbabwean women, including Shaba and Westerhorf, to cope with HIV and AIDS.

Zimbabwe: A Brief History

Zimbabwe is a relatively small country in Southern Africa. Formerly known as (Southern) Rhodesia, it is a former British colony that attained independence in 1980. Since the dawn of independence Zimbabwe has experienced several forms of instability including civil unrest between 1980 and 1987 popularly known as *Gukurahundi*[1] and in which over twenty thousand people were massacred; *Operation Murambatsvina*[2], which saw massive displacement of citizens from the urban areas to the rural areas after demolition of shelter and structures that were deemed improper. The dawn of the new millennium (2000) ushered in a massive economic meltdown, unemployment, absence of rule of law and extreme levels of election and politically motivated violence among other ills. As a collective, the atrocities resulted in massive migration of Zimbabweans to neighboring African countries and everywhere else in the world.

Alongside these forms of instability, Zimbabwe is still struggling to cope with the adverse effects of HIV and AIDS on the economy and on the populace in general. Zimbabwe recorded its first case of HIV in 1985, which means that when Zimbabweans found themselves free from the colonial regime they could not say the same about HIV. While UNAIDS have estimated that around three quotas of all the women with HIV live in Sub-Saharan Africa the 2010/ 2011 Zimbabwe Demographic Health Survey (ZDHS) has established that

1.1 million Zimbabweans out of a total population of about 12 million are living with HIV. While there has been a sharp decrease in HIV prevalence over the past few years in Zimbabwe, at 14 per cent the country still has one of the highest prevalences in the world. Still, more women (18 per cent) than men (12 per cent) are living with HIV. Therefore, more women than men are infected and affected by HIV in Zimbabwe. Generally more women are unemployed, more poor and uneducated, than men in Zimbabwe. The girl child is more likely to drop out of school, to work in the farms and not to go to school at all than the boy child in Zimbabwean homes.

The dire situation of women in this small Southern African country is compounded by gender based sexual violence. The 2010/2011 ZDHS established that 27 per cent of Zimbabwean women experienced sexual violence in the surveyed period; 22 percent of women had their first sexual intercourse forced against their will; and 30 percent of Zimbabwean women have experienced sexual violence since the age of 15. The UN plan for gender (2007) estimates that one in every three women in Zimbabwean is in an abusive relationship while over one out of four have experienced some form of domestic violence. Gender based violence is defined by UNFPA (2005) as "Any act of gender-based violence that results in, or is likely to result in, physical, sexual or psychological harm or suffering to women, including threats of such acts, coercion or arbitrary deprivations of liberty, whether occurring in public or in private life". Research is pointing toward the fact that women are biologically at more risk of being infected by HIV than men. In two separate studies of serodiscordant couples Nicolosi et al (1994) and Padian et al (1991) established that women have upward of twice the probability of infection. In another study Higgins et al (2010) concluded that "… heterosexual transmission accounted for more infections among women than men, suggesting that women might be at greater risk of infection if exposed through heterosexual intercourse" (2010; 436). Besides their biological make-up, women are more susceptible to HIV infection due to gender-based violence and due to being caregivers to family members living with HIV. Due to gender-based violence women generally have no say in sexual matters.

Levels of literacy are relatively high in Zimbabwe. The ZHDS 2010/2011 established that 78 per cent of men and 70 per cent of women in the 15-49 age group attended at least some secondary education. Approximately 2 per cent of women and one per cent of men have never attended formal education. The percentage is likely to be more in favor of men than women in the 50 and above age group because it is only recently that girls are being accorded a near equal chance to go to school as boys.

It is against this backdrop that the stories of Tendai Westerhorf (2005) and Lutanga Shaba (2005) are told; and it is against this same background that many untold stories of Zimbabwean women are in existence. Since the publication of these two stories in 2005, disclosure by people living with HIV has become the trend. These stories have been very influential in the past six years and have coincided with the launch of the National Behaviour Change Programme in Zimbabwe. The two autobiographers have also taken head on the issue of living openly with HIV. For instance, in 2006, a few years after she had disclosed her HIV positive status and a few months after the publication of her story (*Secrets of a Woman's Soul* 2005), Shaba opened a dating agency in Harare[3] for HIV positive people. After announcing on national television that she was living with HIV and just before the publication of her story (*Unlucky in Love* 2005) Westerhorf successfully organized the first ever public Voluntary Counselling and Testing for nine Members of Parliament. This was meant to encourage Zimbabweans to go for Voluntary Counseling and Testing.

Lutanga Shaba; Telling the Untold Story

A lawyer by profession, Shaba is a famed woman activist in Zimbabwe. She has gone public about her HIV positive status, announcing bravely that she is living positively with the virus feared by many. Shaba is well known for mobilizing women to contest in elections, as well as fighting for 50 per cent representation of women in government. She has patronage of the Mama Milanzi Programme which helps marginalized women and disadvantaged young girls in education and skills development so that they may rise above their circumstances. As head of an organization called Women's Trust (Women in Governance and Leadership Trust), she has been getting support from such organisations as the National Association of Non-Governmental Organizations (NANGO) and Women's Coalition, in her pursuit for leadership development among women. She also sits in the National Executive of the Movement for Democratic Change[4] (MDC) since 2011.

Shaba's (2005) semi-autobiography carries an insidious sense of sadness. In *Secrets of a Woman's Soul* Shaba excavates the taboos a mother and daughter break as they are met with frustrations resulting from their surroundings and ambient circumstances. By speaking out on HIV and AIDS, Shaba makes a bold attempt at de-stigmatizing and giving voice to a taboo subject in Zimbabwean society. In *Secrets of a Woman's Soul*, Shaba, through the pseudonym Lingalireni, (affectionately called Linga) refuses to be sparing when she brutally and candidly speaks out about commercial sex, transactional sex, poverty and HIV and AIDS.

Shaba takes an honest look at township life back in the seventies when she was growing up in colonial Rhodesia and traces her life and that of her mother right up to independent Zimbabwe. As the readers follow the narrator's life into a dark abyss of frustrated hopes and lost dreams brought about by extreme poverty and the battle for survival, the choking truth comes to the fore that women have had an incredible burden to lug around since pre-colonial times. The struggle for survival can be clearly seen as the young Linga watches her mother toiling just to live from hand to mouth. At the tumultuous yet tender age of sixteen, the narrator is forced into transactional sex just to support herself and her mother. This brutal realism, which forces her to make an equally brutal decision, shows just how desperate the times were. This absence of choice, option, and alternative is the central paradigm of the problematic discourses of the women in Zimbabwean society.

Lingalireni, and her mother Beata go through some humiliating, painful and traumatic experiences in the form of poverty, sexual abuse, ridicule, rejection, divorce and eventually death for Beata. All these experiences affect both women the same way although they reflect them in their different ways. While Linga puts up a brave front and holds her head up high, smiling over a wounded spirit, Beata, we are told, recoiled and smiled less and less, blinking away tears of distress while going through her daily chores like an automaton. This tendency to avoid stressors and threatening stimuli or to avoid talking about them as a way of protecting one's self-worth and integrity is discussed by Sherman and Cohen (2002). Shaba outlines the horrors of teenage sexuality, orphanhood and infection with sexually transmitted infections and consequently HIV. Through her eyes, we are made to glimpse how much it takes a woman to live through such a bitter experience and still come out sane and standing tall.

Tendai Westerhorf; a Real Life Narrative of Pain

Tendai Westerhorf (nee Kateketa), who has a public profile as a model in Zimbabwe, publicly declared her HIV status and formed the Public Personalities Against AIDS Trust (PPAT) in 2003. Her disclosure was triggered by her conviction that openness about HIV and AIDS issues is a vital tool in the fight against stigma. After three broken marriages, four children from irresponsible and unsupportive fathers, infection with HIV, Westerhorf tells her story of struggle to emancipate herself from the crushing reality of HIV and AIDS using Rumbi as her mouthpiece. Although her road is long and rough, Westerhorf bravely proclaims in the end,

"Today I truly see HIV as the best thing that has ever happened to me" (103). Such an end lends her story the high profile of a statement of encouragement to fellow women whose survival is being threatened by the existence of HIV and AIDS.

Having been a popular model before 2003 and having been married to prominent former Zimbabwe National Soccer team coach Clemens Westerhorf, the disclosure of her HIV positive status attracted a lot of media attention. Soon after the publication of her book (*Unlucky in Love*) in 2005, which attracted vigorous media analyses, Westerhorf told the Zimbabwe Weekend Gazette Newspaper that; "This book has been written very differently from most HIV and AIDS biographies; it takes away the gloomy side of HIV" about her work.

In *Unlucky in Love* (2005) Tendai Westerhorf tells the story of a woman whose marriage ends in a distasteful divorce. Rumbidzai (affectionately shortened to Rumbi), is an HIV positive mother of four who strives to give her life meaning in an environment that is dominated by repressive masculinities. In a bid to outline the nuances of women's vulnerability to HIV and AIDS, their survival strategies, as well as their brave efforts at rebuilding positive identities; Westerhorf delves deep into her private life. She has a personal approach in her semi-autobiography *Unlucky in Love*. Like Shaba, she uses the narrative voice as self-cleansing, pardoning while it gently reproaches her for past whims, dreams, choices and mistakes.

Dimensions of Coping and Resilience

Resilience has been defined differently by researchers coming from different fields. However, what is common in the myriad definitions is that resilience involves the ability to survive challenging situations. It involves the ability to "cope well with adversity" and to "persevere and adapt when things go awry" (Hall 2007). Resilience involves, therefore, choosing and sustaining the choice of surviving and conquering a suffocating situation either at a personal, interpersonal, family, community or any other level. Caldwell (2009) argues that the difference between coping and catastrophe begins with the person's perception of the stressful event or situation as well as the person's perceived capacity and ability to cope with the event. Catastrophe results from the person feeling that they are unable to cope with a stressor or to come out of a situation and therefore the person reacts in a way that is detrimental to their situation. Vera, (2002) a Zimbabwean writer, calls coping or resilience the ability "to endure without having a nervous breakdown".

Resilience is concerned with how the person handles themselves in risky situations and in circumstances threatening or posing unwellness. Adger (2000) defines resilience as the ability by communities to deal with external stressors and disturbances resulting from social, political or environmental change. However, Rugalema (2000) posits that when it comes to HIV and AIDS it is not households that cope but individual members of those households as HIV and AIDS primarily breaks families and forces surviving members of the families to join other households or to be joined by caregivers from other households. Contrary to Rugalema's position, we argue that households still cope with HIV and AIDS as they take on the burden of caring for the surviving members of other households; orphans, widows and the elderly in the true extended African family fashion.

Zimbabwean women as reflected in the sample life narratives under study, suffer different kinds of pain in their families, cultural and work environment and in several ways in the community. They, however, as individuals and collectively, devise several strategies and mechanisms to come out of stressful situations. To survive, to endure, to cope or to be destroyed defines the women's ability, or lack of it, to fight and conquer the circumstances threatening to drown and suffocate them.

Women and girls are the primary caregivers in households affected by HIV and AIDS. HIV and AIDS by nature demand a lot of sacrifices; of time, love, care and resources, and women and girls sacrifice more of all than their male counterparts. In most cases care giving is primarily the burden of women and girls.

While many people are coping with HIV in Zimbabwe directly or indirectly, Zimbabwean women not only have to deal with the pandemic but are saddled with several other stressful issues that they need to contend with. These stressors are the aggressors that steal their peace and threaten their sanity and they include gender based violence, disease, poverty, unemployment and politically motivated violence, which has also affected women and children more than men. According to the 2010-2011 Zimbabwe Demographic Health Survey, young women, women who are employed but not for cash, uneducated women and women with little wealth are more likely to agree with beating with 39.6 per cent justifying wife beating. This can be compared to 33.7 per cent of men aged between 15 and 49 believe that a husband is justified in beating his wife. What is disturbing is that the survey established that men were less likely than women to agree that wife beating was justified. Due to this compromised space that they occupy, "women have become especially susceptible to the disease [HIV and AIDS] as a result of their limited power in sexual encounters" (Wodi 2005, pp.2-3).

Cultural practices and beliefs have also worked in unison to corner the woman into subjugation. Though now happening to a relatively lesser extent and recorded in fewer places, such practices as wife inheritance, forced marriage and appeasing of raging avenging spirits by offering a girl as compensation are still being performed in Zimbabwe. Addressing issues to do with culture is very central to the welfare of communities as culture both poses as a threat to the wellness of women and is supposed to provide coping mechanisms for handling difficulties positively. According to Mechanic (1974) an individual's ability to successfully cope with stressors is determined by the efficacy of culturally-provided solutions to such stressful situations.

Silence as a Negative Coping Strategy

Silence and secrecy have been used by Zimbabwean women as coping strategies from time immemorial and men have admired them for this. However, the Westerhorf (2005) and Shaba (2005) life narratives prove that silence as a strategy of coping only brings more suffering as it helps perpetuate the stressors. Culturally in Africa, women who speak out are despised as they are considered as deviant and recalcitrant. Silence is viewed as the embodiment of true womanhood; therefore a woman who vocalizes the unspeakable and taboo subjects in her life is branded as a disgrace to her clan.

Silence also works to prohibit exposure of such traumatic experiences as gender based violence and rape (Muchemwa in Muponde and Primorac 2005). Silent sufferers of abuse or disease do not seek help from either the law or relevant medical institutions. According to the Zimbabwe Demographic and Health Survey (ZHDS) 2010-2011 only 37 per cent of women victims of domestic violence, be it physical or sexual, have sought help. In *Secrets of a Woman's Soul* Linga (Lutanga Shaba) is shamed into silence but her soul continues to cry out to outlive and forget the vile event. Only through speaking out and getting out of the shell can she attain peace of mind thus telling her life story to Ayesha, a psychiatrist who guides her on the road to recovery.

In Westerhorf's *Unlucky in Love*, Rumbi (Tendai Westerhorf) is married to Horst, a promiscuous foreigner who drinks till dawn and always throws tantrums. Horst (who represents Tendai's real life ex-husband) is a shouting and yelling menace at home yet Rumbi submits to him completely, "handling his temper tantrums and mood swings with feminine grace". Rumbi says, "Horst went out drinking late at night. I said nothing for fear of raising the sleeping bear of his temper" (Westerhorf 2005: 26). The pattern of Horst's behaviour mirrors the harmful effects of patriarchy's authoritarian, insular and aloof nature that causes women pain and emotional upheaval. Vulnerable women in both rural and urban Zimbabwe have been known to tolerate obnoxious behaviour from their partners for fear of raising a domestic furor, or even being thrown out of the house with no clothes, money or food. While culture condones silence in the same way that some religions encourage stoicism and martyrdom; evidence from real life narratives like Shaba's and Westerhorf's illustrate that silence only worsens the existing pain and shuts out potential support systems and escape routes.

As McFadden (1994:9) points out, certain cultures work to oppress women and cause them suffering because of the fertile discourses that support them:

> Culture is therefore a mere stumbling block for women because femininity is reinforced mainly through cultural practices. Notions of cultural appropriateness restrict women to certain roles, restricted spaces, stilted discoveries and limited rights. Power is a notion that clashes with femininity. The idea that being nice equals being female does not coincide with a woman being powerful. The representations of power in our societies have been constructed in ways which exclude women as players.

In *Secrets of a Woman's Soul*, the narrator is forced into transactional sex just to support herself and her mother. This is a destructive mechanism for coping with both poverty and disease.

The trouble with trauma is its lasting nature. It is neither transient nor transitory as the person's psyche holds on to the injury and the wound festers in the secret confines of one's mind and spirit unseen by the public. This is the exact point where positive coping strategies and resilience come into play to ensure continuity and functionality in the sufferers' lives. It is only through an opening of one's heart, pouring out all the past unspeakable blunders, that one can be truly free. This is how Linga gets to Ayesha's couch for help. Only then does she finally accept that she is hurting and carrying deep soul wounds dating back to the time when she and her mother struggled to eke out a living after her father's death. If they do not speak out they otherwise would need professional assistance where such approaches as Trauma and Recovery Framework (Herman 1992) and Narrative Therapy as discussed by White and Epston (1990) from the constructivism and social constructionist movement among others.

Women like Linga and Rumbi refuse to remain silent and speak out their anguish. Consequently they get help to handle their problems with dignity and grace. It seems almost convincing to say education is synonymous with power when one looks at how Linga fights the HIV and AIDS virus in her body. Physically she seeks treatment for her child and for herself while she empowers herself and equips herself with economic survival tools by earning an education so that she can find a niche for herself in the money economy. The fervor with which she approaches her schoolwork is testimony to her determination not to return to the life of want, deprivation and sexual compromise. Linga contracts HIV after a host of other crises coupled with poverty cause her to stumble. It is the same for her mother Beata who stoops to transactional sex after the death of her husband.

Constructive Coping Strategies

There are several instances in both Westerhorf and Shaba where effort is made to de-silence women faced with stressful situations. De-silencing is an empowering mechanism as it gives the sufferer a voice to challenge the taboos of her community and undo years and loads of pain. The act of de-silencing is empowering to women and it is against the prohibitive cultural and traditional practices that keep women in bondage. In *Secrets of a Woman's Soul,* Shaba defies the tradition of silent women and speaks out about commercial sex, transactional sex, poverty and HIV and AIDS. Shaba's and Westerhorf's characters are given voice and a place in society where they can speak out and challenge the culturally imposed yokes that perpetuate the suffering of women and expose them to disease and trauma.

In *Unlucky in Love*, Westerhorf challenges the oppressive masculinities, deconstructs the stereotypical constructions of women in a patriarchal society and especially in relation to HIV and AIDS. Women in the two life narratives just as in Zimbabwean society have been socialized to believe that their fate is determined by male figures in their lives, their spouses, their siblings and their fathers, and that their value is weighed according to the men they are married to. Westerhorf sets out to challenge and deconstruct this deep-rooted belief. For a very long time Rumbidzai is arrested by this belief and her desperate search for the right man to marry, results in three failed marriages.

As one marriage after the other fails, Rumbi strives further to find the right husband due to the stigma associated with unmarried women in Zimbabwe. However, she is disappointed further as the second marriage and the third fail, in the process earning her more stigma and negative labels as she has four children from different men. True to Westerhorf's real life experiences, Rumbi finds herself, appreciates her real value as a woman and makes a decisive decision to ameliorate her life and emancipate herself from the yoke of abusive and oppressive patriarchy. When she finally finds her voice and speaks out Rumbi bursts:

> Who do you think you are Horst, to think you can disappear and come back into our lives just as you please? Go back to Juliet or one of your other girlfriends. You are a piece of shit and I don't need you in my life. You told lies about me and cheated on me but I never cheated on you. Never. You drove past me in the rain and wouldn't even give me a lift. ... Get lost! Get out of my life and don't ever come back! We don't need you! Go hang yourself!
> (Westerhorf 2005; 105).

Rumbi realizes that her problems begin with the man she has been suffering to please and that her emancipation begins with her breaking the silence. She stands firm and kicks Horst out of her life. Westerhorf is de-silencing Rumbi and giving her a voice to challenge suffocating masculinities. She even challenges the church when it fails to be supportive to people living with HIV and walks out of the church, which she does not find as a place for comfort, acceptance, compassion and understanding.

When she tests HIV positive, Rumbi also makes a difficult but emancipating decision to openly declare her HIV status. While she knows the potential stigma that is associated with the positive HIV status in her community, Rumbi goes ahead and declares her status as she strongly believes declaring one's status is the beginning of one's liberation. She uses this as a coping mechanism as she realizes that the fear of the public and carrying a secret is more suffocating that living in the open and having no secret lugged onto one's heart.

In *Secrets of a Woman's Soul*, Linga has to remember how her desperation and destitution landed her in such a compromise of moral standards, what Shaba calls, "a sale of a soul, a shattered dream, a violation to the soul" (Shaba 2005: 69). To show just how deep the wound is, Linga cannot remember without a deluge of tears threatening to drown her.

Challenges in Coping

The absence of alternatives and help from authorities is yet another painful aspect to remember; for there are many 'what ifs' in her scenario. What if the Youth Service Centre staff had taken the 16-year-old girl's case to the police, the social welfare or somewhere instead of giving her Family Planning pills to prevent pregnancy? What if they had given her condoms to prevent what is worse than pregnancy, or even plain counseling. Linga has to replay this scene which was central in deciding her future despite the unbearable nature of the freshness of the pain that she feels anew.

The most painful of all memories is that of ravaging disease. While Linga takes care of the early detected sexually transmitted infections, it is not so with Beata, a woman from another generation that has more taboos than tolerance and openness. She nurses an STI for fifteen years and languishes from an AIDS related sickness till her death when she is so emaciated that she can only be described as a mere shadow of her former self. Beata dies of; "Cardiovascular arrest, Immune suppression, TB, large spleen colon Tumour" (2005: 92). Linga's memory does not fail her as she clearly retrieves the pictures of her mother in her last days "thinning hair, pale skin, reddened lips and skeletal hands". All these signs testify of the deadly pandemic eating away at the conservative woman who has been so stigmatized by gossip that she would rather die than have people know her HIV status. Linga weeps for society's ignorance and selfishness, which created stigma and prejudice amongst those infected with HIV and AIDS. It is the stigma that holds Beata mute concerning her sickness and consequently she dies in this silence.

Upon reliving her mother's experiences as an oppressed and subordinated woman, Linga is set not to see history repeating itself either in her generation or in Chiedza's. When she tests HIV positive, before the birth of her daughter Chiedza, Linga and Simba divorce because of irreconcilable differences. Linga goes on to seek the latest in medical interventions when it comes to HIV positive expecting mothers. No doubt her consciousness on sexual health matters has grown thus giving her voice and a fighting spirit. Through Linga, Shaba gives hope for multitudes of vulnerable women. The story of Linga's fighting spirit, which bears good fruit recreates the identities of vulnerable, downtrodden and abused women and gives them an opportunity for re-birth. Economic, spiritual and sexual empowerment is achieved through going down memory lane. No matter how fierce the expedition seems to be, the results are worth the trouble.

Collective Coping Mechanisms—Social Support Groups

Support groups, as represented by Lutanga Shaba's patronage of the Mama Milanzi Programme, are not new in Zimbabwe especially in relation to HIV and AIDS. As early as 1992 Auxilia Chimusoro, who tested HIV positive in 1987 and revealed her

HIV positive status on national television in 1989, formed an HIV and AIDS support group called Batanai HIV and AIDS Support Group. This support group has survived the years and is still operational in Zimbabwe. Soon after Batanai, Chimusoro co-founded another support group that targeted women and it was called Women and AIDS Support Network (WASN).

Shaba's Mama Milanzi Programme, aimed at assisting women and girls in education and skills development, is in the same fashion offered as a collective or communal coping mechanism. The two authors realize the need for a communal effort in coping with disease, pain and trauma.

When Rumbi turns to her friend Jean in *Unlucky in Love*, Westerhorf is saying the coming together and solidarity of women in the face of stressful situations, in which they cannot be helped by their male partners and male relatives as they are the stressor in the first place, is the recipe for success. She offers women solidarity, more that the church and family, as a collective coping mechanism in which women give each other support. When even the church, which when it comes to HIV and AIDS is of no assistance to people in general and women in particular, cannot give assistance to her, Rumbi's only support is from her friend Jean; a fellow woman. The support she gets from her friend Jean, strengthens Rumbi's resolve to move on.

Both Shaba and Westerhorf challenge patriarchy and all its norms and values, which have kept the woman under slavery for a long time. They give their characters a resolve to challenge poisonous masculinities that threaten to drown and suffocate womanhood. What has made the woman in their novels special is that besides the everyday problems of marital discord, gender based violence, sexual abuse, fending for the family and poverty; they have the extra stressor of HIV and AIDS. Pain or trauma associated with disease brings in a new dimension to the woman's suffering in society. However, Westerhorf and Shaba give the women involved the resolve and strength to exercise resilience and claim victory over vulnerability.

Conclusions

While anguish resulting from disease is presented as an integral part of women's existence as long as they stay loyal to the taboos of their societies; freedom from the bondage of pain, disease and oppressive society is in line with emancipation from colonial, patriarchal and economic bondage. Many women in Zimbabwe show the immense spirit of true "Africana womanism" (Hudson-Weems 2000) by enduring hail and fire and yet remaining steadfast and resilient. The intricate linkages make the woman more prone to suffer than her male counterparts. Given the structure of Zimbabwean or African society for that matter, the woman is headed by the man from home, school, and church to political party. If at any one of these institutions there happens to be a female head by design or accident that woman will likely be the female patriarchy, working hand in hand with the men in oppressing those of her kind.

While decrying society's silent observation of women's suffering, the two women celebrate the resilience of the woman's spirit. Quite successful in portrayal, even as these writers depart from the norm, is the way their characters are forced to rise from the dumps of physical, emotional and mental despair; are given voice and ground in society. The traumatized women remain strong and resilient bringing hope and promise for the future of all those women facing life-threatening crises. Zimbabwean poetry has expressed admiration for such African women, portraying them as strong, proud, beautiful women, determined, enduring, surviving, and going on as if they feel no pain; in their eyes wielding the sword and spear of freedom (Muponde in the poem "Woman in the Shadow" 2010).

There is need for government and organisations working with people living with HIV to continue funding support groups for people living with HIV. The impact of such governmental support is already evident in several cases of disclosure as well as the sharing of stories of survival and victory from women other than Shaba and Westerhorf. Researchers could in the future also invest resources in looking at how integrating men in HIV and AIDS programming improves the coping and resilience of individual women, families and communities in the face of HIV and AIDS.

References

1. *Gukurahundi* is Zimbabwean vernacular term that literally means to wipe away dirt or garbage. Gukurahundi was a massive genocide of perceived enemies of the state that included women and children in the targeted ethnic groups in Zimbabwe.
2. *Murambatsvina* is a Zimbabwean vernacular term that means non-tolerance of filth. This operation was a cleanup campaign that presumably sought to rid the cities and towns of shack shelters and squatter camps where the poor and other people failing to find affordable accommodation had sought refuge.
3. Harare is Zimbabwe's capital city. It is the most populated city in Zimbabwe characterized by people from all walks of life as it acts as the hub for all services.
4. Zimbabwe's strongest opposition political party since independence in 1980; it went into a coalition government with ZANU PF, which had been in power since 1980.

Works Cited

Adger, N. (2000) Social and ecological resilience: are they related? *Progress in Human Geography*. 24 (3) 347-364.

Bryce, J., (2002) "Interview with Yvonne Vera, 1 August 200, Bulawayo, Zimbabwe: "Survival is in the Mouth." *Sign and Taboo: Perspectives on the Poetic fiction of Yvonne Vera* (eds.) Robert Muponde and Mandi Taruvinga. Harare: Weaver Press pp.217-226.

Caldwell, R. & Boyd, C.P. (2009) Coping and Resilience in farming families affected by drought. *Rural and Remote Health* 9: 1088 (Online).

Hall, D. (2007). Interaction. CCCF/Winter.

Herman, M.D, (1992) *Trauma and Recovery*. Basic Books.

Higgins, J.A, Hoffman S and Dworking S L (2010) Rethinking Gender, Heterosexual Men and Women's Vulnerability to HIV/ AIDS. *AM J Public Health*. 100: 435-445.

Hudson-Weems, C. (2000) "Africana Womanism: An Overview" in *Out of the Revolution: The Development of Africana Studies*. Delores P. Aldridge and Carlene Young (Eds.) Lexington Books, pp. 205-217.

McFadden, P. (1994) "Issues of Power and Contestation in the Women's Movement". *Women Plus*, May-August 1997, Harare

Mechanic, D. (1974) Social Structure and Personal Adaptation: Some neglected dimensions. In G.V Coelho, D. Hamburg and J.E Adams (eds.), *Coping and Adaptation* (pp. 32-44) New York: Basic Books.

Moyo, W. & Mbizvo, M.T. (2004) Desire for a future pregnancy among women in Zimbabwe in relation to their self-perceived risk of HIV Infection, child mortality and Spontaneous abortion. *AIDS and Behaviour*, 8 (1) 9-15.

Muponde Robert (2010) http://memorychirere.blogspot.com/2010/06/woman-in-shadow.html

Ngoshi, H. T. & Zhou, S. (2010) Speaking Positions: Zimbabwean Women's Writing in English and the Disease, Pain and Trauma Paradigm. *Imbizo Journal of Comparative Literature* (1) 1.

Nicolosi, A., Leite M.C.C., Musico, M. et al (1994) The efficiency of male-to-female and female-to-male sexual transmission of the human immunodeficiency virus: a study of 730 stable couples. *Epidemiology* 1994; 5 (6) 570-575 (PubMed)

Padian, N., Shiboski, S.C. & Jewel, N.P. (1991) Female-to-male transmission of the human Immunodeficiency Virus. *JAMA* 266 (12) 1664-1667 (PubMed).

Rugalema, G. (2000) "Coping or struggling?" a journey into the impact of HIV/AIDS in Southern Africa. *Review of African Political Economy*. 86, 537-545.

Shaba, L., (2005) Secrets *of a Woman's Soul*. Harare: Weaver Press.

Sherman, D.K. & Cohen, G.L. (2002) accepting threatening information: Self affirmation and the reduction of defensive biases. *Current directions in Psychological Science*, 11, 119-123.

UNAIDS (2010) *Report on the global AIDS epidemic.*

UNFPA (2005) *The promise of Equality: Gender Equity, Reproductive Health and Millennium Development Goals.* New York: UNFPA.

Westerhorf, T. (2005) *Unlucky in Love.* Harare: Public Personalities Against Aids Trust.

White, M. & Epston, D. (1990) *Narrative Means to Therapeutic Ends.* New York: WW Norton.

Wodi, B. E. (2005) Gender Issues in HIV/AIDS Epidemiology in Sub-Sahara Africa. Gender Issues in HIV/AIDS. *Wagadu*, Volume 2.

Zimbabwe Demographic and Health Survey 2010-11 (2012).

Zimbabwe Weekend Gazette (2005) *Westerhorf Unlucky in Love.*

Chapter 19

Resilient Reintegration during Adversities: Case of Young People with Disabilities

Nur Aishah Hanun, Lynne Briggs and Wayne Hammond

Abstract

The increasing interest in resiliency for human development has brought about many studies aimed at identifying factors that facilitate resiliency and how they interact to produce the desired ability to triumph over challenges. However, there is a paucity of literature on studies on resiliency among young people with disabilities (Margalit 2003). This chapter describes the process of resiliency using several case studies of youth with disabilities to illustrate the critical points of the resiliency process and the points of intervention. The concept of biopsychospiritual homeostasis, disruption and reintegration forms the basis for the resiliency process. There are four types of reintegration that are highly dependent upon the external envirosocial factors. Young people with disabilities often experience stigmatization, hence it is a risk or stressor when factoring in attempts for intervention. That it can occur without social interaction is an important characteristic of stigma. The disruption caused by the stigma can be extremely damaging to the psychological well-being of the sufferer. The examples presented in this chapter can be used by educational, medical, mental health professionals and concerned members of the community to assist understanding how resiliency can occur, when and how to intervene to facilitate resilience. Each of these four interventions points discussed in this chapter has specific characteristics that impact upon different points of the resiliency process. Finally, three cautionary notes further guide the reader about specific characteristics of young people with disabilities that, if understood, will assist with intervention efforts.

Key Words

Resilience, disabilities, stigma, resilient reintegration

Introduction

> It is our birth right to activate our inherent ability and will to be resilient—enabling us to weather the impossible and to attain excellence. We just need to know how.—*N.A.Hanun*

The business of facilitating human development is among one of the most diverse endeavours one can embark on. From birth to adulthood, communities worldwide invest heavily in the provision of resources to ensure that the human child is protected, nurtured, and prepared to become an independent member of the society. Providers of services in the field such as teachers, medical and mental health nurses, social workers, counsellors, psychiatrists and psychologists are often regarded as in the frontline thus, inevitably face challenges specific to their occupations. Others, for example policy makers, support staff in schools and hospitals, volunteers in community centres and people in our neighbourhood provide the much needed support that indirectly facilitate in the caring and education of our young.

Parallel to this noble effort, government departments in many countries aim to provide resources and assistance that permeates the entire strata of the society. Despite these considerable efforts often there are still young developing people with unmet needs. That is while their needs in one area may be met given their disability, their specific needs are not fully addressed. Common in this respect are the young people who have disabilities and needs are so varied that it becomes difficult to provide for all if perceived as "at risk".

Disabilities and Stigmatization

People with disabilities are people whose development is regarded as atypical, or outside the range of what is considered physiologically normal or positive development. The onset of their disabilities may be due to a genetic abnormality that occurs prenatally, or at post-natal during the child's developmental phase. Disability can also occur as a result of external environmental contaminants, or physical force that changes the growth trajectory. Often, it's aetiology is not clear. Examples would include physical or mental disabilities, or both—conditions such as learning disabilities, deafness, blindness, autism spectrum disorder and cerebral palsy. No matter the disability, as long as the person is aware that he or she is different from others, there will be the risk of stigmatization (Heatherton, Kleck, Hebl, & Hull 2003).

Stigma is the devaluation of self and can occur either within one's mind, or as a result of negative social experience. As (Goffman 1968) in his pioneering work on social stigma emphasised, stigma has its roots as a social construct and first defined it as "an attribute that is deeply discrediting", "a spoiled social identity" (p. 13).

Thus, while the feeling of being stigmatized is an internal psychological process (Harvey 2001), internally constructed stigma will be confirmed or even amplified when negative social interaction focusing upon negative attribute/s of the individuals occurs. Thus, by simply raising one's eyebrow to another about a limping person can cause, or worsen, stigmatization for that individual.

Various studies relating to stigmatization among disabled individuals have shown that stigmatizing experiences affects a person's self-concept, thus triggering the devaluing extent of disability. This can result in individuals with disabilities viewing themselves as being "in a position of lower status and unworthy of acceptance" (Ladieu-Leviton et al. 1948; as cited in Martz 2004, p. 140). Stigmatized individuals with disabilities also tend to experience the devaluation of character that can lead to feelings of isolation, estrangement and ostracisation from the community, purposelessness and, especially if not working, a lack of self-worth (Davey & Keya 2009; Martz 2004).

Identifying Stigmatization that Signals Need for Intervention

Stigmatization occurring among young people with disabilities often goes unnoticed because it is essentially an internal psychological process. However, there are signs that do show a high probability that stigmatization has impacted upon the individual. Just observing, or listening, to youth with disabilities is not helpful if one does not know what to look for. For example, a degrading remark is made, but a person may not be stigmatized. Being able to identify that stigmatization has occurred would help recognize the need and nature of interventions, which in turn serves to reduce development of emotional distress and psychopathology associated with stigma.

Firstly, responses to stigma include all basic emotions—sadness, fear and anger; and also self-conscious emotions which include shame and social anxiety. The case studies of Val, Pradeep, Chong and Husin (not their real names) which form the basis of this chapter found that *shame* and *sadness* constituted a major portion (64.1 per cent) of the emotional responses to stigma (Hanun et al.,2011). These two emotions were found to cause withdrawal behaviours such as self-imposed isolation aimed to protect from additional exposure to stigma. In contrast, *anger* was found to cause the stigmatized to confront the source of stigma and attempt to cancel out the stigma.

While *fear* inhibits behaviours that will reveal or cause stigma, *social anxiety* functions as a protector of perceived oncoming stigma from unknown or uncertain social environments. An example is the case of Val who believed that she brought bad luck, or even death to those who know her, refrained from befriending people whom she liked because she feared it may bring bad luck to them, thus validating that accusation and invite more stigmatizing remarks from other people. As an example of social anxiety—Chong with physical deformities became anxious each time he went into unfamiliar environments. He consistently had negative expectations of what people were saying about the protruding lump on his head (the size of a golf ball), he became anxious and worried even before he was actually in the environment. His reaction was to wear a baseball cap to cover the lump.

Secondly, one can ascertain when stigmatization has occurred by careful observation of behaviour in the presence of the suspected stigmatizer, whether or not there are debasing treatments or remarks. This is a very important point as stigma is an internal psychological process that can occur with, or without, social interaction. Overt behavioural responses that signal emotional distress include: (a) avoidance (of the source of stigma), (b) denial (of the perceived identity by others which violates their perception of self), (c) try to erase source of stigma (e.g.plastic surgery, cover-ups), (d) ignore (remain within the same environment at the source of stigma, but clearly ignoring it) (e) self-destructive behaviours (committing suicide) and (f) self-isolation (refusing to join social activities with friends, relative or community). It takes practice to develop experience to identify these responses to stigma as they occur. Teachers and social workers, who are by their profession trained to observe behaviours, may or may not be more sensitive than the untrained eye.

The above reactions to stigma describe the reactions of one running away from a threat as a way of coping. These responses do not facilitate the stigmatized individual to triumph over the adversity, but instead they find ways to 'survive' it, hence they put up with the disruptive experience, which in turn does not lead to resiliency.

Facing multiple and chronic adversities (from their disability and the challenges in life), youth with disabilities face a consistently difficult future. One way that parents, educators, and mental health professionals can help is to foster resilient qualities in these at-risk children as one of the most effective ways to positively manage chronic and permanent disability (Spekman, Herman, & Vogel 1993).

A Brief Background on Resiliency Research

Resiliency is generally defined as the ability to overcome adversity. While the elements contributing to resiliency are many (termed as the protective factors—Table 1), achieving resiliency is a dynamic process that changes depending on the interplay between the individual and the environment. Contrary to ego-resiliency[1], resiliency researchers by and large agree that to be resilient is not just to bounce back from adversity, but to develop new skills to handle the adversity and attain additional external support from the social environment (Donnon & Hammond 2011; Hall, & Pearson 2005; Luthar, Cicchetti & Becker 2000; Masten 1994; Rutter 2000).

When triggered by an experience of adversity, it causes the individual to undergo systemic disruption and subsequent reintegration (attempts to recover from the disruption) of the entire self occurs—with the optimum being the state of resilient reintegration[2] (Richardson 2002). The process of resiliency will further be discussed in conjunction with the resiliency model.

Resilience in all categories of children and youth is now seen as crucial to achieve successful future academic and general life outcomes (Hall & Pearson 2005). This can be inculcated by parents, teachers and mental health professionals which services to facilitate young people with disabilities towards normalization[3], and integration into the community, as best as possible (Hanun, Hammond & Kamarulzaman 2012).

The 1970s saw the beginning of research on resiliency by Norman Garmezy (Garmezy 1991; Luthar, Cicchetti & Becker 2000), with the empirical study of atypical schizophrenics and their children. This was the start of what is now known as the first wave of resilience research; the phenomenological study of survivors rather than through academic grounding in theory (Richardson 2002). Other pioneers include the famous longitudinal study of Hawaiian children by Werner and Smith (1982) and conceptions on resiliency from psychiatry (Rutter,1985; 1987; 2000).

The second wave focused on the process of resiliency and the third on application through interventions. Resilience research has now reached the fourth wave, beginning with "integrative research on resilience in children, focussing and on processes studied at multiple levels of analysis and across species" (Masten 2006, p.13).

It was in the second wave that the Resiliency Model was first conceptualised by Richardson, Neiger, Jensen and Kumpfer (1990), which maps out the process of resilience. Through this model, any individual, layman and professionals alike, can have a framework which is not only about understanding at what phase the at-risk individual is in, but also, just as important, where the points of intervention can be implemented, regulated and monitored to facilitate the process of positive resiliency. Figure 1 shows an adapted version of the model Richardson (2002).

The Resiliency Model and Resilient Reintegration

The model in Figure 1 shows when individuals with disability (or any individual) encounter a new challenge, or a new experience that proves to be stressful, there will be an interaction within the internal self (biopsychospiritual homeostasis[4] factor) and external support (I-a and I-b) to try to cope with the challenge/stressor. Depending on the effectiveness of the support, the individual may either reintegrate back to homeostasis or experience a disruption. This disruption is described by Richardson et.al. (1990) as a change in how one feels about and view the world. Outcries like "The system stinks!" or "I thought I could trust my friends" or "This is too hard for me, I can't take it anymore" are common during this phase of disruption.

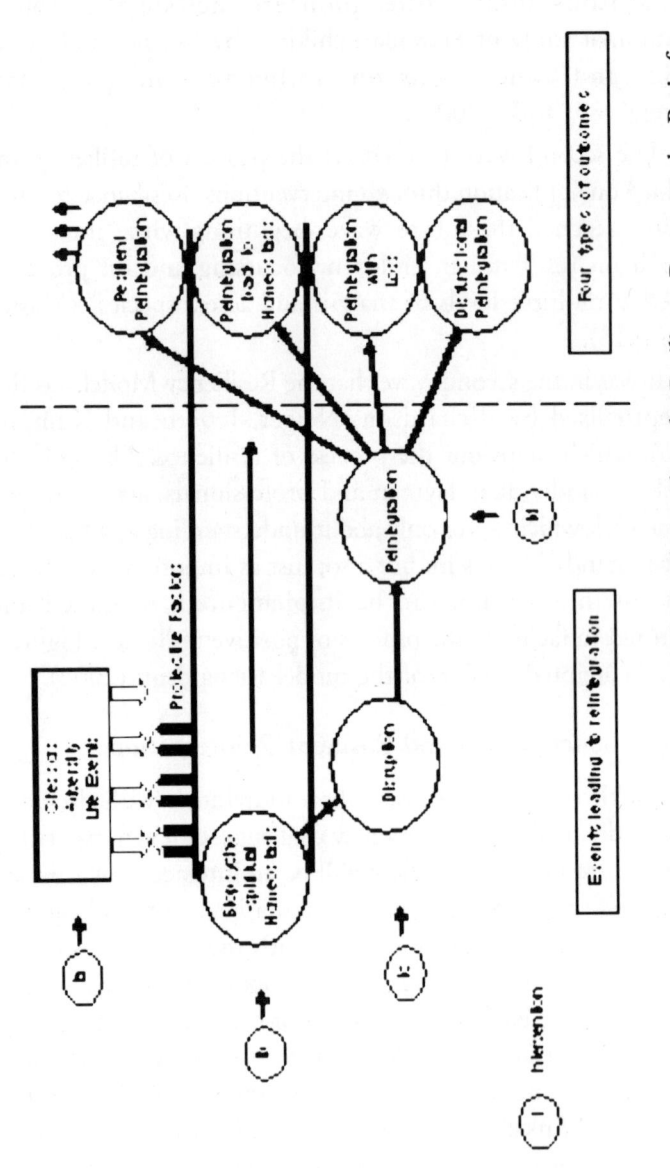

Figure 1. The Resiliency Model—A Framework for Understanding the Resiliency Process and a Basis for Iintervention. Adapted from Richardson (2002).

The disrupted individual will seek to escape the uncomfortable feeling to get out of the disruption. The success or failure of such attempts depend on several factors that is important for the process of resiliency. These factors are resiliency protective factors that consist of internal and external elements. Table 1 shows examples of internal and external protective factors that were found during the first wave of resiliency research.

Table 1 Internal and External Protective Factors[5]

Protective Factors	
Good natured, easy temperament	Internal locus of control
Communicates effectively	Believes in his/her self-efficacy
Sense of personal worthiness	Desires to improve
Sense of control over fate	Problem-solving ability
Assertive/ ask for help	Decision making ability
Healthy expectations and needs	Trust in others/ hope for the future
Productive critical thinking skills	Sense of humour
Ability to have close relationships	High expectations
Delays gratification	Manages a range of emotions
Positive relationships	Flexible
Interpersonal sensitivity	Adaptive distancing
Uses talent to personal advantage	Effective in work, play and love
Positive social orientation	Above average social intelligence
Informal social support	Future orientated

Resilient reintegration (Figure 1) occurs when the disrupted individual navigates their difficult situation and overcomes it through attainment of additional skills and support that then render the person no longer vulnerable to similar future challenges. The new strengths to negotiate adversity are illustrated by upward arrows at the resilient reintegration outcome in Figure 1. To illustrate, when the individual is assisted during a difficult situation and pulled out of it, but then falters again if the same difficult situation reoccurs, then that person is considered not resilient to that particular stressor. For young people with disabilities, resilient reintegration is the ideal option to aim for, as anything less would be to remain vulnerable within their state of dependence and possible despair.

For example, a youth who have become blind need to attain basic life skills that will allow for independent use of resources like cutlery and other aids for the blind to enable them to dine and travel outside their homes independently or with minimal support. This mobility will cultivate a strong positive sense of self, build self-esteem and efficacy, and create opportunities to garner more external networking and support; hence further increasing chances of resilient reintegration during challenges.

Too much support from others will eventually deny the maturing youth of his or her inherent need to attain autonomy and eventual depressive states may take root. Such depressive state can either be maladaptive reintegration[6] and dysfunctional reintegration[7] (Figure 1). Thus, further intervention from family, educational and mental health professionals is needed to assist the individual with the disability to the state of resilient reintegration.

An easy way to identify and differentiate between the types of reintegration is to ask, "If this situation happens again, can you be sure that you will know exactly what to do and have no problems at all to overcome it?" If the answer is a strong "yes", then you would know that resilient reintegration has occurred and can be further confirmed if the individual is able to include new external support/s that can help overcome the difficulty demonstrated with a clear plan, and/or sound problem-solving skills. If the answer is, "I am not sure" or "No! I would be upset if it happens again", then this would indicate that homeostatic, or maladaptive, or dysfunctional reintegration has occurred. The difference between the three is explained in footnotes 3, 4 and 5.

This chapter, using an actual case of a young teenager who tried to commit suicide, further illustrates the concept of resilient, homeostatic, maladaptive and dysfunctional reintegration.

Understanding the resiliency process—Case Studies of Youth with Disability and Stigma

The young lady Val was 16 years old when she tried to slit her wrist. Ever since the age of eight years, the Systemic Lupus Erythematosus (SLE) that had started then had worsen, and it was at this point that she was admitted to a government hospital for two months. She had collapsed into a coma, and was first treated in the Intensive Care Unit (ICU), then later, in an open ward. Her father is in the army reserves and her mother is employed on a factory assembly line. Home was a two bedroom apartment barely 700 square feet. Val either stayed with her grandma or stayed home where food would be left for her on the table till everyone came home. Schooling was no longer an option as she constantly becomes sick. Her three sisters and a brother are all either still at school, or have attained work on completion of secondary school.

The interview continued for almost an hour, and Val has given many instances of stigmatizing experiences that came as a consequence of her SLE. However, a surprise was to come when this seemingly cheerful 18 year old related her story to me.

R: ...okay. Val have you ever tried to smoke or take drugs?

P1: Never.

R: If you feel sad, or angry, d you feel like doing those kinds of things? Smoking or do drugs? Or skip school? Have you done anything like that?

P1: Knife.

R: Meaning? Commit suicide?

OBS: Val nodded.

R: Really? When? Does your mother know?

P1: At the hospital.

R: How old were you then?

P1: 16 years. At that time I was admitted into hospital. No one came. Mom came but only after second visit (*by her family*).

P1: When mum called, she said, "I am tired, having a fever". The nurse also said, "(*The mum*) Have not come to visit for a long time".... (*pause*).... I am not well, I can't (*go home*)..... I don't know when I can leave the hospital.

R: At that time, how did you get the knife?

P1: From long before, at 13 years till 16 years, mum, dad, never knew that I always bring with me a penknife.

R: Oh.... I nodded.

P1: At that time.... will I do it?.... will I do it?.... Aaaa.... like that..... if I do it, then? What is it with me?

OBS: Val showed how she held her penknife, moving it up and down across her wrist.

P1: Did it like this.... slit a bit of my wrist... Aaaa.... blood.... when feeling sad, we don't feel the pain at all.... cut.... blood....

R: Really? (I was very concerned with what I was hearing)

P1: Slit some more.... scratch..... cut..... blood.... don't know.... don't know..... was not aware.... satan.... I do it.... and do it (*slit her wrist*)..... when I looked, it was already cut...

R: So who realised that you were holding the knife?

P1: There was this nurse.... she asked me to acknowledge God... asked me to recite the Ayat Qursi (*Quran verse*)....While I was holding the knife, I can hear people talking... I followed her (*recitation of the*

	Quran).... suddenly I let go of the knife... she (*the nurse*) took it. When she was about to walk out the door, I told her not to tell my parents... she said "okay, but promise not to do this again.
R:	She took the knife away?
P1:	She took it. She said she would not tell my parents, but she will take the knife.... and won't give it back.... 'I take it, and promise me you won't carry a penknife in your pocket again"
P1:	Carry it in my clothes.... I put it between the folds.
P1:	I tried..... from then on, I became strong.... convince myself to be healthy. Able to raise up my will (*to succeed*). From the fall, I pick myself up, my will that was shattered.

Field notes: Later Val explained that the nurse often come to talk to her and gave her encouragement to live her life in a better way.

Orientating this narrative to the Resiliency Model in Figure 1, the *stressor* that had impacted on Val was the fact that her mother, whom she had depended heavily upon, had only once visited her during the whole two months she was in hospital. Negative voices in the likes of "No one came" had repeatedly played within Val's mind and emotions while laying immobilised for two months. At this point, she was still at a state of *biopsychospiritual homeostasis* of her understanding and beliefs of her situation.

However, this painful thought was validated and worsened by her mother's seemingly uncaring and dismissing treatment of her when she called to give excuses of being tired and having fever, for not coming to visit. It worsened even more when Val overheard the nurses' comments about her mother's single short visit when in fact she was rather ill. To be treated callously in a way devalued by one's own kin and parent was difficult for Val to contend. She had no one to vent out her negative thoughts to, and to her, it was stigmatizing that the nurses were talking about her.

This event had led to the *disruption* of her biopsychospiritual homeostasis, the phase described by Richardson et. at.(1990, p. 36) as "unpleasant and even agonising". It is this stage that the person will do almost anything to get out off—including suicide. Disruption leads to the disorganization or a change or shift to the person's understanding, perceptions and beliefs of the situation. This anguished state of being will cause the need to re-establish a new state of biopsychospiritual homeostasis in order to function (Richardson et.al. 1990), driving the individual to act and find a way out. We can see in the Val's narrative when she recalled her thoughts at that point, "At that time... will I do it?... will I do it?... Aaaa... like that... if I do it, then? What is it with me?"

At this crucial point *reintegration* can go in four ways: resilient, homeostatic, maladaptive and dysfunctional. In Val's case, she decided to slit her wrist, leading to what is classified as a *dysfunctional reintegration*. It was also at this phase that the nurse stepped in and provided the much needed external support. During that time, Val was gently coaxed to reflect about God and to recite the holy book (Quran). On her own admission, she did not know exactly how long that 'standoff' lasted, but eventually she let go of the penknife on her own accord.

Through the advice and attention given to her by the nurse, Val was able to harness the strength that was already in her as she described her change, "I tried... from then on, I became strong... convince myself to be healthy. Able to raise up my will (to succeed). From the fall, I pick myself up, my will that was shattered".

It is evident that up till the point that Val decided to slit her wrist, she was still contemplating about her decision. This brings it to an important point for intervention, which can potentially save a life—as it did for Val, even though she already started her intent. This phase of reintegration can clearly be identified by parents, educational and mental health professionals through observing the overt agitated behaviour and listening to what is being said. As this phase is driven by an internal anguish to reduce it, the focus on intervention is first and foremost for facilitation of that aim.

In the case of Val, her spiritual beliefs changed her perception of herself being unwanted by her family to the unconditional love from God, and it became the catalyst to that transformation. Subsequent to that incident, Val had developed several strategies to cope with derogatory and stigmatizing remarks from her family, especially her mother. She writes her anguished thoughts in her diary and at the time of this inquiry, she had 13 diaries and 21 accounts of her mother telling her that she is better off dead than alive as she causes trouble for the family. Despite the stigmatization, Val was able to be cheerful with friends and teachers at the vocational school, and amiable with her family.

It is important to note that evidence from these case studies shows that the reintegration process is unique for every individual and highly dependent upon its context. The individual's biopsychospiritual condition (also called the internal protective factors) is an important element to consider when implementing an intervention. Examples include health and fatigue levels, self-esteem, internal locus of control, sense of humour, spirituality and empowerment. See Table 1.

Points of Intervention

The Resiliency Model has identified four points of intervention that facilitates and promotes resiliency. These points can be further classified into intervention BEFORE adversity and intervention AFTER adversity. As we shall see, there has to be a balance between the two in order to attain the best type of reintegration; that is the resilient reintegration. An imbalance between the two could actually become a barrier to resiliency. This point will be elaborated in the third cautionary note at the end of this chapter. All other types of reintegration should be avoided especially dysfunctional reintegration which will see the individual in extreme scenarios that involves addictive drugs, alcohol, committing suicide and other dangerous behaviours.

The most initial point of intervention is the *envirosocial protective processes* that are done before an adversity with the aim to provide protection for the individual from possible harm. Richardson et.al.(1990) explains that the protection processes includes living conditions such as a private space that contains familiar and comforting things can help when dealing with difficult life events. In addition, this protective process also includes having parents or a responsible adult who would delay or prevent exposure to dangerous substances and negative stimuli.

In the case of Val, living in a two bedroom apartment with four other siblings and her parents did not provide the much needed environment when faced with adversity, so she needed to retreat and absorb comfort from other familiar things. In addition, her mother and siblings have over the years become the source of stress rather than being protective factors. On the contrary, Pradeep has very supportive parents who often guide him on how to behave, they also has the financial means to provide a comfortable home, and to help him become as independent as his disability allows. If this kind of intervention is not provided by the parent or caregiver, then the nearest intervention falls upon the responsibility of other responsible adults in the community, which is the next possible intervention before the onset of adversity.

The *envirosocial enhancing processes* is also carried out before an adversity aimed to build up suitable protective mechanisms. They include enhancing the self-esteem, empowerment, and facilitating coping skills such as effective communication skills. The intervention from the community is best to consist of teachers, school culture, school counsellors, medical and mental health professionals who by their profession are able to promote the development of skills that can help these young people to weather adversity more effectively. Parents who facilitate the attainment of these skills are also an important part of this process. Young people with disabilities often face compromised intellectual abilities that reduce life chances and positive life outcomes. This permanent risk can be buffered and reduced through an educational and health system that caters sensitively to their needs.

Both Val and Pradeep had received timely and sensitive medical intervention through the government health system, and both had attended the vocational schooling that began when they were 18 years old. The school has a major life skills component has been a tremendous influence in their lives. Both had referred their schooling as the most important part of their life, expressed attachment to their teachers and had clearly expressed they would be very upset if they no longer have access to this school.

In contrast, Husin, another youth with disability has experienced repeated disruptions when he attended an academically focused special education school. For him, school was a stressor and a source of constant irritation and reminder of his disability. Thus depending on the perception and suitability of the individual, a potential source of protective factor can instead be the cause of disruption.

This difference illustrates that a source of stress or protective factor can dichotomously exist within a single entity. Using the case of Val to illustrate this point, her mother who should be a crucial source of protective factor (at one time) had instead became a risk factor, and the unfortunate reason for her decision to commit suicide. Therefore, any intervention efforts should always be aware not to overlook the two sides of any situation as this callousness can be a huge disservice to the client.

The succeeding two interventions are done after an adversity has caused the young person to go into the disruption stage. The *envirosocial supportive processes* are the intervention that supports the individual that is undergoing a disruption so that the change of world view becomes a source of positive change and reintegration rather than a source of utter despair. Parents, school counsellors, psychologists, social workers, nurses, just to name a few are often those who come in direct contact with these young people and thus have the opportunity to provide the emotional support aimed at reducing the chances that these people do not choose to carry out dangerous or life threatening responses to their disruption.

All youth with disabilities in the case studies who went to vocational school for young people with disabilities (a total of 7 youths) cited that their school is the source of their happiness. Next to family, school is the second most visited place for young people and thus is a potential major protective factor or in the unfortunate case, a source of adversity or stress. Although teachers may be inundated with responsibilities for educational outcomes, having the knowledge and understanding of the resiliency process can add to the repertoire of skills for teachers into the mavericks/ multi-taskers that many already are.

Hospitals are another place with a high occupancy rate and by those who are already experiencing some kind of illness (a form of risk), and if their situation is compounded by other stressful event, there will be a need for intervention. This point was already illustrated through Val's narration of her suicide attempt. Youth centres, volunteer organizations and community programs also are places where young people (including those with disabilities) often spend their time outside the home. As such, adults and whoever else who can lend a listening ear, and extend a helping hand might also just save a life or provide the much needed envirosocial support for the one deluged by disruption.

The subsequent and final point of intervention is called the *envirosocial reintegrating process*. People who have provided the envirosocial support processes to buffer the disorganization phase are usually also those who provide for the reintegration phase.

After having experienced disruption and disorganization of his/her view of the world, the individual with adequate support will want to rebuild the pieces of his/her life back to a functional state. Intervention at this phase includes assistance with problem solving, helping with contact to resources, and provide feedback to ideas and steps taken to improve their lives.

In the case of Val, the support given by the nurse after her attempted suicide also facilitated her towards a resilient reintegration. Val's own narration, "I tried..... from then on, I became strong.... convince myself to be healthy. Able to raise up my will (to succeed). From the fall, I pick myself up, my will that was shattered". From that point on, Val was able to overcome repeated degrading and stigmatizing treatment and remarks from her mother and siblings.

This evidence also illustrates the critical importance of at least one person who can provide the much needed support. It is crucial for the individual who is experiencing severe disruption to their biopsychospiritual homeostasis. Similar to the findings on the youth with disabilities case studies, of many other resiliency studies also found that in the moment of dire distress and severe disruption, just one person who is able to provide the much needed support can make all the difference between a dysfunctional and a resilient reintegration, and for some, between life and death.

Three Cautionary Notes

Firstly—Reintegration is individually unique. Another case study showed a different reintegration of a different stressor and the context. Facing stigmatization in school, Pradeep went to search for people to help him. In his own word, "I try to find a teacher to help me, if the teacher is not there, I will continue to find people until I find someone who can". In his state of disruption, the drive to reduce that anguished state results in his agency to initiate engagement with people who have the potential to help him. One important difference between Pradeep and Val's situation is that they have very different family backgrounds. Pradeep had a very loving, supportive and financially strong family, while Val came from a family of lower economic status that did not value her as a worthy member of the family.

Secondly—The existence of external support to assist with reintegration is crucial especially for young people with disabilities because it is often that they are also cognitively compromised. This means that they may not be able to adequately problem solve and work their way towards a reliable solution (Margalit 2004). Current studies also show that many may also have sensory integration disorder SID as another risk factor to their development. As a consequence of having SID, young people with disabilities will tend to be hypersensitive and overreact to stressors. Taking a narrative from Pradeep:

R: If you have to be home alone, and there happened to be an emergency: like a fire, or theft, how do you think you will feel?

L1: If alone, I will feel scared... because the kids near my home like to taunt me... knock on my door.... call me out to play ball...hmm... many kinds of things.

R: If they knock, what would you do?

L1: I go into my bedroom... lay in my bed and cover my whole body with my blanket... also close my ears.

R: Why cover your ears?

L1: They call me to come out... "Eh! Came la smoking!"... I feel scared.

Pradeep was already safely locked inside his home, but he still felt threatened by the boy calling from outside that he needed to hide in his bed, and under his blanket. Falling into a 'fight or flight' response from what is normally considered as non-threatening stimuli is a characteristic of SID. Other signs that SID include is reacting fearfully to normal social or non-social stimuli, and that can sometimes be paralysing to the person.

The third cautionary note involves the first two interventions before the onset of adversity or challenge. Parents and caregivers of young people with disabilities may sometimes be providing too much protection and support. These carers may be doing things for the disabled people in their care instead of allowing them to become skilful in basic life skills like eating, dressing, toileting and mobility inside and outside the home. Teachers in special education programs often cite that parents are usually reluctant to allow overnight excursions even though it is carried out within close proximity to their home. Those who are teaching young people with disabilities also need to exercise patience and avoid doing things for them as much as possible.

All these overprotective measures could mean that youth with disabilities lack much needed skills that allow them to be independent, solve problem, build support resources outside the home or outside the normal circle of support. Within the Resiliency Model, this kind of support will show as the overprotected youth, when challenged, get support that will ensure no disruption occurs (all problem solving done by the adult), thus causing biopsychospiritual homeostasis to bounce out of the challenge back into a similar state of homeostasis, with no new skills learnt from that experience (Figure 1).

Over support will not serve youth with disabilities well as it removes the chance to develop new coping skills which are afforded by a challenge, as it is quickly extinguished by the protective adult. Another concern is when unforeseeable circumstances occur. For example, in the event of sudden loss of immediate care and support, the assistance that the disabled youth is accustomed to will be suddenly disappear. This is often replaced by some other support that will definitely be different. Not being used to having to develop coping and problem solving skills, it can be a major disruption that may make it difficult (though not impossible) to come out off, and to attain a resilient reintegration—as the youth is used to having overprotection and support in the past.

Conclusion

The resiliency process is constantly dynamic, and always involves the interplay between the internally situated biopsychospiritual protective factors and the externally situated envirosocial protective factors. Young people with disabilities have to contend with both chronic and permanent disabilities, while needing to be navigating resiliently from oncoming stressors that are part and parcel of everyday life. Parents, care givers, medical, mental health, educational professionals and concerned members of the community can all use the Resiliency Model according to one's own capacity and skills to assist young people with disabilities to grow into the best possible adult they can be.

Finally, as a standard framework the resiliency model could be used for our own selves to assist in understanding the changes that happens during the process of negotiating a challenging situation, and to allow a conscious effort to attain a resilient reintegration and better life outcomes.

References

1. Earvolino-Ramirez (2007) articulated the important difference in meaning between ego-resiliency which refers to a personality trait and resilience which refers to a dynamic process.
2. Resilient reintegration causes an altered state of understanding of the world, successful navigation of the adversity and gaining of additional skills or resources than before the adversity.
3. Normalisation principles provide guidelines on how to treat individuals with disabilities (Winzer 1996). These include; "the society should regard disabled people as individuals with rights and to treat them humanely and fairly", "facilitate normal family and community life for disabled people", "to allow access and chance for typical life routines", "facilitate normal developmental experiences like marriage, independent choices", and "right to work and play in normal surroundings" (Winzer 1996, p. 65).

4. Biopsychospiritual homeostasis—protective factors consist of three components. Biological coping factors include medical conditions, tolerance for pain, rejuvenation (healing) capabilities, fitness levels, and states of fatigue. Psychological and spiritual coping factors include self-esteem, internal locus for control, empowerment, efficacy, good sense of humour, good decision making skills, belief in a higher force, and independence of spirit. Homeostasis denotes that it is in a calm balance and unchanging state.

5. These protective factors are not exhaustive. Adapted from *Resilience: A concept analysis.* (Earvolino-Ramirez 2007). They were identified by pioneers in resiliency inquiry—Anthony E.J. (1974); Benard, B. (1991); Garmezy, N. (1991); Masten, A.S. (1994); Rutter, M. (1985; 1987); Werner, E. E. (1982; 1992).

6. *Maladaptive reintegration*—occurs when the life event is so significant that the individual reintegrates his/her world view to a lower level of homeostasis. Thus they have fewer skills than before the life event. E.g. lower self-esteem, negative expectations, and loss of confidence. Ultimately, the person resigns to this lower state of being.

7. *Dysfunctional reintegration*—occurs when the individual reintegrates using psychoactive substances (drugs, alchohol), withdrawing into psychopathic syndromes, attempts suicide, thus intervention becomes necessary.

Works Cited

Anthony, E.J., & Cohler, B.J. (1987). Risk, vulnerability, and resilience—an overview. *In The Invulnerable Child* (Eds.). The United States: The Guilford Press.

Benard, B. (1991). *Fostering resiliency in kids: Protective factors in the family, school and community.* Portland, OR: Northwest Regional Educational Laboratory.

Davey, G., & Keya M. (2009). Stigmatisation of people with mental illness in Bangladesh. *Mental Health Practice,* 13(3), 30-33.

Donnon. T., & Hammond, W. (2011). Enhancing resiliency in Children Living in Disadvantaged Neighbourhoods. In K.Kufeldt & B. McKenzie (Eds.), *Child Welfare: Connecting research, Policy, and Practice* (2nd Ed.). (pp. 501-514). Waterloo: Wilfrid Laurier University Press.

Earvolino-Ramirez, M. (2007). Resilience: a concept analysis. *Nursing Forum,* 42(2), 73-82.

Garmezy, N. (1991). Resiliency and vulnerability to adverse developmental outcomes associated with poverty. *American Behavioural Scientist,* 34, 416-430.

Goffman, E. (1968). *Stigma—notes on the management of spoiled identity.* New Jersey: Pelican Books.

Hall, D.K., & Pearson, J. (2005). Resilience—giving children the skills to bounce back. *Education and health,* 23(1), 12-15.

Hanun, N. A., Hammond, W. A. and Kamarulzaman, K. (2011) *Stigma and Protective Factors:A Study of Resilience among Youths with Disabilities.* MEd. Sultan Idris Education University, Malaysia.

Hanun, N.A., Hammond, W., & Kamarulzaman. (2012). Hanun, N.A., Hammond, W., & Kamarulzaman. (2012). The role of educators in facilitating resiliency that assists normalization for young people with disabilities. Chris Forlin (Eds). *Future Directions for Inclusive Teacher Education: An international perspective.* New York: Routledge.

Harvey, R.D. (2001). Individual differences in the phenomenological impact of social stigma. *The Journal of Social Psychology,* 141(2), 174-189.

Ladieu-Leviton G, Adler DL, Dembo T: Studies in adjustment to visible injuries: Social acceptance of the injured. *Journal of Social Issues* 1948; 4: 55-62.

Luthar, S. S., Cicchetti, D., & Becker, B. (2000). The construct of resilience: A critical evaluation and guidelines for future work. *Child Development,* 71(3), 543-562.

Heatherton, T.F., Kleck, R.E., Hebl, M.R., & Hull, J.G. (Eds.). (2003). *The social psychology of stigma.* New York: Guilford Press.

Margalit, M. (2003). Resilience model among individuals with learning disabilities proximal and distal influences. *Learning Disabilities Research and Practice,*18(2), 82-86.

Martz, E. (2004). A philosophical perspective to confront disability stigmatization and promote adaptation to disability. *Journal of Loss andTrauma* 9, 139-158.

Masten, A.S. (1994). Resilience in individual development: Successful adaptation despite risk and adversity. In M.C. Wang, & E.W. Gordon (Eds.), *Educational resilience in inner-city America: Challenges and prospects* (pp. 3-25). Hillsdale, NJ: Erlbaum.

Masten, A., & Obradovi'c, J. (2006). Competence and resilience in development. *Ann. N.Y. Acad. Sci.* 1094: 13-27 (2006). 2006 New York Academy of Sciences. doi: 10.1196/annals.1376.003

Richardson, G.E., Neiger, B.L., Jensen, S., & Kumpfer, K.L. (1990). The resiliency model. *Health Education,* 21(6), p. 33-39.

_____ (2002). The metatheory of resilience and resiliency. *Journal of Clinical Psychology,* 58(3), 307-321.

Rutter, M. (1985). Resilience in the face of adversity: Protective factors and resistance to psychiatric disorder. *British Journal of Psychiatry*, 147, 598-611.

_____ (1987). Psychosocial resilience and protective factors. *American Journal of Orthopsychiatry*, 57, 316-331.

_____ (2000). Resilience considered: Conceptual considerations, empirical findings, and policy implication. In J.P. Shonkoff & S.J. Meisels (Eds.), *Handbook of early childhood intervention* (2nd ed., pp. 651-682). Cambridge, England: Cambridge University Press.

Spekman, H.J., Herman, K.L., & Vogel, S.A. (1993). Risk and resilience in individuals with learning disabilities: A challenge to the field. *Learning Disabilities Research and Practice*, 8, 59-65.

Werner, E. E., & Smith, R.S. (1982). *Vulnerable but invincible; A longitudinal study of resilient children and youth*. New York: McGraw-Hill.

_____ (1992). *Overcoming the odds: High risk children from birth to adulthood*. London: Cornell University Press.

CHAPTER 20

"Resilience at Work and in Life"

Andrew Shatté

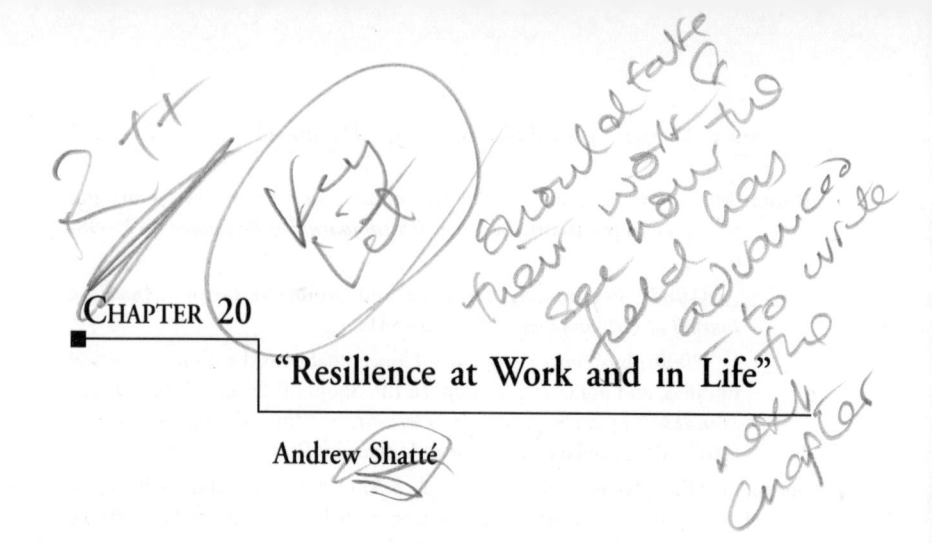

Abstract

This chapter maps the 20-year development of a fleet of programs designed to boost resilience in children, college freshmen, and corporate employees. By adopting a longitudinal view, we afford a glimpse into the role of serendipity in any unfolding research agenda. What began as a depression-prevention initiative for children morphed into resilience programs for people of all ages, as our programs became infused with the then burgeoning field of positive psychology and our increasing understanding of what resilience is. This chapter details the seven factors that comprise resilience and outlines the seven skills that are demonstrated to boost them. Our hope is that this chapter serves as a celebration of the myriad researchers around the world who have devoted their careers to this critical competency—Resilience.

Resilience—The Back Story

In the early 1990's at the University of Pennsylvania, a small group of researchers made a major breakthrough in the depression literature. Aware of the burgeoning epidemic of depression, they developed a program, based on the principles of cognitive therapy, designed to prevent depression in at-risk children. It worked. By the time of the two-year follow-up in 1992, the Penn Optimism Program (POP) had halved the rate of depression in children aged 10-12 years of age, relative to a matched control group (see Jaycox et al. 1991; Gillham et al. 1992).

By 1993, my colleagues and I prepared to take the next, logical step in the research platform. Now armed with an effective anti-depression program, we developed a protocol to train others (psychologists and teachers) to deliver the program to children, in order to effectuate mass dissemination, to provide the inoculation against the epidemic. This work would be our doctoral dissertations.

To this end we certified 10 teachers in suburban Philadelphia and set about recruiting subjects for the 20-children groups the newly-minted teachers would lead. A child's eligibility for the program was determined by her level of risk for depression based on two established risk factors: (1) high conflict and low cohesion in the child's family (as measured by the Child's Perception of Interpersonal Conflict, CPIC, and the Family Environment Scale, FES) and (2) the precocious development of depressive symptoms (as measured by Beck's Children's Depression Inventory, CDI). In the past, places in POP were offered to the 50 per cent most at risk children, based on a median split of a combination risk score.

Of the 150 students we were able to recruit for the Philadelphia study, only about half were truly at risk. In our fresh-faced eagerness, we had readied more teachers than were needed to run high-risk groups. What to do? To keep the teachers motivated and skilled, we decided to assign all children to groups, even if their risk score was so low it was highly improbable that they would ever experience a bout of clinical depression, at any point in their lives.

It was through this circuitous route that we made our discovery. At the end of the 12-week program and through the four-month and eight-month follow-up periods, we observed the typical anti-depressive, prophylactic effects of the program among the high-risk children. But to our surprise, we discovered that the low-risk kids made significant strides relative to low-risk Controls on a slew of measures, including parent, teacher, and peer ratings of their pro-social behaviors. It became clear that POP offered benefits beyond depression prevention. The program instilled a foundational skill set which could be put to diverse uses—to avoid depressive symptoms in children at risk for depression, and to boost pro-social, problem-solving behavior for those not at risk. The program turned out to be something much more fundamental than depression prevention. As we considered the benefits it bestowed, the concept that emerged was resilience. POP boosted resilience, and children could channel that new-found resilience towards what they needed most.

Once we realized that the competency we were boosting was resilience, it prompted a major shift in our thinking. First, we had transitioned from therapists treating the 'sick' to prevention psychologists equipping healthy children with the skills to stave off depression. Second, we had moved our focus from averting the negative (depression) to actively working to lift a positive trait (resilience) in healthy children. So the Penn Optimism Program was renamed the Penn Resilience Program (PRP). We had become positive psychologists.

What is Resilience?

As we began to use the language of resilience at academic meetings and in our therapy and consulting practices, we took stock of how the concept 'hit' people. It became clear that everyone, experts and lay people alike, had an opinion on what resilience means—and that as with snowflakes, no two opinions were alike. We began to see that the concept of resilience is like fine art—no one can describe or define it, but everyone claims to know it when they see it. Resilience appears monolithic—as a singular construct with a single definition. But that obstructs good communication about what resilience is. It was time to distill the concept into its component parts.

A systematic literature on resilience extends back at least as far as the 1950's and the work of Emmy Werner and Ruth Smith in their landmark, longitudinal study of children born behind the eight ball on the island of Kauai.[1] Their emphasis, as well as that of their intellectual descendants, tended to be on how one became resilient and then, once in possession of resilience, how one used it in life. Werner and Smith explored how people use resilience to steer through day-to-day adversity, overcome childhood obstacles, and bounce back from trauma. These are, of course, noble academic pursuits, but they do not answer the riddle of what exactly resilience *is*. It was to this task that we next turned our attention.

The Resilience Factors

In 1997, my colleagues and I formed a training and consulting company endowed with the mission to distribute the training programs we had developed at the University of Pennsylvania to children, college students, and corporations. Under the company's auspices, we began the work of uncovering the factors that comprise resilience.

To pave the way for a comprehensive factor analysis, we scoured the research literature on resilience and related concepts such as hardiness and coping. In addition, we sampled the literature on overcoming, steering through, and bouncing back. Our searches incorporated dictionary definitions and vernacular usages of the word 'resilience' and related constructs, and provided us with a comprehensive view of how 'resilience' is applied to the way people deal with negative forces in their lives. As a head nod to the then nascent field of positive psychology, we included 40 items that tapped into positive traits related to Reaching Out that we conjectured were related to resilience (e.g., the ability to assess risk, take on challenges and opportunities, and develop strong relationships with others).

In this first-pass measure of resilience, we assembled 260 items which we administered to about 1,000 people. The data were subjected to exploratory factor analyses to uncover the solution of best fit. A seven-factor solution emerged most compellingly[2] and was solidified in a subsequent confirmatory factor analysis. The 60 items that loaded most strongly were folded into a psychometric instrument we called the Resilience Factor Inventory (RFI).

The RFI measures an individual's current level of functioning on 7 traits that comprise resilience: (1) Emotion Regulation, (2) Impulse Control, (3) Causal Analysis, (4) Self-Efficacy, (5) Realistic Optimism, (6) Empathy, and (7) Reaching Out.

- *Emotion Regulation*—The ability to control one's emotions, especially in the wake of an adversity, in order to remain goal focused.
- *Impulse Control*—The ability to control one's behavior, especially in the wake of an adversity, in order to remain goal focused.
- *Causal Analysis*—The ability to differentiate all (or almost all) of the causes of an adversity, and determine and act on those over which one can exert control.
- *Self-Efficacy*—A belief in oneself; the belief that one has mastery in the world and will be able to handle whatever life throws at one.

In an ideal RFI profile, Causal Analysis and Self-Efficacy are high. Sometimes, however, the Causal Analysis score is relatively high while the Self-Efficacy score is relatively low. In these instances, the individual may be a good problem solver but does not perceive herself as such. Typically, this is because one's schema, or belief system, about oneself is overly pessimistic and bleak. At other times, the Causal Analysis score is relatively low but the Self-Efficacy score is relatively high. In these instances, individuals are not effective problem solvers but they think they are. Interestingly, this profile is most often seen in salespeople.

- *Realistic Optimism*—The sense that the future is bright, within the confines of reality. The RFI measures optimism, the decision as to whether or not that level of optimism is realistic must be made against the backdrop of the individual's life. This is the only one of the seven factors in which it is possible for the score to be maladaptively high (i.e., for there to be too much of a good thing).
- *Empathy*—The ability to understand what motivates others, to imagine a situation from another's perspective, and to understand the thoughts and emotions that motivate others. This has emerged, perhaps predictably, as a significant predictor of success as a manager. In truth, since we are social beings, it's a core competency for us all.
- *Reaching Out*—The willingness and ability to take on complex tasks and challenges that may make one's life more positive. While many of the other factors adopt the traditional view that resilience is about how we respond to negative events, this factor pursues the positive psychology notion that how we manage positive events is important as well.
- *Resilience Quotient (RQ)*—A summary measure that represents the arithmetic mean of the seven factors.

Having uncovered principal components that form the concept of resilience, the next step was to ensure that we had developed a reliable and valid means of measuring it. To this end, we set about investigating the psychometric properties of the RFI.

Measuring Resilience

Our mission now was to boost resilience, especially for those in need. To accomplish this mission, we needed to ensure that the RFI could reliably and validly measure resilience, and we needed to ascertain whether the RFI was sensitive to increases in resilience as a result of our interventions.

The Validity of the Resilience Factor Inventory (RFI)

Since 1997, our research has established the criterion validity of the RFI in two ways—its concurrent validity and its predictive validity.

Concurrent validity is a measure of the extent to which the new measure, in this case the RFI, stacks up against accountings of the same construct, both questionnaire and 'real-world' measures. Since there was no extant, accepted questionnaire measure of resilience in the literature, we took another tack. Based on our experience as consultants and trainers, we believed that among professions, sales is probably most dependent on resilience for success. So, we hypothesized that successful salespeople would show high levels of resilience.

The resilience factors of Emotion Regulation and Impulse Control, we proposed, would be essential to successfully negotiate the cold call or cold visit. The resilience factor of Causal Analysis would be core to correct interpretation of feedback from potential clients, in order to adjust their pitch—thereby delineating aspects of their performance over which they can exert control. Self-Efficacy and Optimism would be important to remain perseverant through the inevitable rejection. In cold-calling sales, we conjectured, the resilience factor of Empathy, which is important in functions with long-term relationships, would be less focal.

Since sales managers are typically chosen from among the best salespeople, we supposed that sales managers would show higher levels of resilience than the salespeople they manage on all seven factors except Empathy, as specified above.

To test these hypotheses we worked with a Fortune 100 telecommunications company in their sales division. The frontline salespeople and the managers to which they reported completed the RFI. The scores on each factor, as well as an average across all seven factors (RQ), are provided in Figure 1.

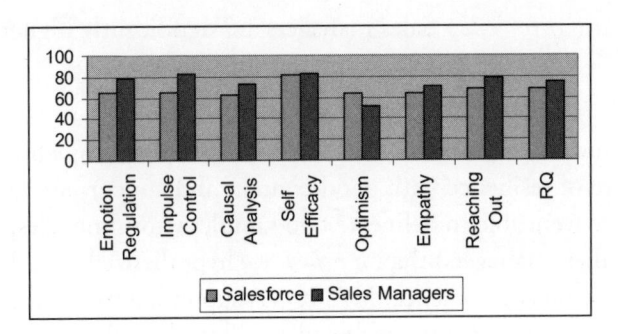

Figure 1

The most stringent test of the statistical significance of group differences is through a Multivariate Analysis of Variance (MANOVA). MANOVA is an inferential statistic designed to handle multiple dependant variables and avoid inflation of an experiment-wise error rate that would result from running multiple t-tests.

Results of the MANOVA analyses are as follows:

Emotion Regulation: Sales managers are significantly higher than salespeople on this factor
$F_{(1,25)} = 7.14$, p=.013.

Impulse Control: Sales managers are significantly higher than salespeople on this factor
$F_{(1,25)} = 12.17$, p=.002

Causal Analysis: Sales managers are significantly higher than salespeople on this factor
$F_{(1,25)} = 12.17$, p=.002

Self-Efficacy: No statistically significant difference

Optimism: No statistically significant difference

Empathy: No statistically significant difference

Reaching Out: Sales managers are significantly higher than salespeople on this factor
$F_{(1,25)} = 13.39$, p=.001

RQ: Sales managers are significantly higher than salespeople on this factor
$F_{(1,25)} = 7.17$, p=.013

This study demonstrates that we had hit upon a psychometric measure of resilience with good content and concurrent validity, since we were able to delineate two samples (frontline salespeople versus their managers) that, *a priori*, we hypothesized would differ on the factors of resilience. MANOVA supported five of the seven hypotheses—that managers scored significantly higher on four out of the six predicted resilience factors (Emotion Regulation, Impulse Control, Causal Analysis, and Reaching Out) and that there were no significant differences between sales managers and salespeople on Empathy. The next question became "is the RFI useful in making predictions about someone's performance?" In other words, does it have good predictive validity?

Sales is one arena in which it is easy to test predictive validity, since there is a direct link between the behaviors of the salesperson and a measurable bottom line. To this end, we examined the predictive validity of the RFI in portfolio sales in the investment industry. The following hypotheses were tested:

1. The more resilient a new recruit was at the time of hiring, the better he/she would perform.
2. The more resilience the new recruit was at the time of hiring, the more he/she would produce in the first nine months on the job.

To test these hypotheses, ncew hires in a large investment portfolio company were administered the RFI and their performance was monitored across the first nine months on the job. Performance was evaluated on two principal measures: (1) the number of customers generated through cold calling and/or cold door knocking, and (2) the dollar value of sales to those customers.

The findings revealed that RQ scores (the arithmetic mean of the seven factor scores) were significantly correlated with the number of customers generated (r = .43, significant at p = .041), and gross commission, a measure of the dollar value of sales (r = .44, significant at p = .033).

We were now armed with a valid measure of the seven factors that comprise resilience. This was to prove immeasurably useful in the work we had begun in the corporate arena.

Resilience for Corporations

Since 1994, we've consulted with and trained personnel in hundreds of organizations in the United States and abroad representing a diverse cross-section of corporate entities, public sector departments, and non-profit organizations. Boosting resilience in adults had become a mainstay of our practice. But like most twists and turns in life, this was due more to serendipity than to entrepreneurial foresight and concerted planning.

In 1994, we entered discussions with a large healthcare provider in the United States with a view to distributing our children's program, the PRP, to the children within their care. We met with a contingent from the healthcare provider to convince them of the merits of the PRP. As it turns out we did not venture with them to distribute the children's program. But in the course of our presentation, someone in the audience mentioned that, to help them meet the demands of their job, they and their staff could use the program. This was met with laughter of assent. And we immediately began to brainstorm what an adult version of the PRP might look like.

The initial program we devised was, like the PRP, based on the principles of cognitive therapy. In developing the program, we identified seven skills designed to boost resilience: (1) ABC, (2) Avoiding Thinking Traps, (3) Navigating Around Icebergs, (4) Challenging Beliefs, (5) Putting It In Perspective, (6) Calming and Focusing, and (7) Real-Time Resilience. Customization of the program for various clients afforded the opportunity for participants to use their newfound resilience for diverse ends—

elevating performance, managing stress, dealing with adversity, becoming a better manager, change management, and many more of the critical competencies required in the modern, corporate world.

The Skills of Resilience

The seven skills were:

Skill 1. ABC

A skill based on the work of iconoclastic, New York psychologist, Albert Ellis. Participants learn about how activating events (A's) conjure up automatic beliefs (B's) in people, which in turn lead to emotional and behavioral consequences (C's; A® B® C). Participants also learn that they develop habits in their thinking that lead them to feel the same emotion over time and over circumstances, leading them to be 'anger people, 'guilt, or 'sadness people'.

There are seven basic emotions that interfere with an employee's productivity and performance; anger, frustration, sadness, anxiety, guilt, shame, and embarrassment. Each emotion has a belief that produces it. For example, a belief that your rights have been violated leads to anger, and belief about some future threat headed your way produces anxiety. A chart of the links between thoughts (beliefs) and emotional consequences (i.e., B-C links) can be found below.

Belief (B)	Emotional Consequence (C)
Violation of rights	Anger
Loss of self esteem or real-world loss	Sadness
Future threat	Anxiety
Lack of resources	Frustration
Violation of another's rights	Guilt
Loss of standing	Embarrassment
Violation of one's own standards	Shame

Participants learn that this is rarely a one-off scenario; that we all develop habits in our thinking. We develop a radar with which we scan the world. Some of us scan for violations of our rights, and our radar 'bleeps' on imaginary violations—incorrect perceptions of how the world is. Those of us who do experience anger much of the time. Others develop a radar around future threat and for them, anxiety is their 'go-to' emotion. As with all radars, if we scan long and hard enough we'll find it. As the famous American author Mark Twain is reputed to have said, "there have been many catastrophes in my life—some of which actually happened".

In learning this skill, participants come to recognize their radar and practice a skill to get around it. This leads to greater Emotion Regulation and Impulse Control—two core factors from the RFI.

Skill 2. Avoiding Thinking Traps

A skill based on the work of the founder of the cognitive therapy model, Dr. Aaron (Tim) Beck. Beck outlined several "errors in logic" to which people are prone. Thus, for this skill, participants are trained to identify the thinking trap that most holds them back, and to develop a technique to avoid the trap when it comes up.

Human beings have 1300 cubic centimeter brains that afford us enormous processing capacity. We also have five highly developed senses: vision, hearing, touch, taste, and smell. In humans, eyes and ears are paramount; through these organs, we take in more information about the world than we can compute, leading us to take necessary short cuts. These short cuts lead to inevitable inaccuracies, or thinking traps. And these traps lower our resilience and interfere with life functioning. The seven biggest thinking traps are:

- *Personalizing*—The tendency to automatically attribute the causes of problems to oneself.

- *Externalizing*—The tendency to automatically attribute the causes of problems to others or circumstances.
- *Overgeneralizing*—The tendency to make global statements about oneself (e.g., "I'm a loser") or the world (e.g., "people are mean") without the evidence to support it.
- *Magnifying and Minimizing*—The tendency to blow up the importance of one piece of a situation while blowing 'down' the importance of others. In humans, who are arguably evolutionarily loaded for the negative, we typically magnify the negative and minimize the positive.
- *Pessimism*—Assuming the worst in a spiral of negative, future threat beliefs.
- *Mind Reading*—Assuming that you know what other people are thinking and feeling without consulting with them, or, more commonly, expecting others in your life to know what you're thinking and feeling without having communicated that to them.
- *Emotional Reasoning*—Using your feelings as a barometer of how the world is. Since our emotions are determined by our thinking and since our thinking can be flawed, our feelings can be an unreliable indicator of reality.

Skill 3. Navigating around Icebergs

This skill is based on the cognitive-therapy concept of deeper beliefs and underlying assumptions (a la Beck) and irrational beliefs (a la Ellis), along with the general concept in the cognition literature on schematic representations (schema). Since the majority of our schema lie beneath the level of consciousness, just as the bulk of an iceberg lies under the water, we dubbed them Iceberg Beliefs.

While Beck & Ellis specialized in the deep beliefs that are risk factors for depression (e.g., if I'm not perfect, then I'm fatally flawed; life is supposed to be easy), we retooled the concept in light of the principles of positive psychology. For us, deep beliefs are double-edged swords with both pros and cons attached to them. For example, the Iceberg "if it's not perfect it's a failure" sets us up for depression, but also drives us to excel. The key to dealing with Icebergs is to navigate around their cons while tapping into their pros.

Skill 4. Challenging Beliefs

This skill comes from the work on explanatory style first developed by Lynn Abramson, Lauren Alloy, and their colleagues at the University of Pennsylvania. The traditional explanatory style literature touts the benefits of optimism (external, unstable, and specific attributions for negative events) and details the deficits, especially in terms of a diathesis for depression or pessimism (defined as internal, stable, and global attributions for negative events). Where we depart from the classic literature is in our belief that all styles, including optimism, have limitations (and that all styles, including pessimism, have upsides). Our focus is on the four most observed styles: (1) internal, stable, global, (2) external unstable, specific, (3) external, stable, global, and (4) internal, unstable, specific for negative events. And our emphasis is on flexibility (i.e., what is key to enhancing resilience is identifying your style and developing the ability to generate alternative attributions that sample the other dimensions of explanatory style.

Skill 5. Putting It in Perspective

A skill devoted to the thinking trap of catastrophizing, in which an individual ruminates on future threats stemming from a setback until they become bogged down on catastrophic, albeit low-probability, negative outcomes. Participants are taught to counter their worst case scenarios with best case outcomes, using each as an anchor to settle on the most likely outcomes. The goal is to establish emotion regulation of the anxiety that catastrophizing produces, and to engender better problem solving.

Skill 6. Calming & Focusing

This skill imparts distraction techniques that can temporarily shunt out negative thinking (via focusing). It also includes breathing and relaxation skills that end overactive sympathetic nervous system functioning (fight or flight) and activate the parasympathetic (relaxation) response.

Skill 7. Real-Time Resilience

Participants learn to challenge inaccurate thinking the moment such thoughts pop into their heads.

The Resilience Skills—A Reformation

By the mid 2000's, as our thinking on positive psychology began to crystallize, we introduced more aspects of positive psychology into the skill set. By 2005, we replaced the last three program skills with the following:

Skill 5. Positive Radar

Participants learn of the connection between thinking style Radars and positive emotions, and practice tracking the following positive emotions:

Belief (B)	*Emotional Consequence (C)*
All's well	Happiness
I have everything I need	Contentment
This task is (just) within my intellectual ability	Interest, engagement
Commitment, connection	Love
Elevated standing with others	Esteem, respect, regard
I have performed well/admirably	Pride

Skill 6. Positive Icebergs

Participants learn of the Iceberg beliefs they have around their core values. In addition, they learn to identify areas of conflict between their behaviors and those values, and between short- and medium-term goals and their values. Finally, they create a life mission statement and practice tapping into positive Icebergs during adversity.

Skill 7. Connection

In 2006, I joined the faculty of the Brookings Institution in Washington, D.C. Brookings is one of the principal sources of leadership education for the United States federal government. I was tasked with discovering why federal government employees, in spite of their poor compensation, low autonomy, and low authority relative to their private sector peers, were significantly more satisfied in their jobs and, as it turned out, also significantly more resilient.

We began our investigation by asking employees in both the public and private sectors why they stayed in their jobs. It soon became clear that their responses could be sorted into three categories that represented different levels of connection to their jobs.

At the lowest level, Level 1, people stayed only for the pay and the benefits. At Level 2, people were there for the pay and the benefits but also liked their work and liked the people with whom they worked. At the highest level, Level 3, people needed the pay and liked the work and their colleagues, but they also believed that what they did made a significant contribution to the greater good. The notion of greater good manifest in myriad ways (e.g., grooming the next generation of employees for their company, contributing to an organization that does good things in the world, creating a product that enhanced the lives of people in their community or even their nation). It soon became clear that connection bestowed true benefits on the connected.

Our research revealed statistically significant increases in job satisfaction, as measured on a self-report Likert, with each step up in level of connection.

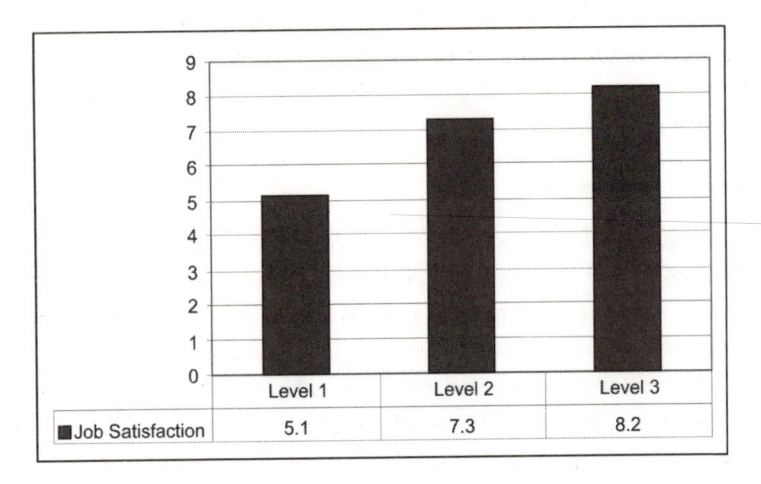

Figure 2

	Level 1	Level 2	Level 3
Job Satisfaction	5.1	7.3	8.2

And we were able to demonstrate statistically significant increases in resilience with each step up in level of connection.

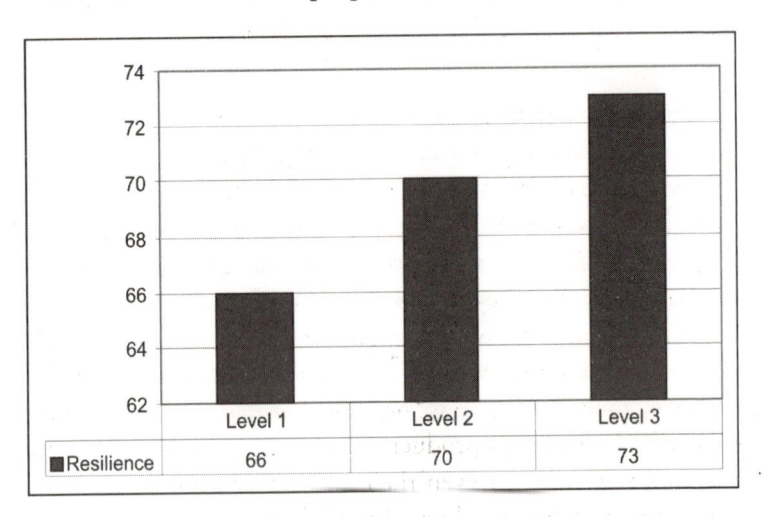

Figure 3

	Level 1	Level 2	Level 3
Resilience	66	70	73

Thus, for *Sskill 7 Connection*—we help participants identify their current level of connection, then guide them to find higher level reasons for staying in their jobs.

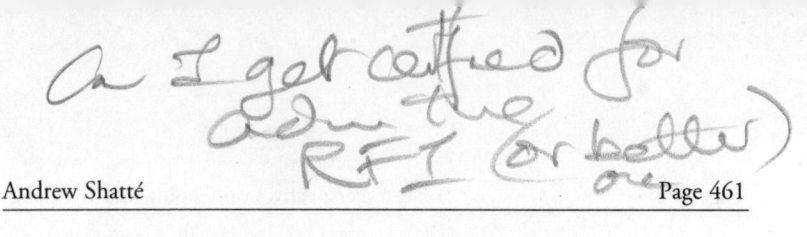

To summarize the progress made towards our mission over time, we distilled down the monolithic concept of resilience and identified its seven component parts. In addition, we developed a psychometric instrument to validly measure resilience. And we developed a training program designed to boost resilience. Now, we needed to verify that the training worked.

Empirical Trials of the Resilience Training

What follows are six case studies of the application of resilience training in a corporate setting.

Case Study 1. Boosting Resilience at Verizon

The Company. This training was conducted with 300 managers in the mid-Atlantic division of Verizon communications.

The Business Issue. These managers oversaw technicians who laid and repaired telephone cable. Their industry and their company had experienced enormous change over the years, including mergers, acquisitions, emerging competitors, and a changing focus away from traditional phones to wireless technology. This was billed as a resilience and change management training.

Intervention. Participants received the first edition of the training in a 1-day format. No follow-up training boosters were provided. To test the ability of the training to increase resilience, participants were administered the RFI both pre-training and at three-months follow-up. Results are presented in the graph (next page).

Analyses revealed statistically significant improvements on five of the seven resilience factors (Emotion Regulation, Impulse Control, Self-Efficacy, Empathy, and Reaching Out) and RQ. The ability of the RFI to detect the effects of an intervention was established.

	Emotion Regulation	Impulse Control	Causal Analysis	Self-Efficacy	Optimism	Empathy	Reaching Out	RQ
Pre-Training	75	78	66	77	60	63	75	70
Post-Training	79	80	67	80	61	67	77	73

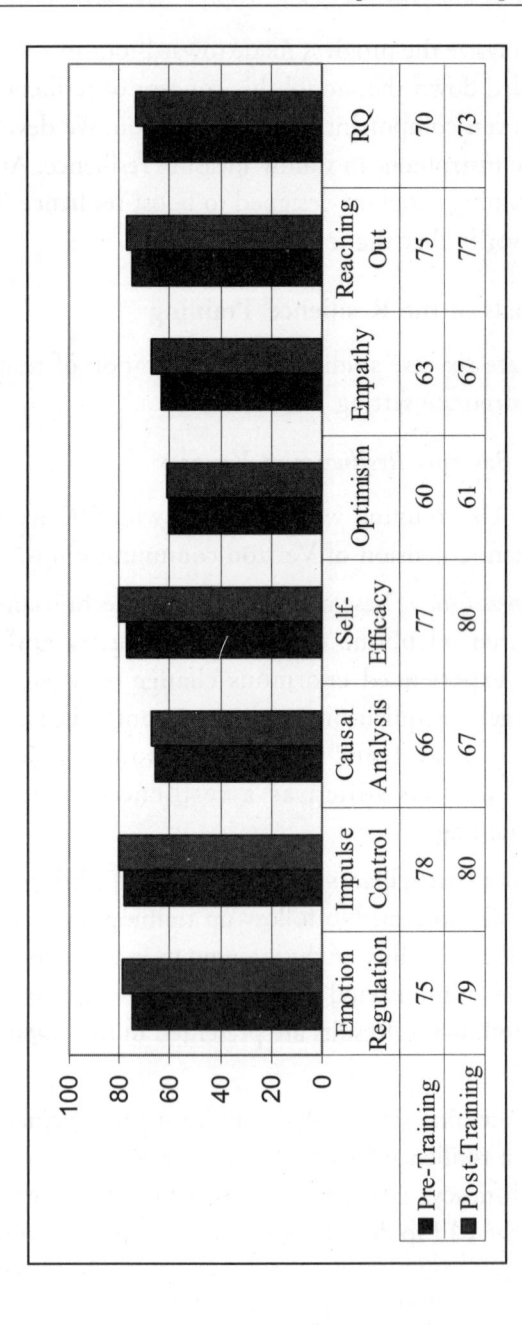

Figure 4

Case Study 2. Boosting Sales at Verizon Information Services

The Company. Verizon Information Services, a $4.3 Billion division of Verizon Communications Inc., is a world-leading print and online directory publisher and content provider. In addition to print directories, Verizon Information Services produces and markets SuperPages.com—the Internet's preeminent online directory and shopping resource.

Business Issue. We worked with a group of sales representatives in the San Juan, Puerto Rico office of Verizon Information Services, responsible for selling Verizon directory advertising to commercial customers in Puerto Rico. Because of the volume of calling required and high levels of rejection, success in this position required a high level of resilience.

In the aftermath of September 11, 2001, Puerto Rico was experiencing the same negative effects on business as the United States. At Verizon Information Services, increased quotas, combined with a shrinking local economy, made an already challenging sales job that much more difficult.

Intervention. In January, 2002, a group of telesales representatives participated in the early edition of our resilience training—a 12-hour program in which they learned the seven skills of resilience. Participants also subsequently engaged in two booster sessions during which they reviewed the skills and worked through live examples of the how to apply them.

Performance on a number of key sales indicators was gathered about six months post-training, and compared with a control group of telesales representatives who did not participate in the resilience workshop.

Results. Results showed that the resilience training group outperformed the control group by both maximizing upside results and minimizing downside erosion of sales and customer base in a difficult economy.

There was no significant different between the group that received resilience training and the control group at pre-test. By post-test, however, the training and control groups differed significantly on the percentage of sales objectives achieved.

	Resilience Training	Control
Pre	102	103
Post	120	105

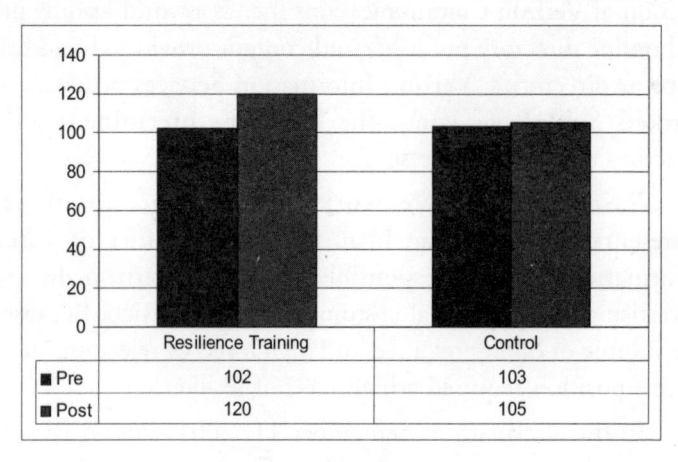

Figure 5

Several other measures showed moderate to very large effect sizes, although due to the relatively small sample sizes, they did not reach statistical significance. These include,

The number of sales closed per day:

	Resilience training	Control
Pre	3.9	5.4
Post	7.6	6

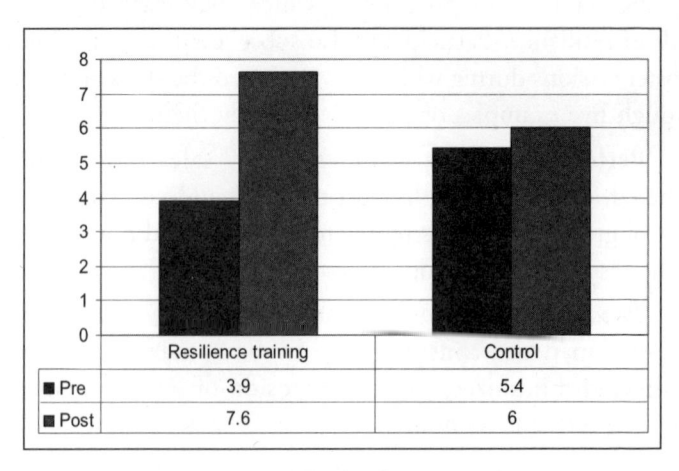

Figure 6

Regarding sales in new markets, both groups showed sharp downturns due to the failing economy. That said, the resilience training group had a lower degree of disintegration than the control group.

	Resilience training	Control
Pre	870	1006
Post	512	402

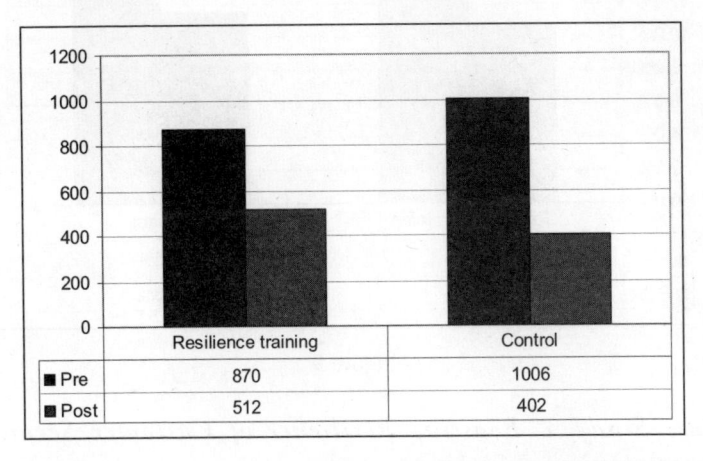

Figure 7

This was also true of the percentage clients lost due to cancellations:

	Resilience training	Control
Pre	11.1%	9.5%
Post	11.7%	13.3%

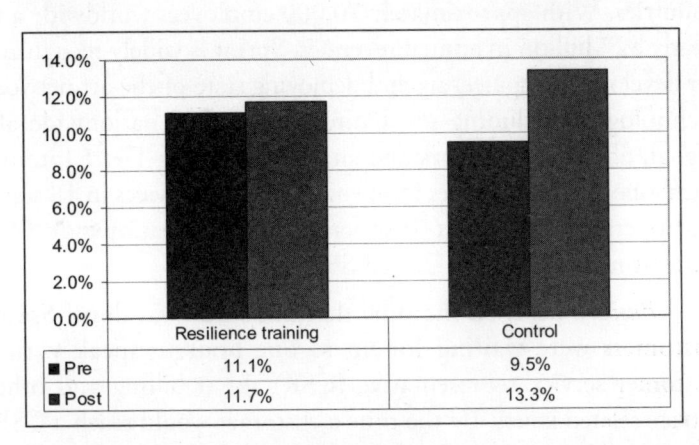

Figure 8

The Resilience group also showed greater improvement in the percentage of closed sales:

	Resilience training	Control
Pre	10.8%	11.5%
Post	15.7%	13.8%

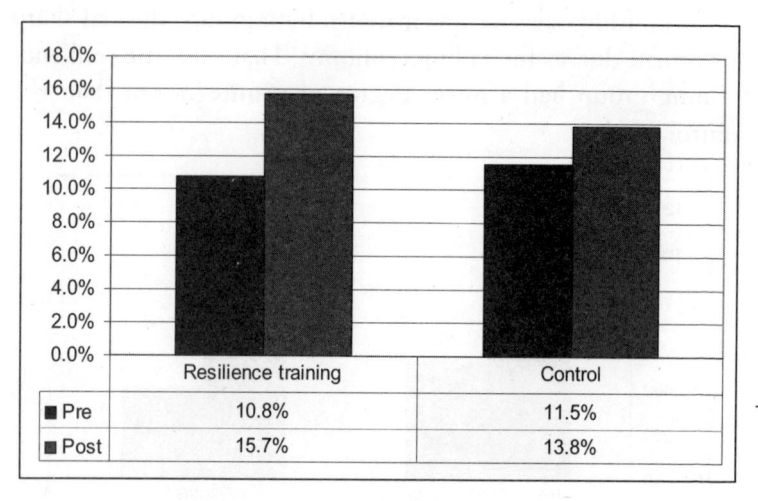

Figure 9

Case Study 3. Boosting Resilience of Customer Service Representatives at Sprint

The Company. Sprint is a global integrated communications provider serving more than 26 million customers in over 100 countries. With approximately 70,000 employees worldwide and nearly $27 billion in annual revenues, Sprint is widely recognized for developing, engineering and deploying state-of-the-art network technologies, including the United States' first nationwide all-digital, fiber-optic network and an award-winning Tier 1 Internet backbone. Sprint provides local voice and data services in 18 states and operates the largest 100-percent digital, nationwide PCS wireless network in the United States.

Business Issue. At the time that this study was done, Sprint customers were waiting for up to one hour to speak with a customer service representative (CSR) about billing and other service related issues. By the time a customer would reach a CSR, they were frustrated and angry, and would often take it out on the CSR. Besides being responsible for resolving customer requests, Sprint CSR's were required to attempt to sell additional services to existing customers. Trying to resolve an irate customer's problem was challenging enough without the pressure of selling additional services. The number and quality of successfully completed customer calls was dropping, and CSR attrition rate was increasing.

Interviews with CSRs showed that many of them were taking the customers' complaints personally, which decreased the CSRs' effectiveness. In addition, a number of CSRs interpreted the addition of upselling to their list of duties as evidence that the company did not value them as employees.

Intervention. Fifteen CSR's were selected for resilience training. The only selection criteria were schedule-based—participants were selected based on who worked that day, and an equal number of CSRs were selected from each supervisor's group to minimize office disruption. No performance measures were included in the selection criteria. Sixteen CSR's were later added as a control group, and consisted of a matched sample based on performance prior to the training, experience with CSR and sales, tenure with Sprint, and supervisor.

The 15 CSRs who attended training received a one-day workshop. In the training, participants learned the Self-Awareness Skills (ABC, Avoiding Thinking Traps, and Detecting Icebergs) and Change Belief Skills 4 and 7 (Challenging Beliefs and Real Time Resilience). No follow-up training boosters were provided.

Results. CSR performance was evaluated on four main variables in the following (descending) order of priority:

- *Mean Call Quality*: The performance of the CSR with clients, based on the CSR's ability to effectively answer the inquiry to the client's satisfaction, as rated by their supervisor on a subset of the monthly calls; ratings were on a 100-point scale and averaged for a monthly score.
- *Mean Sales Units*: A monthly figure for each CSR on the Sprint services they sold to clients who called into the call center—different services were awarded different points.

- *True Calls per Hour*: The number of calls which reached a threshold level of quality within each hour, calculated as a monthly mean for each CSR.
- *Total Calls Handled*: The total calls received by the CSR during each month period.

To establish a reliable baseline, the data for each variable for the three months preceding the resilience training were averaged into a pre-training score. To establish a reliable comparison, post-scores were calculated as an average of the performance on each variable in the three months following resilience training.

It was acknowledged ahead of time that the pilot sample sizes were too small to detect significant differences between conditions. Instead, we examined trends across the four measures of interest as an indication of the training efficacy.

It was revealed that on all four measures, the resilience group tended to outperform the control group.

Below is the data for supervisor ratings of the CSR's quality of call:

	Resilience training	Control
Pre	80.1	81.4
Post	82.1	82.1

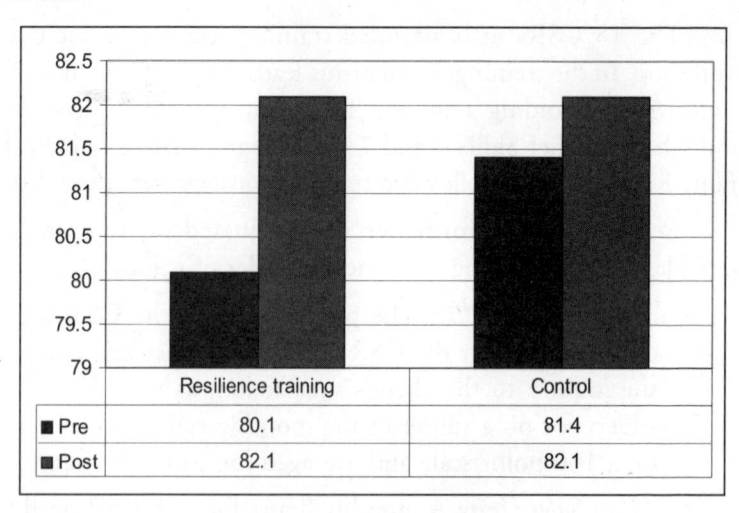

Figure 10

on mean monthly units sold:

	Resilience training	Control
■ Pre	82	76
■ Post	119	101

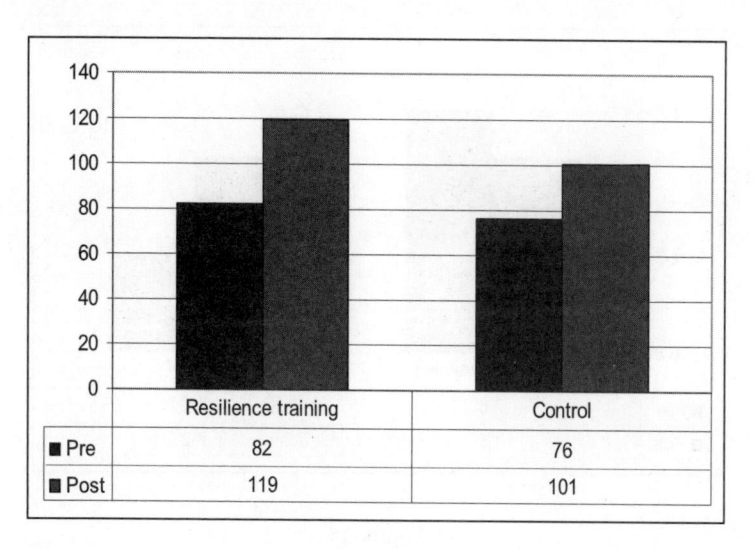

Figure 11

The mean calls handled per month:

	Resilience training	Control
■ Pre	852	795
■ Post	921	775

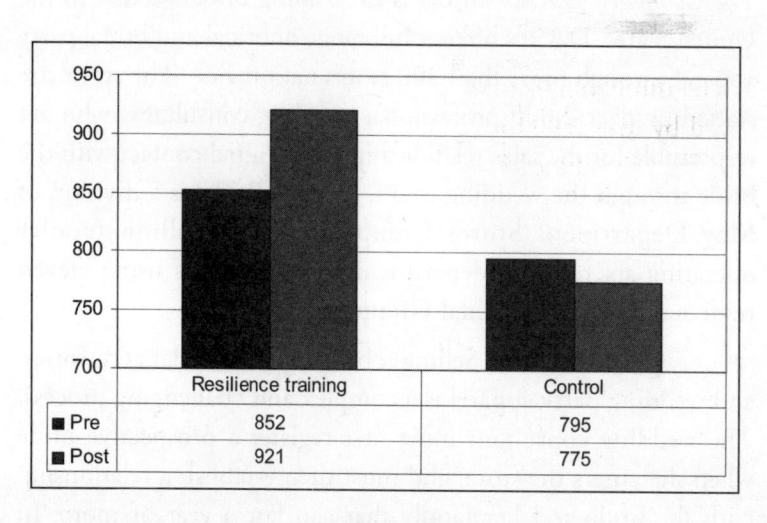

Figure 12

and true calls per hour:

	Resilience training	Control
Pre	7.6	7.6
Post	7.8	7.2

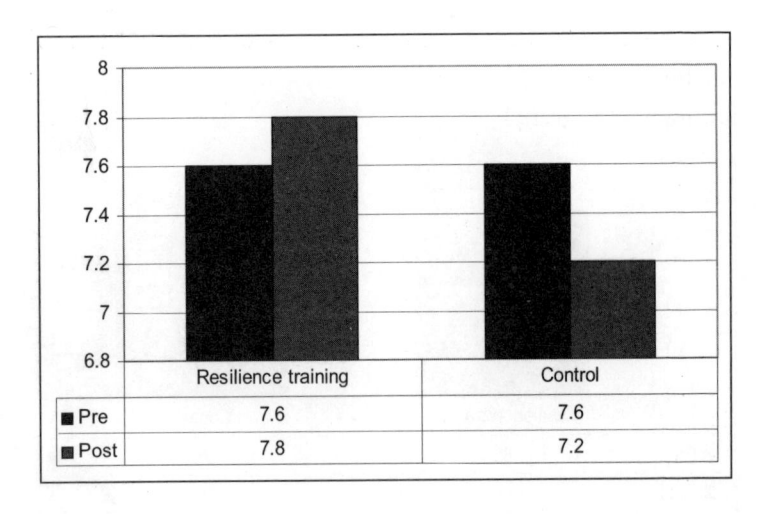

Figure 13

Case Study 4. Boosting Resilience at David's Bridal

The Company. David's Bridal is the leading bridal retailer in the United States. David's offers a full range of bridal and bridal party apparel through more than 200 stores nationwide. The stores are staffed by over 2,000 professional wedding consultants who are responsible for the sales relationship, from initial contact with the bride through the wedding event. David's Bridal is a division of May Department Stores Company, a $14 Billion retailer operating six regional department store divisions using eleven trade names and the Bridal Group.

The Business Issue. Selling a bridal gown, bridal accessories, and wedding party apparel is a complex and challenging process. The wedding consultant must first register a prospective bride when she enters the store, and must then establish a relationship with the bride and her family that can last a year or more. In addition, the industry is extremely competitive, and wedding consultants must walk a fine line between being overly aggressive and scaring the bride away, and being inadequately assertive and losing the business to a competitor.

This is possibly the most emotionally charged environment imaginable for a retail salesperson. Interviews with wedding consultants and store managers indicated that wedding consultants often had difficulty controlling both their emotions and behavior when dealing with difficult brides. Specifically, they would become both angry and anxious, and would often make impulsive decisions about a potential customer's willingness and desire to buy. This would result in missed sales opportunities.

Intervention. We hypothesized that wedding consultants equipped with the skills of resilience would sell more than a no-training, Control group. If a wedding consultant learned to generate more accurate beliefs about why a prospective customer wasn't buying, then more appropriate emotions and behavior would follow and sales should increase.

Approximately 20 wedding consultants from four retail stores in the same region received an 8-hour resilience training program, delivered in two four-hour segments. The program focused on the skills that most impact Emotion Regulation and Impulse Control, the two resilience factors that most needed boosting (i.e., Skill 1—ABC, and Skill 3—Detecting Icebergs). About half of the consultants in the training condition also received a one hour in-store review session with a resilience trainer approximately one month after the workshop.

Results. The wedding industry is very seasonal. Therefore, a simple pre-training versus post-training design is not adequate. For this reason, we decided to use the same time period in the previous year as the control period. Given that the training occurred in the fourth quarter of 2002, we compared sales in the first quarter of 2003 with first quarter sales in 2002. The results are presented in the graph below.

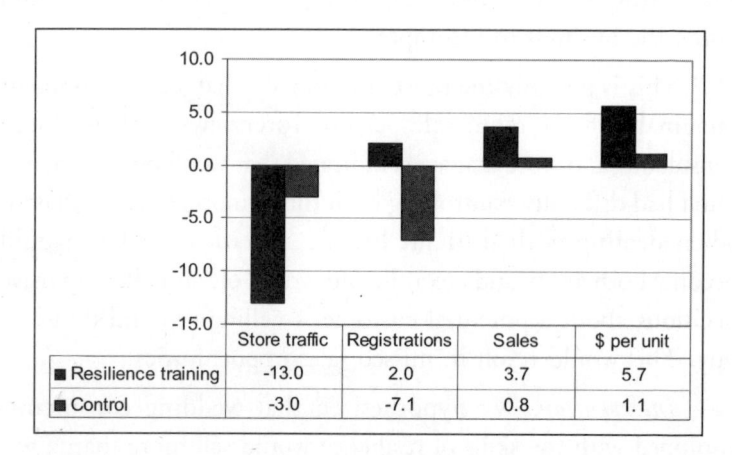

	Store traffic	Registrations	Sales	$ per unit
■ Resilience training	-13.0	2.0	3.7	5.7
■ Control	-3.0	-7.1	0.8	1.1

Figure 14

As the graph depicts, both the training and control groups suffered a downturn in the number of people entering the store (store traffic) from Q1 2002 to 2003, but this was especially dramatic for those in the training group. In spite of that, those in the training group were able to convert more store traffic to store registrations, sell to a higher percentage of people, and sell significantly more per bride.

Case Study 5, Boosting Resilience at Edward Jones Investments

The Company. Edward Jones Investments is a St. Louis-based firm that provides investment and brokerage services through a network of more than 8,000 community-based branch offices throughout the United States and Canada. Edward Jones Investment Representatives (IR's) differentiate themselves from their competitors by working exclusively via face-to-face meetings with their customers.

The company provides extensive training to their IR's in all aspects of investment product sales and customer service, and was ranked No. 1 in *Fortune Magazine*'s Best 100 Companies to Work For in America in 2002 and 2003.

Business Issue. Investment Representatives at Edward Jones do a great deal of cold calling, making most of their new client contacts by literally knocking on doors. After establishing a new client, IR's must build long-term relationships. New IR's come from diverse backgrounds, often do not have prior brokerage or sales experience, and are exposed to situations that are in many cases brand new to them (e.g., high levels of rejection, steep learning curve, commission-based income). Edward Jones' New IR Training group was seeking a way to boost the resilience of its new IR's in order to improve both their short and long-term success in the Company.

Intervention. A group of new IR's participated in an 8-hour resilience training program in February of 2002. The workshop took place immediately prior to the final week of training for licensure as brokers.

This particular IR group had been recruited for training as brokers in August of 2001—a month before the terrorist attacks in the United States on 9-11 that precipitated the stock market crash. By February of 2002 when the training occurred, the stock market had shown no signs of recovery. A diversity of emotions was evident in the group of about 70 people. Some, with violation of rights radars, were angry—"this is not fair". Others, with future threat radar, were anxious—"at this rate I'll never make a living". Yet others, with loss of standing radars, were embarrassed—"all of my friends and family were watching this career change, and they're going to think I failed". Some were frustrated and perceived a lack of resources—"there's nothing I can do to fix this". Others felt guilt (i.e., violation of another's rights)—"I've let my spouse and children down". Some felt ashamed (violation of own standards)—"it's my job to make money for my family and I've dropped that ball."

The training was designed to boost their resilience and enable them to better deal with the inevitable adversities that lay ahead. The objective of the training was to positively impact IR's who had no previous experience in the brokerage industry and no existing clients. The training emphasized boosting the factors of Emotion Regulation and Impulse Control.

Results. Performance was measured at one, three, and nine months post-training, and was compared to a randomized Control Group. About half of the IR's assigned to the training condition received a follow-up call from their resilience trainer approximately six weeks after the workshop.

Subjects were polled on what they did in the wake of being rejected. Their write-in responses were coded for the use of emotion regulation skills. Per the graph below, those who received training used Emotion Regulation skills at a significantly greater rate than those in the Control group.

	Resilience Training	Control
■ % using the skills	92%	32%

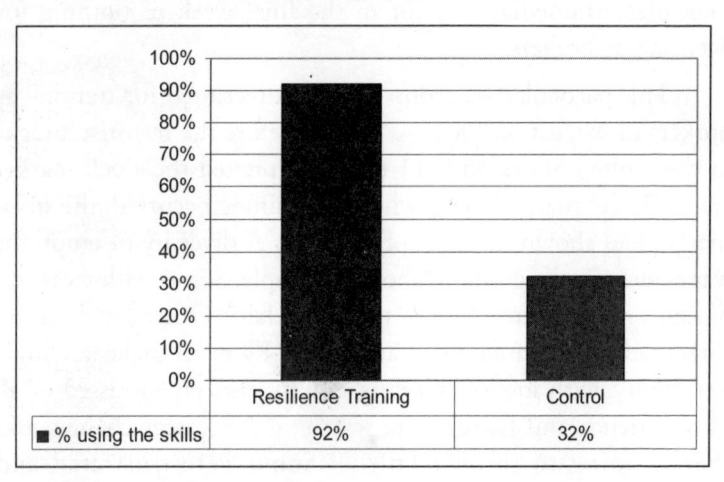

Figure 15

In addition, subjects reported how much negative emotion they experienced after being rejected, on a 1-10 scale. Our work suggests that once one is in a negative emotion at the level of 8 or above, then one is no longer functioning adaptively; that is, no longer acting in goal-focused ways. Regression analyses confirmed that the more participants used the Emotion Regulation skill, the more emotion regulation they showed.

% at 8 or above	Resilience traning	Control
	10%	54%

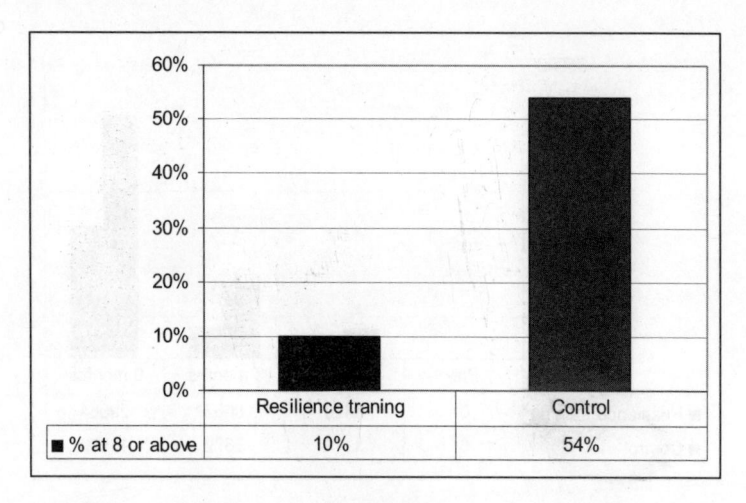

Figure 16

Data analyses indicated that those who received Resilience Training outperformed their Control peers on two key sales measures at all post-training intervals:

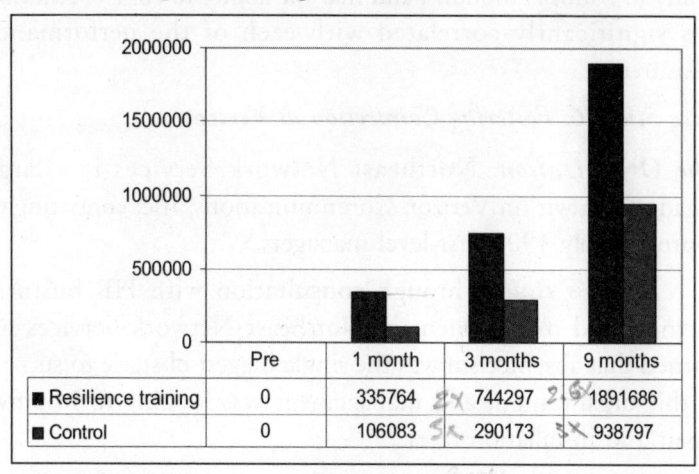

	Pre	1 month	3 months	9 months
Resilience training	0	335764	744297	1891686
Control	0	106083	290173	938797

Figure 17

Assets under management—the average dollar value of the money their clients have requested they manage and also on the gross commissions they earned on the money they made for their clients:

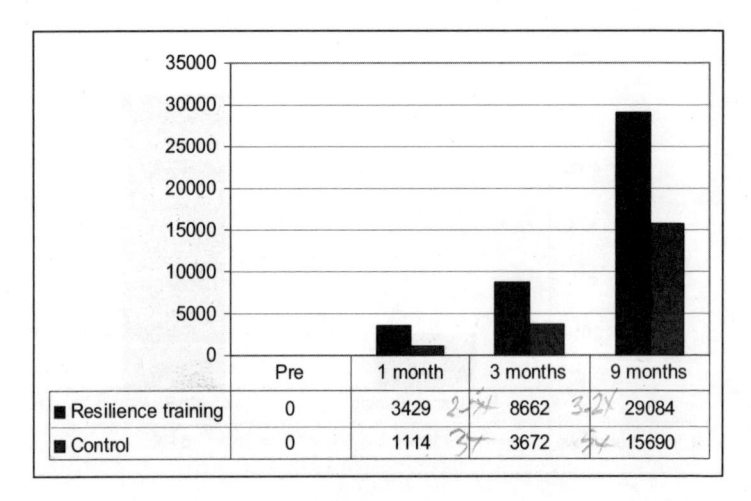

	Pre	1 month	3 months	9 months
■ Resilience training	0	3429	8662	29084
■ Control	0	1114	3672	15690

Figure 18

Proof of concept was clearly established by a series of regression analyses that showed that use of the skill was correlated with the ability to control emotions, and that the ability to control emotion was significantly correlated with each of the performance measures.

Case Study 6. Fostering Connection at Verizon

The Organization. Northeast Network Services is a large organization within Verizon Communications, Inc. consisting of approximately 1900 first-level managers.

Business Issue. Through consultation with HR business partners and management in Northeast Network Services we learned that absenteeism was the single biggest obstacle to success in this organization, and management was looking to improve repair and installation rates.

Intervention. Recall our work on connection to the job and its relationship with job satisfaction and resilience. In the course of consulting with Verizon, we began to notice low levels of connection within certain organizations. This was understandable given the negative events to which these employees had been subjected. In 2000, they went through the merger of Bell Atlantic and GTE to form Verizon—the largest merger in telecom history. In 2005, their pensions were frozen, and in 2006, the pension plan was discontinued. All of this occurred against the backdrop of a significant change in business—the traditional landline industry was being severely eroded by competitors and by a shift to wireless technology. In fact, it is psychologically maladaptive to maintain connection and commitment to an organization that is unable to offer job security.

The drop in connection was evident when we asked employees why they joined Verizon versus why they stayed. Some of the reasons people gave for why they joined the company included the following:

— "Family legacy"
— "Verizon was famous in my neighborhood"
— "Reputation for caring for their people"
— "Would train me in valuable skill set"
— "Did good in the world"
— "Used to do quality work"

Some of the reasons they gave for why they stayed included the following:

— "Too much time in"
— "Pays more than competitors"
— "Health benefits"
— "Close to retirement"

The preponderance of responses for why employees joined the company are at Level 2 (i.e., enjoy the work, the challenge, my colleagues) or Level 3 (i.e., contribution to something greater than self; the greater good). However, the preponderance of responses to why they stay are at Level 1 (i.e., pay and benefits). Thus, connection and commitment among employees had notably declined over the years.

All 1900 first-level managers went through the one-day resilience training.

Results. Data were collected on several connection and performance indicators both before and after the training.

Verizon conducts an annual survey of all employees inquiring about, among other things, their attitudes towards the company. The managers who participated in resilience training posted significant increases from pre- to follow-up on items such as 'I feel valued', 'I have clear direction', & 'I get respect from my reports, peers, and supervisors' at a time when the company generally posted decreases on these items.

Results also showed that absenteeism dropped by 7 per cent. This was calculated to be a $10 million savings. Repair rates went up 3 per cent which was estimated to be a $15.7 million savings.

Installation rates went up 4 per cent which represented a $17.6 million savings. This totals to $43.3 million savings, for which a significant portion has been attributed to the resilience training.

Summary and Conclusions

For twenty years now our colleagues and we have engaged in a systematic program of research to establish the critical importance of Resilience in the corporate sphere. First, we demonstrated that a program based on cognitive-therapy techniques could significantly prevent depression. Then, we established that the program was not a depression-prevention protocol per se, but rather boosted resilience in children—resilience that they could use for diverse outcomes. We tackled this monolithic concept of resilience and distilled it into its seven component factors, and in this process developed a valid psychometric instrument for measuring the concept. We established that the instrument (the RFI) was sensitive to the boosts in resilience the program afforded. And finally, we showed the power of the program to increase resilience and performance in a wide range of corporate industries and job types.

Since 1997, with considerable investments of time, energy, and money, we have created what is, perhaps, the most empirically-validated resilience program in the world. And as advents emerge from the field of positive psychology, we continue to fold those effective elements into the resilience protocol.

In many respects the story of our development of the resilience program is a story of resilience unto itself.

References

1. Werner, E.E. & Smith, R.S. (1955). *Overcoming the Odds: High-Risk Children from Birth to Adulthood*, Cornell University Press.
2. For those readers who have a special interest in factor analyses and psychometric development, the 7-factor solution emerged as optimal by both a scree test (which examines sudden drop offs in the explanatory power of the components or factors) and by selecting those factors which explained variance to the degree of an eigenvalue of one or greater.

Index

A

Acquired Immuno Deficiency Syndrome (AIDS) 400
Acute stress disorder 286
Acute stress risks 284
Addiction 218
Adjustment difficulties 13
Adversity 37
Africana womanism 416
Aggressive behaviours 100
Alcohol abuse 203
Alcoholics Anonymous 231
Appraisal-focused strategies 7
Art therapy 153
Art-making activities 160
Art-making skills 185
At-risk children 158
Attention and executive function 106
Attention Deficit Hyperactivity Disorder (ADHD) 107
Atypical schizophrenics 424
Australian Psychology Council (APAC) 168
Auto-pilot life 268

B

Bhagavad Gita 274
Bible 273
Biopsychospiritual homeostasis 431
Boundary situations 34
Brain plasticity 246
Broaden and build theory 245
Bronfenbrenner 390
Buddhist perspective 18
Buddhist teachings 275

C

Catecholamine activity 374
Catecholamines 374
Causal analysis 448
Child development, context of 126
Child-based interventions 130
Child-centred social policy 148
Childhood sexual abuse 177
Clean language questions 73
Clean Language: Revealing Metaphors and Opening Minds 51
Co-dependence 219
Co-dependence learning 219
Cognitive competence 3
Cognitive developmental theorists 155

Index

Community resilience 135
Community Resilience Framework 308
Community Resilience Profile 313
Community Resilience Questionnaire 310
Community-based interventions 135
Concept of resilience 116
Conceptual clarification 26
Conjoint Behavioural Consultation (CBC) 144
Context resilience 338
Coping responses 6
Coping strategies 6
   appraisal-focused 7
   emotion-focused 7
   problem-focused 7
Core purpose integrity 15
Cortisol 10, 203
Counselling services 167
Covington, Stephanie 212
Crisis reaction 286
Crisis resolution 286
Culture resilience 338
Curiosity oriented approach 252

D

Davidson, Richard J. 47
Depression prevention 446
Devastating diseases 219
Developing inner resilience 71
Development economics 333
Dissociation 10
Dommett, John 3
Doping 10
Dynamic contextualism 40
Dysfunctional reintegration 428

E

Ecological systems theory 125
   exosystem 125
   macrosystem 125
   mesosystem 125
   microsystem 125
Emotion-focused coping strategies 8
   accepting responsibility or blame 9
   disclaiming 8
   escape-avoidance 8
   exercising self-control 9
   positive reappraisal 9
Emotional Chaos to Clarity 212
Emotional distress 388
Emotional experience, intensity of 101
Emotional guidance 261
Emotional Guidance Systems (EGS) 255
Emotional intelligence elements of 49
   empathy 50
   motivation 50
   self-awareness 50
   self-regulation 50
   social skills 50
Emotional Intelligence—Why it can matter more than IQ 48
Emotional interaction 109
Emotional regulation 101, 388
Empathy 448
Enhancing Resiliency in Survivors of Family Violence 207
Environmental stressors 133
Envirosocial enhancing processes 434
Envirosocial protective processes 434

Envirosocial reintegrating
    process 436
Envirosocial supportive
    processes 435
*Everyday Stress Resilience
    Hypothesis* 111
Existential philosophy 26
Existentialism 28
Existenz 31
Extensive resources 159

F

Facing Co-dependence 221
Family-based interventions 133
Family violence 183
Framework for resilience 81
Frankl, Victor 37, 237, 267
Fredrickson, Barbara 245
*From Death-Camp to
    Existentialism* 237

G

Gender differences 10
Goleman, Daniel 48
Grabau R. F. 31
Gross domestic savings 347
Gukurahundi 401

H

Handbook of Adult Resilience 208
Healy, Ann Marie 14
Hebb, Donald 246
Hebb's law 246
Herman, Judith 208
High-risk environment
    conditions 364
HIV and AIDS trauma 400
Hormones 10
Human activity systems 76

Human development 420
Human Immuno Virus
    (HIV) 400
Hyperactivity 106

I

Images of resilience 52
    ambiguity and uncertainty 55
    barriers to progress 56
    bouncing back 54
    determination 60
    drive and motivation 61
    endurance 59
    feeling in control 61
    flexibility 62
    guidance 62
    keeping focus 56
    limited challenges 57
    new growth 54
    overcoming fear 58
    risk 57
    self-management 59
    tolerance 60
Immanent and transcendent
    modes 32
Impulse control 448
Individualised resilience
    interventions 130
Intimate partner violence 203

J

James, William 271
Jaspers K. 28
Jigsaw puzzle of life 5

K

Kindling 157
Kollwitz, Kathe 195
Koran 274

Index

L

Latzel E. 32
Leadership resilience 337
Learned helplessness 377
Learning goals 94
Lerner R. M. 40
Long-term resilience 258

M

Maladaptive behaviour strategies 10
Maladaptive coping mechanism 9
Maladaptive techniques 9
Mama Milanzi Programme 404
Man's Search for Meaning 237, 267
Maslow A. H. 29
Mastery 367
Measuring resilience 449
Meditation 7
Medium of the unconscious 161
Mellody, Pia 221
Mental effort 35
Mental health promotion 141
Mental health services 100
Metaphors 50
Miller R. B. 26
Mindfulness, practice of 7
Moffitt, Phillip 212
Multiple and chronic adversities 423
Multivariate Analysis of Variance (MANOVA) 451
Mutual Regulation Model 111

N

Nation Resilience Questionnaire 339
Negative emotions 106
Neural pathways 205
Neurogenesis 157
Neurological development 104
Neuropsychological abilities 106
Neuroscience 177
Neuroscience research 181
Neurotransmitters 374
No One's Son 3
Norepinephrine 203
Normalization 424

O

Obsessive Compulsive Disorder (OCD) 239
Operation Murambatsvina 401
Optimism 262
Orbito Frontal Cortex (OFC) 106
Organizational intervention 92
Organizational settings 80

P

Panchanatham 2
Participant engagement 93
Penn Optimism Program (POP) 444
Perceptual sensitivity 160
Perfectionism, issue of 9
Performance goals 94
Personal growth strategy 258
Personal Resilience Questionnaire (PRQ) 81
Philosophy 30
Physical aggression 388
Positive adaptive change 237
Positive adjustment 13
Positive psychology 245, 250
Positivity 262
Post-trauma resilience, building of 281
Post-traumatic growth 12, 237

Post-Traumatic Stress Disorder (PTSD) 243, 283
Postmodernism 165
Prefrontal cortex 106
Pro-social behaviors 446
Problem-focused coping strategies 9
Problem-solving skills 15
Psycho-educational programs 168
Psychology, origins of 26
Psychology, clinical practice of 26
Psychopathology 158
Psychosis, confusion of 17
Public Personalities Against AIDS Trust (PPAT) 405

R

Reaching out 448
Realistic optimism 448
Rees, Judy 51
Regulatory resilience 111
Resilience doughnut 130
Resilience Factor Inventory (RFI) 450
Resilience interventions, form of 92
    classroom training 92
    team-based sessions 92
    one-on-one coaching and development 92
Resilience, philosophy of 26
Resilience, representations of 54
Resilience Research Centre 13
Resilience training programme 382
Resilience-promoting schools 142
Resiliency 4
Resilient reintegration 427
Rhor, Richard 225

Rogers C. R. 37
Rothschild, Babette 230
RQ scores 452

S

School-based interventions 140
School-based universal program 140
Secrets of a Woman's Soul 404
Self-actualisation 180
Self-defeating behaviours 231
Self-efficacy beliefs 364
Self-harm 388
Self-medication 10
Self-talk 259
Senior Leadership Team (SLT) 90
Shaba, Lutanga 403
Short-term desires 259
Smith, Ruth 446
Social anxiety 422
Social competencies 167
Social cultural ecology 11
Society-based interventions 144
Sociocultural theory 125
Somatisation 3
Stand By Me 240
Stigma 421
Stigmatization 421
Strange situation test 109
Strength-based programs 382
Strengthening communities 138
Strengths perspective 18
Strengths-based practice 187, 252
Stress hormones 374
Stress management 10
Stress response syndrome 283
Stressful environment 6
Stressful life events 5
Sullivan, Wendy 51

Survivor self   281
Swinging monkey   19

T

The Body   240
The Emotional Life of Your Brain   47
The Naked Now   225
The Principles of Psychology   271
The Resiliency Model   433
Toughness   46
Trauma and Recovery   208
Trauma literature   281
Trauma recovery   281
Trauma treatment   230
Trauma-informed services   213
Trauma-responsive services   214
Traumatic event   3

U

Ultimate situations   34
Un-*not*-ing   194
Unbidden disorganization   17
Uncensored   213
Unlucky in Love   406
Unsafe psychosocial environment   12
Up-skilling strategies   130
Úrîmad-Bhâgavatam   275

V

Victim-survivor continuum   282
Vulnerable populations   14
Vulnerability   95

W

Werner, Emmy   446
Westerhorf, Tendai   406
Women and AIDS Support Network (WASN)   415
World Development Indicators   347

Z

Zippy's Friends   140
Zolli, Andrew   14